BOLLINGEN SERIES XXXV · 34

The A. W. Mellon Lectures in the Fine Arts

DELIVERED AT THE NATIONAL GALLERY OF ART, WASHINGTON, D.C.

1952 Creative Intuition in Art and Poetry *by Jacques Maritain*
1953 The Nude: A Study in Ideal Form *by Kenneth Clark*
1954 The Art of Sculpture *by Herbert Read*
1955 Painting and Reality *by Etienne Gilson*
1956 Art and Illusion: A Study in the Psychology of Pictorial Representation *by E. H. Gombrich*
1957 The Eternal Present: I. The Beginnings of Art. II. The Beginnings of Architecture *by S. Giedion*
1958 Nicolas Poussin *by Anthony Blunt*
1959 Of Divers Arts *by Naum Gabo*
1960 Horace Walpole *by Wilmarth Sheldon Lewis*
1961 Christian Iconography: A Study of its Origins *by André Grabar*
1962 Blake and Tradition *by Kathleen Raine*
1963 The Portrait in the Renaissance *by John Pope-Hennessy*
1964 On Quality in Art *by Jakob Rosenberg*
1965 The Origins of Romanticism *by Isaiah Berlin*
1966 Visionary and Dreamer: Two Poetic Painters, Samuel Palmer and Edward Burne-Jones *by David Cecil*
1967 Mnemosyne: The Parallel between Literature and the Visual Arts *by Mario Praz*
1968 Imaginative Literature and Painting *by Stephen Spender*
1969 Art as a Mode of Knowledge *by J. Bronowski*
1970 A History of Building Types *by Nikolaus Pevsner*
1971 Giorgio Vasari: The Man and the Book *by T. S. R. Boase*
1972 Leonardo da Vinci *by Ludwig H. Heydenreich*
1973 The Use and Abuse of Art *by Jacques Barzun*
1974 Nineteenth-century Sculpture Reconsidered *by H. W. Janson*
1975 Music in Europe in the Year 1776 *by H. C. Robbins Landon*
1976 Aspects of Classical Art *by Peter von Blanckenhagen*
1977 The Sack of Rome, 1527 *by André Chastel*
1978 The Rare Art Traditions *by Joseph Alsop*
1979 Cézanne and America *by John Rewald*
1980 Principles of Design in Ancient and Medieval Architecture *by Peter Kidson*
1981 Palladio in Britain *by John Harris*
1982 The Burden of Michelangelo's Painting *by Leo Steinberg*
1983 The Shape of France *by Vincent Scully*
1984 Painting as an Art *by Richard Wollheim*
1985 The Villa in History *by James S. Ackerman*
1986 Confessions of a Twentieth-Century Composer *by Lukas Foss*
1987 Imago Dei: The Byzantine Apologia for the Icons *by Jaroslav Pelikan*
1988 Art and the Spectator in the Italian Renaissance *by John Shearman*
1989 Intermediary Demons: Toward a Theory of Ornament *by Oleg Grabar*

JAMES S. ACKERMAN

THE VILLA

Form and Ideology of
Country Houses

The A. W. Mellon Lectures in the Fine Arts, 1985
The National Gallery of Art
Washington, D.C.
Bollingen Series XXXV · 34

PRINCETON UNIVERSITY PRESS

In memory of Tood

Published by Princeton University Press, 41 William Street,
Princeton, New Jersey 08540

This is the thirty-fourth volume of the A. W. Mellon Lectures in
the Fine Arts, which are delivered annually at the National Gallery
of Art, Washington. The volumes of lectures constitute Number
XXXV in Bollingen Series, sponsored by Bollingen Foundation

Manufactured in the German Democratic Republic
Published in Great Britain by Thames and Hudson Ltd, London

Library of Congress Cataloging-in-Publication Data

Ackerman, James S.
    The villa : form and ideology of country houses / James S. Ackerman.
      p.   cm.——(The A. W. Mellon lectures in the fine arts : 1985)
    (Bollingen series : XXXV, 34)
    Includes bibliographical references.
    ISBN 0-691-09911-1
    1. Country homes.   I. Title.   II. Series.   III. Series: Bollingen series : 35, 34.
NA7560.A34   1990   89-10785
728.8——dc20   CIP

Clothbound editions of Princeton University Press books are printed
on acid-free paper, and binding materials are chosen for strength
and durability

Contents

Foreword

This book is expanded from six Mellon Lectures delivered in Spring 1985 at the National Gallery of Art in Washington, D.C. It is composed of a general introductory chapter treating the typology of the villa in the Western world since antiquity, and ten chapters that focus on moments of innovation and change in the history of villa building. While I sought to distribute my choices of times and places to provide a wide spread, the limitations of my experience and knowledge forced me to favor Italy, England and America. I most regret the absence of German examples —for example, the villas of Karl Friedrich Schinkel—and of a discussion of the situation in France, where in the *ancien régime* the role of the villa is subsumed into that of the château. A comparison with Japanese imperial villas might have been valuable, but I knew that I should be misled in that enterprise by my ignorance of the language.

I was attracted to the subject originally by the striking contrast between the rich variety of forms in the history of country houses and the perception that the ideology of life in the country and in the villa has remained much the same from the time of late Republican Rome to the present, by contrast to major shifts in purpose and in emphasis in other ongoing building types such as urban dwellings and churches. Accordingly, my interpretations of the idea and the functions of the villa in each epoch constitute the thread that binds the several parts.

Of the many who have helped me with suggestions and criticisms of drafts, I want to thank particularly my wife, Jill Slosburg-Ackerman, Thomas Cerbu, Alfred Frazer, John Harris, Michelangelo Muraro, and Natasha Staller. I want also to thank the Getty Center in Santa Monica for hospitality that eased the writing for one chapter. I am grateful to Emily Lane for her meticulous and inspired copyreading and for the refinement of the translation in Chapter 5 and its Appendix, to my remarkably resourceful research assistants, Daniel Abramson and Ann Gilkerson, and to Barbara Shapiro for her lucid drawings. The book refreshes recollections of many country wanderings with my late wife Mildred and celebrates the many years of her encouragement and forbearance.

1.1 Cast of a Roman relief showing a suburban villa, from Avezzano

1 · The Typology of the Villa

A villa is a building in the country designed for its owner's enjoyment and relaxation. Though it may also be the center of an agricultural enterprise, the pleasure factor is what essentially distinguishes the villa residence from the farmhouse and the villa estate from the farm.[1] The farmhouse tends to be simple in structure and to conserve ancient forms that do not require the intervention of a designer. The villa is typically the product of an architect's imagination and asserts its modernity.

The basic program of the villa has remained unchanged for more than two thousand years since it was first fixed by the patricians of ancient Rome. This makes the villa unique: other architectural types—the palace, the place of worship, the factory—have changed in form and purpose as the role of the ruler, the character of the liturgy, the nature of manufacture have changed, frequently and often radically. But the villa has remained substantially the same because it fills a need that never alters, a need which, because it is not material but psychological and ideological, is not subject to the influences of evolving societies and technologies. The villa accommodates a fantasy which is impervious to reality.

The villa cannot be understood apart from the city; it exists not to fulfill autonomous functions but to provide a counterbalance to urban values and accommodations, and its economic situation is that of a satellite. (The relationship is vividly evoked in a Roman relief which shows a walled town with a villa outside its walls [*1.1*].) The villa can be built and supported either by monetary surpluses generated by urban commerce and industry or, when it is sustained by agriculture, by the need of urban centers for the surplus it produces beyond its own requirements. Consequently the fate of the villa has been intimately tied to that of the city: villa culture has thrived in the periods of metropolitan growth (as in ancient Rome, eighteenth- and nineteenth-century Britain, and the twentieth century throughout the West) and has declined with urban decline— indeed, to the point of extinction, as urban life withered in the Dark Ages from the fifth to the eleventh century in the West. But for two periods in Western history this generalization is invalid: at the apogee of the republican city-state in classical Greece and in the communes of central Europe and Italy between 1000 and 1400. Perhaps at a time of communal idealism the wealthy felt no need for an escape from the city, or perhaps life in the country was still too rugged and unsafe for anyone not raised in its rigors.

As satellites, villas have not always been near to the cities on which they depended: colonial agricultural centers such as those in Gaul, Britain and Africa in Roman times and in the southern United States in pre-revolutionary times were settled in areas almost devoid of urban development and became in themselves industrial and cultural centers, importing the values of urban culture, and often large in scale. Their dependence on the institution of slavery was essential to the economy in both these cases, partly perhaps because the prospect of isolation and dependence did not attract sufficient free labor and partly because slaves cost less and were easier to discipline.

While the acquisition of a villa has generally been possible only for persons of wealth and usually of prestige and power (or at least until the democratization of the type in the nineteenth century), it is nevertheless a bourgeois concept in the strict sense of the word (see p. 63), responding to the perceived needs of the city dweller. The villas of kings and princes, built and supported by public wealth, are essentially hybrids, being rooted in bourgeois attitudes but, by virtue of often unlimited economic means and the symbolic and representational requirements of supreme power, demanding a scale and an elegance in some degree antithetical to the concept. The villa of the Emperor Hadrian at Tivoli is the most notable example.

The ideology of the villa

Today as in the past the farmer and the peasant, whether poor and oppressed or rich and independent, do not as a rule regard country life as an idyllic state, but accept it as a necessary and often somewhat antipathetic condition. In the folklore of all ages, the country dweller, with some misgivings, has longed for the stimulation and comforts of city life. The city dweller, on the other hand, has typically idealized country life and, when means were available, has sought to acquire a property in which it might be enjoyed. This impulse is generated by psychological rather than utilitarian needs; it is quintessentially ideological.[2] I do not use "ideology" in the current colloquial sense to designate a strongly held conviction, but rather in the sense of a concept or a myth so firmly rooted in the unconscious that all who hold it affirm it as an incontrovertible truth: a concept which Marxists interpret as the means by which the dominant class reinforces and justifies the social and economic structure and its privileged position within it while obscuring its motivation from itself and others. The villa is in these terms a paradigm not only of architecture but of ideology; it is a myth or fantasy through which over the course of millennia persons whose position of privilege is rooted in urban commerce and industry have been able to expropriate rural land, often requiring, for the realization of the myth, the care of a laboring class or of slaves.

Because literature is a primary depository of ideological myth, the ideology of the villa in every epoch is richly illustrated in poetry and prose. Indeed, literary works have not merely reflected the villa culture of their time but have promoted villa concepts of later times.

Major revivals of the villa from that of the fifteenth century in Italy to Le Corbusier have been explicitly justified by reference to the Roman writers of the late Republic and early Empire—Cato, Varro, Virgil, Horace, Pliny the Younger, Vitruvius and others. Each villa revival has been accompanied by a revival of villa literature: in the fifteenth century that of Poliziano and Bembo; in eighteenth-century England, that of Shaftesbury, James Thomson, Pope and ultimately the early novel (the writings of Jane Austen seem obsessed with the property and status problems of urban-oriented country

1.2 Paolo Veronese, fresco of a pleasure villa, in Palladio's Villa Barbaro, Maser, 1560–61 (see pp. 102–03)

life); in nineteenth-century America, that of the Transcendentalists, Henry James and Edith Wharton. These and other vital moments in villa history were also marked by literature devoted to the design and improvement of villas and their gardens—an equally rich source for the interpretation of the myth. The villa descriptions by ancient writers were too vague to help in visualizing the appearance of the buildings, so Renaissance treatise-writers (Palladio especially) had to be especially inventive as they sought to revive the type. The publication of villa books in England from the early eighteenth to the mid-nineteenth century was an industry in itself, and there were those for whom it was a primary vocation. In America, from the time of *The Horticulturist* in the 1830s to *Sunset Magazine, House and Garden* and *House Beautiful* in the mid-twentieth century, instruction in the creation and nurture of the suburban villa and garden has attracted a large public.

Painting as well as literature bolsters the ideology: in Pompeian and other Campanian villas the walls were often decorated with ideal garden and villa scenes: it is chiefly from this source that we know of the appearance of the seaside pleasure residences of the type called *villa marittima*. In late medieval country castles, tapestries and wall paintings depicted the delights of country life, anticipating the scenes of social gatherings, music parties and outings on the walls of Palladian villas [1.2]. Eighteenth-century England pioneered a new genre of painting, the portrait of the country house, the popularity of which was stimulated by the visit of the distinguished Venetian topographical painter Canaletto [1.3]. Turner got his start as a specialist in this genre which, though it admittedly gave prominence to the great country houses of the landed aristocracy, must have promoted bourgeois idealization of country life. Seventeenth-century classical landscape painting, particularly that of Claude Lorrain, rose to prominence in the eighteenth century and fostered the aesthetic of the informal English garden, and then of the "picturesque" in gardening and architecture. At the end of the century the first romantic villa designers actually took the imaginary buildings of the Roman Campagna in paintings by Claude as architectural models. The more modest ambitions of the mid-nineteenth-century suburban villa are reflected in early Impressionist painting, especially that of Monet. In all these cases country life is presented in the most favorable possible light.

The content of villa ideology is rooted in the contrast of country and city, in that the virtues and delights of the one are presented as the antitheses of the vices and excesses of the other. The expression is fully articulated in the literature of ancient Rome, where it evolves from an early proto-villa stage in the agricultural treatises of Cato and Varro into the typical mature form of Pliny the Younger's two letters describing to a friend the pleasures of two of his numerous luxurious estates, one, Laurentinum, on the seashore not very far from Rome, and the other, Tusci, in the Apennines in southern Tuscany (see the next chapter, pp. 52ff.). The early stage, related to Stoicism in its ascetic and moral tone, advises the urban man of affairs to acquire a modest farmhouse on a small country property and to cultivate it himself with little or no help; the labor itself is seen as purifying him of the contamination of the city. A similar pattern of evolution is repeated in later times—in the provincial villa culture of Imperial Rome, in the transition from the simple and almost unadorned country residences of the fifteenth century in the Veneto to the elegance of Palladian villas, and in the metamorphosis

1.3 Canaletto, *Badminton House*

traceable in Thomas Jefferson's concept of his farm at Monticello from the modest structure of the 1770s (itself surely influenced by the early Roman writers) to the lavish estate of the early nineteenth century [*1.26*].

In describing the sumptuous Tusci, Pliny set the tone for later writers; his letter (*Epistles*, V.vi.45) concludes with an encomium that clearly delineates the rural–urban antithesis:

> For besides the attractions which I have mentioned the greatest is the relaxation and carefree luxury of the place—there is no need for a toga, the neighbors do not come to call, it is always quiet and peaceful—advantages as great as the healthful situation and limpid air. I always feel energetic and fit for anything at my Tuscan villa, both mentally and physically. I exercise my mind by study, my body by hunting. My household too flourishes better here than elsewere: I have never lost a retainer [slave?], none of those I brought up with me.

Sixteen hundred years later Palladio describes the same benefits from the architect's perspective:

> But the villa mansion is of no less utility and comfort [than the city house] since the rest of the time [the gentleman] passes there overseeing his possessions and in improving their potential with industry and with the skill of agriculture. There also, by means of the exercise that one can get in the villa on foot or horseback, the body may more actively be made to preserve its health and robustness, and there the spirit tired of the turmoil of the city may be greatly

restored and consoled and may peacefully attend to the pursuit of letters and of contemplation. For this reason, the ancient sages used often to retire to such places, where they might be visited by their virtuous friends and relatives and where there were houses, gardens, fountains and similar relaxing places, and above all [*lacuna*] their Virtù, so that they could easily pursue that blessed life so far as it may be achieved here below.

And Le Corbusier, referring to a commission of the late 1920s, stresses the importance—mentioned by the preceding authors, but not in these lines—of the landscape setting:

The inhabitants, who have come here because this rural countryside was beautiful *with its country life*, will contemplate it from the height of their terrace garden or from the four aspects of their strip windows. Their domestic life will be inserted into a Virgilian dream.

The same repertory of the benefits of villa life echoes down the centuries: the practical advantages of farming, the healthfulness provided by the air and exercise—particularly hunting—relaxation in reading, conversation with virtuous friends and contemplation, and delightful views of the landscape.

Social and economic aspects

Le Corbusier's reference to his client's "domain" reminds us that the villa is necessarily the possession of the privileged and powerful class in society, though at certain times in history, as in the mid-nineteenth century, the privilege has filtered down to those of modest financial means.[3] The social structure of most of the villas we are considering involves the proprietor and his guests on one stratum, servants on another, and, in the case of agricultural establishments, farm laborers, often supervised by bailiffs, on still another. For most of Western history the latter, whether free or enslaved, have been bound for their subsistence to the proprietor and to his estate and could not break the bond without great risk. He, however, had no reciprocal obligation toward his retainers. In this respect the farm villa differs fundamentally from the feudal castle, where the relation between the lord and his retainers was contractual and reciprocal; they provided goods and services—including military service—and he provided protection against common enemies. Long after the feudal system had been forced into the background by a money economy and by urban capitalism, the landed nobility resisted abandoning their country castles in favor of villas; this class had no reason to develop a villa ideology until the time came when it became economically dependent on the city.

So, in those areas of the postmedieval Western world in which the feudal system was most firmly established, a villa culture was slow to develop. The situation is clearly delineated in France, where the format of country life for the privileged classes derived from the feudal château. The social character of the château did not change substantially as the monarchy gained in power, drawing the aristocracy into a dependent position at the court, where competition for royal favor made rustic retirement a risky option. Furthermore, the prestige of the aristocracy in France was such that, well into the nineteenth century, bourgeois proprietors modeled their country residences on the aristocrat's château. Viollet-le-Duc's designs for country residences are called "châteaux" while César Daly's, for a lower social stratum, are called "villas."

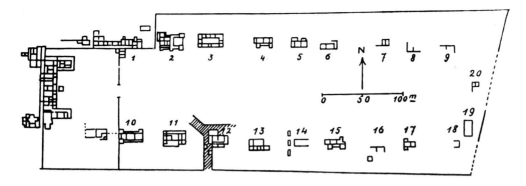

1.4 Gallo-Roman villa, Anthée. The main house is at the end of the central axis; farm, industrial and domestic structures are ranged along the sides.

Economically, as we have seen, there are two categories of villa: one is the self-sustaining agricultural estate that yields not only produce for its own use but a surplus for sale to urban or regional markets sufficient to sustain the proprietor's desired mode of life. The other is the villa described by Leone Battista Alberti as "per semplice diletto," conceived primarily as a retreat (though some cultivation may be pursued as part of the *diletto*), and dependent for its construction and maintenance on surplus capital normally earned in urban centers. The ideology that extolls the country and scorns the city is thus in part a paradoxical response to the dependence of the villa style of country life on the economic resources of the city.

The villa frequently appears in a colonial context, where a powerful empire controls distant territories from whose produce it gains sufficient profit to offset the expense and burden of providing defense and communications. Colonial villas tend to differ in type and scale from those in the homeland: being isolated, they must function as social and administrative units in themselves, often serving as substitutes for towns. Their economy is typically dependent on the production of their estate. The grander villas on the periphery of the Roman Empire—in Gaul, Pannonia, Africa, and elsewhere—mostly built from the second to the fifth century, were more complex establishments than those on the Italian peninsula; some, like the villa at Anthée near Namur in Belgium [1.4] were effectively small villages, containing community baths. The American colonies of the southern Atlantic seaboard were, like Rome's, virtually townless, so that the estates had to accommodate all the communal functions; many included dependent settlements, like their Roman ancestors. Too few of the dwellings and workshops of slaves and freedmen have survived to permit a credible reconstruction of these settlements.

In the course of time, colonial villas in un-urbanized territories often spawned towns, reversing the normal dependence of the villa on the city. The far-flung Imperial villa-settlements of Rome and the American plantation centers had been sited originally in places adapted to communication, transport and, in the case of the Roman examples, defense. As urbanization increased, these considerations encouraged the growth of towns, as we are reminded in the etymological linking of "villa," "village" and the French "ville." These were not the great metropolitan centers that grew up as

1.5 Drayton Hall, near Charleston, S.C., 1738 on

administrative headquarters but more modest market towns. In the southern United States the domestic architecture of these towns retained some of the openness and rural flavor of the villa/plantation residence.

Southern plantation mansions themselves were not designed to express autonomy from the mother country; on the contrary, their owners wanted to affirm in them their close ties to Britain, and had their carpenters build from plans in books recently published in London. This explains the Palladian porch added to the facade of Drayton Hall near Charleston, South Carolina [1.5], which was to have had symmetrically placed outbuildings connected to the central block by Palladian quadrants. The fact that plantation owners had to subdue the wilderness of a new land at great physical and financial risk cemented their attachment to the country life and architectural tastes of the British squire. The absence of a comparable villa development in the north Atlantic colonies is attributable initially to the different social and political origins of the colonists, the majority of whom, refugees from church and class domination, had not attained positions of privilege and status in Britain upon which they could reflect with nostalgia. They had chosen, furthermore, an area more adapted to family farming on small freehold properties, and they had established a society in which there were no slaves, peasants or serfs to support a gentleman farmer or to maintain a pleasure-villa. The contrast between the northern colonial farmer and the southern plantation owner was even greater than that between Cato and Pliny the Younger in Roman times. Cato was a statesman who farmed for ideological and philosophical reasons, while his American counterpart farmed to survive, with a certain Catonian (and Protestant) pride in successful crops and in the sweat they represented, but without those mythic trappings that find expression in the literature, art and architectural symbolism of a true ideology. Eventually, the polarity in both the Roman and the American social and ethical attitudes became the seed of civil war.

The most radical mutation in the history of the villa occurred in the early nineteenth century when the villa ideology became democratized and accessible to the growing body of lower-middle-class city dwellers. The causes were complex: they included the rapid growth of central cities at the expense of the countryside; industrialization; steamboat, rail and trolley transportation; the effects of eighteenth-century egalitarian social philosophy; and romanticism. The development was anticipated in British villa literature of the later eighteenth and early nineteenth century (most effectively by Loudon in Great Britain and by Alexander Jackson Davis and Andrew Jackson Downing in the United States), which first provided model plans for small and inexpensive country houses accompanied by texts promoting those elements of the traditional mythology that suited proprietors below the rank of gentleman [*1.6; 9.9; 10.13*]. Once the villa had been presented in this way as a commodity, it was a short step to its manufacture by entrepreneurs for the open market, and another short step to its mass production on the periphery of great cities and ultimately even of smaller ones. The garden-city movement of the later nineteenth century appropriated as much as possible of villa ideology into its blurred vision of urban and rural values. Ultimately, the term "villa" came to be applied to any detached or semi-detached residence, whether in

1.6 Andrew Jackson Downing, villa in the Italian style, from *The Architecture of Country Houses*, 1850

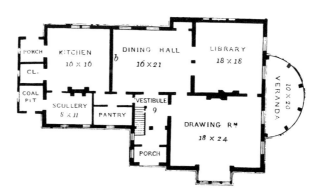

the city, suburb or country, with a little more open space around it than dwellings in the densely populated streets of the urban core. This development, however, did not affect the evolution of the villa in its traditional sense except perhaps in helping to disparage the use of the word "villa" to designate the type. Nineteenth-century country houses in the villa tradition, such as those of Scott, Richardson, Viollet-le-Duc, Voysey and others, were not called villas, and in the present century Le Corbusier was exceptional in his revival of the designation.

Style and form

The distinction between the farmhouse and the villa is not simply one of purpose and of program: it is rooted in different cultures and in different rates of evolution. Just as agricultural practices change more slowly than those of industry and commerce, so the farmhouse changes more slowly than the villa. French historians of the *Annales* school have called this phenomenon of gradualism the *longue durée*, and have opened new historical possibilities in studying its processes.[4] Farmhouses in many parts of Europe today retain forms that have remained unchanged for millennia (though they are rapidly being replaced by contractors' villas and will soon be threatened with total extinction). The debased economic and social position of the peasant, the *contadino*, and the sharecropper have kept them until recent times from altering their agricultural methods or the physical setting in which they lived and worked, but even on the rare occasions when they became wealthy and worldly their sense of propriety and pride of class led them to retain traditional forms.

The villa is quite the opposite: it rarely displays an effort on the part of the proprietor or the architect to conform to past custom (as do most of the early villas of the Medici [*3.3–5*]; more typically, it strains to be the paradigm of the most up-to-date architectural style (as in the Medici's Fiesole villa [*3.12–14*]. The rule is illustrated in all of the following chapters and most decisively by the celebrated milestones of modern architecture: the Ames Gate Lodge at North Easton, Massachusetts [*1.24*], the Coonley house at Riverside, Illinois [*11.3–6*], the Villa Savoye at Poissy [*1.7; 11.16–18*], and the suburban retreats of contemporary designers such as Peter Eisenman [*1.8*], Mario Botta and Robert Venturi. Even though the Renaissance architects sought to revive antique villas and British eighteenth-century villa architects were fanatic Palladians, in both cases the revival was a progressive statement that explicitly rejected a prevailing style. There is hardly a moment in the history of architecture when villas were less innovative than other architectural types. Urban residences sometimes have kept abreast of villas, but generally follow a more conservative tradition, even in cases where urban and rural residences were designed by the same architect and/or for the same patron. This generally is consistent with the proprietor's fashions of dress in the city as opposed to the country.

The villa is less fixed in form than most other architectural types because the requirements of leisure lack clear definition. But two contrasting models were firmly established in Roman times: the compact-cubic and the open-extended [*1.9, 21*]. The former was better suited to crowded suburbs like Pompeii where the line between the city house and the villa was, as in the residences of Le Corbusier or Eisenman [*1.7, 8*],

1.7 Villa Savoye, Poissy, by Le Corbusier, 1928–30

1.8 Falk House, Hardwick, Vt, by Peter Eisenman, 1970

not firmly drawn, and to the initial settlements on the periphery of the Empire where considerations of defense demanded consolidation. The compact Pompeian form, as in the Villa of the Mysteries just outside the city walls [*1.9; 2.7*], is due also to the fact that the villa had not yet gained its independence from urban models by the first century BC; the vagueness of the contemporary writer Vitruvius in describing villas (his main point is that the order of rooms at the entrance differs from that of the city houses) confirms this suspicion. The compact villa, when it faced a farmyard or a view, tended to acquire a loggia along its facade, typically framed in Roman examples between two projecting blocks or towers. This type reappears in the small early Renaissance villa like the Belvedere of Innocent VIII at the Vatican or the Farnesina in Rome [*1.10, 20C*]. Tropical forest conditions produced a variant of the cubic type in the plantation houses of seventeenth-century Brazil and the eighteenth-century Caribbean, a veranda-surrounded block that seems not to have been exported from Europe; it found its way into the plantation-house design of the early nineteenth-century Mississippi valley, as at Home Place in Louisiana [*1.11*].

The open villa is more congenial to the identification of the natural environment with health and relaxation. It expands informally in extended asymmetrical blocks and porticoes and in the varied profiles of changing levels, and often grows like an organism as the wealthy proprietor is tempted to extend the initial structure by adding rooms, courts and porticoes, as Pliny must have done, and Jefferson (who in the course of forty years never ceased to alter the shape of Monticello), and Wright at the Taliesins [*1.12*].

1.9 *(opposite)* Villa of the Mysteries, Pompeii, 2nd-1st C. BC: reconstruction

1.10 Villa Farnesina, Rome, by Baldassare Peruzzi, 1509–11. Drawing, 16th C.

1.11 Home Place, La., 1801

1.12 *(below)* Taliesin, Spring Green, Wis., by Frank Lloyd Wright, begun 1911

To fulfill its ideological mission the villa must interact in some way with trees, rocks and fields, and the two major types I have defined are roughly coordinated with two types of interaction: the compact-cubic villa is often a foil to the natural environment, standing off from it in polar opposition, and the open-extended type is integrative, imitating natural forms in the irregularity of its layout and profile, embracing the ground, assuming natural colors and textures.

A paradigm of the first is Lorenzo de' Medici's villa at Poggio a Caiano outside Florence [1.14; 3.18], which is inscribed within a cube, faced with white stucco to emphasize its total polarity to the irrationality of foliage and rolling hills, and, to underscore this message, raised on a high podium to ensure that the contact of the residents with nature should not be intimate but removed and in perspective.[5] Palladio followed this tradition in the design of an early villa, that of the Godi family in Lonedo [1.13, 4.9], which is also sharply geometrical in form, avoiding even window-frames or mouldings; there is no podium but the entrance stairway leads to the upper floor. (Later Palladian works are more engaged with nature—even the entirely cubic Villa Rotonda in Vicenza [4.18], which is designed to reflect the varied views and which seems to crown the hill on which it is placed.) The effort to respond to nature by antithesis explains the apparently paradoxical appearance of the sharply geometrical and classical Palladian style in early eighteenth-century Britain (e.g., at Lord Burlington's villa at Chiswick [6.3, 4]) in tandem with the invention of the informal English garden. The white

1.13 Villa Godi, Lonedo, by Andrea Palladio, 1537–42

1.14 *(below)* Villa Medici, Poggio a Caiano, by Lorenzo de' Medici and Giuliano da Sangallo, 1485 on. Painting by Giusto Utens, 1598/99

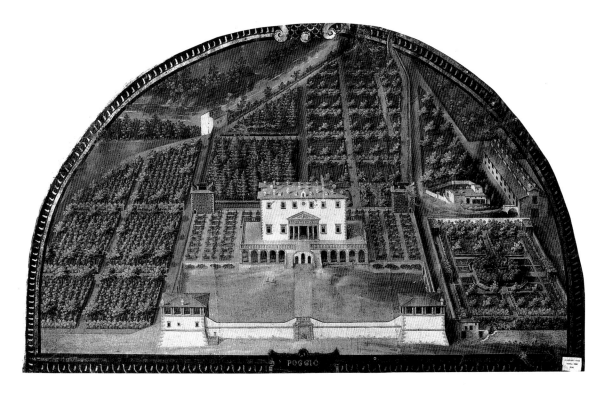

stuccoed podium-villa again became a major twentieth-century paradigm, notably in the Villa Savoye at Poissy [*1.7*] and the Tugendhat House in Brno.

The alternative type, expressing collaboration with the landscape, is exemplified in Pliny's villa descriptions of extended, even sprawling structures, but their appearance is difficult to reconstruct from his letters [*2.10–12*]: Hadrian's villa at Tivoli [*2.9*], bits of which were known to the architects of the Renaissance, and the ancient villa at Piazza Armerina in Sicily [*1.15*] give us a better opportunity to visualize this exceptionally large and lavish "organic" type. Renaissance villa designers were too fixed on the polarity of nature and culture to devise schemes in which the barriers between the two were blurred; what interaction did occur was rather between the architecture and the garden, which remained firmly in the artist's control. The formal garden of the Renaissance was frequently complemented by a "barco," or hunting park, where the irrationality of nature could be accepted; the nature/art dialectic was transferred to the contrast of controlled and uncontrolled greenery and water. An early engraving of the Villa Lante in Bagnaia shows a small "wild" area in the lower right corner [*1.16*]. In non-agricultural Renaissance villas, such as those of the Papal court in Rome, the artifices of the formal garden sometimes took precedence even over the architecture. The Villa d'Este in Tivoli concedes all emphasis to the garden [*1.17*], the building itself being exceptionally inexpressive and bland, while the architecture of the Villa Lante is overwhelmed by garden design. There, for the first time, the central axis of the composition is occupied by landscaping elements rather than a building—highly controlled and allegorized water courses, fountains and stairways—while the shy, cubic residential casinos are pushed to either side.

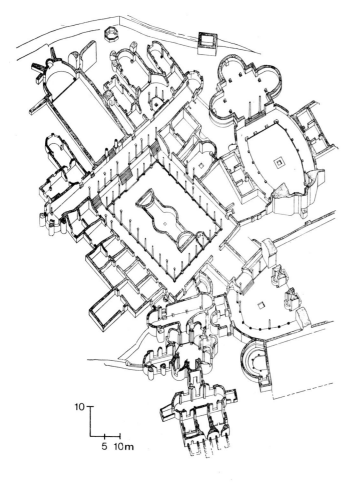

1.15 Roman villa, Piazza Armerina, 3rd C. AD: plan

1.16 (*opposite, above*) Villa Lante, Bagnaia, by Giulio Romano, *c.* 1518–20. Engraving by Tarquinio Ligustri, 1596

1.17 (*opposite*) Villa d'Este, Tivoli, by Pirro Ligorio, c. 1565–72. Bird's-eye view by Etienne Dupérac, 1573

10

5 10m

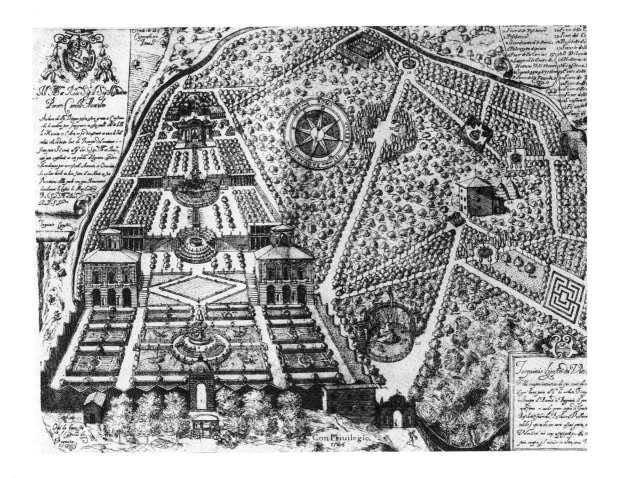

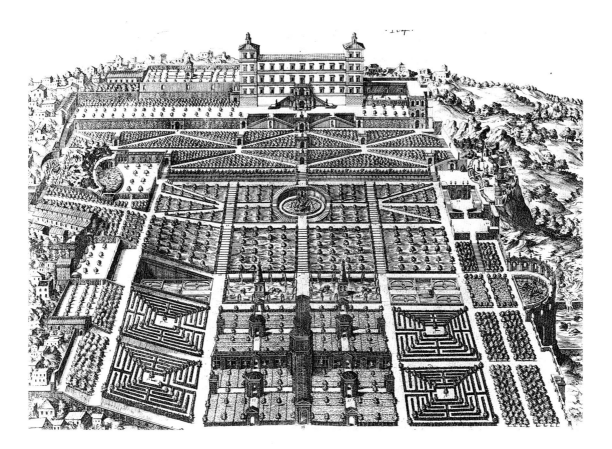

Renaissance designers would have been disappointed and disoriented had they discovered that most Roman villas weren't classical. The normal ancient examples (none of which could be reconstructed before the discovery of Herculaneum and Pompeii) lacked the axial symmetry, rational integration and proportion that supported their conception of the heritage of antiquity [1.15]. Even the villas described by Pliny, which to us seem patently sprawling and irregular, were visualized in the eighteenth century as rigidly symmetrical and rational. Whether Roman villas, like many in later times, expressed their communion with nature by a richness of color and of texture is hard to tell even today because of the condition of the remains. In any event, Renaissance architects, from Giuliano da Sangallo through Bramante, Raphael and Palladio, did give the villa and garden a classical form by imposing a rule of order, number and symmetry that fixed the type up to the moment of naturalist disruption in the eighteenth century (Sebastiano Serlio, in his manuscript for a book on villas and palaces, even classicized the peasant's hut). This achievement greatly narrowed the distance between the two Roman types by pulling the extending arms and wings of the open villa in symmetrical order about a central block, as in the porticoed villas of Palladio.

The triumph of nature over architectural form was ultimately achieved in eighteenth-century England, where the fashion of the picturesque emerged (see Chapters 7 and 9). The desire to make the real environment look like pictures was stimulated by the landscape paintings of Nicolas Poussin, Claude Lorrain, Jacob van Ruysdael and others, in which the architecture, while frequently geometric in its forms, was designed to be seen as part of the landscape and to respond to it in mood [7.2]. Authors of books on architecture and landscape design such as Richard Payne Knight [9.1], Uvedale Price and their heir Humphrey Repton urged clients to build villas that borrowed from the landscape something of its irregularity, its contrasts of light and its shadows and textures. The asymmetries of Gothic proved sympathetic to this aim, and the "Italian villa" style [9.7, 8] abruptly emerged, not from any actual models in Italy, but from the canvases of the French and British painters who had worked there. From this point on, a picturesque, nature-integrating spirit dominates the naturalist lineage of villa architecture—from the publicists Repton, Loudon and Downing to Philip Webb's Red House, Shaw and Richardson, Lutyens, Aalto, Wright, the Greenes, and Maybeck to Moore.

The view

In reflecting on the ways in which villas respond to the landscape one must remember to look not only at them but out from them. The choice of prospect is almost as subject to myth and the rule of taste as the choice of design. I say "almost" because the villa builder is limited in the choice of land formation and flora by the nature of the territory in which he intends to settle and by the property available to him. In the environs of Tivoli, east of Rome, there are examples of three genres of villa siting. Hadrian's vast villa [2.9] extends over a low-lying escarpment at the base of the hills that rise out of the wooded Campagna, barely above the level of the plain; it is a nestling villa, in the lap of the hills, with views just over the treetops. The villa of Quintilius Varus and the Renaissance Villa d'Este are perched high on the slopes—not on the very peaks but high enough to gain a

1.18 View from the Villa d'Este, Tivoli, looking toward the villa of Quintilius Varus

1.19 Horace's Sabine farm

vast panorama of the countryside and distant mountains: a view toward the former from the terrace of the latter [*1.18*] shows both to be commanding, extroverted villas (the famed gardens of the Villa d'Este, incidentally, are barely visible from the villa itself: they drop sharply away, and attention is drawn only to the distant panorama). By contrast, Horace's "Sabine Farm" is back within the mountains on an extraordinary site suited to a poet [*1.19*]: a saddle, only large enough to hold a small cubic structure, deeply embedded between two sharply rising hills, with a valley on one side of the cross axis and conical peaks on the other, atop one of which a village seems almost to cling (the existing one is believed to occupy the site of a Roman predecessor). Surely each of these four structures was designed for what could be seen from them as much as what was to be done in them.

The villa view that in one sense most fully illustrates the urban roots of the villa myth is the one that looks back on the city from a high and distant promontory outside its walls. Such villas once dotted the slopes of Mount Vesuvius when Pompeii flourished, and Cosimo de' Medici built his Fiesole villa on a manmade terrace so that he could enjoy in leisure hours visual command of Florence, the city he controlled politically [*3.13, 14*].

The influence of the visual prospect upon the conception of the villa was intensified in eighteenth-century England where the vogue for the informal garden was extended to embrace the entire agricultural landscape. This was achieved by removing walls, hedges and fences so that the lawn and planted trees merged imperceptibly into pasture and boscage. The innovation was not due entirely to a change of taste, as its promoters believed, but also to a radical change in agricultural economy and society. The Acts of Enclosure led to the elimination of ancient common pastures and peasant tillage as well as many villages on the great estates. They concentrated development of the entire landscape in the hands of the major landowners. Extended fields with cattle and haystacks now could become embellishments of a pastoral elegy [*7.12*].

Survival or revival?

Renaissance villa architects, intent as they were on reviving the ancient villas, did not know of any models on which to base their designs, and were forced to depend entirely on the meagre literary sources. Of these, Vitruvius was of almost no help, and Pliny's

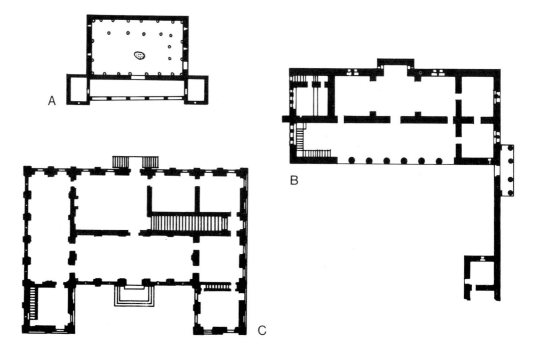

1.20 (A) Gallo-Roman villa at Mayen, 2nd-4th C. AD; (B) villa of Theodoric, Galeata, c. 500; (C) Villa Farnesina, Rome, 1509–11

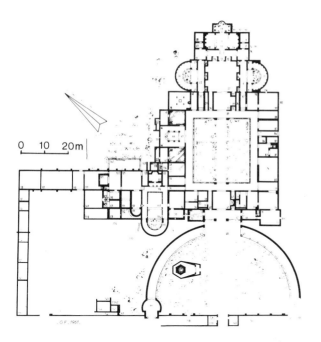

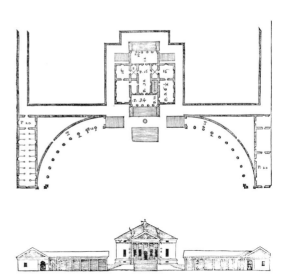

1.21 Gallo-Roman villa, Montmaurin, 2nd-4th C. AD: plan

1.22 Villa Badoer, Fratta Polesine, by Andrea Palladio, after 1556, from *I quattro libri dell'architettura*, 1570

descriptions, though ample, were useful only for projects of great lavishness, such as Raphael's design for the Villa Madama in Rome (about which he wrote a letter filled with Plinian phrases). In spite of this, archaeologists today continue to unearth Roman villas that anticipated Renaissance and later types. Since a *revival* of these ancient forms cannot have occurred, they must somehow or other have *survived* over the intervening centuries through links that have mostly vanished. The persistence of the compact-cubic type may not be especially significant since within the rationalist orientation of Mediterranean culture it is one self-evident architectural solution to the problem of designing a freestanding structure. The U-shaped villa with projecting blocks framing a central loggia, however, is specific enough in form to arouse curiosity about how it traveled from the late Roman Empire to the fifteenth century and beyond. Whatever the answer, it is likely to be more in the realm of folkways than of architectural style. In a characteristic Roman provincial example, at Mayen in German Gaul [*1.20A*], the loggia with extended wings was added in the fourth century to an earlier block. The type was preserved in a sixth-century villa of Theodoric in Galeata [*1.20B*], not far from Ravenna, and emerges again in the typical Venetian–Byzantine palace, whence it passes back into a type of early Renaissance villa that achieves a refined form in Baldassare Peruzzi's Villa Farnesina in Rome [*1.10, 20C*].[6] Another villa, only recently excavated at Montmaurin in the French part of Gaul [*1.21*], anticipated the entranceway flanked with two quadrants of a circle in a style invented again by Palladio for such projects as the Villa Badoer at Fratta Polesine [*1.22*], which passed from there into innumerable houses and villas in Europe and America.

The villa as sign

The villa inevitably expresses the mythology that causes it to be built: the attraction to nature, whether stated in engagement or in cool distance, the dialectic of nature and culture or artifice, the prerogatives of privilege and/or power, and national, regional or class pride. The signifiers range from the siting and form of the building as a whole to individual details and characteristics. Since signs and symbols convey meaning only to those who know what they signify, they are usually chosen from past architectural usage or occasionally are imported from other types of construction, like the ship-railings of Le Corbusier [*11.18*].

Intimate engagement with nature is signified by a site and design that permit the villa to nestle and to extend out into its surroundings, by asymmetrical and open design, colors reflecting the setting, and natural and varied textures. Distancing from the setting, on the other hand, is signified by a compact form, cubic in outline, often with a podium or similar device to elevate the living quarters off the earth, studied proportions, and emphasis on plane surfaces of white or of a light color which disguise the nature of the materials. Ambiguity toward these two poles can also be expressed, as in Frank Lloyd Wright's Kaufmann house in Bear Run [*1.23; 11.22–24*], which poses a dialog between the nature-affirming effects of fieldstone hearth, chimneys and floors laid in irregular slabs linking the interior and exterior, and the contrasting smoothness of the

1.23 Kaufmann house, Fallingwater, Bear Run, Pa., by Frank Lloyd Wright, 1936

1.24 Ames Gate Lodge, North Easton, Mass., by H. H. Richardson, 1880

carefully formed cement balconies, which Wright wanted to paint gold. Claude Nicolas Ledoux's Hôtel Thélusson in suburban Paris was a classical jewel entered through a menacing imitation cave.

The dialectic of nature and artifice is expressed in the paradoxical imitation of natural forms by manmade elements. Rustication, adopted from a small number of Roman buildings of the first century, was a Renaissance device that aimed to give building blocks the appearance of "living" stone as distinct from the ashlar masonry of finely finished surfaces. While late medieval and early Renaissance rustication implied a military and public function, the symbolism evolved in the sixteenth century to conform with the rustic implications of the term, and rustic gates, walls and portals, often with the rusticity created in terracotta, were increasingly used for villas. Sebastiano Serlio, taking up the idea from Giulio Romano, made much of combining rustic and smooth treatments as a way of dramatizing the antithesis of the natural and the artificial [1.28]. The fountain-grotto of villa gardens was a companion motif, in which irregular natural phenomena such as stalactites were reproduced in a variety of plastic materials to which natural objects such as shells and fossils were added. H.H. Richardson used rustication of a vigorous new kind, not intending particularly to refer to the Renaissance, most vividly in the Ames Gate Lodge [1.24] and the Payne House in Waltham, Massachusetts. He was also one of many proponents of shingles as a nature-invoking surface.

1.25 Villa Medici, Cafaggiolo, by Michelozzo, 1440s? Painting by Giusto Utens, 1598/99

The expression of power and class aspiration is evident in the first villas of the Renaissance, which took over the vocabulary of the medieval feudal castle—towers, irregular blocks, battlements and crenellations—such as the Medici villa at Cafaggiolo [1.25; 3.6]. Even a villa as modern as Lorenzo de' Medici's Poggio a Caiano [1.14] was given a walled enceinte with four corner towers decades after its completion, and the equally avant-garde early sixteenth-century Villa Giustinian at Roncade, near Venice, was given a moat and drawbridge [3.23]. Castle-villas returned to favor in the eighteenth century in the work of Vanbrugh and in the early Scottish designs of Robert Adam. While the adoption of Georgian architectural symbols in southern plantation houses affirmed the link of the colonists with their homeland, Jefferson's taste for Republican Roman and Palladian references was intended to express Republican as against aristocratic ideals [1.26]. In nineteenth-century Newport, Rhode Island, the villas of the excessively rich again assumed aristocratic, even regal pretensions.

Regionalism permeates the symbolism of the Florentine villas of the Medici dukedom in the sixteenth century, the British villas of Scott, Voysey and Lutyens, and more recently those of the California school.

Palladio was extraordinarily prolific in devising and combining villa-messages. While his geometric and axial forms and white surfaces express a sophisticated contrast to the organic world, the composition often reaches out into the surroundings [4.10, 13]. While his domes and temple-front facades imply the patron's exalted social status by suggesting classical learning and religious tradition, he could join them to common

1.26 Monticello, Charlottesville, Va., by Thomas Jefferson, begun 1768: garden (west) front

1.27 Villa Emo, Fanzolo, by Andrea Palladio, c. 1564

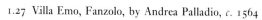

barnyard elements. At the villas Barbaro at Maser [*4.10*], Emo at Fanzolo [*1.27*], and elsewhere, he adapted the loggias flanking the templefront from *barchesse*, traditional agricultural sheds of the Venetian mainland, designed to store farm machinery and implements, produce and cattle. Their role in the Palladian villas was probably not fully utilitarian: the patrons would not have supported the odors and noise. *Barchesse* do not appear at the Villa Rotonda near Vicenza [*4.18*] because it is a suburban villa with no farm functions; here, Palladio tells us, he put temple fronts on all four faces of a domed cube to underscore the focal position of this hilltop site in relation to the surrounding views.

Conclusion

The villa poses a cultural paradox. If the farmhouse resists change because agriculture and farm culture evolve slowly, we might expect the villa to remain even more convention-bound: it is supremely conservative socially, being a luxury commodity available only to persons of privilege and power, and the ideology that sustains the type has changed little over millennia. Yet the mythical nature of villa ideology liberates the type from mundane restraints of utility and productivity and makes it ideally suited to the creative aspirations of patron and architect. Often this creativity has been limited to the sphere of taste, like that of fashion in apparel, which has also been motivated by an unchanging mythology since surplus wealth first offered its temptations. But the villa draws our attention because through the centuries it has articulated concepts and feelings of different cultures with respect to the dialog between city and country, artifice and nature, formality and informality. The villa gives shape to universal human concerns.

1.28 Sebastiano Serlio, Rustic Gate, from *Tutte le opere d'architettura*, 1584

2 · The Ancient Roman Villa

At the close of his Satire on the exasperations of living in Rome (II. vi), Horace tells the tale of the country mouse and the city mouse. The former invites his urbane friend to share a meal in his simple dwelling in the woods, serving the few delicacies he has managed to save—which his fastidious guest barely nibbles—while he himself eats dessicated berries and scraps of lard. The city mouse then persuades his friend that life is too short to be spent in rustic and frugal conditions and that he should join him in returning to town. There, all is luxury, in a great house with sumptuous furnishing and a vast array of remains from a banquet of the night before. But, as the companions are lounging on their ivory couches, there is a tumultuous banging on the door and the hall is filled with terrifying hounds. The country visitor beats a hasty retreat saying that he prefers his cave and his weeds.

In the preceding lines, Horace had complained of his own life in the capital where he is jostled by the crowds, suffers from bad weather and, because of his associations with highly placed persons and even the Emperor, is assailed by petitioners, called as a witness, and subjected to trivial gossip. He dreams of his Sabine villa near Tivoli where he can relax with the books of the ancients, sleep or simply rest, forgetting mundane cares, and where he can enjoy simple and plentiful wine and food, discussing with his guests matters of substance such as the nature of good and the question of its highest form.[1] Horace's image is not merely particular to him; almost all of the Roman writers who touch on the subject of country life depict the city in an unfavorable light.[2] Martial compares the constant noise and annoyances of city life, which disturbs his sleep (*Epigrams*, XII. 57) with the quiet of the countryside, where he has a farm; Juvenal (*Satires*, III. 160) compares the high cost of life in Rome, especially for the poor, with the simplicity of country life, were "no one wears a toga until he's dead." The toga apparently was the Roman equivalent of the suit and the necktie, and it was often referred to in this sense; Pliny the Younger, as we have seen (above, p. 13), listed among the advantages of Tusci, his villa in the Apennines, that there was no need to wear a toga there. Martial exaggeratedly claims that in Rome four togas are worn out in the summer, while one suffices for four autumns on his modest villa at Nomentum (*Epig.* X.xcvi.11); elsewhere he refers to "tunicata quies," repose in an ordinary tunic (*Epig.* IV.lxiv.10).

Pliny the Younger was a very wealthy senator and a writer of the first century AD who owned numerous properties and two palatial villas, while Horace was a celebrated poet of the previous century, the son of a freed slave. His modest villa–farm had been the gift of his patron Maecenas. Martial (*c.* AD 40–*c.* 104), also a poet, owned a small rural holding, evidently much more rustic than that of Horace, comparable in its own sphere to that of the country mouse. But despite the markedly different economic positions of the three, they shared a common attitude toward country life and, with a few others of their time, contributed to formulating for posterity the essential features of an ideology. Defined as an antithesis to urban life, its essential elements were the simplicity and the informality of country living, the healthfulness of the air and the opportunity for exercise (especially in hunting and fishing—though Pliny does confess to fishing from a couch), the scope for undisturbed intellectual and creative activities, leisurely conversation with friends, and the delights of contemplating the natural and cultivated landscape in different seasons and conditions.

What defines this complex of attitudes as an ideology is the fact that it can be maintained only by privileged persons whose income, whether large or small, is not dependent on the rigors and risks suffered by those full-time country dwellers who have to wrest a living from the soil and to suffer the tedium of a life in isolation. History records little evidence that farmers, peasants or slaves—who have no option but to stay put—experienced the charms of rural life depicted in the villa literature. Indeed, it was typically by the sweat of the laborer's brow that the delights of rusticity were made available to the proprietors.

But faint echoes of this contrast transpire through the literary encomia. The rigors of winter in the stormy countryside are described by Martial (*Epig.* VII. xxxv), who retains, however, the greatest affection for his villa. A letter of Horace dismisses—with what today seems crude insensitivity—the grumbling of the overseer of his Sabine villa (*Epistles*, I. 14) who is longing for the city with its games and baths and is complaining of the heavy farm work (perennial sentiments: witness the World War I song, "How're you gonna keep 'em down on the farm, after they've seen Paree?"). Columella (*De re rustica*, XII. Preface, 9) complains that the spoiled women of his time are bored in the country and look on a few days' sojourn at the villa as a "sordid business." Similarly, in later centuries, many of the attractions of country life identified in the literature have not been accessible to women.

For the large landowners, the country landscape may be clouded by the uncooperative attitude of peasants and tenants; Pliny writes from Tuscany that he has escaped there in order to be free to do as he wishes, but instead he is assailed by the complaining petitions of the peasants (*Epist.* IX. xv.1.3). Horace claims in the letter to his foreman that he likes to do a moderate amount of work on his farm, which was tended for practical purposes by the foreman and a moderate number of slaves. In his *Epode* II, which begins "Beatus ille qui procul negotiis / ut prisca gens mortalium / paterna rura exercet...", he focuses on the rewarding toil of the farmer and his wife and the pleasures of simple country food, probably in imitation of Cato and the agricultural writers to be cited below. The fame of this piece was rekindled by the free paraphrase of a later villa enthusiast who would not have found pleasure in wielding a hoe, Alexander Pope, in his *Ode on Solitude*:

> Happy the man, whose wish and care
> A few paternal acres bound,
> Content to breathe his native air,
> In his own ground.

Whose herds with milk, whose fields with bread,
Whose flocks supply him with attire,
Whose trees in summer yield him shade,
    In winter fire.

Blest! who can unconcern'dly find
Hours, days and years slide soft away,
In health of body, peace of mind,
    Quiet by day . . .

But in Horace's poem the perspective unexpectedly shifts in the last quatrain, where it emerges that the speaker is the usurer Alfius, who, having called in all his loans to acquire a country place, puts them out shortly after and remains in his despised vocation, in town.

Otium

The *negotiis* (from *negotium*) of Horace's first line (business, affairs, preoccupations) is the perennial antithesis of *otium*, the ideal condition of country life in the minds of urban Romans.[3] Pliny, in describing the benefits of his Laurentine villa on the seashore outside Rome, exclaims (*Epist.* I. ix. 6): "O sweet and honorable *otium*, lovelier than any *negotium*!" ("O dulce otium honestumque ac paene omni negotio pulchrius!"). If we must find a single English word for *otium* it would be seclusion, or serenity, or relaxation, but the ancients thought of it rather as an opportunity to engage, often intensely, in worthwhile physical and mental pursuits. The concept was sustained in early Roman times by the teachings of the Greek philosopher Epicurus (341–270 BC), which rejected glory, military enterprise, politics, and the crowd. Epicurean themes were sustained in the first century BC by the poets Lucretius, Catullus and, as we have already seen, Horace.

Pliny the Younger gives a vivid image of the relevance of the concept to the understanding of villa life in his description of a typical summer day at his more remote villa, Tusci (*Epist.* IX. xxxvi). He wakens at sunrise and meditates in the dark for a time, often planning the day's writing. Then he calls his secretary and dictates what he has composed; later, walking or sitting in the garden or portico, he returns to work, and again dictates, after which he goes for a drive in his coach, still concentrating on his writing. He continues:

Then I sleep a little more, and then walk, and then read a Greek or Latin oration aloud and with emphasis, not so much for my voice as for my stomach, though it strengthens both. Now I walk again, am oiled, exercise and bathe. Then if I am dining either with my wife or with a few friends, a book is read and after dinner a comedy is performed or the lyre is played. Again I walk a little with members of the household, a number of whom are well educated. . . . Friends come from nearby towns, sometimes bringing a welcome interruption when I am tired. I hunt a little, but not without taking my notebooks so that if I catch nothing I can still bring something home. I also devote time to my tenants—not enough from their point of view— and their boorish quibbles make our literary pursuits and urbane occupations more attractive by contrast.

Roman society was originally agricultural, however, and the conservative, libertarian spirit of the independent farmer and patriotic public servant survived in a segment of

Roman intellectuals of the late Republic and early Empire. Influenced by the Stoic tradition, they had only contempt for the Epicurean ideal and for the sort of country life it implied. They advised frugality, simple food and living accommodations and hard work. Their views are represented in the agronomical treatises and by Cicero and Pliny the Elder (uncle of the author of the *Epistles*). The major surviving agricultural texts represent three different stages and three centuries in the evolution of the Roman villa/farm: those of Marcus Porcius Cato (234–149 BC), Marcus Terentius Varro (116–27 BC) and Lucius Columella (first century AD).[4]

Cato, one of the distinguished statesmen of his day, wrote his short *De agri cultura* in the aftermath of the Punic Wars, when the countryside and its livestock had been wasted, rural manpower decimated and the peasant and freeholder ruined and driven into the cities by the pillaging of the armies, the competition of slave labor and cheap produce imported from the provinces. The agricultural economy was restored by two alternatives to the operation of traditional family farms.[5] One was the purchase by urban middle-class investors, like Cato, of moderate-sized farms to be worked by slaves. The other was the gathering of large properties (*latifundia*) by much richer city dwellers who had profited, often illegally, from the wars. These were ranches and plantations—made available both by the collapse of the peasantry and subsequently by confiscation of the property of those defeated in the civil strife of the first century BC—which were transferred from crop cultivation to grazing or, in the more southern areas, to wine and oil production. Plutarch (*Life of Tiberius Gracchus*, 8) refers to the country around Cosa in southern Etruria, the area of Settefinestre [*2.4, 5*], as "poor in free men, filled instead with *barbarici* slaves used by the rich to cultivate their property, after they chased away the farmers." That strategy was deplored by the agronomists as destined to weaken Rome by rendering it dependent for grain on provincial imports.[6]

Cato was deeply committed to affairs of state and to personal financial involvements, and his book addressed others like himself who sought to profit from their agricultural investment. He approaches the villa as if it were a factory for the production of certain commodities, and in his recommendations for the management of the staff of slaves he is calculating in his generosity and harsh in his administration, recommending reducing rations for slaves assigned to light work and selling those who are old or sick. He prescribes frequent supervisory visits by the proprietor, who depends on an experienced slave-foreman called the *vilicus* to carry the responsibility for the effective management of the estate.[7] But his image of the villa-residence, from what may be gathered from his sketchy description of it (*De agr.* XIV. iv), provides only basic shelter and does not recommend any but the most minimal comforts. This type is commonly referred to as the *villa rustica*. Such a building is described more fully by Varro (*Rerum rusticarum*, I. xiii. 1ff.). Apart from its ample kitchen, it is designed for the convenience more of the animal than of the human occupants: evidently the proprietor is not expected to spend time there. It is placed near the manure heaps for convenience. An interlocutor in Varro's Book III asks for clarification on the definition of a villa, pointing out that the same term is applied to the simple *villa rustica* and to the comfortable *villa urbana* (modeled on the city house) encorporated into the working farm, such as Varro's own at Reate. Varro allows that this is true, but insists that all villas may be economically productive and that in any event the elegant modern type designed for pleasure is degenerate.

Cato's attitude toward the country appears to be wholly unsentimental but for one theme that runs through his text and those of the other agronomers, the idealization of the traditional husbandman (*De agr.* I. iv): "But it is from the farming class that the strongest men and sturdiest soldiers come. Their calling is held to be the most exalted, and their living the most stable; they excite the least envy and are least likely to harbor evil thoughts." Varro writes, in the introduction to his second book (*Rer. rust.* II. i), "It is not without reason that those great men our ancestors preferred country people to city-dwellers; for just as in the country those who live in the [luxury] villa are lazier than those who are working in the fields, so they believed those who stay in town to be more indolent than those that live in the country." Pliny the Elder writes (*Naturalis Historia*, XVIII. iii, 13), in his account of early Roman agriculture, "The rural tribes who possessed farms were the most highly regarded, while it was a disgrace to be transferred into a city tribe because of the disapproval of inactivity."

The opinion of these determined farmers (echoed by Jefferson, p. 206) constitutes a competing ideology to that of *otium* and is fused with the view that life in the country, when led by the refugee from the city, ought to be Spartan, frugal, self-denying. This ideal was a survival of an age of independent husbandmen; it already was difficult to maintain when proprietors came to be city-based. Ultimately, in the age of elegant country houses after the mid-first century AD, it became anachronistic.

Virgil and country life

Virgil wrote two works devoted to life in the country that have been admired and read for two millennia: a pastoral poem in ten episodes called the *Eclogues* or *Bucolics*, from 42 to 37 BC, and, immediately after, the *Georgics*, a poetic treatise on agriculture in the tradition of the agronomers. Both poems were composed within the orbit of Octavian (later the Emperor Augustus) and reflect the impact of his policies on farm management. Both idealize and mythologize country life—but in a new way that curiously fuses the opposing ideologies of the authors discussed above. Like the agronomers, Virgil represents the life and labors of the husbandman and the shepherd as the optimal and most ethical existence but, like the city-based villa owners, he represents farming as a calling free of care and unwanted distractions which offers even the farmer the opportunity for *otium*. In contrast to Pliny the Younger, however, Virgil's *otium* is the reward for hard physical labor.[8]

The *Eclogues* constitute the paradigm of Arcadian literature (the term "Arcadians" appears in *Ec.* X. 31); shepherds and peasants or simple farmers inhabit an ideal countryside, joke with one another, or compose songs to heroes and beautiful boys and girls; mythology and legend enrich their leisurely existence. The universe of the *Eclogues* is idyllic and abstract. But in two of the ten poems (I and IX), the actual world enters. In the first, a dialog between Meliboeus and Tityrus, the former complains of having lost his farm by expropriation when, after the civil wars that brought Octavian and his allies into power (especially after the victory at Philippi in 42 BC), small farmers were dispossessed as land was redistributed to soldiers who had fought with Octavian. Tityrus, on the other hand, like Virgil himself, had gone to Rome and (probably through the protection of Maecenas, who was an intimate and adviser of Augustus) won the right to repossess his property. He speaks glowingly of Augustus for having brought peace to the peninsula. The Ninth Eclogue returns to this theme: one of the protagonists says "I hear Menalcas [read Virgil] saved all with his songs." There is a curious tone of unconcern in the face of this catastrophic dispossession; the ideal joys of the countryside have the power to compensate for the utter ruin and exile of country people around Mantua, where Virgil lived. Moreover, Virgil does not permit the reader to place his characters on the social scale, except to make clear that they are not great landowners: Tityrus once had a large herd, but lives simply; Meliboeus has lost a humble cottage with a turf roof; others work for a proprietor and might be slaves.

The *Georgics* is a more worldly work, since its aim was partly to instruct the reader in the fundamentals of farming. The nature that Virgil extolls in the poem is one tamed by men. A passage in Book II of the *Georgics* epitomizes Virgil's idealization of this nature. I quote from Dryden's 1697 translation:

> The World was hatch'd by Heav'ns Imperial King:
> In prime of all the year, and Holydays of Spring.
> Earth knew no Season then, but Spring alone:
> Then Winter Winds their blustring Rage forbear,
> And in a silent Pomp proceeds the mighty Year.
> Sheep soon were sent to people flow'ry Fields,
> And salvage Beasts were banish'd into Wilds
> Then Heav'n was lighted up with Stars; and Man,
> A hard relentless Race, from Stones began.
> Nor could the tender, new Creation bear
> Th'excessive Heats or Coldness of the Year
> But chilled by Winter, or by Summer fir'd,
> The middle Temper of the Spring requir'd,
> When Infant Nature was with Quiet crown'd.
>
> . . . .
> For what remains, in depth of Earth secure
> Thy cover'd Plants, and dug with hot Manure;
> And Shells and Gravel in the Ground inclose;
> For thro' their hollow Chinks the Water flows:
> Which, thus imbib'd, returns in misty Dews,
> And steeming up, the rising Plant renews.
> Some Husbandmen, of late, have found the Way,
> A hilly Heap of Stones above to lay,
> And press the Plants with Sherds of Potters Clay.
> This Fence against immod'rate Rain they found:
> Or when the Dog-star cleaves the thirsty Ground.
> Be mindful when thou hast intomb'd the Shoot,
> With Store of Earth around to feed the Root;
> With iron Teeth of Rakes and Prongs, to move
> The Crusted Earth, and loosen it above.
> Then exercise thy struggling Steers to plough
> Betwixt thy Vines, and teach thy feeble Row
> To mount on Reeds, and Wands, and, upward led,
> On Ashen Poles to raise their forky Head.

On these new Crutches let them learn to walk,
Till swerving upwards, with a stronger Stalk,
They brave the Winds, and, clinging to the Guide,
On tops of Elms at length triumphant ride . . .⁹

Like the arguments favoring life in the villa, this envisages the rustic delights of a golden age at the time of the Sabines, the Etruscans and the first Romans, in contrast to the exasperations and responsibilities of modern urban life. Virgil, who experienced a civil war and, as suggested in the *Eclogues*, was threatened with the loss of his own rural homestead, knew better than most how hazardous and demanding farming could be. Yet here the "earth unbidden pours forth its easy sustenance," and "boughs offer the fruit that the fields yield up of their own accord," while the farmer enjoys "secure rest." Of course, nature's prodigality is gained at the cost of hard labor and a frugal existence.

The *Eclogues* and *Georgics* reflect, each in its own way, the agricultural situation on the Italian peninsula in the Augustan period. We have seen that already in Cato's time small farms were disappearing, and that in the following century wealthy investors were acquiring great tracts of land and converting them, to the distress of the agronomers, from cultivation to pasturage. In the *Eclogues*, lesser farmers are also being dispossessed by land redistribution which, though it may simply shift the ownership of the smallholding, also represents large-scale centralized land planning. The first two books of the *Georgics* are devoted to cultivation and the third to pasturage. It is in the Book III (l. 41) that the author refers to the "haud mollia iussa"—the not-so-light yoke—of Maecenas (to whom each book is dedicated), a phrase that has been interpreted to mean that the theme of the poem as a whole, and especially of the book on pasturage, had been set by the Roman patron, despite Virgil's resistance, in order to support the land policy of the powerful landholders, and presumably of the head of state. René Martin has proposed plausibly that the reference to the patron's requirements refers only to the third book, and that Virgil originally had intended to conclude his poem with the paean to nature quoted above from the close of Book II.¹⁰

The change in agricultural economy from the family farm to the great estate is one that was to be repeated in future centuries. In the fifteenth century, the early Medici put together large properties by systematically acquiring small farms from their impoverished neighbors (see Chapter 3), and the landed aristocracy in seventeenth-century Britain enacted Acts of Enclosure to consolidate the small farms that had survived from the Middle Ages (see Chapter 7). In both cases the enterprise was related to the emergence of a particular kind of country house. Both of Virgil's books inevitably were addressed to the class represented by the great landowners—Seneca complained that Virgil, in the *Georgics*, "Sought not what was truest, but what could be most appropriately stated, and wished not to instruct farmers but to delight readers" (*Epistles*, LXXXVI. 14ff.)—and this helps to explain the idealized presentation of country life and the falsely idyllic depiction of the farmer's existence. The characters in the *Eclogues* might be wealthy aristocrats playing the role of shepherds, like the courtiers of Marie Antoinette at the Hameau in Versailles. Virgil does not overtly take the part of the proprietors: in addressing his reader as if he were contemplating becoming a cultivator or a shepherd, he draws together the two traditions of Roman writing on country life, that of the farmer-agronomers and that of the city dwellers seeking and praising *otium* in a country estate.

The typology of the Roman villa

The term "villa" may have been relatively new at the time Cato was writing: Pliny the Elder (*Nat. Hist.* XIX. xix, 50) wrote that there is no mention of the word in the ancient Twelve Tables of the Law. Vitruvius, the author of the only surviving ancient treatise on architecture (*De architectura*, written before 27 BC), offers a sketchy and inadequate description of a villa residence: "In town, the atrium is customarily right behind the entrance portal, while in the country, in the *pseudourbana* type of residence, peristyles come first and then the atrium surrounded by a paved portico" (VI. v.3). Beyond saying this, he describes only barns and other farming buildings.

A more useful definition of villa nomenclature is given in Columella's *De re rustica* (I. vi. 1), an encyclopedic treatise on agriculture of the first century AD. The *villa urbana* is the dwelling of the proprietor,[11] the *villa rustica* contains the dormitory of the foreman and slaves (with an underground prison for chained slaves) and the stables and pens, while the *villa fructuaria* is the structure for processing and storing wine, oil and grain (functions which in most excavated villas are encorporated into the *villa rustica*). The core of the *rustica* is a large kitchen. The *urbana* is elegant, with separate winter and summer apartments, baths, and promenades. The *villa suburbana*, passed over by Columella because it is not designed for agriculture, is a retreat near the city [*1.1; 2.7*]. Martial refers to the type, comparing his humble villa to the estate of a friend on the edge of Rome which is large enough for wine production and so extensive that the noise and disturbances of the city do not reach it (*Epig.* IV. lxiv). Finally, the *villa marittima*, also not primarily agricultural, appears at the seashore and often extends out into the water. The literary sources do not give much information on the type except to establish its frequency along the shores of the Bay of Naples, but it is represented in many Pompeian wall paintings [*2.14, 15*]. The paintings show primarily porticoes rather than dwellings and farm buildings; the desire to contemplate the sea was as strong as the taste for mountains and greenery.

Columella's predecessor Varro disapproved of the luxury of the *villa urbana*, which was just beginning to be sought in his time. "With respect to its buildings," he wrote (*Rer. rust.* I. xiii. 6) "a farm is certainly more productive if built rather according to the thrift of the ancients than the luxury of the moderns. . . . Now they want to have the largest and most elegant *villa urbana* and to compete with those of Metellus and Lucullus to the damage of the public." Lucullus's villas drew widespread criticism from contemporary authors, as indicated by the passage from Velleius Paterculus:

> As for Lucullus, who was otherwise a great man, he was the first to set the example for our present lavish extravagance in building, in banquets, and in furnishings. Because of the massive piles which he built in the sea, and of his letting the sea in upon the land by digging through mountains, Pompey used to call him, and not without point, the Roman Xerxes.[12]

Varro returns to this subject in the preface to his second book, on animal husbandry, saying that because modern proprietors no longer work on the farm, "they want citified

Greek *gymnasia*," sometimes more than one, and believe that they do not have a villa if it "does not ring with many Greek names" such as *palaestra*, *apodyterion* (dressing room), *peristylon* (loggia), *peripteros* (colonnade), etc. Cicero (106–43 BC) also has a character in a dialog express his distaste for modish villas: "I scorn [*contemno*] magnificent villas, marble pavements and decorated ceilings." In a similar vein, Seneca (54 BC–AD 39, in one of his letters (*Epist*. LXXXVI, 4ff.), describes the ancient towered and fortified villa built by the general Scipio Africanus in the second century BC. This revered leader "worked his own land as was the custom of our ancestors," and was satisfied with a cold bath in a dark basement, which Seneca contrasts to the ever increasing luxury and heat of public and private baths in his own time.

All the agricultural writers were disturbed by the declining involvement of villa proprietors in farming. Both Cicero (*De senectute*, XVI. 56) and Pliny the Elder recall that all senators were once farmers, and Cicero adds that Cincinnatus was behind the plough when called to assume the dictatorship. Columella quotes with approval the lost treatise of the earliest agronomer, the Carthaginian Mago, to the effect that "One who has acquired land should sell his [town] house, lest he continue to favor the city *lares* [household gods] rather than those of the country," and the senior Pliny repeats the same passage (*Nat. Hist*. XVIII. vii. 35) following the statement that the rural tribes of early Rome were held in the highest esteem while those that had settled in the city had fallen into ignominy (XVIII. iii. 13). Cato's concept of a villa was one devoted almost exclusively to agricultural functions; the main structure would have required, in addition to storage areas, stalls for animals, wine and oil presses and other utilitarian spaces, accommodations for the *vilicus*, cells or a dormitory for the slaves, and some modest accommodations for the proprietor on the occasion of his brief visits of inspection from the city. In such establishments, the distinction between the *villa rustica* and the *villa urbana* defined by Columella did not necessarily apply: the two were often fused in one, as in Vitruvius' chapter on the working villa (VI. 1ff.), which is concerned more with animals, storage and presses than with people. (He seems to be speaking of a much more elaborate establishment in another chapter when he mentions that the sequence from atrium to peristyle in a villa is the reverse of that found in city houses (VI. v. 3).)

Surviving villa remains of the Italian peninsula[13]

Among the excavated remains of Roman farmsteads, instances of villas in which the two functions are combined greatly outnumber those in which they are distinct. The great majority of these, however, seem to have been the principal residence of the proprietor, as suggested by the frequency of amenities such as ample central peristyles, wall paintings and mosaics and, occasionally, a bathing suite. There were few densely inhabited metropolitan centers other than Rome, and the population was spread over the countryside. Judging from the remains, most of these farms were modest in size.

The earliest villas that have been excavated, of the later second century BC, were simple farmhouses in which, as in the modern Italian *casa colonica*, no clear distinction can be made between the spaces occupied by the owner and those assigned to the laborers. In a model of such a villa at Boscoreale, near Pompeii [*2.1*], the large court to

2.1 Villa, Boscoreale, 1st C. BC: modern model

the right of the entrance is entirely devoted to containers for the fermentation of wine. Wine presses are in the low wing to the rear of the building. There is no atrium or peristyle; the entrance gives directly onto a small open court. Bedrooms are in the tall block behind the fermentation court. Of these villas, Varro wrote (*Rer. rust.* I. xiii. 6–7):

> In the old days a villa was praised if it had a good kitchen, roomy stables, and cellars for wine and oil proportioned to the size of the farm . . . whereas nowadays efforts are aimed at providing as handsome a dwelling house as possible. . . . Also they took care that the villa should have everything else required for agriculture. . . . while nowadays they have their summer dining room face the cool east and their winter dining room the west rather than, as owners used to do, to see on what side the wine and oil cellars have their windows.

Storage, pressing facilities, barns and stables were joined within the same walls with comfortable and even sumptuous accommodations for the proprietor. At the so-called "Villa of Publius Fannius Sinistor" at Boscoreale, near Pompeii,[14] the proprietor's quarters were ranged about the central peristyle colonnade and there was a bath on the east side, while to the west of the entrance was a room for pressing wine and oil. What appear to have been a barn and kitchens face the entrance court to the east of the entrance. The stables and possibly other elements were arranged below grade, and there was a second story over the kitchen and perhaps elsewhere. A summer *triclinium* or dining room has a large window facing east, as in Varro's description, and one to the north, while the winter *triclinium* faces onto the atrium and is closed on the northern side. A similar overall plan was found in a less elegant villa at Russi, near Ravenna, showing that the type was not restricted to Campania, where the majority of remains have been found. The need for security is the chief reason that the majority of the rustic villas of the first century BC were as tightly enclosed within their rectangular perimeter as a city house. This villa, moreover, by contrast to those without agricultural functions in the neighborhood of Vesuvius discussed below, does not, except for its summer *triclinium*, exploit views of the Bay of Naples.

Two sites at which the *villa rustica* is a separate structure from the *villa urbana* have been excavated and published recently: San Rocco, at Francolise, near modern Capua in southern Italy, and Settefinestre, on the coast near Orbetello in southwestern Tuscany.

The San Rocco villa [*2.2, 3*] was built on two hillside platforms, the upper, northwestern terrace being occupied by the residence or *villa urbana* and the lower by the *villa rustica*.[15] Both are supplied with large barrel-vaulted cisterns. The two rectangular blocks had the same orientation but different axes and were divided by a narrow roadway that could be closed off for security. The villa was remodeled and greatly enlarged in about 30 BC. In its earlier phase, of about 100–90 BC, the dwelling block had ten rooms disposed in an L, with no peristyle, as against the forty rooms of the later stage. The later *villa urbana* was designed like a city house [*2.6*], with an axial sequence introduced by a columnar vestibule/porch at the entrance from the roadway, continuing through a roughly square peristyle to a square *tablinum* (reception room) flanked by a *triclinium* and an *exedra*, and along a narrow passageway to the exterior and a stairway leading down through the platform to ground level. Probably one could have seen straight through the villa along this axis to a bit of sky beyond. In the second half of the first century, baths were added on the north side. Open porticoes on the south and west overlooked the countryside and the distant sea from the height of the platform (see below, p. 85). The smaller *villa rustica*, on the southeast, had two courtyards divided by a long common living and dining block and served both for agricultural purposes (pressroom, threshing floor, storage) and for housing the *familia*.

At Settefinestre, built principally in the second quarter of the first century BC, there were also two cubic structures, the *rustica* and the *urbana*, but here they were connected at one corner [*2.4, 5*].[16] The *villa urbana* was also built on a high terrace to compensate for the slope. For all its elegance it incorporates an industrial area along the eastern third of the block, with a latrine for a large workforce, rooms for pressing olives and grapes and a mill. Baths are placed in the northern end of this section. The domestic portion has the canonical axial spaces that create a perspective through its center and out to an *exedra* opening through a columnar porch onto a loggia (that runs all along the northwestern stretch of the terrace), and beyond to the valley below. Several rooms were decorated with murals of the second Pompeian style (*c.* 90–45 BC). The loggia, which can only have been intended for relaxation and enjoyment of the view, continues along the southwestern edge. An imposing portico of fifteen arches on piers below the loggia faces the principal garden, which is enclosed by an odd turreted wall that metaphorically reflects the fortified villas of an earlier age, as did those of Tuscany fifteen hundred years later [*3.3–6*]. The wall was known in the Renaissance, and drawn by a fifteenth-century visitor. (see also below, p. 85). The *villa rustica* has not been excavated fully, but appears to have had two large open courts and perhaps quarters for the slaves. Slave quarters are difficult to identify unless rows or courts of cells isolated from the domestic core appear in the plan. In other cases they may have been placed in the stables or in upper stories that have not been preserved.

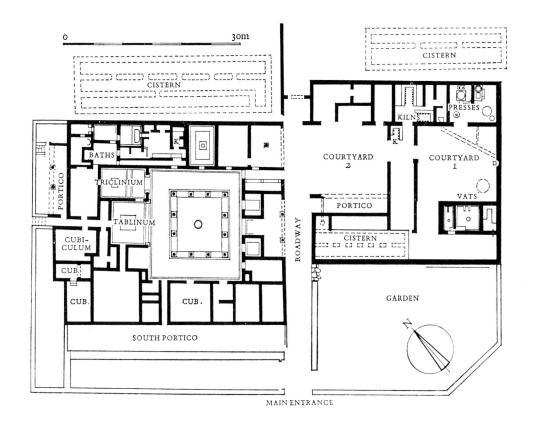

2.2, 3 Villa of San Rocco, Francolise, as enlarged in *c.* 30 BC: plan and perspective reconstruction

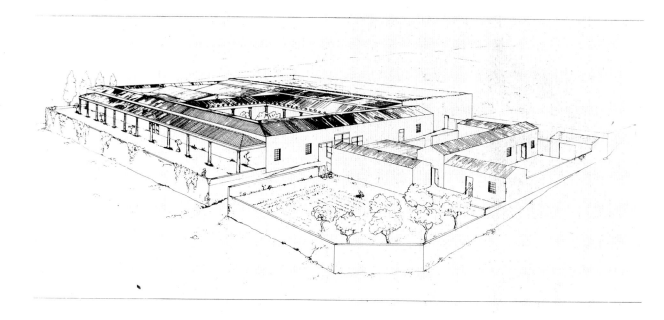

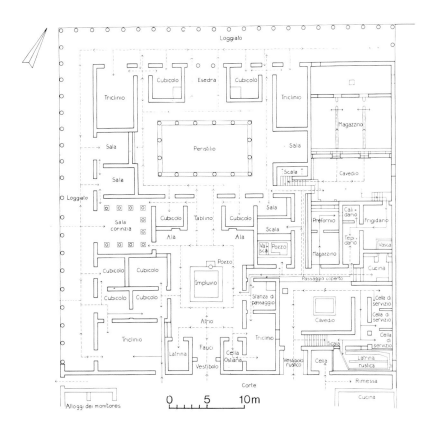

2.4, 5 Villa, Settefinestre, *c.* 75–
50 BC: plan of the *villa urbana*
and bird's-eye view
reconstruction of the complex as
a whole. The northwestern
loggia, at the top in the plan,
appears at the lower left in the
reconstruction, facing the garden
enclosed by the turreted wall.

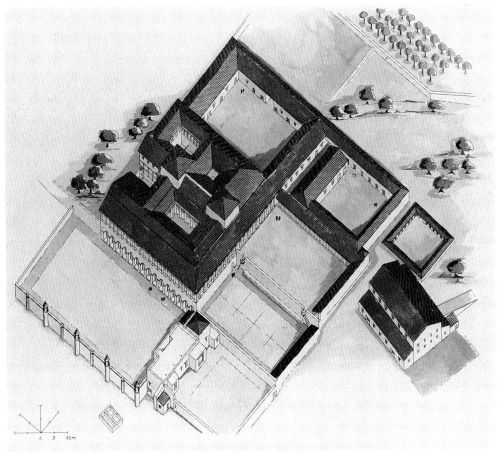

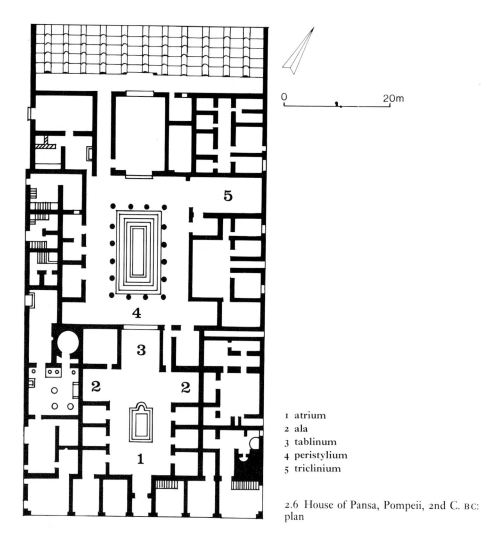

1 atrium
2 ala
3 tablinum
4 peristylium
5 triclinium

2.6 House of Pansa, Pompeii, 2nd C. BC: plan

The proprietors of most of these combined-function villas were probably constantly involved in agricultural concerns and shared only in part the ideology of the owners of luxury villas. They had no Pliny to speak for them, but their attitude must normally have been close to that expressed by Varro and Columella.

Much of what we know about pleasure-villas of the late Republic and early Empire has come from the excavations at Pompeii, Herculaneum, Boscoreale and the surrounding settlements, all buried in the volcanic eruption of Mount Vesuvius in AD 79. This area, skirting the coast of the Bay of Naples, including the neighboring district of Baiae (where less excavation has been possible), was the pre-eminent holiday resort of Romans during that period.[17] The circumstances of the disaster, which buried the communities under ash, a hail of volcanic stones and waves of lava and mud, and was followed by earthquakes, nevertheless left much of the ground floor masonry of many buildings relatively intact, and protected it from the decay to which most other Roman construction has been subject.

The several suburban villas in the outskirts of Pompeii [2.7] and Herculaneum were related in plan to the houses within the walls [2.6], most of which were built on rectangular plots with one side on the street, while the other sides abutted neighboring

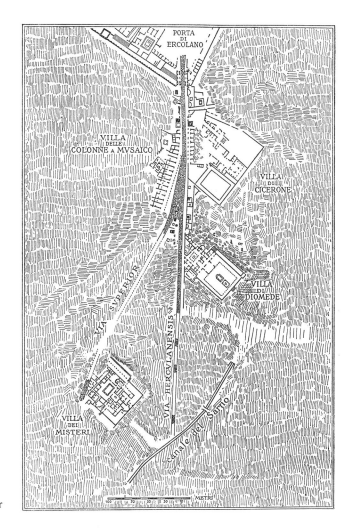

2.7 Suburban villas, Pompeii,
2nd-1st C. BC: plan. The villa
of the Mysteries is at the lower
left.

houses.[18] The entrance is on an axis along which the public spaces are aligned: an
entrance hall (*atrium*), an open court (*peristylium*) surrounded by a colonnade,
occasionally a vestibule (*vestibulum*) before the atrium or a *tablinum* after, and, at the
end, an *exedra* or a dining hall (*triclinium*). Some of the grander houses had large gardens
at the rear. While the houses were rarely built symmetrically about this spine, care was
often taken to provide a visual perspective from the entrance to the rear, framed by
openings in the successive partition walls.

The early villas, like the *villa urbana* of San Rocco [2.2], follow the house tradition
[2.6] and are generally contained within a compact cubic shell, though they are in the
open country. Along an axis, more or less central, public spaces are arranged in
sequence. The Villa of the Mysteries at Pompeii [1.9; 2.7]—named for its fine murals
depicting the celebration of Dionysian mysteries—which was rebuilt over a span of two
centuries differs in being supported on a high platform with an internal *cryptoporticus*
(covered walkway) and external blind arches that compensate for the slope in the terrain,
and in having exterior porticoes on three sides. The orientation appears not to have been
chosen primarily for the best view, but in accordance with the centuriation (land
surveying system) of the area: other villas had similar orientations. The entrance

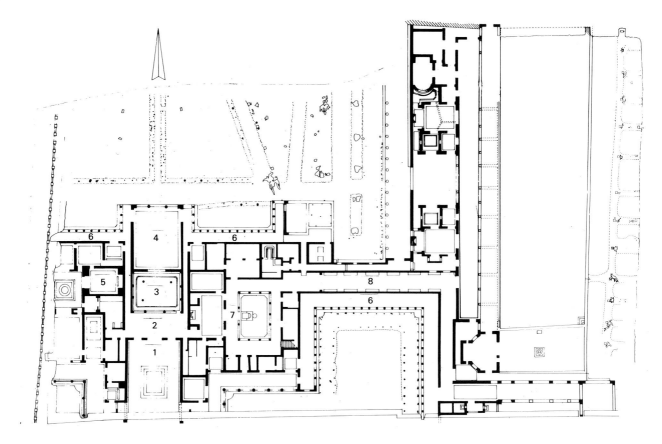

2.8 Villa, Oplontis, 1st C. BC–1st C. AD: plan.

vestibule, on the east side [*1.9, top*], gives directly onto the peristyle, which in turn opens onto the atrium (the reversed sequence is the chief criterion given by Vitruvius (VI. v. 3) for distinguishing villa from house plans). A *tablinum* follows the atrium, but here, atypically, the visual continuity is interrupted by a wall through which one could pass only by small side doors (this kind of blocking of an axial perspective is found in some contemporary architectural wall paintings of the second style, such as those from the "Sinistor" villa). The culmination of the axis is an open-air *exedra* built perhaps in the first century AD. It served as a lounge or *triclinium* overlooking the Bay, which again freed the visual perspective to extend outwards to the horizon. Between AD 14 and 63, just before the volcanic disaster that buried the city, a farming wing with slave quarters, a wine press and wine storage was added to the villa at the northeast corner. Alterations were still under way at the time of the eruption.

The most luxurious example of this type in the area is one started in the first century BC which has been excavated recently at Oplontis, near Pompeii [*2.8*].[19]. Here the city form is greatly expanded by the addition of a bath establishment (5), a large peristyle on the east side (7), a *cryptoporticus*-like passageway (8), and open porticoes around the exterior (6). The axis of public rooms is introduced by a large atrium (1), followed by what is probably a *tablinum* (2), an enclosed garden with engaged columns (3), and, at the apex, a great hall opened to the Bay by a two-columned pedimented porch, which may or may not have been a *triclinium* (4). In contrast to the Villa of the Mysteries, where the *tablinum* wall blocks physical and visual access to the panorama beyond, here one has on entering a view along the central axis through the villa to the rear garden. An extending eastern wing, rare in Pompeian villas, was added to the compact main block in the first century AD.

The Villa of the Mysteries and the Oplontis villa adapt the internal organization of the Campanian city house, but their freestanding and semirural setting prompted two innovations that I have already pointed out in two farm-villas, San Rocco [2.2] and Settefinestre [2.4]: the room that terminates the central axis, rather than being an element of closure oriented inward toward the peristyle, faces outward to embrace the view; and colonnaded porticoes are attached to portions of the perimeter to provide a protected engagement with the natural environment. Although spaces for agricultural use were added to the Villa of the Mysteries late in its history, these residences, like the suburban villas of modern times, were not centers of substantial agricultural enterprise and were probably not used for hunting and other sports.

From the late first century AD on, villas intended primarily for *otium* or pure pleasure became the norm rather than the exception. Independent farmers (other than soldiers rewarded for their services by a grant of small subsistence plots expropriated from peasants like Virgil's Meliboeus) had long since lost the competition with slave labor, and huge ranges for the raising of cattle and sheep replaced modest steadings of the sort we have been examining. Nevertheless, few grand pleasure villas have been found other than a number of sumptuous ones built by emperors, of which Hadrian's at Tivoli [2.9]

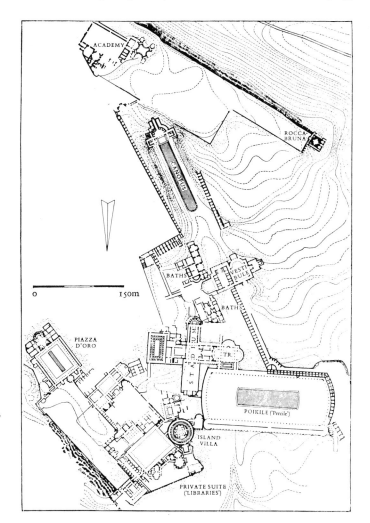

2.9 Hadrian's villa, Tivoli, 2nd C. AD: plan

is the best known. We are better informed about the lesser ones from literature than from excavation.

Our best informant is Pliny the Younger. Like many others of his class, he owned extensive property, and on at least two of his holdings he built or purchased luxurious villas. One, Laurentinum (his "Laurentine" villa), was on the seashore seventeen miles outside Rome, at Vicus Augustanus. The other, Tusci, was in Tuscany on the southern slopes of the Apennines overlooking the Tiber, at Tifernum Tiberinum, near modern Città di Castello. The former was used on weekends, exclusively for recreation; it had no farming functions. The latter, planned for more extended summer vacations, had vineyards and other profitable crops. Pliny described these two retreats in great detail in his letters, which were written for distribution as literary compositions.[20]

The letters take the form of a stroll through the buildings at each site; they emphasize the visual experience, particularly views of the landscape and the sea and diverse effects of sunlight. We get an impression of the variety and relative dimensions of the many rooms and walkways, but it is difficult to visualize the overall design, and through the centuries many widely diverging reconstructions have been proposed. Those of Winnefeld in 1891 [2.10, 12] are as persuasive as any.[21] The difficulty apparently arises from the fact that the villas were not designed initially with a cohesive overall plan, but grew by accretion. Individual portions had a consistent axis, but only a part of the design emerged from a core. To some extent this may have been a product of uneven terrain, but it is a characteristic so common in Imperial villa architecture that it virtually identifies the style of that era. Hadrian's villa at Tivoli [2.9] is the *locus classicus* of this approach to design, where each portion is integral to itself and does not conform physically to the design of contiguous structures, though there might be an optical linkage.

The Laurentine villa (*Epist.* II. xvii) is the easier of the two to visualize [2.10, 11].[22] It was more compact and less "modern," being a variation of the Pompeian suburban type [2.7]. Pliny describes the entrance (II. xvii. 4ff.):

> The villa is ample enough for my needs but not extravagant to manage. There is an atrium at the entrance [1], simple but not drab, then a *porticus* in the shape of the letter "D" [2] which surrounds a small but cheerful court. This makes a fine retreat in bad weather, being protected by windows and still more by the overhanging roof. Opposite the center is the cheerful *cavaedium* [3, a variant of the atrium], and then a rather lovely *triclinium* [4], which runs out toward the shore and, when the sea is whipped up by the southwest wind, is lightly washed by the breaking waves. It has folding doors and windows of equal width so that on the sides and front it seems to command, as it were, three seas. At the rear it looks back through the *cavaedium*, with its colonnade, the portico behind, and the atrium onto the woods and distant mountains.

Major bedrooms flank the dining area, one of which has an "apse" or curved wall with windows that take in the sun at all times of day. The rooms alongside this (8, 9) are equipped with steam heating. There is a gymnasium for the servants/slaves, and an ample bathing section (13–17) with two steam rooms between the hot and the cold pools. Nearby is an open ball-court (19) on the far side of which is a towered suite (20, 21: presumably most of the villa is one-storied) with another dining room that has a view of charming villas along the coast to the north.

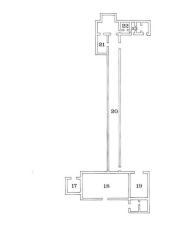

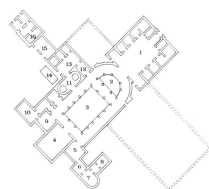

1 atrium
2 area
3 cavaedium
4 triclinium
5 cubiculum amplum
6 cubiculum minus
7 cubiculum in habsida curvatum
8 dormitorium membrum
9 cubiculum politissimum
10 cubiculum grande
11 cella frigidaria
12 unctorium
13 hypocauston
14 piscina
15 sphaeristerium
16 turris
17 turris
18 apotheca
19 triclinium
20 cryptoporticus
21 heliocaminus
22 cubiculum noctis
23 hypocauston

2.10, 11 Pliny's Laurentinum, 2nd C. AD: as reconstructed by Winnefeld (plan), and by Leon Krier (perspective)

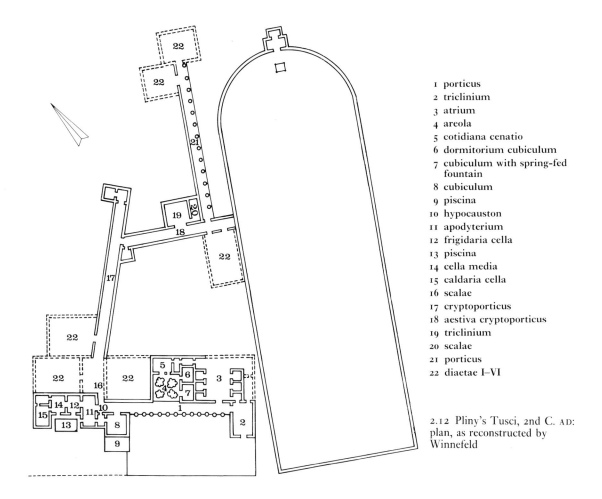

1 porticus
2 triclinium
3 atrium
4 areola
5 cotidiana cenatio
6 dormitorium cubiculum
7 cubiculum with spring-fed
   fountain
8 cubiculum
9 piscina
10 hypocauston
11 apodyterium
12 frigidaria cella
13 piscina
14 cella media
15 caldaria cella
16 scalae
17 cryptoporticus
18 aestiva cryptoporticus
19 triclinium
20 scalae
21 porticus
22 diaetae I–VI

2.12 Pliny's Tusci, 2nd C. AD:
plan, as reconstructed by
Winnefeld

Somewhat removed from these portions, though not necessarily in a separate group of buildings as shown in Winnefeld's reconstruction [2.10], is another tower and dining area, and a *cryptoporticus* (20) "almost as large as a public building." It runs parallel to the shore with many windows looking over a terrace (*xystus*, probably planted with a formal garden) out to sea, and fewer on the opposite side overlooking the flower- and kitchen garden. This wing has other heated bedrooms.

The description of Tusci (*Epist.* V. vi) begins with an evocative description of the landscape. The site is an "immense amphitheatre which only nature could create; the broad plain is ringed by mountains on the crown of which are ancient stands of tall trees, and various kinds of hunting may be found there." Both the hills and the plain have rich soil, with vineyards on the slope as well as on the flat, imposing manmade patterns on the scene, then meadows filled with flowers and varied grasses, and finally the river. The passage (V. vi. 13) concludes: "It is a voluptuous experience to look down on this scene from the mountain. You seem to be seeing not real land but rather a painted scene of exceptional beauty, and wherever the eye turns it is refreshed by its variety and precision."[23]

The villa [*2.12*] is set just below the summit of a hill at the foot of the Apennine range, facing south, so that it invites the afternoon sun into the main entrance portico (*porticus*, 1) which is broad and correspondingly long, and has many rooms connected with it as well as an old-fashioned atrium (3). In front of the portico there is the terrace-garden (*xystus*) of boxwood, as at Laurentinum (where it also extends from a portico), and below it, a garden with elaborate topiary work figuring animals and also a circus-shaped area with many topiary designs (*gestatio*). The major dining room (2) is at the end of the portico, looking out on the *xystus* and the adjacent meadow on one side and the hippodrome on the other. A small court (*areola*, 4) with a central fountain and plane trees gives onto the portico; around it are arranged the private bedrooms (one of which has a small fountain and a fresco depicting birds sitting on branches [*cf.2.13*] and informal dining rooms (5–7).

At the end of the portico is a sequence of bathing rooms with areas for cold, temperate and hot bathing, the last of which has itself three pools (11–15). A *cryptoporticus* leads out from the baths (17: it is not clear how this relates to the other areas), and there are two other promenades, one called the "summer *cryptoporticus*," on higher ground connected to another dining space, and one overlooking the vineyard (19, 20, the position also unclear). Beneath the latter is a subterranean passage that preserves icy air even in summer; it must have been the model for Jefferson's underground pantries and kitchen at Monticello (see Chapter 8). Beyond the dining room extends the open *porticus* (21: there is no evidence for placing this alongside the hippodrome) with suites of rooms at its ends (22).

The hippodrome is an elaborate garden shaped like a circus (not to be confused with the *gestatio*), similar to the later one placed alongside the Flavian Palace on the Palatine Hill in Rome. It was planted with both evergreen and deciduous trees, including fruit,

2.13 Garden mural from the Casa di Livia, Rome

topiary box shrubs forming a variety of figures and obelisks, lawns, roses and, in the center, an area imitating wild nature. This last is a detail that particularly impressed British landscape designers of the eighteenth century as they shifted from classic to picturesque principles; Robert Castell attempted rather clumsily to depict it in his reconstruction of 1728 [7.7]. There is a marble seat perched on a fountain at the curved end with a marble pergola, and a cistern is used to float delicacies for dining in vessels shaped like birds and beasts. This faces a bedchamber entirely of marble in which, gazing out at the trees and bushes, one feels as if one were in the wilds, though without risk of being drenched by the rain.

Pliny's repeated descriptions of the views that may be had from the windows of various rooms in both villas suggest that the planning may have followed the line of the most favored vistas. In the small bedroom at Laurentinum, for instance, you had "the sea at your feet, villas at your back and woods at your head" (*Epist.* II. xvi. 21). The various apertures frame the views of the sea, the mountains and the cultivated fields as if they were pictures, aestheticizing nature in the fashion of contemporary wall painting, in which fictive architectural elements normally frame the view into the distance.[24] *Varietas* is the underlying principle in the selection of a site that offers many different views, and subsequently in the provision of the doors and windows at different angles and heights.[25] Here again the aim anticipates the taste for the picturesque (see Chapter 9).

While the blocky, circumscribed form and the axial emphasis of the Pompeian villas still appear to have affected Pliny's Laurentine villa, Tusci had a loose articulation of parts in response to the irregular topography. But the difference also represents a different taste, emphasizing informality and a more casual approach to nature. It is characteristic of the majority of villas built after the mid-first century AD, but was anticipated already before the eruption of Vesuvius in AD 79 in the many "maritime" villas built along the borders of the Bay of Naples and the Mediterranean sea. These apparently were mostly luxury villas, but some were also managed for profit; contemporary sources refer to wine production and the cultivation of fish in seaside aquariums.[26] Often steep cliffs forced architects to build on many levels and to connect the parts with ramps and stairways.[27] Few of these villas have been well enough preserved or thoroughly enough excavated to reveal more than the general site plan, but they were a favored subject of Pompeian painters during the late years of that city.

The villas appear in small-scale wall paintings of the fourth style (AD 62–79) as the main features of a seashore landscape.[28] They do not represent actual buildings, but they do testify to the interest in maritime villas and to the evolution in the design of buildings for leisure from the contained blocks of the early Pompeian examples [2.7] to the open forms of the later first and second centuries AD.

One type [2.14] is actually found more frequently in Gaul, Britain and Germany [1.20A]: the portico villa with symmetrical forward projections. The buildings are usually on a raised platform, face the waterfront, and have airy colonnades across the entire front and occasionally the sides and rear as well. Many, like the examples illustrated here, have an upper story. The majority of the villas depicted in paintings are not as symmetrical and regular as these, however; many have loose arrangements of blocks [2.15], almost always with loggias along the front, and often with freestanding or attached towers. A mosaic from Carthage, in present-day Tunis, represents a villa complex with a similarly casual composition [2.16].

2.14, 15 *(opposite and below)* Maritime villas from Pompeian murals, *c.* AD 62–79

2.16 Mosaic of villa life from Carthage, 4th C. AD

The casual disposition of the fictive maritime structures is found in a few remains of actual villas dating from the mid-first century on.[29] Among these are the villas of Domitian, one near Sabaudia and another at Castelgandolfo, both on steep inclines overlooking the sea.

One that has been better preserved and more profitably excavated than most is that at Val Catena on the island of Brioni in Istria [2.17].[30] Here a protected inlet was developed as a harbor from which the produce of an exceptionally large villa could be shipped. The grand house on the heights to the south of the inlet (A) has an open terrace 11 meters wide all across its front. The residence itself—which is divided in two by a central wall without apertures—is closed and blocky and has none of the bold openness of the port structures. The elaborate building on the north shore is a bath (B). A terrace extending from C to D gives access to a sacred precinct (E) at the head of the waterway.

That the greater openness and informality of second-century planning appears even in inland villas on relatively level terrain is illustrated in the imposing complex of Sette Bassi on the outskirts of Rome [2.18].[31] The original core of the residence conforms to Vitruvius' description of the *villa pseudourbana* (see above, p. 42). It was constructed some time after AD 139 and is composed of a great peristyle [2.17, *lower left*] and a block of building behind it on its long axis. The peristyle entrance, however, is not on that axis, as earlier practice would lead one to expect, but in the center of the long exterior wall, so that one turns ninety degrees to the left to enter the building. There is no atrium, but a niche-like foyer at the entrance behind which cubicles of middling size are densely packed. To the right of the foyer is a sequence of bathing rooms. A few years later a tract

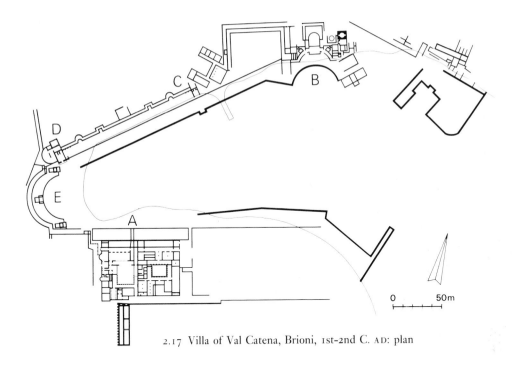

2.17 Villa of Val Catena, Brioni, 1st-2nd C. AD: plan

2.18 Villa, Sette
Bassi, after AD 139:
modern model

of more ample rooms with a large *exedra* overlooking the garden was added on the side of the peristyle opposite the entrance. The rooms here have large windows, in contrast to the narrow ones in the earlier block, and reveal an increased desire to engage with the natural environment just as Pliny had documented in his letters. In the next campaign, a majestic walkway 320 meters long, with many windows between paired columns, was constructed on the far side of the complex, forming a garden-hippodrome on the level of the basement of the residential quarters. Finally, a three-story palace complex on imperial scale was constructed in front of the earlier buildings [*2.18, lower right*). The asymmetrical outer facade is dominated by the huge reception hall, while the garden facade has a loggia extending its whole length. With the addition of the palace wing, the complex came to resemble more the Flavian Palace than even the most luxurious country houses of earlier times.

The few villas I have examined represent a small portion of the remains from Roman times. I intended to illustrate only the types of structures referred to in the contemporary writings. The literary as well as the archaeological evidence comes almost entirely from the late Republic and early Empire, a period of rapid development of the Roman villa. We know very little of villas on the Italian peninsula after the beginning of the second century AD apart from a few built for emperors, which had to serve representational and ceremonial functions that set them apart.

I have also omitted villas in the Roman provinces, which archaeological activity and aerial surveys over the last half-century have made better known than those in Italy. They too were functionally and economically different, being isolated from urban centers, and most were built or rebuilt after the second century.

The evolution of the Roman villa in Italy was intimately linked to economic and cultural changes in the period of the late Republic and early Empire. In that time, the Italian peninsula evolved from a self-sufficient to a dependent position in agriculture. The institution of slave labor, combined with the importation of provincial grains and foodstuffs, contributed to the collapse of small farms, whether owned by farmers who could not afford to keep slaves, or wealthy city dwellers like Cato, who had his farm managed and worked by slaves whom he supervised on the occasions of his regular visits. Many wealthy landowners acquired large ranch-like estates (*latifundia*) and converted them to stock raising and pasturage; none of these has been associated securely with villas. With this transition came also the first villas devoted exclusively to rest and recreation, with no agricultural functions. The Romans did not devise another term for this type.

A significant ideological change was prerequisite to the formation by city dwellers of a myth of country life that was to survive from Roman times to the present. In Cato's time, and among conservative writers of later generations, the country estate represented primarily a sound investment with an opportunity to increase one's profits by hard work, even physical labor, in a spare and frugal setting. Farming, and country life in general, was associated with the simple virtues of idealized ancestors.

A contrasting, Epicurean ideology that was to become the more influential in later generations transformed the country dwelling into a setting, often of great luxury, for the enjoyment of *otium*, the relaxing improvement of the mind and body. These changes had a great impact on the form of Roman villas, which evolved from compact, enclosed forms dependent on city houses (encouraged by concern for security) to loosely arranged gatherings of rooms, porticoes, cryptoporticoes, baths and towers, that might be constructed additively, over time. The earlier types were kept geometrically regular on uneven terrain by being supported on masonry platforms, while the later ones adjusted to the lay of the land by shifting axes and levels.[32]

In the course of this evolution, villa design turned by degrees from an urban introspection and isolation from its environment to an extroversion that made variety of aspect a major motivation. Villas like those of Pliny turned inside out, as the interior atrium and peristyle gave way to the exterior portico and *xystus* (though the spirit of inwardness was preserved in portions of Hadrian's villa [*2.9*] and in the villa at Piazza Armerina in Sicily [*1.15*]). They not only embraced the natural beauties of the countryside and seashore but themselves became objects of aesthetic worth. The new awareness of the delights of prospect emerged contemporaneously with the depiction of the natural environment in art, and villa owners frequently doubled the pleasures of contemplating nature by procuring landscape paintings as mural decoration. Painting and building also interacted in the development of perspective, as architects conceived sequences of doors and windows along axes that framed the view and painters developed techniques of converging orthogonals and receding planes.

These changes, most importantly the increasing autonomy of rural from urban forms, which took place over no more than one hundred years, were fundamental to the development of the country residence in future Western culture. Although civilized rural life was hardly possible after the collapse of the Roman Empire, the villa, when it reappeared, preserved the values and to some extent the forms that emerged from this climactic century of Roman civilization. Before the first excavations of the mid-eighteenth century at Pompeii, Herculaneum and other sites, later Westerners knew the Roman villa and the ideology associated with it exclusively from literary texts. But Roman ways of building in the country were somehow preserved unconsciously in Mediterranean farm buildings and in the Byzantine world to help Renaissance patrons and architects in their effort to re-establish the architectural forms of antiquity.

3.1 Benozzo Gozzoli, imaginary Florentine villa, from the *Adoration of the Magi* in the Medici Palace, Florence, 1459

3 · The Early Villas of the Medici

No Roman villas survived the collapse of the Roman Empire in the course of the fifth century. In the period that followed, the great cities were sacked and burned, and for about five hundred years most of the population of Europe clustered around the strongholds of the bishops and lords who offered hope of defense. In such a situation there was no opportunity for the growth of towns. Today there is not a major European city in which one can see a single stone of a street or secular building laid between the fifth and tenth centuries except for the few unearthed by archaeologists. We know no more of the physical character of settlements in this period than we know of those of Paleolithic man.

What we call the medieval city is the city of the later Middle Ages only, of the tenth to thirteenth centuries, and it was the artifact of a quite different society from that which preceded it. The rulers and the feudal nobility did not foster urban growth: their power was based on the land and on an agrarian economy. The city revival was the work of traders, craftsmen and manufacturers who established a communal type of government free of royal, imperial or ecclesiastical control and strong enough to defend itself against outside aggression. These city makers came to be called "burghers" or "bourgeois," because *Burg* and *bourg* mean citadel or fortress. It was this class of people who created a monetary economy that provided surpluses available for investment. When the feudal monopoly of the ownership of land outside the cities had begun to be shaken and the countryside had become sufficiently safe, the new class revived the villa—as distinct from the farmhouse and castle—to provide a place for relaxation and exercise and an investment in agriculture.

In late medieval Italy, while most aristocrats possessed a dwelling with a defensive tower in the resurgent towns, their principal seats were fortified castles on their own property in the country. These were symbolically and functionally centers of power and influence; they were rarely rebuilt to conform to current tastes because their age itself was a pre-eminent value—a sign of the antiquity of the line, of the precedence of the nobility with respect to the bourgeoisie, of the stability of tradition in a time of change. A crucial difference between the *rocca*, or fortified castle, and the villa was that the former was the seat of the proprietor's political and economic power and the latter was the place to which the proprietor would go to find respite from the responsibilities and cares of power, or management, in the city.

The favorable assessment of country life and the associated distaste for urban values and conditions disappears from written records in the West with the fall of the Roman Empire and emerges again only in the fourteenth century. The revival was stimulated and given focus by the most influential writer of the age, Petrarch (Francesco Petrarca), a Tuscan by birth, a great scholar of classical culture, a confidant of rulers and a major presence in the politics of his day. His great work in praise of the rural life, the *Vita Solitaria*, was started in 1346 in a cottage in the Vaucluse, outside of Avignon, which was then the seat of the papal court. The essay opposes the frenzied pursuit of urban ambitions and professions (*negotium*) to the peace and the potential for self-realization of life in the countryside (*otium*). Many of Petrarch's letters, which he carefully crafted for wide dissemination, are studies of the same contrasting conditions, and they detail the many pleasures to be derived from the sights, the sounds and the tastes of country life. He does not define the rural life as one of leisure: on the one hand, it is devoted to the development of *humanitas*, the most arduous of all tasks since it involves both intense study and dominion over the unruly spirit; on the other, it offers the opportunity for action, in agriculture and hunting. But, while Petrarch revives aspects of the ancient themes of villa life, he also preserves essential elements of the monastic tradition— solitude, chastity, celibacy—departing from it chiefly in the ultimate goal, which for Petrarch is the realization of an ideal humanity, rather than union with God. The life Petrarch proposed was not that of the villa: like Thoreau's five centuries later, it was too hermitic, too divorced from society and, incidentally, unrelated to any particular architectural setting. But no texts were more important for the revival of the ideology of the villa in the following centuries.[1]

Florence was a paradigm of the change from the countryside of the feudal fortress to that of the villa. Its emergence as a major center began a little later than most—the burst of building dates from the thirteenth century—but it gave the rest of Europe a model for the formation of a capitalist economy and a city-state. Already by the mid-fourteenth century the fashion for villa building had developed to the point that the chronicler Giovanni Villani would describe it disapprovingly as a craze:

> There was no ordinary or great citizen who had not built or was not in the process of building in the country a grand and rich estate with an expensive layout and handsome buildings, and much better than in town. And in this all were guilty and because of the unreasonable cost they were thought to be mad. And it was such a magnificent show that most foreigners not familiar with Florence, coming from outside, believed that these rich buildings and beautiful palaces in a three-mile band outside the city made a city in the style of [ancient] Rome.[2]

Renaissance bird's-eye maps of Florence show the hills to the north dotted with suburban villas of the kind to which Villani referred. We know of them also from a literary masterpiece written in the time of Villani, Boccaccio's *Decameron*. The ten stories in this collection are told by members of a group of wealthy young Florentine ladies and gentlemen who escape the terrible plague of 1348 by taking refuge in the family villa of one of their number, a most luxurious retreat two miles outside of the city, with splendid gardens.

There are no surviving villas from the fourteenth century, but we can imagine that they were not very different from those depicted in the background of the frescoes of the *Adoration of the Magi* in the Medici Palace in Florence, painted by Benozzo Gozzoli in the late 1450s [*3.1*]. Like the contemporary villas of the Medici family itself, Gozzoli's are composed of straightforward medieval elements such as towers, silhouettes with

3.2 Gonzaga castle, Mantua

military crenellations, defensive perimeter walls and moats and irregular plans, combined with Renaissance details, such as colonnaded loggias.

This commitment to medieval forms emerged paradoxically at a time of intense engagement with the revival of Roman antiquity in all aspects of the arts, sciences, humanistic learning and government. Any affluent Florentine who commissioned a palace or a chapel in town would have demanded that it reflect the design of ancient buildings, to the virtual exclusion of medieval features.

In this respect Florence differed from the many cities that were ruled by hereditary *signori*, such as Mantua, where in the fourteenth century the Gonzaga family had built a fortress-palace [*3.2*] close in style to those illustrated by Gozzoli [*3.1*], and continued to feel comfortable in it after they too had become among the most enthusiastic converts to the antique revival. I shall suggest that perhaps a little of the *signori* psychology affected the grand families of republican Florence when they left the dust of the city behind them.

This may be one reason why ancient villa life was revived in such a medieval form. Another reason is that the country was still not quite safe from bandits and marauders,

3.3 Villa Medici, Trebbio, *c.* 1427–33. Painting by Giusto Utens, 1598/99

which made it seem prudent to build (or, in the case of the Medici villas, to rebuild) in a modified castle tradition.

The two earliest Medici villas, at Trebbio [*3.3*] and at Cafaggiolo [*1.25; 3.4–6*], were near the route leading directly north from Florence toward Bologna, in a mountainous and fertile valley called the Mugello. The Medici had owned property there since before 1359, when they were farming the area for grain and wheat, and there were fourteenth-century structures at both sites before the Renaissance campaigns. Giorgio Vasari attributed the two villas to the Medici architect Michelozzo di Bartolomeo, but no direct evidence for the date of construction has survived. According to the most recent deductions from the records of agricultural activity at Trebbio, it was built some time in the period 1427–33.[3]

It is still uncertain how much of the existing structures preceded Michelozzo's intervention, but the many features common to the two villas (and to the third Medici castle–villa at Careggi [*3.7–11*]) suggest that while pre-existing foundations may have dictated the placement of some major masses, most of the visible portions of the interior and exterior were executed in the fifteenth century. These include the stuccoed exterior

3.4–6 Villa Medici, Cafaggiolo, *c.* 1443–52:
painting by Giusto Utens, 1598/99, showing the
estate from the east; plan (with east at the bottom);
and east front

surfaces, the window and door frames, the vaulted interior spaces, the projecting crowns of the towers and the machicolated passages that top the main blocks. They constitute elements of a "modern" style alternative to the *all'antica* mode of Michelozzo's Medici Palace in Florence. A number of civic and religious buildings were also designed by Michelozzo in this more conservative style, such as the Palazzo Comunale at Montepulciano (begun in 1440), where the tower and main block have similar projecting passages with crenellations.[4]

Cafaggiolo and fourteen surrounding farms were bequeathed by a collateral branch of the Medici family to the heirs of Giovanni di Bicci de' Medici in 1443 and came to his son Cosimo in a division of the estate in 1451.[5] The villa was described in 1456 as "A place for habitation at Cafaggiolo outfitted as a fortress with two towers and a drawbridge and a moat around it. And a piazza in front and garden behind." At this time it was the center of a property that included thirty-one farms.[6] A massive tower in the middle was still standing in 1598/99, when the estate was represented in one of the series of paintings of Medici villas by Giusto Utens [*1.25; 3.4*].[7] The painting also shows that the existing frame of the entrance portal and the arched entrance to the court on the right were not part of the original design [*cf. 3.6*]. Another change, as indicated in the plan [*3.5*], was the addition in the sixteenth century of a substantial block to the rear of the villa, overlooking the garden, with a loggia on the upper story of the north side. Before this time the principal court to the rear (which may not have had the two-room block that now fills one corner) probably had only a low wall on the garden side and received ample direct light. Today, surrounded by three-story-high walls on all sides, it is a dour and inelegant space. The long vaulted entrance gallery, on the other hand, is airy and noble, as are the ample and well proportioned rooms on the ground floor. Details in these apartments such as brackets and moldings suggest, by their greater refinement, that the villa was designed later than that at Trebbio.

A recently discovered chronicle reporting the visit to the Cafaggiolo villa by Pope Eugene IV in 1436 suggests that Averardo de' Medici may have completed the rebuilding before the Medici exile in 1433; but if Cosimo was the instigator, as suggested by Vasari, a more probable date would be between the 1443 extinction of Averardo's line and the official distribution of property in 1451.[8]

The purpose of the kind of villa structure represented by Trebbio and Cafaggiolo was to serve as a center for the collection and distribution of the agricultural production of the surrounding farms, which the family continued to annex throughout the century.[9] Cosimo and his successors did not see them as symbols of power and prestige. But, though Michelozzo's work still retained a severe fortress character, these dwellings did serve the function of the villas of antiquity as a place of escape from the city and a healthy setting for relaxation and good fellowship. Lorenzo the Magnificent spent much of his youth at Cafaggiolo, and later maintained close contact with his bailiff there in correspondence that shows an informed interest in dairy farming.

During the twelfth and thirteenth centuries the agricultural economy of central Italy had been radically altered by the widespread dissolution of feudal ties. The dramatic growth of urban centers weakened the grip of the rural *signori* and created a demand for farm produce that the feudal system could not provide. Peasants were gradually freed from serfdom and came into possession of the property they were able to cultivate by their own labor. But few had sufficient resources to protect themselves against the hazards of farming, and city dwellers with surplus capital were eager to purchase their property and their services. From the late thirteenth century in Tuscany, peasants made contracts with the investors that did not call for cash payments in rent but for the equal sharing of the farm's production, an arrangement called *mezzadria*. The majority of buyers were citizens of modest means who sought a small farm as a defense against the recurrent famines, and it was largely from these urban investors that the Medici and other rich entrepreneurs amassed great estates during the fifteenth century, when the threat of famine had receded.[10]

There were numerous motives for the extent and the pervasive pattern of investment in agricultural estates by the Medici and other wealthy Florentine financiers and bankers. While the average yield from agriculture in the Florentine countryside in the mid-fifteenth century was around six percent, at a time when far higher percentages could be realized from banking and trade, farming was a way of diversifying investment that, in spite of the vicissitudes of war and weather, was not subjected to the same fluctuations as the urban markets. Real property could also be offered as collateral. Besides, the building of estates by acquiring individual farms adjacent to a villa residence brought with it a prestige rooted in the medieval regard for landed property.

A villa residence also offered, as it had for the young protagonists of Boccaccio's *Decameron*, a refuge from the periodic plagues of the period. The Medici in particular must also have felt the need for a protected retreat in the event of violent opposition to their power. Maybe this caused them to favor a fortress-like architecture in the years following their exile in 1433. The fact that they installed retainers or family members in many of the farms surrounding their villas suggests a desire to build a power-base resembling that of the medieval feudal *signori*.[11]

Finally, the agricultural produce of the villa was as helpful to the economic management of the great family palace, with its large force of servants and attendants, as it was to the small landholder. This is the first point made by the head of a Florentine family in Leone Battista Alberti's widely read dialog on family government, which also reveals some of the class tensions fueled by the encounter of the new monetary economy with the traditional barter system:

> *Gianozzo:* I would make every effort to have estates from which my house could be kept furnished with grain, wine, wood and straw, all much more cheaply than by purchase in the market. I would there raise flocks, pigeons, chickens and fish as well. . . . I would very much like to have the whole place united or to have the parts close together, so that I could often pass through all of it without going too far out of my way. . . . This also reduces the number of peasant families one has to deal with; it is hard to believe how much wickedness there is among the plowmen raised up among the clods. Their one purpose is to cheat you, and they never let anyone deceive them in anything. All the errors are in their favor; they try constantly and by every means to get and obtain what is part of your property. First the peasant wants you to buy him an ox, goats, a sow, a mare also and then sheep too. Next he asks you for loans to satisfy his creditors, to clothe his wife, to dower his daughter . . .[12]

The Medici villa of San Piero at Careggi, acquired from Tommaso Lippi in 1417, differed from the earlier castle-type residences more in function than in form [*3.7–11*]. It was a small suburban villa, on the populous slopes of the hills to the north of Florence

3.7 Road front. The wing to the right of the small door that leads into the courtyard [*3.10*], with the large rusticated portal, was added in the 16th C.

3.8 View showing the garden front [*3.11*]. From Giuseppe Zocchi, *Vedute delle ville . . . della Toscana*, 1774

Villa Medici, Careggi,
remodelled by Michelozzo,
1430s on

3.9 Plan: entrance front, bottom; garden front,
left. Solid lines indicate the original building;
dotted lines, later extensions—the range seen on
the right in *3.7* (right), and the loggia of the left
in *3.11* (top).

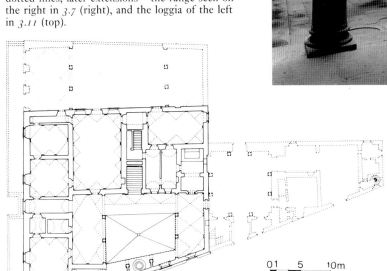

0 1   5   10m

3.10 The court

3.11 The garden front

(a nearby castle–villa, towered like those in the Mugello, appears in the background of Giuseppe Zocchi's eighteenth-century view [*3.8*]), within perhaps an hour's ride by horseback, and could be used as an alternative residence for a casual short visit or for state occasions. A banquet was given there to entertain Francesco Sforza in 1439, and in 1459 his son Galeazzo Maria wrote a letter describing the amenities of the villa and its garden. More frequently it was used as a refuge, or as a place to recuperate from illness (Lorenzo the Magnificent chose to spend his last days there). It was also an agricultural center: the family acquired eleven surrounding farms between 1437 and 1456, and twenty-seven farms were declared in the 1480 tax rolls.[13]

The remodeling of the villa by Michelozzo, recorded by Vasari, may have extended from the 1430s through the 1450s and beyond, and the building underwent substantial changes in the sixteenth century, with the addition of a wing on the east side [*3.7*, right, with the large rusticated portal].[14] Evidence of different building campaigns is visible even on the older portion of the facade along the road: the arches of the corbel table to the far left, toward the garden, where the line of the facade is slightly deflected, are narrower and more regular and are apparently later than those to the right.

The garden facade is symmetrical about its central portal [*3.11*], and has more of a Renaissance appearance than the street facade. The window frames have probably been altered since Michelozzo's time. The two-story loggia at the left end of the garden front and another loggia facing it across a small court are not visually or structurally coordinated with the main block of the building, and have the appearance of a later addition [*3.9*]. They may have been added by Lorenzo de' Medici later in the fifteenth century, or less probably (given the Quattrocento style) by Alessandro de' Medici after Republicans burned the villa in 1529.[15]

The regularity of the court is disrupted by the angular facade wall that bends with the road; the line was probably preserved from the pre-existing building. On the interior of this wall, Michelozzo placed a projecting passage cantilevered out over octagonal columns and capitals in a conservative style [*3.10*] intended perhaps to distinguish the old portion of the villa from the new. This side of the court was believed until recently to have survived from the fourteenth century. The arches of the other two arcades of the court are supported by columns and capitals characteristic of Michelozzo's mature classicizing style. We do not know whether the two modes were employed contemporaneously or successively.[16]

In contrast to the Mugello villas, then, Careggi has a mixture of the conservative and the *all'antica* styles—apparently not simply because it was constructed slowly, but to convey a message. Only Michelozzo in this period would have been satisfied with the juxtaposition of octagonal and classical column shafts in the small compass of the court. In the same years, he was building the majestic Medici Palace in Florence, the first major monument of the *all'antica* style in Florentine domestic architecture. The messages projected by the two dwellings seem inconsistent. The villa is traditional, modest to the point of recessiveness, and irrational in form, while the palace is innovative, dominating and classically regular. They signify the two poles of Medici policy at mid-century, the one to rule from behind the scenes through intermediaries rather than to take offices of leadership, and the other to ensure that their real power was made apparent.

The modest character of the villa was determined also by Cosimo's aim to use it primarily for intellectual recreation in the form of humanistic symposia and learned conversation rather than for political purposes. I suspect that Cosimo had in mind an emulation of the country residences described by Petrarch at Vaucluse and Arquà. Some of this spirit is conveyed in his letter to the Neoplatonic philosopher Marsilio Ficino:

> I came to the villa at Careggi not to cultivate my field but my soul. Come to us, Marsilio, as soon as possible. Bring with you our Plato's *De summo bono*, which by now I suppose you have translated from the Greek tongue into Latin as you promised. I desire nothing more ardently than to know the route that leads most conveniently to happiness. Farewell, and come not without the Orphean lyre.[17]

Comparable functions must have been contemplated for the villa at Fiesole, which Cosimo commissioned for his son Giovanni shortly before 1455 at a site only slightly farther from the edge of Florence than Careggi. A letter written to the humanist Francesco Filelfo by Bartolomeo Scala in the autumn of 1455 relates that

> I set out in the afternoon for Fiesole, where Giovanni was rusticating, absorbed in his building. . . . He read [your letter and poem] very carefully and then spoke most warmly in your praise, saying he had written to you that very day, and urging you, if you thought him worthy of the kindness, to undertake the work of interpreting Petrarch's poems, which in themselves are somewhat obscure. . . .[18]

The Fiesole villa, however, was only large enough for small gatherings and could not accommodate more than the intimate family. Probably it was used for short visits. It had no connection with agriculture, and was not an adaptation of an existing structure; the site was chosen for the panoramic view, and a massive substructure had to be built to support the building and the garden on the steep hillside. It appears from a detail in a late fifteenth-century fresco by Domenico Ghirlandaio [*3.12*] and in an eighteenth-century drawing and print from Giuseppe Zocchi's series of views of Tuscan villas [*3.13*] that the original platform was considerably shorter than the present one. Michelozzo thus was free of constraints imposed by medieval walls, foundations and towers, and could build in an advanced style.[19] The two views show also that this style was much more chaste than the present building indicates, and more so than that of any other domestic building of the time. The villa was a cubic block covered in off-white stucco, with four-arched loggias on both sides. A basement story opened onto a lower platform at the rear. Vasari reports that it was

> founded upon a base on a slope of the hillside with the greatest expense, but not without great utility: having in the lower part vaults, cellars, stables, storerooms and other handsome and commodious habitations; and above, beside the chambers, public halls and other rooms, he made some for books, and certain others for music.[20]

This is the first of the Medici villas completely open to the exterior and without a central court. The arches are not molded and the windows are unframed. The only relief elements are bands at the top of the loggia piers. The many changes made in the sixteenth century left few traces of Michelozzo's conception [*3.14, 15*]. On the entrance side, the loggia bay to the far left was walled in, a block of rooms was added along the right side, and all the surface features were altered. There is virtually no evidence to support a reconstruction of the original ground plan, except that the depictions of Ghirlandaio and Zocchi [*3.12, 13*] make it clear that with open loggias at both front and rear the principal *salone* probably occupied the full depth of the main floor. Nor do we know anything about the garden, but it is likely that formal parterres were laid out on the terrace before the entrance loggia; this may have been the first formal garden in the Renaissance to be conceived as an extension of the architecture.

Assuming the accuracy of Ghirlandaio's representation, this villa was dramatically dissimilar to its predecessors in symbolism as well as in form. This is due less to its later date and the evolution of Renaissance architecture than to its distinct role as a suburban villa without an agricultural function, the scale and form of which was accommodated to the choice of a site with a panoramic view. No military features and no reminiscences of medieval architecture were admitted. Nor, for that matter, was there an effort to refer to the classical tradition. The Fiesole villa is an abstract, purist structure designed, by virtue of its geometry and light, creamy color (to judge from Ghirlandaio) and smooth texture, to stand off from rather than to merge into its natural environment. In this it became the source of Poggio a Caiano and of a multitudinous progeny of light-colored, smooth-surfaced cubic villas from Palladio's Rotonda to Le Corbusier's Villa Savoye.

Villa Medici, Fiesole, by Michelozzo, commissioned shortly before 1455

3.12 Detail from Domenico Ghirlandaio, *The Assumption of the Virgin*, Santa Maria Novella, Florence, 1486–90

3.13 The villa after 16th-C. alterations. Detail of a preparatory drawing by Zocchi for his *Vedute delle ville*. The villa appears at the bottom right, seen from the southwest.

3.14 View from this southeast. The entrance front is on the right, as in *3.12* and *3.15*.

3.15 Plan

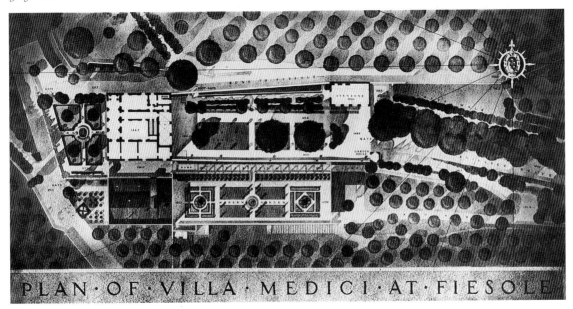

3.16 Leonardo da Vinci, landscape drawing, 1473

In some respects, the Fiesole villa conforms to the precepts of Alberti's *De re aedificatoria*, which was finished at about the time of its construction though not published until 1485. Alberti based his book on the schema formulated by Vitruvius early in the first century BC. Alberti calls for a villa to be on a height, to make its forms more grand, and with a garden and light all around. His villa, however, would have been considerably more imposing than Michelozzo's, and he would not have approved the absence of any references to Roman architecture. But the dictum of Alberti most relevant to Michelozzo's innovations at Fiesole is his vigorous attack on the traditional castle–villa: "It seems improper to me," he writes, "that spires and battlements be placed on the buildings of private citizens, for these are suited to fortresses and particularly to those of tyrants, and are foreign to a peaceful citizenry and a well constituted republic because they signify a threat of fear and oppression."[21] A letter written from the Fiesole villa by the poet Angelo Poliziano to Ficino gives a vivid image of the attractions of the retreat:

> When you are made uncomfortable by the heat of the season in your retreat at Careggi, you will perhaps think the shelter of Fiesole not undeserving of your notice. Seated between the sloping sides of the mount, here we have water in abundance and, being constantly refreshed with moderate winds, find little inconvenience from the glare of the sun. As you approach the house it seems surrounded by trees, but when you reach it, you find it commands a full prospect of the city. Populous as the vicinity is, I can enjoy here that solitude so gratifying to

my disposition. But I shall tempt you with other allurements. Wandering beyond the limits of his own property, Pico [della Mirandola, the humanist philosopher] sometimes steals unexpectedly on my retirement, and draws me from the shade to partake of his supper. What kind of supper that is you well know; sparing indeed, but neat, and rendered graceful by the charms of conversation. But be my guest. Your supper shall be as good, and your wine perhaps better, for in the quality of wine I shall contend for superiority even with Pico himself.[22]

Ficino, in turn, wrote in 1488:

When once I and my noble master Pico della Mirandola were wandering among the hills of Fiesole, we saw spread out beneath us all Florence—fields, houses and, in the middle, over the Arno, mist, and on the other side, steep mountains. We imagined a house placed on the slopes of the hill in such a manner as to escape the fog of Boreas, but without putting it in the crevice, to allow it to receive breezes when the weather is warm.[23]

One aspect of the function that had not been a factor in previous country building was the weight given to the extensive view. Clearly, the patron chose the site because it commanded all of Florence and a great stretch of the Arno valley, though a contemporary letter quotes Cosimo as having said that he preferred Cafaggiolo because there everything he could see belonged to the family.[24]

In this respect the Fiesole villa anticipated a re-awakening interest in the aesthetic values of the natural landscape documented in the famous drawing of the young Leonardo da Vinci, dated 1473 [3.16]; here the artist imagined himself on just such a hilltop surveying a valley. At the same period, Mantegna, in the Camera degli Sposi in Mantua, placed a building with a neo-antique loggia, perhaps a villa, outside the city walls on a platform on the slope of a steep hill. It would have commanded a sweeping

3.17 Andrea Mantegna, imaginary villas, detail from a fresco depicting the ducal family in the Camera degli Sposi, Ducal Palace, Mantua, 1474

view. This structure is so frequently cited as an example of Mantegna's antiquarian interests that the appearance of a pair of castle villas in the adjoining fresco panel [3.17] (close in style to that in Gozzoli's fresco [3.1], but more fortress-like), one with a traditional tower under construction, has been largely overlooked. The juxtaposition suggests that sustaining two distinct villa styles contemporaneously was not an idiosyncracy of the Medici family, but an accepted way of expressing the cultural ambivalences of that time.

Soon villas began to be frescoed with bird's-eye perspectives of actual cities; Pinturicchio was called to paint views of this sort in the arcades of Pope Innocent VIII's Villa Belvedere in the Vatican, which was built in 1487.[25] The frescoes in the *salone* of the Villa Farnesina in Rome (begun in 1509) were designed by the architect–painter Peruzzi to give the illusion that one looks through a colonnade toward the city across the Tiber.

The extraordinary innovation in form and function at the Fiesole villa consists in the replacement of the economic values of the earlier Medici properties—income, security, the provisioning of the city palace—by ideological values that made an image of the landscape, exalting it as something other than the natural environment, the theater of daily life. Aesthetic and humanistic values found expression at Fiesole: the appreciation of a hilltop view for its own sake (earlier, as in Petrarch's letters, the landscape was interpreted morally), the visual command of the city from the relative isolation of the suburb, the *locus* for the enjoyment of undisturbed *otium*. Michelozzo's simple arcaded cube was the first modern villa designed without thought or possibility of material gain.

In spite of its semi-urban site, the Fiesole villa was felt to be in harmony with the Virgilian literary *topos* that on the one hand depicted the sights, sounds and odors of the countryside as ultimate pleasures, and on the other represented the bucolic life as one of joy unalloyed by care or hardship. The tradition was masterfully revived by Lorenzo de' Medici's close associate, the humanist–poet Poliziano, a professor in the Florentine Studio from 1485 on. His readings of ancient authors were enriched by encomiums of their work in poems which he gathered in a volume entitled *Silva*. One of these, "Rusticus," which celebrated the bucolic works of Virgil and Hesiod, was actually written in the villa at Fiesole and closes with praise of its view over Florence and the Arno and of the hospitality and patronage of Lorenzo. Another, dedicated to Homer, is given the name of the old villa, "Ambra," that Lorenzo had bought at Poggio a Caiano and that he occupied while a new one was under construction. It concludes with the revival of another side of the literary villa tradition, the celebration of the virtues of husbandry, as represented by Lorenzo's establishment of a model farm, centered on a dairy, during the decade before the initiation of the new villa.[26] Lorenzo joined at Poggio the material pursuits of the early villas with the ideal aims of the Fiesole retreat.

Lorenzo extended the properties he had inherited in the area of Poggio a Caiano after purchasing the old villa Ambra from his in-laws, the Rucellai, in 1474, returning to Cosimo's policy of developing villas as agricultural enterprises. In harmony with this policy, his program began with the building of the farm structures rather than with the residence. The principal enterprise was a complex called the Cascina, begun in 1477 near the bank of the Ombrone river within sight of the villa. It is an imposing structure, which survives (though extensively remodeled in the sixteenth century) and still functions. A great square central court is bordered by porticoed barns with stalls on three sides, and by dwellings and other functions on the fourth. There are four corner towers, and a moat surrounding the whole.

Lorenzo's priorities may indicate not only his special interest in agriculture, rooted in his childhood at Cafaggiolo, but a major shift in Medici investment policy away from banking and trade toward the acquisition and exploitation of real property.[27]

According to Vasari, Lorenzo ordered numerous models of the villa to be made, and that of Giuliano do Sangallo was "so different from the form of the others and so consistent with Lorenzo's invention [*capriccio*] that he began immediately to have it carried out." The date is uncertain; we know that Giuliano was employed by Lorenzo in the fall of 1485 to make another model for Santa Maria delle Carceri in Prato (Giuliano's previous work had been devoted to woodcarving and cabinet- and model making and not to architecture). A letter of Michele Verino, who died in 1487, notes that the foundations were completed at the time of writing.[28]

Giuliano da Sangallo was commissioned to supervise the work, and while many elements are attributable to him, there is convincing evidence that Lorenzo himself conceived the essential aspects of the villa. He was profoundly interested in architecture: in 1481 he had written for drawings of the Ducal Palace at Urbino, and in 1485 for a *modello* of Leone Battista Alberti's unfinished church of San Sebastiano in Mantua. He advised on the design of the villa of Poggio Reale and of the palace of King Ferdinand in Naples. As Poggio a Caiano was being started, he insisted that each chapter of Alberti's *De re aedificatoria* be sent to him as it came off the presses.[29]

Alberti's Ninth Book, which deals extensively with villas, must have encouraged Lorenzo to consider designing the facade of Poggio around an entrance in the form of an ancient temple porch: "The tympanum [pediment] in private buildings should not be made so as to approach in any respect the majesty of a temple. But the vestibule may be improved by a slightly elevated porch and even improved by the dignity of a tympanum."[30] This passage is particularly relevant to the study of the Medici villas because it immediately precedes the polemic against castle–villas quoted above. In transposing the pediment to domestic architecture, Alberti intended to give the dwellings of important citizens a solemnity and magnificence previously reserved for sacred edifices. Poggio, like the Fiesole villa, was cubic, stuccoed, and painted off-white, and was sited on a hill in order to enjoy a panoramic view and also to be itself viewed, as is evident from photos taken from the later Medici villa at Artimino [*3.18*]. But Poggio is raised on a one-story arcaded platform not dictated by the topography. This support, which houses service functions, is distinguished visually from the courtly elegance of the residence above by unstuccoed red brick piers, arches and broad pilasters that suggest a more earthy character. The concept may have been stimulated by Alberti's San Sebastiano, which is raised one story over a grid of square piers like those at Poggio. The platform decisively separates the inhabitants of the villa from the natural environment that insistently surrounds it—the hills and valley are isolated for detached contemplation, as the sea is contemplated from the decks of a modern ocean liner. A prerequisite of this decision was the idealization of the landscape that had accompanied the origin of landscape drawing and painting and that had generated in Lorenzo's closest circle the revival of pastoral literature, a revival in which he himself participated as a poet.

3.18 View from the Medici villa at Artimino

The distinctive feature of Poggio a Caiano in comparison to its predecessors is its grandeur. The earlier Medici villas near Florence had not sought to convey dynastic statements to the world at large; they revealed a desire for the quiet of anonymity and, except for the one at Fiesole, for communion with the informality of the natural environment. Poggio was meant to be admired.

A drawing of about 1550 and a painting by Utens [3.20; 1.14] show elements of the design that were changed later [3.19]. The two flights of stairs leading from ground level to the elevated promenade and entrance originally extended perpendicularly from the facade, and the arches between them were supported on the same type of piers as the platform arcade. The arrangement recalls the raised choirs of Italian Romanesque churches such as San Miniato in Florence, access to which was normally gained by straight lateral staircases. The disproportionately large and elaborate clock over the entrance was originally a small acroterion of uncertain purpose, and the windows had heavy stone mullions of a type much employed in Rome in the late fifteenth century.

The facade is divided into three sections by the disposition of the openings: a compact block of four windows above the porch in the center (the porch itself has two windows on either side of the entrance door) is flanked by a stretch of unpenetrated wall terminating in a single-window bay. There was no precedent for this rhythmic treatment in Florence, though there were earlier Tuscan castle–villas in which a compact central section was flanked by corner towers one bay wide. Venetian palaces and villas were more likely sources; their facades are typically composed of a densely fenestrated central section separated from single-windowed outer bays.[31] This designates a distinction in

3.19 Facade

Villa Medici, Poggio a Caiano, by Lorenzo de' Medici
and Giuliano da Sangallo, 1485 on

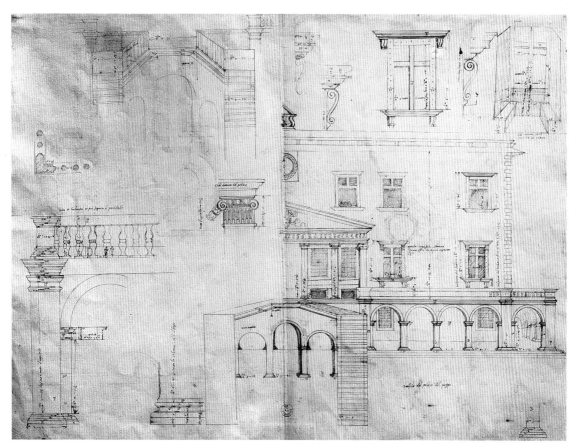

3.20 Details of the facade elevation. Drawing by an anonymous artist, *c.* 1550

function between the public spaces that make up the central spine and the private chambers along the sides, and the Poggio plan provides a comparable separation [*3.21*].

The temple-like portico at Poggio is a symbolic motif set onto the facade without essentially affecting its form (it even crowds awkwardly against the window frame to the left), in contrast to Palladio's practice of developing the entire facade design from the Roman temple front [*4.10, 18*]. The coloring of its glazed terracotta frieze (mainly white figures on a blue ground) and the broad and squat proportions were perhaps intended to refer specifically to the Etruscan (that is, Tuscan) temple. The frieze, now removed from its place, is, like the portico itself, a unique *all'antica* invention, possibly by the major sculptor of Lorenzo's court, Bertoldo di Giovanni. As recently decoded, its complex subject-matter is derived principally from Claudian and Ovid, and deals with the general theme of the cyclical return of Time (years, seasons, day/night) and celebrates the beneficent rule of the Medici dynasty. In its pastoral and agricultural references it is in harmony with the revival of pastoral poetry and painting in Lorenzo's circle and with Lorenzo's agricultural enterprises.[32]

Lorenzo and Giuliano da Sangallo did not even attempt to justify the colonnade and pediment structurally: the porch behind it is covered by a transverse barrel vault, an element that, notwithstanding its *all'antica* stucco coffering studded with Medici symbols, never occurred in such a context in Roman temples. And with good reason: if it had been built in masonry, as it feigns to be, it would have been unstable. Barrel vaults of this kind were to become a speciality of Giuliano da Sangallo; they are found at the Villa Tovaglia, in the vestibule of the sacristy of Santo Spirito in Florence, and in the Palazzo Scala. Vasari reports that Giuliano built one in his own home in Florence as a trial for the vault of the *salone* at Poggio, which covered a span that Lorenzo had feared would be too great for safety.[33] Lorenzo may have conceived the idea of such vaults, but the research seems to have been done by Giuliano, who revived both the Roman technique of precast terracotta units and the complex systems of design that linked individual tiles into overall patterns.

Giuliano recorded the basement plan in a sketchbook now in the Siena Library [*3.21*]. It is approximately square, arranged in three tracts which extend laterally and are bound together by a central longitudinal axis. Openings are laterally aligned so that in proceeding along the central axis one may see through the doors on the right and left and through a pair of rooms to exterior windows and beyond. This coordination of a plan by axes and by the simple proportions of the individual rooms was new to Tuscan architecture and reflects the influence of Alberti. The plan is generated from the concept of a grand barrel-vaulted central *salone* of 2:1 proportions which extends through the two upper stories. To give the *salone* ample light from the exterior, the rooms that flank it at basement level [*3.21, left and right*] are eliminated above the platform, so that the short sides of the *salone* become outer walls, and the villa takes on the form of an H [*3.18*].

This imposing, virtually regal, hall is as striking an innovation as the facade pediment. It suggests that Lorenzo intended to extend the private realm of his family into the public space of authority. Later palace designs carried out by Giuliano for and under the influence of Lorenzo—the suburban Medici Palace in Via Laura, Florence, and the palace for King Ferdinand of Naples—also feature grand halls as the focus of the

Villa Medici,
Poggio a Caiano

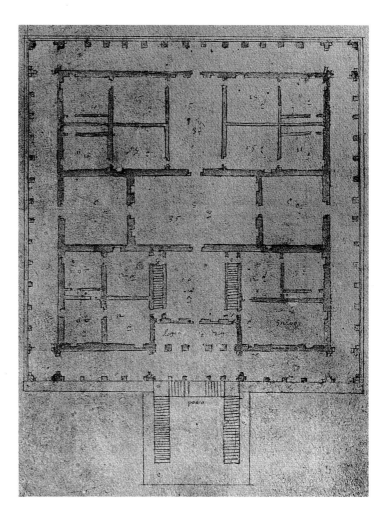

3.21 Basement plan. Drawing by
Giuliano da Sangallo

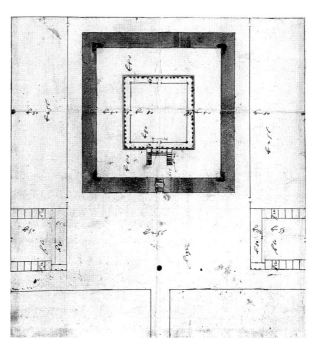

3.22 Project for a moat. Drawing by
an anonymous artist, before 1521 or
after 1530

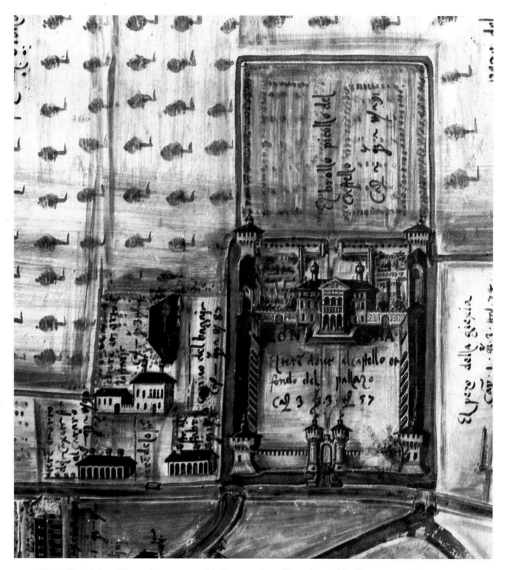

3.23 Villa Giustinian, Roncade, *c.* 1510: bird's-eye view. Drawing, 16th C.

composition (though, since both have central courts, the hall is at the end of the central axis).[34] The grandeur of all these projects testifies to Lorenzo's intention to create a type of domestic monument with dynastic implications, quite distinct from the character of earlier Renaissance domestic architecture.

The existing enclosure of the hilltop site by a wall with four corner towers [*1.14*] apparently was not envisioned originally. A drawing, made perhaps for Leo X before 1521, or after the second Medici reinstatement in 1530, shows the site without an enclosure and proposes a moat rather than a wall around the villa [*3.22*]. In this project, which probably was rejected, there is one slim bridge, perhaps a drawbridge, over the water. The moat, which had been a feature of the farm block of 1477, must have been considered more for security than for symbolic reasons, though an association with the earlier castle–villas would have been inevitable.[35]

A similar combination occurred in the design of the Villa Giustinian in Roncade, just north of Venice [3.23].[36] This villa was also innovative and unprecedented in style; like Poggio it featured a classical pediment. It was placed within a walled enclosure that looks like a medieval fortress with its corner towers, drawbridge and crenellations. The enclosure was meant from the start as a barnyard, but the architect and clients intended to give a different, more military and perhaps feudal impression. Moreover, the pediment at Roncade is more casual and less symbolic than the one at Poggio, which was designed as part of a complete classical temple porch.

We do not know whether Lorenzo had intended to have a moat built at Poggio, but it would have conformed to the design of at least one ancient structure, the Villa of the Mysteries outside the walls of Pompeii, of the first century BC [1.9; 2.7]. This was also a moated, cubic villa with a platform on which the residence was placed.[37] Apart from the incidence of the moat, which was exceptional in antiquity, the platform villa has been identified by archaeologists as a major villa type of the Italian peninsula. The type was generally cubic like the buildings at Fiesole and Poggio, and oriented toward views. One, the recently excavated San Rocco at Francolise near Capua (discussed above, p. 45), has no moat, but a high podium that can be seen from a distance, as it is near the top of a hill and commands a distant view [2.3].[38] To take advantage of the view there is a small three-bay portico on one side, rather like those at Fiesole, and a terrace at the top of the platform extending the whole length of another side.

A third ancient example, the Settefinestre villa in Tuscany (also discussed above, p. 45 [2.5]), is exceptional in that major portions of it were visible in the Renaissance. A drawing of the later fifteenth century, recently identified, shows a portion of the perimeter wall and of the arched supports of the platform [3.24].[39] The villa, which is one story high, is on sloping ground. On the lower side toward the enclosure wall it is raised on a platform one story above ground. The supporting arches are similar to those of Poggio, and barrel-vaulted corridors pass through the platform from side to side (at Poggio these are below ground level, within the sub-platform).

3.24 Roman villa, Settefinestre: the turreted garden wall. Drawing by an anonymous later 15th-C. artist

The discovery of this drawing proves only that a fifteenth-century draftsman was interested in such remains, and not that Poggio and similar structures were consciously derived from the Roman platform villa. I prefer to think of the connection as representing the capacity of a culture to preserve such a type subliminally, conveying it perhaps through vernacular versions. A similar instance is found in the survival of the more pervasive provincial Roman loggia–villa with projecting wings, which re-emerges in fifteenth-century Venice and Rome.[40]

The other villa–palaces planned by Lorenzo and Giuliano for Naples and Florence were also of the platform type, and it was not specific to Tuscany; another example, of the sixteenth century, is the Villa de' Vescovi at Luvigliano near Padua, designed by Palladio's precursor Falconetto or by his patron Alvise Cornaro [3.25]. Its one-story superstructure makes it close to the Roman antecedents. That the type was not specific to the Renaissance is demonstrated by the Villa Savoye at Poissy, Le Corbusier's best-known country residence, of 1928–30, which certainly is tied to the classical tradition as well as being a *machine à habiter* [1.7].

Work at Poggio a Caiano was halted before the central *salone* could be vaulted, with the death of Lorenzo in 1492 and the overthrow of the Medici by a popular uprising shortly after. It resumed only with the triumphant return of the family two decades later, shortly before Lorenzo's son, Cardinal Giovanni, was elected pope as Leo X. After the repression of another republican coup by a second Medici pope, Clement VII, in 1530, the family's populist pretensions had to be abandoned. With the support of the great powers of Europe they became hereditary rulers of Tuscany for more than two centuries. In the second half of the sixteenth century they established as many villas as they had in the fifteenth. The buildings followed the chaste cubic style of Poggio, while attention was lavished on the gardens, which were celebrated and emulated throughout Europe. The design of Poggio affected Florentine suburban villas right up to recent times.

In the nineteenth century, when "Italian villa" style became equal favorite with Gothic among the suburban builders of the romantic period, some features of Poggio were mixed in with some features of its more medieval Medicean predecessors to produce the ideal picturesque dwelling of the British and American middle class. The efforts of Andrew Jackson Downing, represented in his "Italian villa" [1.6] (compare it to Cafaggiolo [3.4]), to overcome the pernicious influence of the pervasive Greek Revival architecture of the early nineteenth century helped to lead American domestic architecture in exactly the opposite direction from that of the Medici—away from classicism into the picturesque. Ironically, the most earnest efforts of the Medici to re-establish a classical Roman style of life in the country inspired in modern times a vigorously anti-classical taste.

What are the implications of the sequence from early country houses that retained a medieval vocabulary and irregularity to a moment only about forty years later when this casualness was decisively rejected, and for good? Cosimo de' Medici and his humanist friends and guests were as eager as Lorenzo to restore the culture of the ancients, but they did not feel uncomfortable gathering together in a quasi-medieval setting so long as it was remodeled with modern doors, windows and loggias. Yet Cosimo and his architect Michelozzo would not have dreamed of such a compromise in the city. The Medici

3.25 Villa de' Vescovi, Luvigliano, by Giovanni Maria Falconetto or Alvise Cornaro, 1529

Palace in Florence had to be the Poggio of urban architecture, and it was equally influential. Alberti, on the other hand, could not accept this ambiguity, and his polemic against the castle style must have been covertly directed against the impact of Cosimo's villas of the second quarter of the fifteenth century.

Cosimo's patronage followed the tradition of Petrarch in emphasizing the more casual, the more anti-urban aspect of the villa ideology. Moreover, all these country places had buildings on them when earlier Medici bought them, doubtless from members of the hereditary Ghibelline aristocracy whom their Guelph party had defeated, and the new villas were built up around old cores. But perhaps the choice was prompted by another motivation. I suspect that Cosimo and his friends, for all their desire to project a Renaissance image, did not mind suggesting through the look of their villas that they had added the power and privileges of the medieval agrarian lord to the power of the modern urban banker and industrialist. Cosimo's grandson Lorenzo no longer needed the support of tradition; he was looking ahead, to the time when his family was to play its role on a worldwide stage, as princes of the state of Christendom.

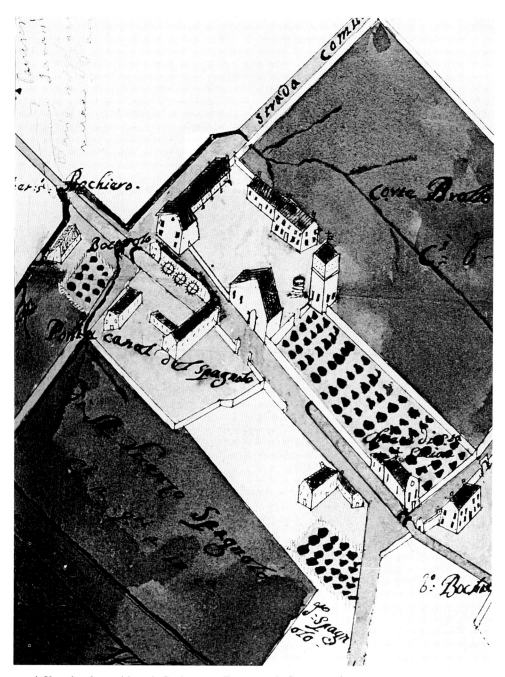

4.1 A Venetian farm with 15th-C. elements. From a 17th-C. manuscript

4 · Palladio's Villas and their Predecessors

Palladio, in his pioneering *I quattro libri dell'architettura* (*The Four Books of Architecture*), published in 1570 when he was sixty-two, writes about the practical functions of his buildings, how he intended to symbolize these functions, about his patrons and how he wanted to accommodate his designs to their sites.[1] He was also interested in form, otherwise he would not have been the most imitated architect of all time. But he did not write much about it. He was publishing a richly illustrated book, believing that pictures would speak more vividly than words. He was right: those pictures, and the drawings preserved in London and Vicenza,[2] sparked survivals and revivals of his work from the time of his death until the present day.

To see these villas in context we must first step back a century or so for a brief look at their ancestors, the farms and dwellings of the Veneto in the fifteenth century. The Veneto is the present-day name of the province, which is a somewhat reduced descendant of the great Venetian Republic of the Renaissance. The island of Venice had begun to expand into the mainland—they called it the *terraferma*—in the fourteenth and fifteenth centuries, annexing former imperial cities at a rapid rate. The countryside, with its great alluvial plains enriched by the foothills of the Alps, had been fertile farmland since pre-Roman times, though vast areas were made swampy by the many rivers and streams descending from the hills. The Venetian advance into this territory was motivated first by a desire to assure a steady food supply, and secondly by considerations of defense which, as we know from our own usage, can be indistinguishable from aggression.

In the course of the fifteenth century, two types of villa dwelling emerged in the Veneto (Renaissance writers used "villa" to refer to the whole estate; Palladio calls the proprietor's residence a "casa di villa"). One, the more common, was the working farmhouse, a modest structure located within a farm court made up of a number of utilitarian structures bordering an open central area, frequently paved [*4.1*]. Almost all of these complexes possessed, in addition to the dwelling, what the Venetans (the inhabitants of the Veneto) call a *barchessa*, a long barn with one side entirely open toward the central *piazza* under an overhanging roof supported on piers, posts or arches, and containing stalls for animals, storage spaces and housing for the laborers on the closed side. One or more dovecots in the form of high towers, usually square in plan, were also standard elements, in addition to various other storage and utility structures less standardized in form. The complex was normally enclosed within a lower wall with an entrance gate opening onto an access road. Where such settlements were used by patrician families for the country sojourn known as *villeggiatura*, the residences often were given a certain elegance by the adoption of salient features from the design of Venetian palaces, such as carved Gothic window and door frames. It seems likely, however, that the owners would not have spent much time in such a purely utilitarian setting with few of the amenities to which they were accustomed in city life.

The second type of rural residence was by contrast designed to satisfy the demand for such amenities, and it descended not from the farmyard but, like the early Tuscan villas, from the medieval castles of the area. The castle–villa, as represented in an engraving of what must have been the most imposing of them, the Barco della Regina near Treviso [4.2], retained the high surrounding crenellated walls, corner towers and imposing entrance gateway of medieval castles designed to withstand sieges, though these were now reduced to a merely symbolic function. Farming equipment and stock might be housed within the enclosure, along the inner face of the wall. But the residence was unambiguously the focus of the complex and the reason for its being. So it was conceived

4.2 Barco della Regina Cornaro, Altivole, 1490 (destroyed). From a contemporary engraving

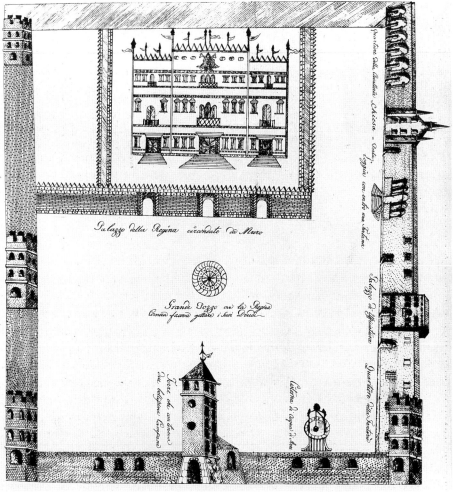

4.3 Villa Porto-Colleoni, Thiene, after 1447?

as a work of art. Those that survive must have been designed by architects, and they conform to the taste current in Venice and the *terraferma* cities in the early Renaissance.

The Villa Porto-Colleoni in Thiene, north of Vicenza, probably built in the 1440s, is the purest survivor of the type [*4.3*].[3] It ingeniously combines a principle of late Venetian Gothic palace design—the central expanse of windows illuminating a *salone* that extends from the front to the rear—with a ground-floor loggia framed by projecting corner towers reminiscent of a provincial ancient Roman villa type [*1.1, 20A*]. The roofline is characterized by crenellations (those of the central portion are now partially masked by the modern roof) that were intended to recall the medieval ancestry and probably to suggest links to the pro-Imperial Ghibelline feudal aristocracy, which retained its power in the area of the Vicenza. Though the dwelling was the center of a vast agricultural estate, the space enclosed within the surrounding walls is not large.

The castle–villa survived into the sixteenth century, and even into the lifetime of Palladio. The Villa Giustinian in Roncade just north of the Lagoon was designed for a great Venetian family about 1510 [*3.23*].[4] The proprietor's residence cast off the retrospective architectural character of its predecessors and is the most imposing surviving version of Early Renaissance *all'antica* style in Venetian territories. The inventiveness of its anonymous architect equals that of his distinguished contemporaries Mauro Codussi and Tullio Lombardo. While the surrounding walls are conventional in design, the palace itself is unprecedented in its two-story loggia crowned by a pediment, and in the basic cubic form and airy lightness of structure. This building more than any other reveals the vigor of the indigenous achievement of the Veneto at the moment when it was curbed by external events.

At this point politics entered to dominate the course of Venetian architecture by causing a break in its evolution of such length that a resurgence of its great tradition was no longer possible.[5] In 1509 the League of Cambrai, which included the Papal States, the Holy Roman Empire, the French Monarchy and the Duchy of Milan, was formed to oppose Venetian advances on the *terraferma* by military force. Its armies overran the mainland territories of the Venetian Republic and penetrated as far as the shores of the Lagoon, within sight of observers in the campanile of San Marco. Though the threat of total defeat soon subsided and ultimately little territory was lost, the war dragged on until 1517. By the time the Venetians were ready to initiate large private building projects, a generation of architects had expired. Their successors had to be imported from Rome, which in turn had been devastated by a hostile invasion in 1527. The most successful of the Roman émigrés were Jacopo Sansovino, originally from Florence, and the Veronese Michele Sanmicheli, both of whom became official designers of the Republic. During the 1530s both made innovative contributions to villa design as well as to the urban areas of Venice and Verona.

The patrons of the new *terraferma* villas were of two sorts: Venetian patricians, some of whom had had great land holdings in the previous century, but had rarely built ambitious dwellings on them, and mainland aristocrats whose feudal title to their land reached back to the Middle Ages. Residences on feudal villas were often fortified castles too uncomfortable for modern tastes.

The greatly increased importance of the *terraferma* was due to an economic revolution that made land and its agricultural products more important to Venice in the sixteenth century than it had been in earlier periods.[6] Increasing numbers of landholders found it worthwhile to spend at least part of their time supervising work on their farms. A superficial manifestation of the change was the rapidly developing taste for the relaxing charms of the country, seen as an escape from the city, which was referred to scornfully by the patrician diarist Girolamo Priuli when he wrote in the early years of the century:

> Since the noblemen and citizens of Venice had enriched themselves, they wished to enjoy their success and to live in the *Terraferma* and elsewhere, devoting themselves to pleasure, delight and the country life, meanwhile abandoning navigation and maritime activities. These were certainly more laborious and troublesome, but it was from the sea that all benefits came. We can judge the damage inflicted by the *Terraferma* on the city of Venice from the way in which her intoxicated nobles, citizens and people bought estates and houses on the *Terraferma* and paid twice as much as they were worth. They paid 20–25 Ducats per *campo* of land, which yielded less than 3–4% per annum, and subsequently erected palaces and houses on these estates which consumed large sums of money. . . . Nonetheless, there was no man of

4.4 Daniele Barbaro, Patriarch-elect
of Aquileta. Portrait attributed to
Paolo Veronese

means, among nobility, citizenry or populace, who failed to buy at least one estate and house
on the *Terraferma*, especially in the Padovano and Trevigiano, for these were nearby regions
and they could go and stay there and return in a day or two.[7]

Priuli's view was jaundiced; he longed for the great age of Levantine trade when Venice
was a city of daring merchants, and before she had to compete with the Turkish advance
or with Atlantic powers who sailed around Africa. What he failed to anticipate was that
in an inflationary age, land would become the best possible investment and the
reclamation of marginal land the most profitable industry. Further, in an age of
expanding territory and population, there would be a premium on maintaining an
adequate food supply without having to resort to costly purchases from abroad, one of
the pre-eminent concerns of the Republic. Ultimately, the land proved to be more
profitable than the sea.

But the hope of profit was not all that enticed Venetians into the land, nor, Priuli
notwithstanding, was it merely the opportunity to rest on weekends or to escape the
plague. An attitude was becoming more common that made the countryside worthy on
its own account rather than simply as an antithesis to the city. The proprietors of major
estates were becoming increasingly sympathetic to that awareness of a landholder's
responsibility toward his properties in cultivation expressed by ancient Roman authors
discussed in Chapter 2. The most supportive of Palladio's patrons, Daniele Barbaro
[*4.4*], had read the agronomical texts of Columella, Varro, Cato and (Rutilio) Palladio,
and cites them in the villa chapter of his translation and commentary on Vitruvius.[8]
Those writers had depicted agriculture and horticulture as occupations worthy of a
gentleman and even, in contrast to urban occupations, capable of promoting moral
betterment. A generation after Priuli, the Venetian nobleman Roberto di Spilimburgo,
in his *Cronaca* of 1540, called land investment "the finest and most suitable commerce,
that proper to gentlemen."[9] Consistent with this reappraisal was a shift in attitude

toward the peasant (see Chapter 5), who was depicted elsewhere in Europe as either comic or villainous (*villano* is an Italian term for peasant). Peasants and shepherds in Venetian painting and literature appear as convincing and worthy people and the Venetian landlord attempted to maintain cordial relations with his farm laborers as a prudent policy.

Alvise Cornaro, who coined the term *santa agricoltura*, was the herald of this realistic–humanist reappraisal:

> At this very time [his eighty-third year], I still go every year to revisit my friends whom I find there, and I take pleasure in being with them and conversing with them, and through them with others who are there, men of fine intellect: with architects, painters, sculptors, musicians and farmers, since our age is rich in such men. I see the works they have recently made and see again earlier works, and I always learn things that I take pleasure in knowing. I see the palaces, gardens, the collections of antiquities. . . . But above all, I take pleasure in the voyage going and coming, as I consider the beauty of the sites and landscapes through which I pass. Some on the flat, others hilly, near rivers or springs, with many beautiful habitations and gardens around them.[10]

It came naturally to this technologist of a new era, the pioneer of modern land reclamation, to class farmers with artists as the practitioners of the manual arts whose fine intellects were elevated above the common herd. Cornaro's love of the cultivated landscape was consistent with his belief that nature awaited the improving hand of man. Few aristocrats would have shared such radical views, but increasing numbers in Venice and the *terraferma* cities were purchasing farmland or adding to inherited holdings and

4.5 Villa Garzoni, Pontecasale, by Jacopo Sansovino, after 1536

Prospetto Generale

4.6 Villa La Soranza, Treville di Castelfranco Veneto, by Michele Sanmicheli, before 1540 (destroyed)

building there a kind of villa capable of accommodating both a life of luxury and the functions of a farm. As we have seen in the villas of the Medici (Chapter 3) and the castle–villas of the Veneto, the combination was not itself new, though these seem to express rather what I suppose to be ambivalence toward the charms of the countryside, an ambivalence rarely revealed in Palladio's generation.

The Villa Garzoni at Pontecasale, south of Padua [4.5], built by Jacopo Sansovino some time after 1536, was one of his earliest private commissions in the Veneto. We know that Alvise Garzoni was of a wealthy Venetian family that had purchased extensive lands in the area in the mid-fifteenth century; also that, together with the monks of the Abbey of Santa Giustina in Padua and with the canons of Candiana Cathedral, he took part in a pioneering consortium to carry out land reclamation in the area in 1540.[11] The Garzoni obviously encouraged Sansovino to propose a quite new type of design, and he attempted to oblige, but had some difficulty in deciding what a villa ought to be, since he had probably never before stayed long enough in the farmlands of the *terraferma* to become aware of the traditions there. He picked up enough tradition to surround the area with a wall reminiscent of the *castelli* and to build majestic *barchesse* alongside the villa in a different, simpler classical style. But the villa itself is a grandiose palace, the facade of which is Venetian on the flanks and Roman in the middle. It is one of the most breathtaking buildings of its time, but somewhat out of tune with its function, and Sansovino was not called to execute further villa commissions.

Michele Sanmicheli was the first to come to terms definitively with the new exigencies of the country seat for great landholders. Of his villa structures two—both destroyed—were recorded by Vasari in his *Lives of the Artists*: La Soranza [4.6] in Treville di Castelfranco Veneto (before 1540), and that of Girolamo Cornaro in Piombino Dese (after 1539). By contrast to Sansovino's they were simple cubic structures, the former having an arched loggia separated by a short distance from the *barchesse* as in the main structure at the Villa Garzoni.[12]

Sebastiano Serlio, another refugee from Rome to Venice, received no architectural commissions, perhaps because of his nasty personality. But he made an incalculable contribution to the history of architecture by grasping the potential of the Venetian book-publishing industry to produce, in separate books starting in 1537, a practical treatise on architecture that raised the printed image to the level of the printed word.[13] This stroke of genius was, needless to say, an essential preamble to Palladio's *Quattro*

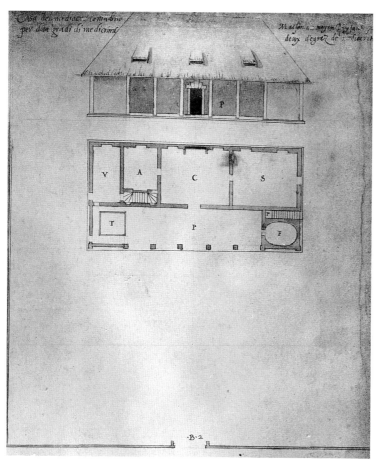

4.7 Sebastiano Serlio, project for a villa of a prosperous peasant, from his unpublished Sixth Book of Architecture, 1540s

libri published thirty-three years after the first of Serlio's books. Further, the treatise launched an entire genre of professional manuals illustrated with plates that had true instructional value, the most famous of which was the extraordinary anatomical work of Vesalius, *De Humani Corporis Fabrica* of 1543, the plates of which were also designed and cut in Venice.

Serlio's Sixth Book, on domestic architecture, never reached the press, but finished manuscripts survive in Munich and in New York.[14] This volume was composed in France, where the author had gone in search of work, so it contains no Italian villas of the type I have discussed. It offers a chain of country dwellings, one for every economic stratum from peasant to prince, but leaves a sharp break between the farmhouse of the prosperous peasant [4.7] and the most modest merchant's country house, which makes no concessions at all to agriculture, being a mini-château. The simple thatched structure may reflect the local vernacular in its materials, but the composition is classical, with porticoes and the symmetrical, tripartite system of Sanmicheli's La Soranza [4.6].

In seeking to meet the practical and expressive demands of a new kind of client, the architects of the Venetian Renaissance would surely have revived the ancient Roman villa had they known what it looked like, not only because of their passion for antiquity, but also because the ancient traditions of the gentleman-farmer had been conveyed through literary channels. But as we have seen no Roman villas had been excavated, and the written sources were ambiguous about their form. Yet there is a curious similarity between the type of villa built on the periphery of the Roman Empire and a basic Early Renaissance type that makes one wonder whether the tradition was not carried along subterranean channels to resurface after one-and-a-half millennia [*1.20A, C*].[15]

If Sanmicheli's villa concept was too severe and Sansovino's too grandiose, Palladio turned the virtues of both into a formula for villa design that was exactly adapted to the aims of his clients. He responded to the new demands with his perfect balance of magnificence and agricultural function, of the villa tradition of the Veneto and ancient Roman elegance, and his excitingly varied solutions covered an impressive portion of the map of the *terraferma*, as he responded to calls from both Venetian and provincial patricians. His villas are geographically clustered in the eastern part of the Veneto in sites within short distances from Venice, Vicenza or Padua, and for the most part near to rivers or canals [*4.8*].

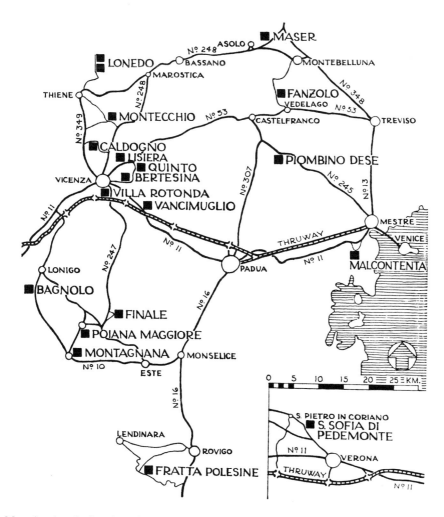

4.8 Map showing the location of villas by Palladio

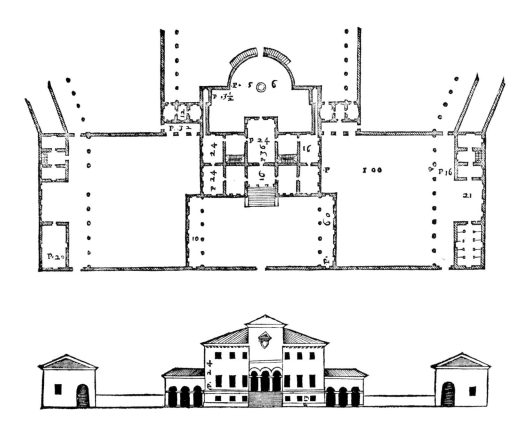

4.9 Villa Godi, Lonedo, by Palladio: plan and elevation, from *I quattro libri*

Palladio's design for one of his earliest villas, at Lonedo [*1.13; 4.9*], may have been stimulated by the innovations of Sanmicheli. It is certainly as plain and as simply articulated. The plan of the Lonedo villa is slightly irregular, because it had to accommodate existing farm buildings. The structures are surrounded by a perimeter wall which recalls the *castello* walls of the previous century. The site commands a spectacular river view to the south, and calls to mind one of Palladio's instructions for locating villas:

> Don't build in valleys enclosed between hills because buildings in hidden valleys, apart from being invisible from a distance and having no view themselves, lack dignity and majesty. . . .
> They are contrary to health because the rain settles there and sends out vapors that affect the mind and body and weaken the spirit and degenerate the joints and nerves.[16]

The Villa Barbaro at Maser [*4.10–15*] represents a more developed stage of Palladio's ideas for the elegant country residence.[17] He incorporated into it the principal features of a typical farmyard of the region [*4.1*], the dovecot and the *barchessa*, the first being placed in elegant pavilions at the two ends of the composition, and the second being transformed into serene arcades flanking the central block. The dwelling block is distinguished by a splendid stuccoed Roman temple-front that emphatically does not recall the odors and confusion of the farmyard: Palladio explains in the *Quattro libri* his reasons for turning to Roman religious architecture for motifs applicable to the villa dwelling:

> I have made in all the villa buildings and also in some of the city ones a pediment on columns for the front facade in which there are the principal portals. The reason is that these porches announce the entrance of houses and lend much to their grandeur and magnificence. They make the forward part more eminent than the other parts and are most convenient for the insignia of arms of the builders, which one usually places at the center of the facade. Also the ancients used them in their buildings, as one sees in the remains of temples and of other public edifices, which in turn got the motif in all probability from house architecture.[18]

Palladio's study of Roman antiquity was the architectural equivalent of the humanists' study of ancient literature: he was seeking first a vocabulary and a form of expression, but also, as this passage shows, an explanation of the historical evolution of ancient forms.[19] These interests must have been stimulated by his early acquaintance with his patron Giangiorgio Trissino, who was responsible for giving the young Palladio his first introduction to the city of Rome, and by his membership of the Accademia Olimpica, a society for the promotion of learning and drama, composed principally of noble Vicentines, whose acceptance of a craftsman like Palladio was an exceptional event in Renaissance society. In mid-career, Palladio wrote a guidebook to the antiquities of Rome and an edition of Caesar's *Gallic Wars*, and, late in life, he prepared a volume of reconstructions of the ancient baths of Rome (published only in the eighteenth century in England, at the instigation of Lord Burlington).

This background explains why Daniele Barbaro, one of the two brothers for whom Palladio designed the villa at Maser, sought the architect's collaboration as the illustrator of his commentary on the *Ten Books of Architecture* by Vitruvius.[20] The volume, which appeared in Venice in Italian in 1556, was the first scholarly study of a treatise that had had a profound effect on Renaissance architecture, and Palladio's influence must have made itself felt through the text as well as in the woodcuts. Here Palladio made his first attempt to establish a canon of the ancient orders, and it is intriguing to follow the changes and refinements from these plates to those of his own *Quattro libri* of 1570.

The villa mansion at Maser is sited on a gentle slope at the foot of the hills that rise above the flat fields of the Veneto to announce the Alps to the north [*4.10*]. From the window in the center of the temple-like facade, the Barbaro brothers could look out over the orchards of their estate and watch their peasants at work [*4.13*] and, if they were to turn around to take in the great cross-shaped *salone* of the *piano nobile* [*4.12*], they could enjoy the illusionistic frescoes of Paolo Veronese which filled each bay with landscapes containing romantic Roman ruins that provide a poetic version of antiquity to complement the classicism of the architecture and the rusticity of the view [*4.14, 15*].[21] Through the door at the rear of the *salone* the proprietors could step out onto a terrace against the hillside into which the architect had set an elegant "nymphaeum"—a grotto-fountain rich with figural imagery [*4.11*]. This symbolic evocation of the ancient world also served functional uses, as Palladio tells us in the text of the *Quattro libri*: the water flows from the fountain fish pond into the villa kitchen, and from there first into the garden for irrigation and ultimately to the orchard on the far side of the public

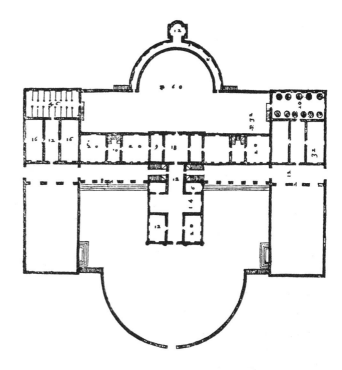

Villa Barbaro, Maser, by Palladio, 1557–58

4.10 *(left)* South front

4.11 *(below left)* Nymphaeum

4.12 *(above)* Plan of the principal floor, from *I quattro libri*

4.13 *(below)* View out from the *salone*

road.[22] In one of the small rooms at the corners of the main hall Veronese painted the scene of a contemporary castle–villa from which ladies and gentlemen are departing in a carriage, perhaps for a pleasure tour of the countryside [1.2]. The building, with its crenellated skyline, is curiously old-fashioned in contrast to the innovative character of the actual one by Palladio; it has four corner towers linked by loggias, recalling the villa of Poggio Reale in Naples, of the 1480s. But the long avenue of trees leading to the entrance is a modern feature. I cannot explain the anachronistic aspect, but it underscores the conservative character of villa life and the persistence of the ideology of *villeggiatura* that reached back to ancient Roman times.

Life in the country, as depicted by the sixteenth-century authors who will be discussed in the following chapter, was praised primarily for benefits enjoyed by the male proprietors of the villas: relaxation from urban cares, reading, conversation with

4.14, 15 Villa Barbaro, Maser: *salone*, with frescoes by Paolo Veronese, 1560–61

one's peers, hunting, and fishing. But time spent with the family also played a part, and villa life may have contributed to a greater participation of women and children in the benefits of wealth: villa frescoes of the time of Palladio showing contemporary scenes suggest that they played a role in the recreational diversions, for example in the performance of music. The fusion of these perceived social benefits with the economic advantages accruing from the agricultural enterprises of the villa brought about the widespread diversion of Venetian and Venetan interests from the traditional involvement with maritime trade and military service to investment in land.

The ownership of extensive agricultural land by city dwellers narrowed the gap that distinguished them from the landed aristocracy and, by a curious legal development, could even entirely erase that gap. One of the families for whom Palladio designed a villa, the Repeta of Campiglia, had bought a large fief from the Bishop of Vicenza in the thirteenth century, and in 1516 the Venetian Doge confirmed the family rights to the "noble fief with the titles of Marchese and Count."[23] Thus, the possession of the property brought with it enrollment in the ranks of the nobility, so long as the title could be confirmed by an authorized representative of the Holy Roman Emperor. In 1437 the Emperor had made the Venetian Doge an Imperial Vicar, and by 1516 a successor added to this the privilege of making feudal vassals in Verona, Vicenza and Friuli. Palladio's design for the villa mansion is, considering this situation, exceptionally modest. The elevation [4.16] is of only one story and is without embellishment other than the pediment (detached here from any temple-support that might give monumental justification to its use).

By the mid-sixteenth century, the Repeta family, imperial title notwithstanding, had developed a strong attachment to the Protestant heresy, which implied a rejection of wordly display and perhaps even an anti-aristocratic position.[24] This is reflected also in Palladio's account of the elevated moral tone of the villa decorations:

> On the side facing the stable are rooms, some of which are dedicated to *Continence* and others to *Justice* and others to other *Virtues*. It was made thus because this gentleman, who willingly receives all those who come to seek him out, may lodge his visitors and friends in the room to the virtue of which their inclination of soul most disposes them.[25]

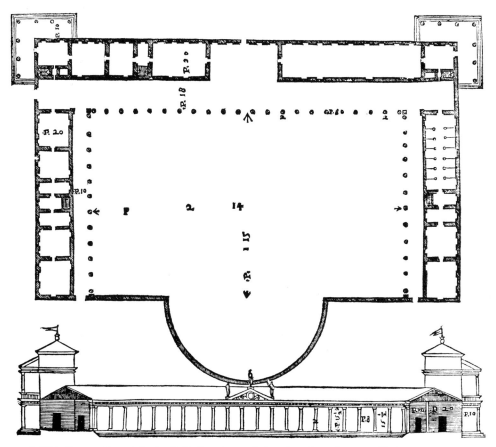

4.16 Villa Repeta, Campiglia, by Palladio: plan and elevation, from *I quattro libri*

4.17 Villa Saraceno, Finale, by Palladio, 1546

The Villa Emo in Fanzolo [*1.27*] belongs somewhere between the elegance of Maser and the simplicity of Campiglia.[26] Here the forms of Maser are modified by reducing ornament to a minimum: windows are without frames and sculpture is restricted to the interior of the pediment. To judge from the themes of the frescoes inside by Zelotti, the builder was also concerned with the traditional virtues. Here again, Palladio emphasized practicality in discussing his design:

> The storerooms, granaries, stable and other villa areas are on either side of the owner's house, and at the ends are two dovecots, which provide utility to the master and ornament to the place, and one can go everywhere under cover, which is one of the principal things one seeks in a villa house.

It is hard to know how literally to take the architect's claim that these buildings combine the living and working functions. It seems unlikely that the patrician owners would have welcomed the odors, noise and mess involved in housing farm animals within their loggias, as is done in the Venetian *barchesse* on which these loggias were modeled, but it would have been wasteful not to have employed them for storing tools, vehicles, stakes, birding nets and other necessaries of farming. Some of the smaller residences like the Villa Saraceno in Finale [*4.17*] must have operated more like the traditional farm courts [*3.23; 4.2*]. The lateral wings and the round dovecots shown in the *Quattro libri* project for the Saraceno were never executed,[28] and the reduced size of the finished portion probably prevented the isolation of any agricultural functions from the dwelling. Like a number of other villas in the *Quattro libri*, the Saraceno was planned to provide grain storage in the loft under the roof and other types of storage in vaulted areas below. The kitchen would have been within the porticoes to one side of the central residence.

The text of the *Quattro libri* is exceptional in the Renaissance for its unceasing reference to practical functions and for the sense it conveys of an architect disposed to respond imaginatively to the needs of each client as well as to the general demands of the several architectural genres. This explains on the one hand why each villa is so different from the others and on the other why a majority of them still serve the functions for

4.18 Villa Rotonda, Vicenza, by Palladio, 1566–70: view from the east

which they were built originally—in some cases only recreational functions, but often in other cases agricultural ones as well.

The best-known of all Palladio's country houses, the Villa Rotonda [4.18], in a sense is not a villa at all: in the *Quattro libri* it appears in the book on palaces, partly because it is just on the outskirts of Vicenza, and partly because it had no agricultural function—it was built purely for pleasure by Monsignor Paolo Almerico, a retired official of the papal court, who wanted it as a place to entertain his fellow Vicentines. The farm buildings attached to it today are later additions. Thus Palladio described it in terms of its situation and of the delights of the views it offered the owner and his guests:

> The site is one of the most pleasant and delightful that one could find because it is at the top of a little hill with an easy ascent and is bathed on one side by the Bacchiglione, a navigable river, and on the other is surrounded by other most agreeable hills which give the aspect of a great theatre: and all are cultivated and abound in most excellent fruits and the best vines. Thus, because it enjoys beautiful views on every side, some of which are limited, others more distant, and still others that reach the horizon, loggias have been made on all four sides.[29]

The site, then, suggested the design, a highly unorthodox proliferation of temple-fronts emerging from a cube intended to be crowned by a fully visible hemispherical dome. The ensemble paradoxically reflects nature in a model of the most distilled refinement, combining the Renaissance absorption with the classical past and the millennial Christian-sacral associations of the cupola.

I have tried in discussing Palladio's villas both to illustrate the work of a great and influential architect and to emphasize through that work the various ways in which effective architectural design relates to the needs and to the ideologies of a society—or at

least of that portion of a society that sponsors building. I have emphasized the extent to which the particular aim of the Palladian country house was to give magnificence to the once humble agricultural complex, symbolically joining the substructure of work to the superstructure of consumption.

I close with another, in some ways contradictory, thought that while we steadily increase our understanding of the architecture of the past, we may still be aware of only part of its essence, the part accessible to reasoning. There is another part, reached by the five senses, and this, given our academic indoctrination and suspicion of emotional self-indulgence, is, for all of its immediate accessibility, the harder for us to receive.

There is a myth perpetuated by universities and intellectual journals that to *understand* a work of art is truly to grasp its message, to engage with it. But we know from our experience in life how far apart understanding and engagement can be and how possible it is to love another person or to respond to a building without adequately understanding them, or to understand them without feeling. The experience of Palladio's buildings can be greatly enriched by knowing why and how they came to be, how contemporaries saw them and what the architect himself said about them, but they speak for themselves in multiple ways through their creation of and response to ambiences and conditions of light and atmosphere and through their scale, proportions, textures, colors and so on. They can be different every time we see them.

Perhaps these observations can be used to support the fantasy of the untrammeled artist–genius creating the great masterpiece through sheer sensitivity. But that would ignore our discovery that what gave Palladio freedom and inspiration to build exciting structures was the knowledge of the boundaries in which he had to maneuver—the tradition of the distant or immediate past, the specific demands of clients, the choice of materials and of a site. Liberty has meaning only in a context of restraint.

5 · The Image of Country Life in Sixteenth-Century Villa Books

In just the years during which Palladio was building villas in the Venetian *terraferma*, an innovative literary genre first made its appearance: the essay, letter or dialog on villa life.[1] The genre was inspired by the Roman treatises on agriculture and on other writing in praise of the villa that we examined in Chapter 2, particularly the poems of Horace and the letters of Pliny the Younger. Yet the texts were not intended primarily as basic agronomical treatises in the tradition of Cato, Varro and Columella, but rather as reinforcements to the particular style of life being lived in the country by members of the urban middle class and lesser nobility—the very people who employed Palladio. These appear to have been primarily purchasers of agricultural land near the town in which they lived. Their bailiffs and peasants raised crops and pastured animals (there is no mention of slaves), and they visited their villas at more or less frequent intervals to relax and to supervise work for short or long stays, according to their interests.

The villa book, which made its appearance around 1540, was already in decline in the first decades of the following century, following the depression in the agricultural economy that had prevented most of Palladio's villas from being completed.

In a sense the villa life and ideology of the Italian Renaissance is another example of the humanist *renovatio* of ancient culture as it was known through surviving texts in all fields. This applies particularly to the earliest encomiums of country life, such as those of Petrarch and of Leone Battista Alberti. But the sixteenth- and early seventeenth-century texts, though they display an easy and impressive familiarity with the ancient sources and share much of their subject-matter, were profoundly different in attitude. Their spirit is hedonistic or materialistic and lacks the morally elevated core of their models, whether the Stoic severity of the agronomers, Cicero and Pliny the Elder, or the idealization of Lucretian *otium* on the part of Virgil, Horace and the younger Pliny. The later Renaissance writers represent villa life only as a restorative relief from the evils, restrictions and responsibilities of the city, and a chance to hunt, play games and perform a little healthy and productive work. They seem not to seek opportunities for self-improvement. Rather, they carry into the country an obsessive preoccupation with tensions generated by a social ambience of barriers and conflicts between the classes and the sexes. On the whole they were insensitive and at times antisocial.

Only one of the authors focused on the typology of villas: Anton Francesco Doni, author of a very rare volume published in Bologna in 1566 entitled *Le ville del Doni*, was a Florentine scholar best known for a bibliographical study, *La libraria*, and another work of classification, *I marmi*. In consonance with these interests, he gave his work on villas a typological structure, defining five species of villa according to the social class of the proprietor:

> Our Princes and *Signori*, in order to separate themselves from the great noise of the crowd, make beautiful Villas [i.e., dwellings] in their Villas [i.e., farm properties] ... which are near or far from their Cities whichever pleases their Excellencies, and they are made so beautiful, rich and comfortable that they are no different from the palaces and beautiful structures within the City. ... I relate these to the second type of our modern gentlemen. ... The third class of villa dwellers are the Merchants, those who have enough cash. To them the villas come as a surplus benefit [? *di strabalzo in mano*]; they use them on certain days for recreation more than anything else. Artisans, less comfortably placed, who live by their hands, have their villas made on other grounds, in order to help them save, because they go there with a salad and a loaf of bread, as if they could not manage to live continually in the City. The peasants are the last, and they enjoy the Villa by necessity, and are the first villa dwellers, and there they must sweat on the mountains, hills, plains and valleys, and there they labor with joy.[2]

Doni's taxonomy is artificial. He shows no familiarity with the agricultural and economic nature of the villa, being a courtier whose knowledge appears to have been restricted to visits to elegant villas of the aristocracy and wealthy bourgeoisie, many of which he describes.[3] His fourth and fifth category are abstract concepts included in order to demonstrate a parallel hierarchy between the building types and social class, much as Sebastiano Serlio had done in the manuscript of his Sixth Book of Architecture, of about 1550 [*4.7*].[4] In actuality, almost no artisan of his time could have afforded a piece of rural property or have been able, as Doni suggests,[5] to maintain it by sending his wife and children (who would also have been in the work force) there during the summer, and his depiction of the idyllic house and life of the peasant is a fantasy that obscures the almost universal reality of dingy huts, hunger and misery (not to speak of the anomaly of classifying as the peasant's villa a property to which the title normally was held by the landlord).

Even if we dismiss the suggestion that villas could be built or bought by the working classes after the mid-sixteenth century, it is still unsatisfactory to type them strictly by social class. Not only could wealthy members of the bourgeoisie build as elegantly as the nobility, but they frequently bought estates from old patrician families. Indeed, apart from cases of successful land reclamation, it would have been difficult to acquire good farmland with resident peasants in any other way. Sometimes the property was a fief surviving from the feudal era, and the purchaser could apply to be granted the noble title that had gone with the land. In central and northern Italy, however, the seigneurial rights of the feudal system, which bound the peasant to the lord as a serf, had not survived.

As in the slave-economy of ancient Rome, the proprietor depended heavily on his bailiff (*massaro*) for the effective direction of his agricultural enterprise. The estate was normally worked by peasants (*contadini*, *villani*) on some kind of sharecropping arrangement. Their precarious income was earned by the sale of produce on the market, not in wages. But this gave them little freedom: they were taxed by the State and the Church, and proprietors often cheated them of traditional rights such as common land. The landholding class regarded them with suspicion and oppressed them severely, but occasionally saw an economic advantage in being civil toward them.

A large number of North Italian agricultural authorities speak on behalf of the group of affluent bourgeois who have bought, or are considering buying, a villa estate; like their ancient models they hold differing views on the virtues of such a purchase. I have focused on the four authors whose work seems to me to offer the greatest insight into villa society (other books of the period that I have consulted, by Tarello, Agostinetti, Barpo and Bonardo, are rather more occupied with technical material).[6] Giuseppe Falcone, in *La nuova, vaga, et dilettevole villa* (Brescia, 1559), is a vigorous proponent of the tradition of Varro and Columella, insisting that the proprietor be committed to full-time supervision of his estate. Agostino Gallo, in *Le dieci giornate della vera agricoltura, e piaceri della villa* (Brescia, 1564), by contrast, though he provides extensive instructions on farming procedures, represents villa life as one of relaxation and diversion. (A translation of his Day VIII, on the delights of the villa, is printed in an Appendix below, and I shall give page references to that when discussing Gallo here.[7]) The others, Alberto Lollio, *Lettera . . . nella quale . . . egli celebra la villa e lauda molto l'agricoltura . . .* (Venice, 1544), and *La villa: dialogo di M. Bartolomeo Taegio* (Milan, 1559), allow for a compromise between these options. Taegio is the only one of the group who follows Pliny the Younger in representing villa life as an opportunity to pursue a scholarly and philosophical *otium*.[8]

The pre-eminent response to country life in writers of the period is one of delight in the sights and sounds of the natural environment—significantly, not the agricultural landscape. Most of them, like Lollio (fol. B iii^r), break into an excess of ecstatic prose:

> Free of troubles and of the molestation that usually disturb human breasts, a man may rest content with that which he has, and live with a tranquil mind, always however employing and exercising the most precious gift of intellect, speculating as best he can on the insatiable appetite of prime material, the firmness of the earth, the rarity of the air, the flow of the waters, the transparency of fire and the splendor of the comets; the milk of heaven, the making of snows, the falling of rains, the freezing of hailstones, the breath of the wind, the power of earthquakes, the crash of lightning, the color of rainbows, the renewal of the plants, the variety of fruits, the propagation of animals, the nature of fish, the character of stones, the industry of man, the brilliance of the sun, the light of day and the shadows of the night . . . contribute to the contemplation of the prime cause in which perfectly and indivisibly—almost in a purest mirror—are collected and reflected the being and conservation of all things.
>
> In the villa, I say, one tastes infinite pleasures in accord with the variety of the seasons that are offered to us one after the other. Here you arrive at faithful Spring, ambassadress of Summer; all the trees, as if in competition one with another, alter again their bark and dress again in greenest boughs: adorning themselves with such a beauty and variety of flowers that beside the sweetest odors emitted by everything around, afford incredible joy and delight to whomever observes them. As birds sing their loves with sweet and dainty accents our ears are filled with lovely melody . . . [the other seasons follow]

Similar pleasures are cited by Gallo (below, p. 130) who, however, becomes truly transported (below, p. 127) in his arias to the sunrise and sunset which, he says, appear so much clearer than those in the city, as we

> watch and wonder at the cheerful birth of the beautiful Dawn, gazing at her divine brightness as it gradually lights up the sky, until the Sun (heralded by his first flashes, like streaks or sparks of blazing fire) with his resplendent beams strikes first the proud peaks of the highest

mountains, and little by little emerges from the sea until he is completely visible to us mortals in all his splendor.

Taegio's list (p. 119) is the most dense with delights:

> Nor would I ever believe that anyone would be so indiscreet as to deny to me that in the villa one gets inestimable pleasure from the open, clear sky which with a vivid, almost smiling, splendor, invites us to joy. And that one gets great enjoyment in seeing a happy, fruitful and festive hillside, with a thousand retired recesses where it seems that quiet and felicity reside, and in hearing the rustic songs of simple *villanelle* and the sound of the waxed pipes of the shepherds. And what shall I say of the sight of the rough plowmen [? *bisolchi bosolchi*] when, adorning the ploughs with fresh flowers, they give a sign of pleasant *otium*? And why should I not speak of the hunters, when they follow the fugitive game and when they stretch their nets in the reddening eastern dawn? And where do I speak of the various kinds of animals that wander at their pleasure through fields painted in a thousand varieties of color, where the summer breezes, dancing among the flowers, make the tender berries tremble softly?

As this speech concludes, the interlocutor in the dialog observes that the amenities of such a place move people to lasciviousness, and that holy persons have always flourished better in rocky deserts.

The elevated style of these passages suggests an inspiration from poetry and a taste favorable to idealized landscape painting. It differs from the style of other parts of these texts; in Gallo's dialog, for instance, it follows his more earthy admiration of the food produced on his farm (below, p. 127—the dairy products, the various fowl and meats, and the fruits.

Lollio recounts a variety of the more practical advantages (fols. B ix^v–x^r):

> The benefits are so rewarding that I never stay there except joyfully and willingly. And first of all because of the air, the chief sustainer of our existence, which in those places I find purer and much superior and more beneficial to my complexion than that of Ferrara, which is heavy and humid in nature and consequently filled with malignant vapors. And how important this is to one's health I think you understand.
>
> As for habitation, I have there a good and very spacious house where, this year, I have added certain rooms that will be extremely cool in the summer and most useful in winter, so that I can stay in great comfort. As to living there is no doubt that one has here the finest and most delicate meats, the whitest bread, the finest fruits, ample and perfect wines. And at all times one has a plenitude of all those necessary things in life.
>
> At the villa, enjoying the satisfying and sweet liberty, I gain contentment from going, staying, doing, and living according to my own lights, without suspicions or fears that any of those ignoramuses (which is the worst one can say of them) will sneer behind my back or joke about me as they are accustomed to doing about anyone they see to be different from themselves.
>
> And because I always have stayed distant from ambitions and have never cared for the smoke, the shadows and the favors that cost so dearly and that are crowned by so many worries and anxieties, finding great contentment in the condition in which the great goodness of God has placed me, I can remain with a relaxed and tranquil mind, impelling myself with all my power, in accordance with the good precept of Socrates, to be the person I wish to be seen as being.

Falcone (Preface, fol. i^v) speaks of the pleasure of eating his frugal meal outdoors:

In your villa, you eat what is at hand—dry bread seems cake—at any time you please, and as much as suits you, outside under the pergola or under the loggia of the portico, or in the open air, or in the kitchen garden, or the ornamental garden, or at the fountain. . . . This is why I am inviting you to the villa: to come from *otio* to activity, from gluttony to sobriety, from enmity to quiet, and to holy peace; from lascivious pomp to a restrained and positive life. But you, proud as you are, want not to work your villa, but to leave it in the hands of sorry bailiffs, assassins and butchers of the soil.

Before we hear more from Falcone, I must point out that he has altered the meaning of *otium*, which figured so prominently in the ancient Roman texts, where it means retirement for the purpose of study and other self-improvement. Falcone's *otio* is sloth, and is the almost inevitable condition of urban life. He is the Stoic, who expects the proprietor to take up permanent residence at the villa, to engage directly in farming and to live energetically and healthfully. He also registers the same relief as ancient authors felt at not having to be concerned about proper clothing (Preface, fol. iv):

You can dress simply and cheaply without having to keep up appearances. Far from the courts, you can attend to your devotions untroubled by litigation and the disturbances of the city. You go into the country to keep *otio* at bay with healthy exercise—which gets the fire lit, the air purified, the water sweetened, makes the earth productive and the gold shine . . .

Further on (p. 22) he warns, however, that "frills and stylishness of clothing should be entirely avoided," in the proper tradition of villa life, and that peasant men and women should dress in the "rustic style."

Gallo (below, p. 128) enjoys going without servants, a hat or a cloak, and is delighted not to have to tip his hat to people he doesn't like. There are many informalities permitted in the country, and Falcone presents an intriguing catalog of them, calling them "privileges," perhaps in ironic reference to seigneurial privileges (p. 3):

Here you have the very real and extensive privilege of being able to walk on foot not only on your own estate but through the surrounding countryside as well, wearing thick boots and carrying a stick in your hand to leap over ditches and keep off large dogs. Other privileges are: having to light a fire under the pot only on Sundays, eating lots of garlic and onions, and not having to wash your hands before meals. When it is cold you have the privilege of warming yourself in the stables and talking with the peasants about estate business past and to come. The owner has the privilege of going about the villa with a *podarina in mano* [*meaning unclear*].

When you meet your plowman you have the privilege of sharing a bite with him. In the villa you have the privilege of carrying a dry log on your shoulders if you need to make the fire burn more brightly, without losing face with your friends.

You have the privilege of being able to ride on the saddle blanket, not bothering with saddle and bridle, without risking your reputation. And if you are not booted and spurred you will not think it odd to ride any old horse, or even a donkey, rather than go on foot.

Further privileges are: being able to drink mixed or watered wine almost all the year, which is better for the digestion and allows you to sell the pure wine; using nut-oil lamps instead of candles; and burning twigs and green wood while you sell the big pieces of dry wood to the highest bidder. When *Madonna* decides to do the laundry, you have the privilege of letting her find wood where she can without touching your pile. *Madonna* in her turn has the privilege of sending for butter and ricotta when the peasant woman is milking . . .

Many of these "privileges" are occasions to break a strict social code, and Falcone, who is the most democratic of his fellow authors, seems to enjoy the prospect for its own sake. His mischievous delight in eating onions and garlic and coming to table with dirty hands sounds like a small boy's attempt to outsmart his mother. Others of the privileges that strike the modern reader as Spartan or overly frugal represent a reaction against the great emphasis in Renaissance urban life on propriety and formal display.

Anton Francesco Doni, by contrast, dreams of the most lavish display, admitting he has no means to support it (p. 24):

> Here I make fish ponds for trout and carp, plant stands of orange trees and build working fountains. I battle with architects and engineers and commission painters, sculptors and stuccoists, as if I were a grand duke. I don't want my building to be modest; I want to be able to entertain ten great lords at the same time. If I can't do that, I would rather throw my money into the Arno.

Lollio's encomium of the villa refers to the "ignoramuses" who are apparently to be found in the city and not in the country, and this introduces a second theme, the denunciation of the physical and social atmosphere in the urban centers. Similarly, Gallo records, in a personal note at the start of his villa encomium in the expanded edition of his book published in 1569,[9] the particular professional burdens which, as a jurist, he has avoided by escaping into the country: the reading of many confused cases, which overcrowds the mind, and is not to be compared with reading Plato, Philo and Seneca; and the company of lawyers, government officials, faithless notaries, and murderous doctors. He adds:

> How very wise were those ancient Greeks, Romans, Africans and others, who gave up their high positions as things that impeded their true well-being, in order to live in their villas, poor in worldly treasures but very rich in their untrammelled spirit, sound intellect, clear conscience and good will.

We saw in Chapter 2 that the *topos* of negative descriptions of the city was established by ancient authors; but the sixteenth-century writers are not simply echoing a theme in the customary manner of humanist scholars: they bring to it a virulent sense of disgust generated by the decayed ethical and social ambience in Italian centers of the period. Lollio expands (fol. B xr):

> But in those times when I take no other fruit or diversion from the villa (whence I draw an infinite number), I enjoy at least this consolation, that I have fled and cast off as far as possible the insolences, the hates, the distractions, the annoyance, the boredom of many who know no other way and get no other pleasure than in impeding and disturbing the peace of others.

And Falcone (Preface, fol. i):

> It seems to me that the city, if I am not mistaken, for the most part today is nothing other than a patent theatre of misery and filled with every infelicity, and so it happens in those persons in which the good and blessed life, because of *otio*, lapses and languishes.
>
> For them, the element fire, which is so active, is extinguished, the air becomes infected, the water is poisoned, the earth made sterile, gold is blackened, iron rusts, every room and lodging is ruined, the mind fattens, the human body sickens, the horse becomes defective, the ship is wrecked, the soldier becomes as a rabbit, the voice becomes raucous, the wine turns, the ruby discolors, the wood becomes worm-eaten and the cloth stained.

Whence, in a later discussion, I shall reveal that where *otio* enters, there enters also destruction, great damage, ruin, scorn and infamy.

Taegio's approach is ironic (p. 110):

The joys and pleasant spectacle of the city are robberies, burglaries, assassinations, favoritism, conspiracies, injuries, betrayals, false depositions by witnesses, false documents of notaries, lies of lawyers, corruption of judges, ambition of councillors, imprisonment of the worthy, condemnation of the innocent, and oppression of the poor, of widows, and of children. I am silent on the lovely sight of the hangman, of the jailer, of the police agents, of the pincers, of the fetters, of the chains and of the prisons. I am silent on the cruel and horrible spectacles of the killing of those condemned by the courts, I am silent on the agreeable encounter with certain cancerous tricksters who, feigning a shuffle, let loose Saint Anthony's fire on those who do not give way to their importunities... I am silent on the sweet harmony of the mournful voices of the poor, who die from hunger throughout the city to the shame of humanity. ...

The interlocutor, Partenio, breaks in to ask about such benefits of the city as the superb palaces, with their priceless furnishings, the statues, paintings, theater and other public entertainment, the sight of beautiful and adorned noblewomen. Vitauro, the principal speaker, replies that in the palaces of great kings there is only labor and pain, while quiet and joy reigns in the huts of the poor. As for (ancient) statues and pictures, he says, they only remind us how low we have fallen, while modern ones portray people who are only rich and not virtuous.

Gallo is equally negative in his characterization. His principal discussion (below, p. 129) begins with the depiction of a society that devotes itself to staining the reputation of decent people and is concerned primarily with financial gain by fair or foul means. The streets are filled with a cacophony of shouts and with an underworld of "bawds and whores reeking of musk, crooks and sorcerers who ensnare you, soothsayers and diviners who tell your fortune, cheats and cutpurses who deceive you, mercenaries and swaggering soldiers who bully you, and hypocrites and confidence tricksters who swindle you." Still worse, one is forced to witness gruesome and sadistic tortures and executions for which "the main square of the city is turned into a slaughterhouse." Indeed, the principal speaker in Gallo's dialog, Giovanni Battista Avogadro, gets so overwrought in his characterization that his interlocutor, Cornelio Ducco, has to get him back onto the track of his discussion, saying, "I do beg you to stop talking about these unpleasant subjects, and to go back to the reason why you enjoy such a cheerful life here."

Gallo's attack on the city concludes with a passage (below, p. 130) in which he affirms that two generations earlier the cities were made far more habitable by a spirit of mutual cooperation within the population; they were places of "peace, charity and faith." His claim that this condition no longer prevailed in towns after the middle of the century conforms with the published records of urban affairs which show an alarming and often incredible growth, from about the second quarter of the sixteenth century—the period of increasing domination of foreign powers—of the exercise of malevolent self-interest and criminal activity on the part of those in power to the detriment of all segments of society.

In their comments on the city, the writers' principal focus is on the breakdown of community and cordiality, primarily among the privileged members of society. To a lesser degree they refer to environmental ills such as noise and bad air. They rarely depict the city as the seat of institutions, public ceremony, entertainment, education, commerce, and other benefits of civilization. One brief comment by Lollio (fol. v[r]) is all we hear in praise of urban life:

> And I should never deny that cities are made for the habitation and commerce of men and are rather like schools in which one learns fine achievements and praiseworthy customs and in which one acquires the laudible accomplishments of the sciences and the virtues.

Contemporary civic documents support the more negative view. In his study of class differences in the Venetian State, which at the time extended from the Adriatic to Brescia, Angelo Ventura identified the many areas in which the ruling class ("gentlemen" and wealthy bourgeoisie, each constituting about five percent of the population) exercised illicit power and exploited public funds.[10] The most relevant for the interpretation of the villa literature was speculation on grain. The cities maintained granaries from which the indigent could be fed in times of drought and widespread hunger, and required the producers to deposit, for a set price, a portion of their harvest in these public stores. The producers preferred to export or to engage in black-market sales and, most disruptively, to hoard grain in the hope of forcing up the price. This speculative enterprise was especially widespread in times of famine. The rich gambled with the lives of the poor. Given that most of the villa properties in northern Italy were producers of grain and wine, at least some of the owners must have numbered among those who evaded their legal responsibilities to the urban majority. It is conceivable that they and spokesmen like Gallo exaggerated the evils of city life partly in order to justify this kind of profiteering.

In the composition of the city councils and of the various offices, even when there was broad representation by election, a small number of privileged people grasped power and favored their friends and families in the assignment of offices. This led to further abuses, as in property assessments for purposes of taxation, which frequently minimized the value of the rich holdings of major landlords and overestimated the property of artisans and peasants. The Monti di Pietà, public trusts partly funded from general taxes to enable needy people to borrow at low interest rates, were regularly the target of embezzlement by members of the governing group, which also supported private ventures with other public funds. Justice was contravened by being entirely in the control of judges selected from the same stratum, who were notoriously lenient toward members of their class and severe toward the helpless, as in the inhuman treatment of the victims of their sentences cited by Gallo. The glue that had held the various parts of society together in earlier generations had become unstuck, and the cities were now battlegrounds of conflict between the rich and powerful and the poor and helpless. The anti-urban diatribes of the villa-lovers suggest that hatred and suspicion were growing not simply between different classes, but within the privileged groups themselves.

While all the villas described in the texts are working farms, the authors differ on the amount of time, energy and expertise the proprietor should devote to agriculture as against the pleasures of recreation and social diversion. Falcone is a vigorous spokesman for intense entrepreneurial involvement, and addresses (Preface, fol. iii) a hypothetical devotee of *otium*:

> Why are you burdened with debts? Why do you not work your villa? Because of *otio*. Oh, you tell me, I am a gentleman [*gentilhuomo*]. You are a good-for-nothing [*stentilhuomo*] and your ineffectiveness makes others ineffectual. Adam was a gentleman, and God ordered him to work, both in and outside the earthly Paradise. The Holy Fathers of old worked. The learned Romans attended to their villas, working them with their own hands to cultivate them well, not disdaining labor, and you who scorn it are a *poveraccio* and ignorant.

He describes the responsibilities (pp. 9, 20):

> To avoid disorder it is essential that the proprietor be expert, know how to do everything, so that he shall also know how to command. It is necessary that he always, or as often as possible, be personally present in every major matter and that he understood everything, see everything, touch everything, trusting as little as possible, especially the peasants, who because of their vile nature are enemies of their masters [*padroni*]. . . . In the evening, in the presence of the entire work force [*fameglia*] you should order and command everything that is to be done the next day so that everyone may, as soon as he has arisen, get about his work without losing time, and see that each one obeys without grumbling.

Taegio's dialog opens with a discussion of this matter. The villa proprietor begins (p. 1):

> VITAURO I have been continuously at the villa, and I plan to return right away (if I can expedite the task that has impelled me to come to the city [replacing a new foreman who has died]).
>
> PARTENIO You believe then in spending the greater part of your time in the villa?
>
> VIT. So I do, and I am most resolute on the point.
>
> PART. I am amazed that a man like yourself, so civil, affable, agreeable in conversation and elegant in manner, who could live comfortably in the city, wants to stay in the villa most of the time.
>
> VIT. And I am also amazed that one as experienced and of such sound judgment and well educated as yourself appears not to know what great felicity one enjoys in the villa.

There then ensues the familiar account of the simple pleasures of country life and of the disadvantages of the city.

Lollio is more permissive (fols. iv, v), responding to the ancient Carthaginian writer, Mago, who advised selling one's city house in order to be continuously in control of the villa activities:

> But would I say that one must stay continually in one's villa? No. But I should say (considering the pleasures and the benefits that agriculture brings us, and in conformity with the precepts of Columella) that a good and diligent father of a family never should let a month pass without returning to his villa, since the eye of the proprietor (as Pliny says so well) is an insurance and a fruitful presence in the fields.

Descriptions of the recreational pleasures of villa life follow the lead of ancient Roman writers and, with the exception of Gallo's, lack originality and a ring of authenticity. They fall into three categories: social (conversation and games, music and dance);

reading and study, and hunting and fishing. Lollio (fol. B ixᵛ) offers a typical overview:

> As for private pleasures . . ., in our house music of various sorts is played every day. And we
> engage in every sort of proper and delightful game. Sometimes we dance for recreation and to
> delight the company. Here we read books with pleasure and we discuss various matters. In
> sum, one has here all those entertainments and diversions that one can decently desire. All in
> all, I have no fear of being thought arrogant in making a comparison, eager as I am to say that
> as in Athens the house of Isocrates was called the School, the factory of oratorical art, so our
> house here may be called the armory of diversion, the fount of pleasures and (to put it in a
> word) the very hostel of joy. Besides this, I believe that we should not underestimate the
> convenience afforded by [the proximity of] the city and surrounding places, since our villa is,
> as it were, a center placed in the midst of many cities and villages in the area around it, with
> Ferrara on the east, Modena and Reggio on the west, Bologna to the south, and Mantua to the
> north, none of these areas being more distant than one day's travel, not to speak of the many
> villages which, as you know, are much more easily accessible.

Gallo's speaker, who apparently spends most of his leisure time with visiting male
friends, refers in a similarly conventional passage (below, p. 131) to occasional visits
with the gentlewomen of the family to stroll, exchange riddles and jokes, and dance.
Conversation and games are depicted by Taegio as a kind of mental sport for the exercise
of brain muscle (p. 149):

> but occasional conversation among respected persons who gather together at times for mental
> recreation, with games, mottoes and decent jokes, pleases me greatly because the mind, tired
> by literary studies, is calmed by such relaxation and thus is prepared with greater vigor to
> return to its virtuous activities.

He also recommends finding a companion with whom to discuss one's writing and
reading.

Gallo speaks of another kind of gathering of villa gentlemen (below, p. 132)
apparently at a country tavern, where a group of companions (it is uncertain whether
women are present) share a meal, obviously much drink, and tell stories. The master
storyteller is a kind of Münchhausen character who spins incredible yarns; Gallo retells
one of these that sets everyone present rolling about on the floor helpless with laughter.

Taegio warns the proprietor inclined to intellectual pursuits that "too much study
destroys and even corrupts the health of the body because the deep thought and
melancholy of the scholar draws the spirits to the head . . ." (pp. 141f.). Like all the other
authors, he refers to hunting, fishing and bird-netting as among the basic benefits of
villa life. Some of the appeal is due to the fact that these sports had been pursuits of
aristocratic landholders since antiquity, and to engage in them was felt to confer some
measure of nobility. In Gallo's dialog, a general hunt (that is, for a variety of beasts) is
planned in the woods of a neighboring *signore*. Detailed accounts of hunting and fishing
are given by Gallo in his Day IX (which follows the text reproduced below). In Doni's
aristocratic villa, a hunt for large game is arranged on one day, with nets and dogs, the
next day brings a bird hunt with falcons, and the third day a hunt for small game—hares
and foxes.

Gallo's description of a fishing outing (below, pp. 125–26) is the most vivid and
unusual of any of the accounts. The fishing is not done by baiting the prey on a line, but
by draining a pond and capturing the fish by hand or with farm tools (in Doni's account,

nets are used). Moreover, the villa dwellers do not take part in this sport, but watch from the edge the absurd antics of the peasants as they try to capture the slippery victims.

Peasant-watching also provides princes and *signori* with entertainment in Doni's essay (p. 42) where, after dinner, the court watches a free-for-all fight among peasants until only one survives standing. While Gallo treats the peasants as comic characters, Doni admires their bravery and expertness. This is followed by races between girls and then boys, and a stage comedy, music and dance. The next day (p. 44) jousting matches, followed by spearing of rings, are arranged, and in the evening a soccer match.

In the process of representing work and recreation at the villa, the literature gives a unique insight into social relations in the later Renaissance. The speaker in each of the essays, whether he is the author or a fictional character, is a "gentleman," a wealthy member of the bourgeoisie (no distinction appears to be made between professionals and those of commercial origin) whose country estates—in most cases apparently purchased rather than inherited—has provided him with a new full- or part-time vocation. His position is quite different from that of the Medici, who had roots in the country as well as in the city, and wielded great political, economic and social power. Our gentlemen had to feel their way in an unfamiliar environment, learning how to behave toward their bailiffs, their peasants and a landed aristocracy that looked on them with condescension or scorn.

They appear at ease with gentlemen of their own class, as is best illustrated by Gallo's story of the outing at a tavern (below, p. 132); but Gallo's speaker treats members of the aristocracy with deference, and seems to be keenly aware of his inferiority to them (e.g., below, p. 133). Probably there was little contact between those who had recently purchased villas and members of the landed nobility.

Throughout Europe, the peasant had been feared and hated since the Middle Ages. Oppressed by poverty and misery, subject to recurring famines and the depredations of war, illiterate and potentially violent, the peasant class vastly outnumbered other classes and was seen as a potential threat to stability and peace. Chaotic and bloody peasant revolts were frequent in the fifteenth and sixteenth centuries, for example in Friuli in 1511 and throughout northern Europe in 1525.[11] There is an extensive medieval and Renaissance literature that vilifies and satirizes the peasant,[12] who appears in visual art and on the stage mostly as a buffoon. To some degree, the villa books follow this pattern; the obsessively frugal Falcone, who insists on watering his own wine, instructs the reader (pp. 49–50):

> When the *contadino* brings material into the granary, take care, since if he sees nobody in the house, he will easily rob you—of bread, wine or other things; he grabs anything. The *villano* is like an unreliable animal and it is advisable to keep an eye on his hands.... In the kitchen there should never be a fire to warm oneself, because the peasant's stove is the barn; thus much wood may be saved, and if the *padrone* finds the peasant at the fire in the kitchen, he should scold him and chase him out into the barn to clean up the cattle, to arrange the hay, where he can eat in the manger, wash and rub the cows' tails, heating himself even better without kitchen wood.

G. Bonardo (*La richezza dell'agricoltura*, pp. 69v ff.) devotes an entire chapter to the problems to be anticipated from dishonest *fattori*, mentioning such practices as telling the *padrone* that animals have died that have in fact been sold, skimming produce from the stores, and selling part of the seeds while claiming that the reduced yield is due to the exhaustion of the soil. (In contrast, Giacomo Agostinetti's *Cento e dieci ricordi che formano il buon fattore di villa* is directed in part to protecting the *fattore* from entering into unfavorable contracts with the *padrone*.)

But while peasants are the cause of some suspicion and anxiety, the writers are aware of the benefits to be gained from considerate treatment. The same Falcone recommends (p. 11):

> While the *signor padrone* is in residence out in the villa with all his noble family, he should be respectful to every insignificant peasant in the villa or territory, being toward them loving, pleasant, sociable, affable, not commanding them haughtily or in anger nor saying anything in any way hurtful or insulting. Because a man is like a horse, and does not want to be governed haughtily. Indeed, it's good to keep them happy and satisfied so that they work better, more and with better will . . .
>
> It is not necessary, however, to be too familiar with them for there is a danger of shattering what they ought always to revere and value. Because in the end it happens that too much familiarity breeds contempt. It is not always necessary for them to understand more than a few of your plans. It is necessary sometimes to pretend to do as they say, so that they will glory in it and work.

Gallo's Avogadro, speaking of his peasants (below, p. 125), claims that he makes a point of

> supporting them in times of trouble, and helping them to educate their children in literacy and manners appropriate to their place in society. We give them money and household goods if they find it difficult to provide their daughters with dowries. . . . These count as true acts of charity, because they [i.e., the peasants] are not deceived by the rogues and swindlers that one finds everywhere these days. . . .

His companion points out the contrast of this generosity to the practice of gentlemen everywhere who bully them "until they have lost property and life and honor."

Taegio recommends occasional visits to the peasants to discuss villa matters (p. 149):

> PARTENIO Now, as to conversation with gentlemen, I know how I ought to comport myself, but since there are a greater number of *villani* in a villa than of gentlemen, how would you propose that I behave in dealing with them?
>
> VITAURO It would not displease me that occasionally you should go to discuss things with the peasants—on holidays and rainy days, and in the season when the peasants have leisure [*divenuti ociosi*] because of the onset of lazy winter and are awaiting to enjoy the fruits of their past labors.
>
> PART. Tell me, on your life, what you talk about?
>
> VIT. I talk about the way in which husbandmen break and plow the earth, the time to fatten and the manner of irrigating the fields, about the quality of the land, of the vigor of the seeds . . .

Camillo Tarello (*Ricordo*, fol. 71v f.) writes an impassioned appeal to landowners to encourage literacy among the peasants, concluding:

> Reading, learning and applying what is learned will give farm workers a healthy, lively, joyful

and long life, nourishing these poor husbandmen with good food, with few aggravations and less work than usual.

This marked change of attitude toward peasants had begun to be revealed in the early sixteenth century in literature and the fine arts in northern Italy, especially in Venetian territories, where peasants had been instrumental in saving the Republic from defeat by the combined forces of the European powers and the Papacy. They are now represented sympathetically, as sentient and occasionally even noble individuals (e.g., in the prints of Villamena), whose wretched condition has not removed their humanity. They appear as sympathetic and exemplary characters in the early sixteenth-century *novelle* of Matteo Bandello, a Dominican friar who gave up orders to move into court society. His *contadino*, by virtue of his poverty and simplicity, appears as innocent of the temptations and vices that attract courtiers and the bourgeoisie, and may even display nobility of spirit, though more typically he appears as a virtuous rustic.[13] The same is true late in the sixteenth century in the rural genre scenes of Jacopo Bassano.[14]

By contrast to these artists, who sanitized and idealized peasants to appeal to an urban and courtly audience, the Paduan Angelo Beolco, known as Ruzante, pioneered written dialect comedies and dialog sketches for the theater beginning in the 1520s, which were to become a source for the *commedia dell'arte*. The central character, who reappears, as in the *commedia*, in different pieces, is the peasant Ruzante, a profane and comical braggart who usually is abandoned at the end by his wife or lover and is beaten by hooligans because his poverty and ignorance make him the quintessential loser (*La Betía, Bilora, Il Parlamento*). An early comedy, *La Pastoral* (1521), stages an uproarious encounter of Ruzante and a group of Arcadian shepherds whose declamations in exaggeratedly elevated triplets satirize the genre of Arcadian literature and are made to seem ridiculous in contrast to the peasant's earthy, scatological outbursts. The meeting between the stylish, courtier-like shepherds of the humanist poetic theater and the rough rustic is a literary counterpart to Palladio's fusion, in the design of his mature villa structures, of the noble temple-like residence with the common rural *barchessa* or porticoed barn [*4.10*]. Beolco's peasant is comical, but he gains the reader's sympathy and respect as a fellow human being.[15]

Women did not figure at all in ancient writings devoted to the villa. Most of the sixteenth-century books, by contrast, show a considerable preoccupation with women, but as only minimal contributors to the pleasures of villa life. The passages devoted to women betray more distaste and distrust than companionship or affection. Children are never mentioned.

The gentlewoman is in some ways as oppressed as the peasant by the domination and condescension of her husband. Gallo's claims that women prefer the villa over the city because the life is freer and less encumbered with obligations (below, p. 128) may be wishful thinking: women are given no role other than managing the family and are not even permitted to engage in the two most prized rewards of villa life, reading and hunting.[16] Taegio writes (pp. 122f.):

Because women are naturally more fragile than men and naturally more inclined to evil than to good, I tell you that they have need more of reins than of spurs, and more of servility than of liberty. The woman who reads puts herself into too great danger. I know of some who have a gentle spirit to whom, when they read, the responsibilities of women suddenly seem boring, and they let themselves be overcome by sleep, and when they read the stories of Boccaccio they don't put them down, feeling an infinite sweetness. And so for all the aforesaid reasons and examples, I conclude that the *otio* of letters is for men, not women, the duty of whom is to learn to manage the family well and not to read.

Falcone warns (p. 189):

Women are not permitted to go hunting, an obvious occasion for encounters like those of Dido and Aeneas and other unchaste ladies.[17]

This preoccupation with chastity and the insistence on the inferiority of women had not been a feature of medieval feudal society, when women could wield power and inherit property, and, if courtly literature reflects actual behavior, could dominate men in (extramarital) love relationships.[18] Bourgeois ideals and the revival of ancient learning and culture in the Renaissance helped to relegate women again to the inferior position they had held in ancient Greece, and greatly to reduce interest in courtly and physical love. The motivation of the misogynism in the passages quoted above is the writers' conviction that, because women are slaves to nature, they are more likely to betray than to keep faith.

In Gallo's dialog, when Avogadro is reminded by Ducco of the fashionable city women who attend various entertainments and stand at the window or doorway (below, p. 128), he sees these activities as a certain path to vice, and launches into a revolting outburst:

Every bad daughter should get death for a dowry, worms for clothes, and a tomb for a house. Unfaithful wives should have their eyes gouged out, their tongues cut out, and their hands chopped off—or rather they should be wiped off the face of the earth altogether, burnt alive!

This pathological impulse for vengeance seems especially extreme in a person who immediately after (below, p. 129) expresses compassion for condemned criminals who are similarly mauled. Curiously, Ducco, who introduced this train of thought, asks him to drop it and to return to the pleasures of the villa.

The mistrust of women's capacity for chastity parallels the mistrust of the peasant. But while the writers are aware that considerate treatment of the latter encourages loyal and cooperative behavior, they do not suggest that an affectionate and understanding attitude toward their wives might encourage their loyalty (Falcone does advise, p. 21, against "injuring" one's spouse in private or public). Because women lacked the capacity for physical and economic retaliation that mitigated the impulse to oppress peasants, they could be subjected to a physical and intellectual confinement that must have been more likely to promote than to prevent a breach of faith.

Gallo's Avogadro complements his vicious vengefulness against women in a sketch of chivalrous *fêtes champêtres* with the virtuous ladies of the villa (below, p. 131), whom the gentlemen occasionally join for a stroll, light and lively conversation spiced with jokes and riddles, and chaste dancing. These occasions appear to be more the dispatch of a responsibility than a real pleasure, and the speaker recounts with far more enthusiasm the outing with his male friends (below, p. 131).

Women of the servant or artisan class, however, may be assigned more essential roles in the operation of the villa. The bailiff's wife (*massara*) who, according to Taegio (p. 17), "should not be so beautiful that love or jealousy tempt him to abandon his work, nor so ugly that distaste for her tempt him to seek others," doubles as a housekeeper and a farmer, and the responsibilities assigned to her by Falcone (p. 16f.) are intensely, even excessively demanding:

As the principal care of the villa property, outdoors in the countryside, is the job of the men, so the principal care of the house devolves on and is suited to the women, to the chief woman of the house. Otherwise, as is said, the woman makes like a man: but the woman would kill the man [*la donna fà l'huomo: ma la donna amazzarebbe l'huomo*]. I say then that in the villa it is the office of the working woman, the bailiff's wife, first to attend to herself, as a devoted woman and fearful of God, to raise her children well, and others of the household, to be obedient to her husband, patient, and loving with everyone, discreet, with good control, not jealous, to love the villa and not often leave the house and her courtyard. She should be strict with wrongdoers; not contentious; she, and her daughters as well, should avoid dancing and music parties, keep the house, clothes, linen and portico clean. The things in the house should not be scattered all over but each should have its place. She should not entrust the keys of the granary and storeroom to anyone, and should keep an eye on the youth, especially the females. She should be the first to rise, and get to work . . . and the last to go to sleep, and in the evening should organize what has to be done in the house the next day. She should work without grumbling because service done in that way is not welcome. Chattering women should not come into the house, and should be sent off right away. In everything she does, she should support her husband. She should willingly serve neighbors, should spur the young people to work, saying, "do you see me?" "do you see your father? What's to be done?" She should not swear, or say common and foul words. Wood scattered around the court should be gathered in bundles to heat the oven.

She should keep close count of how many eggs, chickens, capons, butter, and cheese she has sold. She should not long for fancy clothes but should keep very clean. She should make soap for washing hair and private parts on Saturday with a ladle of good, cold ashes in a pan of water, boiling it down to one quarter and not more; it will come out perfectly smooth. On Sunday she should have everyone change clothes, with white shirts, doing the laundry but without wasting soap or wood, not involving many women in the work, but all the girls should do washing. When in the portico she should watch that the chickens and animals do not waste the feed.[19] If she lends something to neighbors, she should see that it is returned as soon as possible. As soon as meals are over, she should clear the table, so that the house does not look like a tavern. She should keep the small linens in order.

She should put the hens in the coop at the right time, and know how to castrate the young roosters . . . she should make houshold bread, and not keep many puppies. Bread is not to be eaten fresh, but firm and hard . . .

The bottle of good wine is not to be touched, but watered wine used continuously; a little pure may be kept for intense hot weather. At table the little that there is should be eaten in peace, in silence, after saying the benediction. All should savor a single nut. No one should sit at table until the whole family has come home.

The little ones should be put to sleep before the workers return home in the evening. The bailiff's wife who runs the house earns five soldi and doesn't know it. [*Perchè la massara ch'attende de cà/Guadagna cinque soldi e non lo sa.*]

In addition, the *massara* gets the milk and makes butter, ricotta, cheese, and does the salting. She feeds the small animals, tends the kitchen garden, keeping out the animals, watches that food does not spoil, bakes, and cares for bees. The *padrone* does the larger buying, but the *massara* the small things.

The treatment of women in the essays occurs at a period in which the persecution of women for witchcraft had greatly increased. But the villa authors attribute to women no power whatsoever, whether evil or occult—only weakness. Their fear of betrayal by their wives and daughters may well have been related to insecurity about their own image in the world. They had to maintain "face." We have no way of knowing the extent to which the fear was justified, but given the restraints imposed on women, it seems improbable that the instances of sexual promiscuity matched the anxieties expressed.

The villa essays invite comparison to a similar genre of contemporary literature, the books on the courtier. The tone and content of the Renaissance courtier book was set by Castiglione's celebrated *Cortegiano* (Venice, 1528), which depicted an ideal of elevated moral behavior and fixed for the future a definition of gentility. Our authors, in contrast, though they address "gentlemen", are resolutely bourgeois, their behavior materialistic, insecure and, at times, almost boorish. The *padrone* of the villa books is at once a sycophant and a bully, who senses his inferiority to aristocratic acquaintances, oppresses everyone who supports him, and yet feels that at any moment the lid may blow off the boiling pot.

Appendix
The Advantages of Villa Life

A discussion between the noble gentlemen Messer Giovanni Battista Avogadro and Messer Cornelio Ducco in the month of May 1553 on the delights of the villa and how it is better to reside there than in the city.

From Agostino Gallo,
Le dieci giornate della vera agricoltura e piaceri della villa, Day VIII
(Venice: Giovanni Bariletto, 1566, fols. 138ʳ–151ᵛ)

CORNELIO DUCCO Messer Giovanni Battista, you have very kindly persuaded me to interrupt my journey so that you could honor me at your table; and since your friends have left us alone to amuse themselves in this shady garden, moved by my love I feel I must tell you how warmly I appreciate your courtesy. Not only have you given me the opportunity to see this place, which is truly worthy of a prince, with its sumptuous house, its charming garden, extensive pergola and large fish pond; you have also given me the chance to tell you how astonished many people in the city are who, knowing you to be a cultivated man, cannot help finding fault with you for abandoning them and coming to live on this little estate.* Now, because I am extremely fond of you, I should love to hear the reasons that led you to this decision. And I want to know all the more because I am sure that you did it only after much thought, and not on impulse, as the others believe.

GIOVANNI BATTISTA AVOGADRO My dear Messer Cornelio, I know you have always had my good name at heart, so I can do no less than tell you frankly why I came to live here. I see that our companions are nearing the gate of the garden where they are going to take their accustomed siesta, so I shall be able to give you a full account. Let me say to begin with that if those who criticize me knew the reasons that persuaded me to settle here, they would not blame me at all. Instead, they would inscribe over my door those words which were justly written over the door of Cato the Censor when he gave up his high position in Rome in order to enjoy the remainder of his life quietly on his little farm: "Cato, you are truly fortunate since you alone know how to live in this world."

You know from long experience what my life was like before, and how everything went wrong for me because of bad company. When shame finally made me realize this, I decided to abandon that whole world and retire here, determined to live in as civilized a fashion as I could for the time that remained to me. The more I feel the joy of every hour, the more I think that just as my former life was a constant hell, the present one is like paradise. Here my neighbors are civilized, courteous and peaceable, and they love me far more than I deserve; indeed we share everything to such a degree that our possessions belong more to our friends than to the people who own them.

We go hunting together, or birding; we talk, read, sing, make music, play games, or eat together, as you saw this morning. And if by chance a quarrel should break out, everybody else immediately makes an effort to smoothe it over, and we become friends again just as before.

COR. DUCCO I am as pleased to hear these reasons why you left the city and retired to this beautiful estate as I am gratified more than I can say to hear that you have kept a holy peace among you. How happy Christendom would be if this blessed mode prevailed in every town, village, and estate, instead of the diabolical mode that actually exists, with Satan's tongues

---

*Occasionally in this translation the word *villa* has been rendered as "estate," or "country," since "villa" in Italian comprehends those meanings, whereas in English it more narrowly suggests the house.

stirring up discord between one man and another, and doing all they can to provoke anger and argument and then boasting about it as if it were something to be proud of.

GIO. BATT. AVOGADRO Another thing: we are contented with our peasants, because they love us and honor us. Woe betide any who is rash enough to offend us or to commit some foul deed in our territory, for we would all get together at once and drive him off our land.

COR. DUCCO That is not a bad way of seeing that the estate is kept free from troublemakers. It is certainly unfortunate when landowners support such people because of quarrels and rivalries among themselves. No wonder scandals occur when that happens, especially when part of the gentry fraternize with these corrupt peasants and brazenly defend them whatever crimes they commit, both in private and in public. Just as those people are to be blamed who treat their peasants like slaves, so we should praise those who, while being genuinely fond of the good ones, will have nothing to do with the bad.

GIO. BATT. AVOGADRO I must tell you that we make a point of supporting them in times of trouble, and helping them to educate their children in literacy and manners appropriate to their place in society. We give them money and household goods if they find it difficult to provide their daughters with dowries, so that they have a better chance in life. These count as true acts of charity, because they [i.e., the peasants] are not deceived by the rogues and swindlers that one finds everywhere these days, who go around with all sorts of pious stories and play on people's superstitions in order to make a dishonest living.

COR. DUCCO It would be lucky for the poor everywhere if there were more gentlemen like you in every village, who would actually help them rather than—as so many men do, moved by the devil—bullying them until they have lost property and life and honor.

GIO. BATT. AVOGADRO I refrain from saying what I could about that. But can you imagine the satisfaction I get from all the advantages of this site? It is no more than a mile and a half across in any direction, yet it excels any other in all Lombardy.

First, the air is evidently very good. We are five miles from the city. Then, produce is abundant: millet, vegetables, vines and hay—not much flax, though its quality is as good as that of the rest. As for trees, not only are the fields exceptionally well planted, but the roads too are lined with them, so that when the sun is blazing you can go through the whole countryside in the shade.

Then, the many wonderfully clear streams—what can one say about them? You cannot visit any part of the country or turn anywhere without finding canals, rivers, aqueducts, streams or running water of some sort. They seem almost to be competing with one another. Your gaze goes from one to another unceasingly, except that one runs at midday, another in the evening, another in the morning, another all the time. Many of them flow above or below each other, coursing so smoothly through their channels that they seem to have been created by art deliberately to amaze anyone who looks at them.

COR. DUCCO I confess that I have seen many villages in Lombardy well supplied with water, but never one equal to this for the number of streams and their variety, charm and utility.

GIO. BATT. AVOGADRO The waters are cool at present but fairly warm in winter, so that they are good for the animals. These are now eating our hay, of which we need a large amount, since there are more than five hundred cattle and a substantial number of sheep. And apart from the fact that these waters give us pleasure because of their beauty, they are also extremely agreeable and useful for fishing. Of all the diversions that we offer the friends who come to seek us here this is the greatest and most pleasurable.

When we want to gather the fish we can quickly drain a canal, stream or brook. Our friends greatly enjoy the many wonderful things that can happen in fishing. There is nothing in the world to compare with the sight of men and women, young people and old, large and small, coming from all directions, barefoot, and carrying nets, goads, and a whole array of implements—hoes, shovels, spades, gourds, buckets, conches and other shells—to help with the fishing. As soon as the water has been diverted elsewhere they wade in and pounce: fish are slithering about, eels wriggling away, lampreys digging themselves into the mud, frogs jumping, gobies hiding, and crayfish burying themselves.

The most melancholy man could not keep from bursting out laughing when he sees the endless antics of these good folk as they fish. One of them closes off the water or drains the pond; another runs, jumps, falls, gets up again; another laughs, sings, makes a catch and then doesn't know how to keep hold of it; another shouts and makes faces and does nothing but joke with the others. Often three or four or more make a grab for the same fish and fall over one another in the mud and water. When the others see how frustrated they are and watch them getting up all wet and muddy, they burst out in a great roar of laughter and shouting, clapping and banging their shovels and spades and things together. To tell the truth, I do not know anything that is so good to cheer you up when you are depressed.

Who can help laughing to see these good people sometimes mistaking snakes for eels, lizards for lampreys, and toads for frogs? If that happens they hang on to these disgusting creatures and chase after anyone they know is scared of them. Then there is an even greater racket than before, with people running away, children crying, girls shouting, women scolding and threatening not just with words but with sticks, hoes, stones and other things, to defend themselves and others.

So, Messer Cornelio, now that you have heard me so attentively, tell me what you think of our rustic comforts and diversions.

COR. DUCCO I think very highly of them. They are ideal pastimes for gentlemen, noblemen, princes, indeed any refined spirit. And I get even more satisfaction from hearing you describe them so well, so that I feel I have seen them and taken part in them myself.

GIO. BATT. AVOGADRO I wish you had been here on the eve of St John's Day [Midsummer], when, before the third hour [9 a.m.], you would have seen three carriages going by, containing the distinguished ladies Signora Isabella Martinenga, Signora Nostra Cavriola and Signora Barbara Callina, and several gentlemen, all going to dine at Dello with the noble gentleman Carlo Averoldo, a true lover of horticulture, as his exceedingly remarkable gardens testify. When they saw that some of us landowners had drained the Garzietta pond and that a big crowd of men and women were fishing there, they stopped by the gate of the noble Nascini family to ask the ladies where they could get the best view of the antics of these simple people as they fished, and they laughed so much that I thought they were going to burst. When our womenfolk [presumably the peasant women] had seen the entertainment, they set themselves up on the bank with pans in order to cook the various fish, and the ladies looked on, enjoying themselves more than I can describe. The women offered them fried fish [which they declined] and live shellfish in pretty baskets together with a quantity of fine shrimps, and said: "Since your graces decided not to eat this catch with us, we beg you to accept at least this small present, and to think not of its humble nature but of the hearts of those who lovingly offer it to you." The ladies accepted very gratefully, as if it had been a gift of great value, and replied: "You are all very much to be envied, since you enjoy yourselves so much on this rare estate. May God preserve you in this condition for ever." After these affectionate words had been spoken, the drivers urged the horses on with their journey.

COR. DUCCO Those noble ladies were lucky to have come across you when you were doing such amusing things, and you were equally lucky, since it gave you the opportunity to be gracious to them and to honor them with your courtesy.

GIO. BATT. AVOGADRO Now, to return to the benefits of fishing. Apart from its entertainment value, it also allows us to get as much fish and shrimps as we want, and we are almost always able to send considerable quantities to our friends. What we keep for ourselves we eat at its very freshest, which is the right way to eat any good fish.

COR. DUCCO Certainly there is no comparison in flavor between a dead fish and one that has been put in the pan alive.

GIO. BATT. AVOGADRO To continue with my account of the advantages we enjoy here, we get great satisfaction from the fine dairy products that are plentiful all the year round. We produce good cheeses and butters, though we also eat less expensive things like ricotta, farmer's cheese, junkets and creams—sometimes just as they are, sometimes flavored in various ways to make them tastier. And of course there is plenty of veal, beef, chicken, and doves, ducks, geese, peacocks and turkeys. We have not only good cheeses and salted meats, but also excellent fruit and vegetables—citrons, lemons, oranges, asparagus and artichokes.

What can I say about the pleasure we get in the country from the days themselves, which are brighter, clearer, and longer than they are in the town? When it is only just dawn there, the sun has come out here. And likewise when it sets, darkness immediately descends on the town, whereas here you can see for nearly an hour longer without needing a lantern.

And again, how can I convey the great pleasure of those who not only have the happiness of living here in the country but who love the precious brilliance of the day more than the darkness of the night? They begin to rejoice as soon as they hear the awakening cock before dawn; impatient with lying in bed, they get up and stand outside, even in the hot weather, to watch and wonder at the cheerful birth of the beautiful Dawn, gazing at her divine brightness as it gradually lights up the sky, until the Sun (heralded by his first flashes, like streaks or sparks of blazing fire) with his resplendent beams strikes first the proud peaks of the highest mountains, and little by little emerges from the sea until he is completely visible to us mortals in all his splendor. To the pure in spirit it is like a staircase by which we can ascend and enter the holy courts of heaven and contemplate those highest reasons that cannot be adequately described in human language. Then we render infinite thanks to the great Bailiff of the Universe who out of his goodness alone has given us, among innumerable gifts, this brilliant light to help us in all our needs.

And what of the time when he sinks in the western sea? Those who live on country estates are virtually the only people who can watch the sunset, and see the ineffable splendor that blazes out above the earth, above the water, above the mountains and above the clouds, transfiguring them in a galaxy of colors and sometimes turning them so red that they and all the rest of the sky seem on fire. These are experiences that few or none in the city can ever know (except those who stand guard at the castle or high on the city walls), both because the surrounding houses are too tall and because townspeople simply do not care about such things, as we do who live in the country. People in towns either do not get up until the sun has already risen, or if they do get up early (like the wool-spinners and weavers, the blacksmiths and other working people), they have to stay shut up indoors. So there is bound to be a great difference between the lives of the laborers on the estate, who ordinarily work in the bright sun, and those of the townspeople, who work in dark shops and gloomy houses. It is no wonder that the former are always healthy, robust and vigorous-looking, while the latter are downcast, thin, listless and likely to die young.

COR. DUCCO Your delightful description has given me great pleasure; and I cannot resist telling you that from my own little house in Piedmont, which as you know has a splendid view because it is on the top of a hill, you get a wonderful sight of the treasures of the dawn, which I have often enjoyed when I was seeking to get cool in very hot weather. At those times I have gained enormous pleasure from closely watching the variety of colors that appear from moment to moment in the eastern sky and shine like the clearest crystal over our hills, which then seem to be painted in the finest blue, intermingled with the dazzling rays of the sun. Indeed, I cannot express to you a hundredth part of the joy that I have felt and that has uplifted my spirit.

GIO. BATT. AVOGADRO You are surely right to praise your own hilltop, but the one here called Ciliverghe seems to me much more beautiful because it is crowned not only with houses but also with gardens, meadows, vineyards, fish ponds and other fine things. Is there anyone who would not seek to enjoy that view which extends from the distant mountains in the north to the plain of Brescia, stretching out for miles, and on to other territories? It is an ideal place from which to admire and meditate on the effects of dawn and of sunlight, the beauty of the heavens, the pattern of the stars, the phases of the moon—the serene air, the lofty mountains, the bewitching hills, the fertile valleys, and the spaciousness of the slopes and countryside.

COR. DUCCO O blessed hill! It has belonged to the noble Apiana family for more than a century, and is now even more beloved, tended and embellished than ever before by the worthy judge and orator Messer Lanterio and his brothers.

GIO. BATT. AVOGADRO Another great advantage of living in a villa is that in the morning you can be fifteen or twenty miles on your way on horseback before they have even opened the gates at Brescia. And similarly in the evening, we can linger as long as we like, and no one is going to lock us out, as they invariably do in the city, as soon as it strikes ten o'clock.

Is there anything to compare with the freedom and ease that we enjoy? In the city you are expected to go about well-dressed and attended by servants, and to be full of a thousand courtesies, showing deference to all sorts of people whom you do not respect at all. I am not speaking of those who deserve it—I never mind showing my respect for them at all times—but I must admit that I do it very unwillingly in the case of others who are completely worthless but are so puffed up with pride that they take offense if you fail to pay homage to them as they think proper. Here, on the other hand, I can go out or stay at home, without servants, without a hat, without a cloak, dressed in any way I choose. In the city people look down on you if you do not behave as they do, but here nobody envies us or scoffs at us or criticizes us or tells us how we ought to live. These privileges are no less welcome to our ladies than to ourselves. They are much happier leading their own lives here and decorously enjoying themselves in precious freedom than being constrained by the kind of social conduct that is expected of a married woman in the city.

COR. DUCCO You should be grateful to them for behaving in this praiseworthy fashion. I know many women who are so involved with life in the city that they would never agree to leave it. They want to be able to go wherever they like at any time, they want to dress up in the latest fashions, make themselves beautiful and wear perfume. They go around, bursting with vanity, wishing to be admired and flattered by everyone that sees them, thinking of nothing but dashing here and there wherever their fancy takes them. They turn up wherever there is a dance, a comedy, a tragedy, a joust, a feast or a tournament. Otherwise they spend most of the day standing in their doorway or looking out of the window, as if they had lost either their wits or their sense of shame, and they are invariably a source of scandal all over the town. Things were not like this in the old days; it only started after the barbarians corrupted us with their bad ways—not just in this part of the country but everywhere throughout Italy.

GIO. BATT. AVOGADRO I would to God that women did not behave like that (those who do, I mean, for there are many others who are models of propriety). But this plague seems actually to be spreading all the time, thanks to blind husbands and foolish fathers who are really the ones to blame. The only way to stamp out this corruption in our society is to impose the full penalties of the law on these evil women. Every bad daughter should get death for a dowry, worms for clothes, and a tomb for a house. Unfaithful wives should have their eyes gouged out, their tongues cut out, and their hands chopped off—or rather they should be wiped off the earth altogether, burnt alive!

COR. DUCCO Please, I beg you, no more of such thoughts, which lead nowhere. Tell me more of the contentment that you enjoy here.

GIO. BATT. AVOGADRO Here at this villa you do not hear people slandered, as you often do under the loggia in the city, or in workshops or other places. I am not speaking now of vicious people, but of ordinary respectable men and women who have no hesitation in blackening the reputation of honest wives, chaste widows, well-brought-up girls and even nuns! And they seem to enjoy talking about sordid things, like the price and warehousing of grain, money-making, money-lending, swindles, and other shady deals.

People here are not ambitious, envious, proud or underhand; they are not disloyal, hot-tempered, vindictive or murderous; they are not cuckolded by their wives; still less will you find them acting as false witnesses, dishonest notaries, lying officials, false lawyers, unjust judges or devious legal clerks.

Here you are free from bawling streetsweepers and garbage collectors, jostling porters and wine-carriers, bawds and whores reeking of musk, crooks and sorcerers who ensnare you, soothsayers and diviners who tell your fortune, cheats and cutpurses who deceive you, mercenaries and swaggering soldiers who bully you, and hypocrites and confidence tricksters who swindle you.

Nor, finally, will you see here debtors languishing in jail, criminals dragged off by force, swindlers sent to the galleys, slanderers having their eyes put out, blasphemers having their tongues slit, malefactors being branded on the face, false witnesses having their hands cut off, murderers being beheaded, thieves being hanged by the neck, traitors being quartered, and assassins being tortured with pincers and flayed. These are sights that wring one's heart, and move one to pity and loathing and extreme horror—especially when, as sometimes happens, the main square of the city is turned into a human slaughterhouse.

COR. DUCCO I do beg you to stop talking about these unpleasant subjects, and to go back to the reason why you enjoy such a cheerful life here.

GIO. BATT. AVOGADRO Who would want to live anywhere but in the country? Here we have complete peace, real freedom, tranquil security and sweet repose. We can enjoy pure air, shady trees with their abundant fruit, clear water, and lovely valleys; we can make use of the fertile farmland and the productive vines, as well as appreciating the mountains and hills for the view, the woods for their charm, the fields for their spaciousness and the gardens for their beauty.

Another source of enjoyment is being able to watch the hard work of the farmers and the obedience of their teams, as they skillfully plow and sow the fields, and then the crops growing well and being harvested; and also to hear the songs of the peasants, the pipes of the shepherds, the rustic bagpipes of the cowherds, and the sweet singing of the birds.

COR. DUCCO This is what I really like to hear; it makes me understand even more how enjoyable it is to live in the country.

GIO. BATT. AVOGADRO Since it gives you pleasure, let me tell you more about what a free life we lead. Here is how we spend a typical day. We begin by attending Holy Mass. After that we greet one another and usually go for a walk in the direction of our handsome main road, which is not only long and straight for many miles but very wide too, and provided with a fine inn, built by our illustrious lord in 1484 to mark the spot where he concluded a peace treaty with the Duke of Calabria. Beyond that, it is densely lined on both sides with trees and there are clear streams along it. And as we stand gazing out in all directions and enjoying the beauty of that broad canal, we invariably see people coming and going, from other villas, from Brescia, or from Cremona. We often take pleasure in getting them to talk about what they are planning to do or have just done. More often still, we see friends passing by and nearly always hear some piece of news and invite them to join us in a congenial meal.

Sometimes at that hour we go to the estate at Poncarale which, as you know, has lovely hills, delightful views, dense woods, beautiful gardens, sumptuous rooms and clear water. There are respectable people there and we make up parties together, sometimes there and sometimes here. Poncarale is the mother of our estate, so we are very fond of it, and greatly commend its position, placed by Nature almost in the very center of our region, where with its fine buildings like a tall fortress it surveys and commands all this beautiful plain.

COR. DUCCO Who could look at that charming hill without admiring it as a thing of rare beauty? I assure you that whenever I see it (especially when I am coming from Quintianello in Piedmont, as now, or returning there) I gaze at it without ever tiring of it, and think it the best view in the province. It is no wonder that the gentlemen here take such delight in it virtually all the year round.

GIO. BATT. AVOGADRO How can I express the satisfaction that we get from the pure air here, which is so refreshing to the spirit? We find it wonderfully stimulating and at the same time it soothes the brain, purges the mind, calms the spirit and strengthens the body.

And it is impossible to reckon the value of the great sense of contentment we feel when we rest our eyes on the high mountains, the agreeable hills, the great diversity of trees, the green fields, the lovely gardens, the delightful rivers and streams, and so many other things. Our city, for all its magnificence, cannot see such things, and fails almost completely to appreciate them as we do.

Moreover, in the city you hear no bird-song. Here the birds sing day and night, especially from March to October. [In the city] if you want to hear the song of a particular bird you have to keep it in a cage and feed it. But while our birds sing freely in the wild, those who are caged only sing under duress, afraid that if they stop they will be starved to death. So it is no wonder that the singing of ours is more joyful and sonorous and sweeter, and that they sing their love-songs with marvellous exuberance, while the poor town birds sing, or rather lament their unhappy lot, knowing that they cannot warble in the woods or in the tops of the trees, by lovely dells or clear waters. So we villa dwellers resemble our birds in their freedom and happy life, and city dwellers resemble theirs in being imprisoned and depressed. But from this it follows that townspeople are not as intelligent as birds, because they could leave the city if they wanted to, but do not, whereas the poor birds would gladly escape from their cages if they could, to enjoy that precious liberty so extolled by countless famous writers of antiquity.

What else can it be that persuaded so many Romans to give up their high state in order to live and die in their villas, if not the clear realization that only here can one find that treasure of liberty, plus all the delights that every sensible man in the world could enjoy?

Similarly, why is it that for hundreds of years all the leading figures of France, Flanders, Bohemia, Poland, Hungary, and other countries have preferred staying on their well-appointed estates to spending their time in the cities? It can only be that they too know full well that villa life is more restful and more contented than life in any town whatsoever.

And who prompted our lords of Roccafranca, Barco, Villachiara, Virola and Pralboino, the more opulent gentry [*magnifici cavalieri*], and so many other nobles to live in their villas, if not that experience had taught them that they enjoy there another kind of liberty, other sorts of pleasures, and a different order of delight than they could find in towns? Towns today are full of strife and stress, and not what they were in the happy days of our grandfathers and great-grandfathers. With their disciplined way of life, those men saw that peace, charity and faith were valued above all else. If those venerable old men could come back to life now, with the power to punish those who make it impossible to live in peace and tranquillity, they would, I am quite sure, give them what their crimes deserve.

COR. DUCCO Although I get more and more pleasure from your explanation of what makes villa life so happy, it seems to me (forgive me if I offend you) that you go too far when you speak ill of our city, which has always enjoyed the highest reputation for honor and piety throughout the world.

GIO. BATT. AVOGADRO If I said things that are like the opinions of certain people, whom I shall not name, then I should be a most ungrateful citizen, since there are certainly many more upright townspeople than bad ones. I am only saying that the argument for living on an estate (especially a small one) is strengthened when one realizes that the country is in general freer of evil men than the towns are.

COR. DUCCO I am sure that your intentions were good. Now tell me how you spend your time throughout the year.

GIO. BATT. AVOGADRO First of all, I usually get up at dawn, and these days I join my companions at that hour to go out hawking. We roam all over the countryside, crossing slopes, climbing cliffs, scrambling over banks and across vineyards, waterways, bushes, meadows, fields of millet, areas of scrubland, and other places. Sometimes we keep together, sometimes we separate, in order to catch as many partridges as we can. We keep this up until after the third hour. Then we come home and often we eat together, as you saw us doing this morning. Over the meal we talk about what we have discovered and caught, and the contrary and favorable things that happened to us, and other diverting topics, until it is time to rest or to attend to some necessary business. After that we often find ourselves getting together again to read, play cards or board games or chess, sing or play musical instruments, as you will see shortly when the ninth hour has struck. So we modestly while away this time until quite late, keeping out of the heat as much as we can at this time of year. After we have amused ourselves in this way, we walk in a group to visit this friend or that, to see the beauties of his flower and kitchen gardens, his ponds, or his fountains combined with pleasant retreats. There we sit and talk, not altogether seriously, in the open air. This evening I hope to show you similar things. I am sure you will enjoy them, and decide that for good breeding, sound administration and good manners this tiny estate is the equal of our city or any other place.

And what would you say if I told you that sometimes, at the same hour, we come across our ladies in the midst of their own amusements, strolling about the estate to see some of the charming sights I have mentioned, or chatting beside some pool or clear fountain? We greet them with proper ceremony and then we talk with them in a bantering way, mingling ingenious arguments with pleasantries and innocent jokes. Sometimes one of us sits down to play the lute or the viol or some other instrument of that sort. Then you see the wife taking her husband by the hand, the father his daughter, the son his mother, the daughter-in-law her father-in-law, the brother his sister, the uncle his niece, the grandfather the grandmother, and so on, until they are all dancing joyously and chastely. If only God would grant that all dancing today was of that sort we should avoid a great deal of the licentiousness and scandal that is now so widespread throughout Christendom! At the end of these pleasant excursions we accompany the ladies one by one with sweet conversation back to their rooms.

COR. DUCCO You describe these excursions so vividly that I am quite transported and hardly know whether I am seeing them in a dream or listening to you telling me about them. But I am sure that everything you have said is true.

GIO. BATT. AVOGADRO I assure you that what I have told you and what I am going to tell you is just the simple truth. I confess that I enjoy harmless tricks myself, but I would never be capable of devising one, let alone of playing it on you.

COR. DUCCO Since you mention funny stories, I was rather surprised that you did not laugh at table when that gentleman Emilio said that he had jumped over the canal in four leaps to rescue his hawk from a hound, without getting his white boots wet.

GIO. BATT. AVOGADRO That was in fact perfectly true. The water is very low just now because of the drought, and he is light on his feet. But you would really have had something to laugh at if you had heard our beloved Gavaccio telling us about the miraculous events that occurred when he and his wife were crossing the river Chiese.

COR. DUCCO I do not know that gentleman personally, but I have often been told that there is no one to beat him at telling stories. I would love to hear this one, if you could be bothered to tell it to me.

GIO. BATT. AVOGADRO The local young people had hired a couple of pipers for a dance on the feast of San Bernardino. I invited several gentlemen, and among them I wrote to him in Carpenedolo. When almost everyone had gathered together, and we had washed our hands and were sitting down at table, lo! he appeared, much to everyone's delight. There was a rush to embrace him. I cannot tell you how pleased we all were to see him: we were sure that he was just the sort of spice our supper needed. The valorous *condottiere* Signor Camillo Avogadro took him by the right arm and Messer Giovanni Antonio Cavallo, his lieutenant, by the left, and they placed him at the head of the table. And no sooner had he sat down than he began to speak:
   "My lords, before you start eating I beg you to listen to what I have to say, because I am about to stun you with the account of what happened to me this morning as I crossed the Chiese. But since I am very much afraid that you will find it totally incredible, I entreat you with all my heart that if you ever believed anything I ever said, you will believe this." Expecting another of his tall tales, we fixed our eyes on his face and he continued: "Not wanting to miss the courteous invitation of my dear patron Avogadro, early this morning I mounted my horse, accompanied by my wife. We arrived at the river and set about fording it, she following behind. When we had got to the deepest part, somehow, I don't know how, she fell off. At once, in the middle of the stream, I dismounted, picked her up in my arms, put her back in the saddle, retrieved her hat, her veil and her shoes that were floating away in all directions, and got back onto my horse – all so quickly that the rushing water did not get us the slightest bit wet!"
   When he had finished this extraordinary piece of nonsense we burst out laughing so uncontrollably that we had to get up from the table and go off and roll around on the ground. And while we were laughing so uproariously, he also rose from the table and began to swear that every word he had said was true. And the more he repeated these oaths, the more helplessly we laughed, until he, seeing how things were, and that all his swearing, no matter how insistent, was in vain, finally said, as if worn out: "You know, my lords, although I did tell you the truth, yet this tale is so difficult to believe that I must admit I can't bring myself to believe it either." When we heard that it sent us into such fits of laughter that our chests and jaws positively ached and you could have pulled out all our teeth without our noticing. Finally, when it pleased God, we returned to the table where for two hours on end we did nothing but laugh, not at this story only but at other stupendous tales that he told us with the same earnestness, all concocted in the same way. I can only say that if some of the other guests from outside had not started arriving for the dance, I do not know when we should ever have stopped.

COR. DUCCO What do you think is going on in his odd mind when he is telling these lies? Does he do it just to make people laugh? Or does he think they are going to believe him? Or does he really believe the stories himself?

GIO. BATT. AVOGADRO We have often wondered about this ourselves, and those who have known him longest always say that as he never laughs when he is telling them he must actually think they are true.

COR. DUCCO This is a fine humor, not only more remarkable than all the other humors, but just the medicine for all those who suffer from humors as I do.

GIO. BATT. AVOGADRO He also boasts extravagantly of being able to treat all kinds of illnesses, in men, women, children, horses, oxen, cows, sheep, dogs, hawks, goshawks and falcons, and of knowing how to exorcize spirits and ward off curses and spells—and, on the other hand, how to use charms and incantations himself to deform or kill any person or animal whatsoever. But all this is nothing. He can also hold his own in disputes with learned astrologers, chiromancers, geometricians, cosmographers, arithmeticians, and experts in logic, natural science, canon law, theology, and every other branch of learning that ever was. He knows that people think these men are in fact sophists and shams, so he at once launches into a torrent of scholarly jargon, mixed up with bits of cabbalistic lore (at which he is an expert), all with such verbal fluency and deafening rhetoric that he totally confuses the scholars and reduces everybody else to paroxysms of laughter.

COR. DUCCO You make me even more anxious to meet this amazing intellect. If you deem me worthy to be introduced to him I think he will do me more good than the much praised baths of Acquario, where I went last year.

GIO. BATT. AVOGADRO I hope I can arrange for you to enjoy his company in two or three days' time, when he has returned from treating some birds and horses for certain gentlemen in Bornato and Callino, and I know that you will find the merry disposition of this excellent and unusual man very much to your liking. Apart from the fact that you can believe hardly a word he says (something that in itself gives pleasure), he is universally considered to be kind, courteous, loyal, and full of many virtues. We shall appreciate him all the more because tomorrow morning our companions are off hunting, for wolves, boar, roebuck, deer and other animals that are to be found in the biggest woods around Brescia. They will start in the woods of the lords of Vrago, Roccafranca, Barco and Villachiara, and then go on from place to place until they reach Virola, Pralboino, Gamba, Asola, Carpenedolo and Clavisane. This will be an expedition worthy of a great prince; there will be many noble lords present and a vast number of gentlemen and others who will have the best hounds in this region. Hunting out the game in the Martinenghi woods alone will take at least four days, maybe more.

COR. DUCCO These lords are truly rich in great woods and fertile lands that are the flower of the territory of Brescia. More than that, one might observe that just as the most ancient family has the richest holdings of any in the province (with annual revenues of eighty thousand *scudi*), so it is the richest in valiant, magnanimous and famous men. Some of them have bravely fallen in our own lifetime, serving in the glorious wars of our most illustrious lords and other princes. But there are now more of them than ever who will make themselves immortal by their prowess.

GIO. BATT. AVOGADRO I see that it is time to draw this discussion to a close. Our friends, as usual, are beginning to gather together one by one in the great hall. We had better join them in order to take part in whatever pleasures are in store, as you will see.

COR. DUCCO That would please me greatly, as I want very much to witness the manners of this virtuous society.

6.1 Marble Hill, Twickenham, by Henry, Lord Herbert, 1724–29: garden facade

6 · The Palladian Villa in England

Rural society and economy from the Elizabethan period to the early twentieth century gave country houses in England a cultural importance greater than in any other place and time. The power of the privileged classes of Britain was rooted in the land, though often it had to be supported and confirmed by enterprise in the city, and especially in London, the seat of government and the court. The mansions and parks of aristocrats, gentry, merchants and manufacturers which cover the countryside usually served as the principal residences of their owners, whose income typically derived from the rents or agricultural development of the estate of which they were a part. The owners often had houses in London as well, which might be occupied "for the season" and during sessions of Parliament (the involvement of the peerage in government was stimulated by the exclusive right of its members to seats in the House of Lords). This way of life is reflected in English literature of the eighteenth and nineteenth centuries, especially the novel, which to an extraordinary degree is occupied with the life and social interactions of the occupants of country houses.[1]

These country houses were not thought of as "villas" during the Renaissance and Baroque periods because the mansions that embodied the dominant styles from the Elizabethan age to the reign of Queen Anne (1702–14) were too grandiose to suit the rustic associations called up by the word [6.2]. But at the end of Anne's reign and in the first years of the ensuing Georgian era, influential intellectuals joined liberal aristocrats in fostering a radical change of taste which demanded a naturalness and a classical purity

6.2 Castle Howard, by Sir John Vanbrugh and Nicholas Hawksmoor, 1699–1712: south front

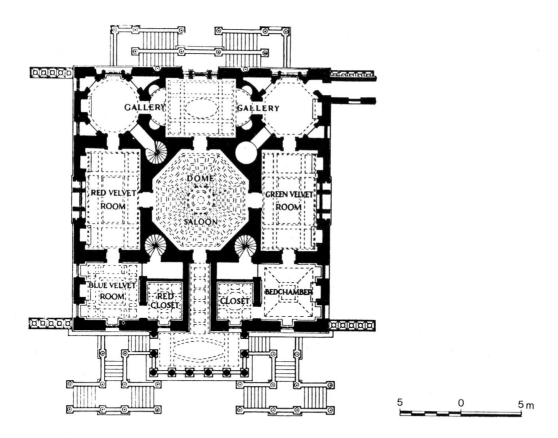

that made the Mediterranean villa a desirable model of form, dimension and spirit. Palladio and Inigo Jones [6.8], the early seventeenth-century importer into England of the chaste classicism of Palladio and Scamozzi, were taken as the orthodox purveyors of the classical tradition, and the vigorous contemporary Baroque style of Wren, Vanbrugh, Hawksmoor and others was all but stifled by the Palladian surge.[2]

The villa at Chiswick, on the outskirts of London, which Richard Boyle, 3rd Earl of Burlington, designed for himself in 1725, can be taken as a paradigm of the resurgent Palladianism.[3] It is modeled freely on Palladio's Villa Rotonda [4.18] in being a cubic structure of about the same size surmounted by a dome, but differs in having one portico—on the entrance facade [6.4]—rather than Palladio's four. The villa also resembles the Rotonda in function, having been intended as a place for entertainment, relaxation, study and contemplation—thus reviving the Plinian image of villa life.

The side [6.5] and rear facades of Chiswick are autonomous. The rear [7.8, *bottom right*], with its row of three Venetian windows, comes directly from a drawing by Palladio in Burlington's collection. The building was not conceived in three dimensions but rather as an assemblage of plane surfaces. Freestanding walls extending from either side of the front and rear facades reinforce the impression, and the planning of the garden discouraged circulation around the villa [7.8]. Burlington, like other gentlemen amateurs, had difficulty in translating his drawings and his copies of details from book illustrations into the density, textures and responsiveness to light of actual architecture, and to some extent this was true even of contemporary work by professionals in his circle.

The main facade of the Chiswick villa illustrates Burlington's shortcomings and

6.3–5 Chiswick House, by Lord Burlington, 1727–29: plan of the principal floor *(opposite)*; south (entrance) facade; and west front

strengths. The fluted Composite columns that he copied from illustrations in the *Quattro libri* or from Palladio's drawings after the antique seem overdetailed and too academic. Palladio himself would have thought them too elaborate for villas, but he had the benefit of the rich warm light of the Veneto, while Burlington had to deal with a less beneficent climate. When Burlington put the books aside he overdid inventiveness, as in the mannered double-ramped stairway leading to the portico, and the basement finished with a rather constipated form of rustication called vermiculation. Still, the villa has a nice prismatic character, which is reinforced by the design of the cupola drum as an octagon rather than the usual cylinder. The detailing, particularly of the orders, has an elegant crispness that suggests the intervention of William Kent. The contrast between the imposing concept of the villa and its tiny scale is engaging.

The plan [6.3] is freer than that of the Rotonda because it is symmetrical around only the one axis from front to rear. The corridor leading to the domed hall is external, extending the portico, so that the main portal opens directly into the domed hall. But visitors must normally have entered at ground level through doorways on each of the four sides. The plan at this level is basically the same as the one above, except that the two larger rooms each have piers dividing them into three parts, and the hall has an inner colonnade. Burlington and his guests could also enter on the upper story through a "link" structure built in 1730–33 to connect the villa to the Jacobean family dwelling (indicated on eighteenth-century plans of the grounds [7.8]).

On the upper story, three distinct tracts cross the axis: at the facade, a disposition of small square private rooms, at the center, the larger public rooms, and at the rear the elaborately shaped triad of rooms for Burlington's gallery: a central one with apsidal extensions at either end, a circular room on the left and an octagonal one on the right.

The interior decoration of the main story is surprisingly ornate by contrast to the exterior and ground floor, and not at all Palladian. It was carried out by Burlington's protégé William Kent, who had been studying painting in Italy for several years before his return to England in 1719. Kent's decorative style was essentially Italian Baroque, as we know from other works as well, involving richly carved swags, ribbons, putti, mirrors, medallions, often gilded, which leave no wall surface unbroken, and elaborately modeled mantelpieces. Some of the Chiswick mantelpieces follow designs by Inigo Jones, uncharacteristically more Baroque than Palladian.

Except for the domed chambers at the ends of the gallery at the rear, the walls of each room are covered in vivid figured velvets of uniform primary colors, and the ceilings are lavishly ornamented with intersecting gilded beams and recesses with paintings by Kent on humanistic themes alluding to the arts patronized by Burlington. The Blue Velvet Room in the facade tract [6.6] is the most imposing, with beams sustained by projecting consoles of a grandeur that makes them overscaled for so modest a space. In a sense, the design of the interior echoes the style of the garden, where certain Baroque elements (straight *allées*, rectangular pools) are retained, and where the visitor is drawn through a sequence of distinct experiences and associations, as suggested by vignettes in Rocque's plan of the grounds [7.8].

The classical purity of the Palladian style is not quite digested in the Chiswick design. On the interiors of the upper level purity was cast off, as was to be the case in other works of the Burlington circle. It was difficult to emulate Palladio's interiors, partly because

6.6 Chiswick House: Blue Velvet Room, by William Kent

Palladio himself did not illustrate them in his book, and partly because the decoration in most of his best-known villas was assigned to fresco painters who preferred a vocabulary more elaborate than his.

Lord Burlington, Chiswick's owner and designer [6.7], inherited huge estates in England and Ireland while still a child.[4] His education, like that of other peers of his time, was crowned by a year-long Grand Tour accompanied by half a dozen secretaries, connoisseurs and artists, starting in the spring of 1714, when he was twenty. His principal goal was, typically, Italy, where he spent six months visiting classical sites of interest for their literary and historical associations or for their architecture, and collecting works of art and books. When he returned to London in 1715 to celebrate his twenty-first birthday, he had already decided to devote his life and great wealth to the patronage and promotion of the arts and at the same time to become himself an amateur practitioner of architecture.

During Burlington's absence abroad, Queen Anne had died, and the Tory clique of her later years had given way to a resurgent Whig party that brought George I from Hanover. The new establishment of liberal Whigs was inspired by Enlightenment principles, and instituted a government that increased the power of Parliament and pursued an aggressive policy abroad. Burlington, though he was not much interested in a political career, was a member of this group and held responsible government posts until, like many in his circle, he could no longer support the policies of the King's chief minister, Robert Walpole, in the 1730s. His departure from court did not diminish his commanding position as an arbiter of taste, which lasted until mid-century; the generosity of his patronage ultimately exhausted his great wealth.

Burlington's artistic aims were still in embryo at the time of his return from Italy. He had not been struck by Palladio and had passed through Vicenza without visiting its monuments. But in 1715–16 he was to receive the initial volumes of two lavish new publications that gave a visual focus to the new ideas current among his circle of intellectuals. They were Giacomo Leoni's English edition (with extensive "improvements" on the original) of Palladio's *Quattro libri*, the *Four Books of Architecture*, and the first of an eventual three volumes of *Vitruvius Britannicus* by the Scottish architect Colen Campbell.[5] Campbell's book consisted of one hundred engraved plans and elevations of important modern buildings in England, and an introduction in which he formulated the guidelines of the Palladian movement of which Burlington immediately became a partisan. Campbell rails against Baroque architecture as represented by the work of Borromini (who "endeavoured to debauch mankind with his odd and chimerical Beauties"), Bernini and Fontana. He diplomatically refrains from criticism of the contemporary English Baroque masters Wren, Vanbrugh and others, and even includes examples of their work. He illustrates five designs of Inigo Jones, through whose work Palladio had virtually become endowed with a British character, making his architecture attractive to the new nationalistic leaders.

Burlington and his friends refined Campbell's rather simplistic Palladianism by assimilating it into the literary and philosophical attitudes of the "Augustan" literary circle. This group of writers was steeped in the Roman literature of the late Republic and early Empire, especially Horace, Virgil, Pliny and Vitruvius.[6] We have seen in Chapter 2 how the Romans had promoted the ideology of country life and the richness of nature.

6.7 Richard Boyle, 3rd Earl
of Burlington. Portrait by
George Knapton

Similarly, the new architecture affirmed the purity and simplicity of early Roman
buildings, whose moderation and avoidance of display appealed to the Whig liberals:
Alexander Pope, in his *Epistle to Richard Boyle, Earl of Burlington* (1731), wrote: "''Tis
Use alone that sanctifies Expense,/And Splendour borrows all her rays from Sense."[7]
Palladio was useful not only because he had published his own buildings—favoring
villas and palaces and ignoring churches—but also because he provided scholarly
studies and reconstructions of Roman buildings and decoration. The subtlest aspect of
the new Palladianism was the revival of the Platonic concept that architecture could
imitate nature by exemplifying the principles of harmony in the universe. This led to the
emphasis on geometric form, on symmetry and on proportions that characterizes the
new style of architecture.

Burlington immediately hired Campbell to remodel Burlington House, his palace in
Piccadilly, apparently in place of James Gibbs (a far better architect, but a Catholic Tory
compromised—in Whig eyes—by mildly Baroque sympathies), who had already done
one wing. Campbell became his client's architectural tutor, assisting him in his initial
architectural experiment of about 1717, the first of the decorative garden structures at
Chiswick. This "Bagnio," now destroyed, was a collage of Campbell-like Palladian
motifs.

Burlington was by now so committed to the new style that he felt the need to see
Palladio's work at first hand, and in the summer of 1719 he set out for Venice. Stopping

6.8 Inigo Jones, preliminary design for the Queen's House, Greenwich, 1616

in Genoa on the way, he met William Kent, who had agreed to find draftsmen to record the buildings and who accompanied him on his tour.[8] The friendship between the two had begun in Rome during the previous trip while Kent was there studying painting. Though Kent was coarse and ill-educated, he was to become Burlington's intimate companion and collaborator, residing for thirty years in Burlington House.[9]

Burlington reached Venice in October, where he was impressed by Palladio's church of San Giorgio, and went from there to Vicenza and to a number of villas in the countryside around. He bought a copy of the *Quattro libri*, which he annotated with comments on the buildings, and at the villa at Maser he purchased a large corpus of drawings from the owner, a descendant of the Barbaros who had been Palladio's original clients. On returning home, he purchased the Talman collection of drawings by Inigo Jones [*6.8*] and Palladio which Jones had collected, and a smaller collection of Palladio drawings that had belonged originally to the Bishop of Verona. (Altogether, these form the core of the Burlington–Devonshire Collection of Palladio at the Royal Institute of British Architects).[10] The drawings provided a storehouse of Roman motifs and reconstructions as well as Palladio's projects, and greatly increased awareness of the scope of Palladio's achievements among English designers of the ensuing generation, few of whom bothered to follow Burlington to the Venetian *terraferma*. Burlington himself plumbed them for the publications he sponsored: Kent's *Designs of Inigo Jones*

(1727), Isaac Ware's edition of the *Quattro libri* (*The Four Books of Architecture*, 1738), and his own *Fabbriche antiche* (begun in 1730), based on Palladio's studies for reconstructions of the ancient baths.

Rudolf Wittkower has shown that Burlington's sponsorship of book publication was part of his concerted effort during the 1720s to become an influential cultural leader.[11] He had protégés in all the major arts: Kent in painting; Campbell, replaced by Kent and the draftsman Henry Flitcroft, in architecture; Pope in poetry; and an Italian sculptor, Guelfi; he founded an academy of music. His success was mixed: Campbell vanished from his orbit, Guelfi failed to live up to expectations, and the academy collapsed. He used his power to establish Kent as a painter, getting for him a precious royal commission at Hampton Court Palace, but the results were disappointing and Kent soon found his true métiers as an architect, decorator and landscape designer. Burlington's fame as an arbiter of taste grew after the completion of Chiswick to the point at which he virtually carried on an architectural practice (which was felt by Lord Chesterfield to be beneath the dignity of a peer[12]).

Among the many architectural projects in which Burlington became involved at this point the most impressive is Holkham Hall [*6.10–12*].[13] The client, Thomas Coke, later Earl of Leicester (who had been to Italy with Kent in 1714 and 1716), was an equally avid amateur, and was co-author of the design with Burlington and Kent. Holkham was on a vast estate in Norfolk, then within sight of the sea, a barren waste that like many villas in Palladio's Veneto had been partially reclaimed from swampland. The designers wanted to use the purist vocabulary and modest scale of the Palladian tradition to moderate the effect of grandeur communicated by great mansions of the preceding generation, such as Chatsworth and Castle Howard. They treated the central block as a Palladian villa to which they added towers at the four corners. Indeed, Campbell had already projected a revival of the four-tower scheme (a feature of Renaissance royal palaces throughout Europe) at nearby Houghton, for the powerful Prime Minister Robert Walpole, which is similarly distinguished by Venetian windows on the main floor [*6.9*].[14]

Beyond the towers the collaborators added smaller semi-autonomous villa units (one containing the family residence and library and others utility functions) which project forward and are linked to the central block by passages of the kind that connected the Chiswick villa to the Jacobean house.[15] What was gained in simplicity by these devices was lost in cohesion: the many blocks and bays resist being grasped as a coherent whole and the jump in scale from the wings to the central mass is not felicitous.

The interior is distinguished by a magnificent two-storied hall adapted from Palladio's reconstructions of the apsidal Roman Basilica and the Egyptian Hall, which Vitruvius had described as "suitable for festivals and entertainments" [*6.11, 12*]. It is an ingenious conflation of these classical buildings (which are longitudinal, being modeled on the temple type) and the cubic halls of recent houses such as Vanbrugh's Castle Howard or Campbell's Houghton (where Kent had executed the interiors in the late 1720s). The basilical apse contains a grand staircase leading from ground level to the public rooms on the main floor. Here an Ionic colonnade of lavishly red-veined alabaster carries, over a rich entablature and cornice, a coved coffered ceiling. The colonnade follows the curve of the hemicycle at the head of the stairs, recalling the

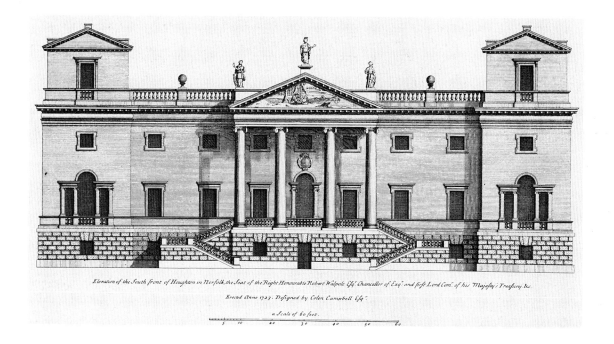

Elevation of the South front of Houghton in Norfolk, the Seat of the Right Honourable Robert Walpole Esq. Chancellor of Exq. and first Lord Com. of his Majesty's Treasury &c.

Erected Anno 1723. Designed by Colen Campbell Esq.

a Scale of 60 feet.

6.9 Houghton Hall, by Colen Campbell, begun 1722: park front, as published in *Vitruvius Britannicus*, III, 1725. The corner towers were never executed.

6.10, 11 Holkham Hall, by Lord Burlington, Lord Leicester and William Kent, begun 1734: south front, and plan of the principal floor

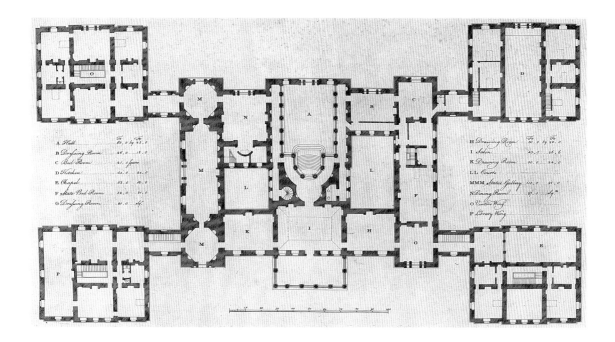

		Ft	Ft
A	Hall	80.0 by	45.0
B	Dressing Room	26.0	18.0
C	Bed Room	21.0 square	
D	Kitchen	44.0	24.0
E	Chapel	52.0	48.0
F	State Bed Room	32.0	31.0
G	Dressing Room	21.0	sq

		Ft	Ft
H	Drawing Room	30.0 by	44.0
I	Salon	40.0	36.6
K	Drawing Room	30.0	24.0
LL	Courts		
MMM	Statue Gallery	110.0	21.0
N	Dining Room	37.0	sq
O	Visitors Wing		
P	Library Wing		

6.12 Holkham Hall: hall

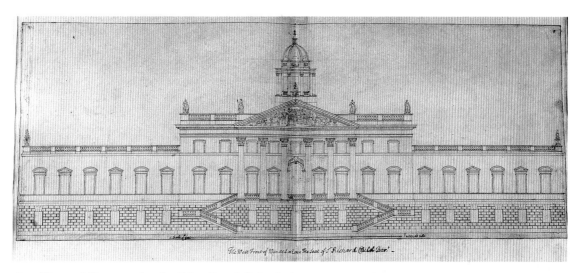

6.13 Wanstead House: project by Colen Campbell for the house as executed, *c.* 1715

curved columnar screens in the apses of Palladio's Venetian churches. Behind this screen a niche within the apse contains the portal leading to the saloon. The concept typifies the nature of the collaboration among the designers. Coke chose the order from the Temple of Fortuna Virilis in Rome (according to an annotation in his copy of Desgodets), and perhaps the formal conception; Burlington had applied his experience in building a version of Palladio's Egyptian Hall for the Assembly Rooms at York, in 1731, which however is severely classical and has no apse. But the realization was surely Kent's, as indicated by the rich detailing and the innovative fantasy that mediates between a Palladian and a Baroque mode. Though Burlington and Kent could not have known it, basilical halls with colonnades and apses were a feature of the entrance blocks of grand imperial Roman palaces such as that of the Flavians on the Palatine Hill in Rome; the form simply re-emerged from the unconscious reaches of the culture like those villa forms discussed in Chapter 1. As Wittkower pointed out, the long gallery with apsidal ends that leads to octagonal rooms in the corner towers repeats the gallery arrangement at Chiswick [6.3]. Kent's Baroque style at Chiswick is also recalled in the use of brightly colored figured velvet for the saloon and major public rooms.

Colen Campbell's priority as a Palladian interpreter protected him from whatever damage he might have suffered from his falling-out with Burlington. He had come to practice law from his native Scotland in about 1711, and by 1718 was Chief Clerk of the King's Works and Deputy Surveyor under Wren's successor William Benson. His earliest designs, for Wanstead, in 1713–20 [*6.13*], at once established his reputation and launched the new style. Wanstead, which was later destroyed, was the huge country mansion (seventeen bays in width with a central pedimented portico) of a commoner who had inherited money made in the East India Company. It was more dependent on drawings by Jones (plans for a palace at Whitehall, etc.) and a plate in Vincenzo Scamozzi's *Idea della architettura universale* of 1615 than on anything by Palladio, who had not published any palace or villa of this scale. It is unlikely that Campbell knew

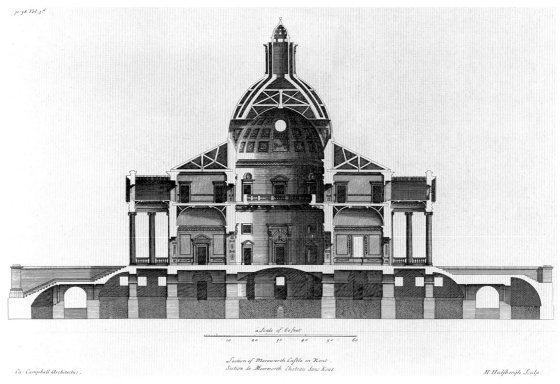

6.14, 15 Mereworth, by Colen Campbell, designed 1722: section, and view from the southwest

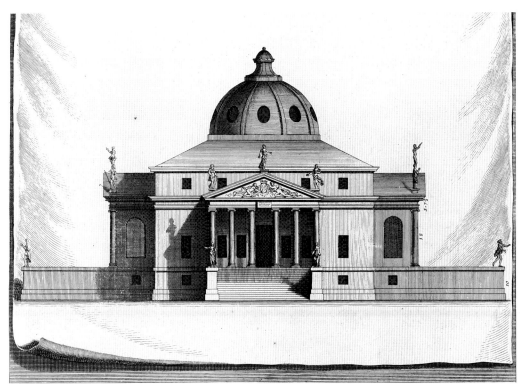

6.16 Giacomo Leoni, Palladio's Villa Rotonda, from *The Four Books of Architecture*, 1715/16

anything of Palladio's work before Leoni's edition of the *Quattro libri* started to appear in 1716, three years after the first Wanstead studies.

Campbell anticipated Burlington's revival of Palladio's Rotonda by three years in his design of 1722 for the villa at Mereworth in Kent, for John Fane, later Earl of Westmorland [*6.14, 15*]. Mereworth, which, like the Rotonda and Chiswick, was planned principally as a casino for entertainment, was much closer to Palladio's model, retaining its four freestanding porticoes—only two of which have exterior stairs—and its drumless cupola. This cupola, raised above the hemispherical profile, like St Paul's in London, was not based on Palladio's illustration, much less on the actual building [*4.18*], but on the version of it published by Leoni, with its oval apertures [*6.16*]. The plan is organized transversely rather than in depth in order to extend a gallery across the whole rear of the building. The spaces to the left and right of the circular central hall were awkwardly partitioned into two parts in order to provide additional rooms. The architect also followed Palladio in the smooth stucco surfaces of his walls (the surfaces at Chiswick are drafted in imitation of masonry) and column shafts. The proportions differ markedly from those of Chiswick because the latter lacks an attic story [*6.4, 15*].

At least two more emulations of the Rotonda were built in the 1750s, at Foots Cray and Nuthall Temple, but the type was not well enough adapted to residential requirements to excite a widespread vogue. A more practical and successful model was found in another Palladian villa-type without a central dome or entrance corridor. It was

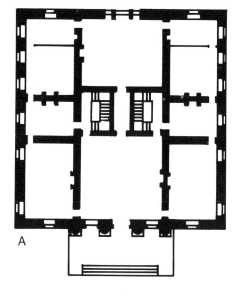

6.17 Plans of (A) Newby (now Baldersby) Park, by Colen Campbell, begun 1718; (B) Stourhead, by Colen Campbell, 1720–21; (C) Marble Hill, Twickenham, by Henry, Lord Herbert, 1724–29. At Newby and Stourhead the hall is at the front (bottom)

A

0   10   20   30   40 ft

divided in depth into three sections, normally two rooms deep [4.9], the central section containing an entrance hall in front and a parlor behind. The tripartite division would be reflected on the front and often on the rear facade by the same disposition of parts as was employed at Mereworth, though the pedimented portico might be four columns wide or be engaged to the wall rather than freestanding [6.17]. The principal floor would be set on a low basement containing the kitchen, storage, servants' quarters and other service functions. This disposition limited the potential size of the structure. Proprietors who needed more space or who wanted to build in the grand manner of the previous generation had to choose between extending the single lateral bays into long wings containing enfilades of rooms, breaking the proportional coherence of the Palladian scheme, as at Wanstead [6.13], and adding more self-contained blocks and thus sacrificing visual unity, as at Holkham [6.10].

By the 1740s, the dilemma came to be reflected in architectural terminology: a "villa" became a small block five bays wide (1–3–1 [6.17]) intended as a retreat, while the larger traditional type intended for display and entertainment continued to be called a "country house." The model for the "villa" was Palladian but the inspiration may well have come from a drawing by Inigo Jones in Burlington's collection for the Queen's House, Greenwich [6.8]. The English villa had originated as a suburban residence on a modestly sized nonagricultural plot in the Thames valley within reach of London. Concentrations of the new type formed along the river banks at Richmond and Twickenham, not far from Chiswick. Of these, the Countess of Suffolk's Marble Hill was the most celebrated [6.1, 17c]. But villas also appeared in rural and agricultural contexts, Stourhead being an example [6.18; 7.20]. In the course of the eighteenth century, as increasing numbers of nonaristocratic clients commissioned country

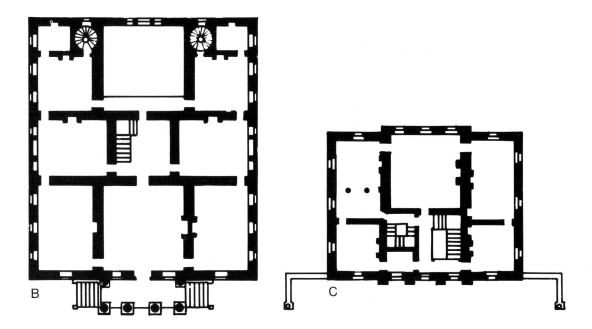

residences, the villa became the standard form for the privileged classes, for both social and economic reasons. The Palladian type dominated until mid-century and thereafter was increasingly challenged by less classical and less formal styles.[16] The change confused traditional usage, according to which, as we have seen, a villa was the agricultural estate itself (Palladio pointedly excluded the Rotonda from the section of his book dealing with the "casa di villa" because it had no agricultural function).

Campbell's first truly Palladian design, and the first example of what was later to be called a villa, was for Newby (now Baldersby) Park [6.17A], begun in 1718 on a design derived, except for the placement of the stairs, from Palladio's Villa Emo. The plan is square and divided into three sections. The hall is also square and the parlor which reflects it on the rear is 24 × 30 feet, a harmonic proportion of 4:5 recommended by Alberti and Palladio as equivalent to a major third in music (the proportion of the other principal rooms is 2:3, a fifth).[17] The parlor is lit by a Venetian window that makes the central accent of the rear facade. The building is as close as possible to ground level (the plan shows only four steps) and has no basement. The temple-motif at the center of Newby's facade is formed by engaged half-columns, not a freestanding porch, probably for reasons of economy. Campbell's adoption of the Palladian villa plan involved the modification of traditional features of the country house. The hall became much more modest in relation to other rooms as the style of life no longer demanded a grand ceremonial central space. There was no need for an enfilade of rooms and anterooms of increasing privacy, since only two chambers could be put on either side of the public rooms.

The Newby model was followed closely at Stourhead (1720–21), the estate of Henry Hoare, a successful banker who was active in London [6.17B, 18, 19].[18] Hoare wanted a

6.18 Stourhead: east (entrance) facade

place for retreat and relaxation, not a great country house, so Campbell proposed the suburban form, though the site would have been a day's ride from the capital. Stourhead was celebrated later in the century for its landscape garden, which I shall discuss in the next chapter. Campbell must have gained this commission because the owner was the brother-in-law of the Surveyor of the King's Works, William Benson, a designer of meagre talent, but a pioneer in the Inigo Jones revival, who had ousted Christopher Wren in 1717 and had hired Campbell as Deputy Surveyor. The plans of Stourhead, Newby and Marble Hill are remarkably similar [6.17], though at Stourhead the depth is increased in order to accommodate the stairs in a closed inner hall and to expand the saloon to the size of the principal hall. The symmetrical disposition of rooms again observes the simplest of Palladio's proportional precepts, being either square or 2:3. Stourhead, like Mereworth, is raised on a high base with openings into a basement level.

Campbell proposed both a freestanding and an engaged portico in the plates of *Vitruvius Britannicus* and proceeded to build the latter. (The present freestanding one, based on Campbell's alternative design, was erected *c*. 1840, to balance the two wings that had been added on either side of the main block at the turn of the eighteenth century.) Stourhead's rusticated basement, double-ramped stairway and elaborate window frames are more indebted to Jones and later seventeenth-century architecture than to Palladio, who would not have thought refinements of this kind suitable for rural buildings.

6.19 Stourhead: rendering of the south front by Colen Campbell

A pair of watercolor views of Stourhead done in the short time between its completion in 1722 and the beginning of the initial landscaping campaign show the eastern and southern facades with an exceptionally ascetic treatment of the garden [6.19]. Though the house is in the open country, the private garden is tightly enclosed within walls, like Dutch city-gardens of the seventeenth century; but the treatment is entirely architectural, breaking the severity of the enclosures with nothing but an oval plot of grass before the entrance front and a circular pool ornamented by a single statue at the center to the south. There is no precedent in either Palladio or Jones for this wilful rejection of communication with nature, and it is particularly curious at Stourhead, which twenty years later was to become, under the guidance of the junior Henry Hoare, the most compelling landscape garden of the eighteenth century.

The Palladian formula followed by Campbell at Newby Park and at Stourhead became a paradigm for smaller villa designs up to the mid-eighteenth century. The best preserved of these is Marble Hill [6.1, 17C], started in 1724 for the mistress of the future George II, Henrietta Harding, later Countess of Suffolk.[19] The designer was another gentleman-amateur, Henry, Lord Herbert (subsequently 9th Earl of Pembroke), who afterwards was responsible for the celebrated Palladian Bridge at Wilton [6.20]. He left the drawings and execution to a professional architect, Roger Morris.

At Marble Hill the central portico on the entrance facade has become vestigial: four pilasters on the upper story support a pediment and frame three large windows on the main floor and three small square ones on the upper floor. There is no flight of monumental stairs, so that the entrance is at ground level, in the basement story. The garden facade [6.1], facing the river, follows Palladio in not having a temple-front motif. It is exceedingly reserved, without ornament other than the modest articulation framing the openings and the arms in the pediment. Even the basement rustication of the central portion of the entrance facade is absent: the sheer surface of white wall is broken only by two flat masonry bands that encircle the house just below the windows of the main floor. The hall is like one of Palladio's palace atriums (Thiene and Iseppo Porto palaces in Vicenza). The hall and the two-story Great Room above it are square; other rooms are proportioned 1:1, 1:2, 1:3, and those on the sides are carefully designed to produce symmetrical lateral facades of three window bays, a refinement that had not been observed by Palladio.[20]

A style as dependent on academic theories as the Palladian revival was bound to produce a theoretical apology, and did so in the writings of Robert Morris, whose first book, *An Essay in Defence of Ancient Architecture*, appeared in 1728, shortly after the completion of the first Palladian villas.[21] Morris, a relative of Roger Morris the builder of Marble Hill, states his position in terms of the antithesis posed in contemporary discussions of painting and literature between the Ancients and the Moderns. Morris favors the Ancients—the Romans and the Renaissance classicists who revived their principles—represented chiefly by Palladio. His Moderns, whom he does not identify, appear to be those who followed Baroque or traditional models; they are guilty of "A Redundancy of those smaller Ornaments, which divide and scatter the Angles of Sight into such a multitude of Rays crowded together, that the whole appears a perfect Confusion."

Morris defines his general goals in terms of concepts of order achieved through equilibrium, proportion and the integration of independent parts:

> Nothing can raise the Mind to a more advanced Pleasure, than to behold the agreeable Symmetry and Concordance of every particular separate Member, centred and united in the Oeconomy of the Whole; with the consentaneous Agreement of apt Materials, regulated and adapted in a due Proportion to the distinct Order proposed, in such a variety of Beauties, whose Dispositions are likewise concurring with the Rules prescribed by its ancient practitioners, which were ever founded upon Reason.

His specific goals were articulated in detail in the *Lectures on Architecture* of 1734, which he greatly expanded in 1736. These focused on instruction in the three basic classical orders (his purism extended to excluding the Composite and Tuscan) and on a simplified form of the Renaissance system of proportions based on musical harmonics. But they also announce the wedding of strict classicist architecture with the informal English landscape garden (discussed in Chapter 7), and in this respect validate Morris's claim to have been a disciple of Lord Shaftesbury. Lecture V, on siting, calls for a setting of

> uninterrupted Vistas and Avenues, an agreeable River, or some opening Lawn, or at least a distant Groupe of Hills and Vales diminishing from the Eye by a pleasing Gradation: I say such an agreeable Spot of Ground, where Nature wantons in Luxuriance, is the first Care of a Builder, and by a proper Design composed to blend Art and Nature together, must

6.20 Wilton House: Palladian Bridge, by Henry, Lord Herbert, 1737

consequently render it the Delight of the Inhabitant, and give an unspeakable Pleasure to the Eye of every Beholder.

Nature, however, is not simply a foil for architecture, since

> Art never more agreeably pleases us, than when she has a Resemblance of Nature: Therefore, by a kind of Sympathy and Attraction, when both are blended or mingled together, so as to be preserved without starting into Extreams, they must necessarily give that Pleasure to the Senses, which alone can flow from the nice Hand and Skill of the Designer.

Consequently, the same lecture proceeds to suggest that the choice of an ancient order should reflect the character of the surrounding landscape—Doric for a site near the sea, Ionic for "the cheerful Vale," and so on. But what ultimately binds strictly and chastely classical buildings to the informal environment is that they also represent nature, in reflecting through their proportions and harmonies the highest order of the universe.

Palladianism represented the pre-emption of architectural design by symbolic goals: the communication both of Roman Republican liberty and simplicity and of British tradition as rediscovered in the Palladian style of Inigo Jones. It was not bound to buildings of a particular function, and was adapted to country houses of the same size as their Baroque predecessors and contemporaries and to small suburban and rural villas of dimensions comparable to Palladio's original models. Because of the simplicity of Palladian elevations, the style encouraged aristocrat amateurs to become architects [see, e.g., *6.20*]. But they left the design of the interiors—for which there were few models among Palladio's illustrations and drawings—to the professionals, who generally made them unregenerately Baroque.

The Palladian re-revival was the conscious confection of a motley but collegial group of exceptional men brought together by Enlightenment ideals—liberal Whig peers and gentry, wealthy financiers, poets, essayists and scholars. Many of them engaged in serious architectural and landscape design, though professional architects (who exerted their influence as much through books as through buildings) were essential to the mix. Leoni's English translation of Palladio and Campbell's *Vitruvius Britannicus* launched the Palladian movement; but the momentum was sustained by the cultural influence of the patrons and amateurs more than by the vigor or convenience of the actual buildings. Burlington, the most influential of the influencers, promoted the style not only by designing for himself and for his friends but by sponsoring book publication— Palladio's reconstructions of the Roman baths, Isaac Ware's English translation of Palladio (intended to counteract the imprecisions of Leoni's version), Inigo Jones's drawings, and Robert Castell's study of ancient villas based on literary sources. The impact of his enterprise was celebrated and magnified by Pope's *Epistle to Lord Burlington*:

> You show us, Rome was glorious, not profuse.
> And pompous buildings once were things of Use.
> Yet shall, my Lord, your just, your noble rules
> Fill half the land with Imitating-Fools.[22]

This appropriation of the destiny of architecture by outsiders has been called "The Rule of Taste," but that designation is off the mark. Burlington and his associates were less interested in taste or in controlling the art world than in political, moral and aesthetic principles that could be expressed through buildings and landscape designs. The first Palladian villas, palaces and churches were vehicles for stating a point of view (though, as inevitably happens, many designers of the second wave aimed simply to conform to the fashion: Pope's "imitating fools"). Nor were Palladian patrons primarily interested in promoting architecture as an art: they resolutely overlooked the presence of three of the greatest architects in British history—Vanbrugh, Hawksmoor and Gibbs. In fact, the figure of the gentleman-architect would not have emerged had architectural quality been the pre-eminent consideration, and the great lords would not have lowered themselves to the level of professional practice if architecture had been seen as simply an art. Only when architectural design could be perceived as a moral and conceptually expressive enterprise could it acquire sufficient status to justify their involvement.

The choice of Palladio as a model uniquely suited the needs of a gentleman-designer. His published architecture was simple and imitable and it offered an easily grasped repertory of basic motifs. The woodcut plans and elevations of the *Quattro libri* (which were technically primitive for their time) and the large corpus of drawings in Burlington's collection were executed in a minimal style that eased emulation, and they provided an ample anthology of inventions, particularly for villa design.

Why was the Mediterranean villa ideal revived in England and not in France, Spain, Germany or any other Western nation? The most apparent reason is that country life and economy in mainland Venice of the Renaissance was much closer to that of eighteenth-century England than to that of other European lands. In both, aristocrats and rich commoners, typically active in the politics and commercial affairs of a metropolitan capital, acquired or inherited—through primogeniture—large rural landholdings. They had substantial financial interests in agriculture, rents and other exploitations of land resources. They could call on a fixed labor force that was slowly evolving from the conditions of feudal peasantry, and they benefited from a growing population with an increasing need for agricultural products. In both places, the country house was transformed at a moment of far-reaching land-reform, which in Venice was based on reclamation and in Britain on Enclosure (see pp. 182–83).

The situation in both virtually demanded the development of large-scale agricultural holdings in place of the traditional family allotments, and this confirmed the wealth and power of many landholders. The Whig patrons of the early eighteenth century also admired the republican constitution of Renaissance Venice, one controlled by an elite in many ways like themselves (though the Venetian patriciate, unlike the English, was not open to newcomers), with an effective system of checks and balances that limited the powers of the several branches and of the (elected) head.

Venice, furthermore, as the only Catholic state that consistently asserted its religious independence from Rome and resolutely protected freedom of inquiry, appealed to the Englishmen who feared the restoration of a Catholic monarchy.[23] Briefly, the dynamics of capitalism helped to bind the aspirations of the landed elite of two states across the intervening centuries and differentiated them from the still feudal world of the rest of Europe.

Intellectually, moreover, villa owners in the two states were alike in their immersion in the literature and antiquities of Rome: they pictured villa life in the spirit of Virgil, Horace and Pliny the Younger, and in both times they revered Palladio not just as a classical architect but as a scholar, interpreter and restorer of the ancient past, and of life in the villa.

For all the similarities, however, we must admit that using the designation "villa" for both the Italian model and the British imitation is misleading. There is no question that Chiswick and Palladio's Rotonda are buildings of the same type and should be given the same name, but Palladio proposed no name for such a suburban pleasure pavilion. His "casa di villa" was the proprietor's house on a farm, and the English equivalent of that was the great country house.

What distinguished the English country house from that of the Veneto was that it served, or was designed to serve, as a principal residence, and that its proprietor was not immersed in agriculture, preferring in the design of buildings and gardens to hide the evidence of crops, herds (except for an occasional decorous selection of picturesque sheep or cattle), labor and other reminders of his economic underpinnings.[24] British proprietors, particularly members of the peerage, were generally wealthier and more secure than their Venetian counterparts, and they could build large showplaces designed for lavish entertainment that welcomed admiring tourists as well as invited guests—occasionally in throngs. This made the scale of most buildings palatial and discouraged the kind of reference to farmyard origins that was congenial to Palladio's patrons, whose background was commercial or military–aristocratic, and who had never been courtiers. The distinctions that made it possible to call Chiswick a villa and to exclude Campbell's Wanstead or Holkham Hall (which matched the scale of Chatsworth or Stowe of a generation earlier) were not clearly formed in the language of the early Palladians: Campbell still used "villa" in the Palladian sense of a rural/agricultural estate. It was Gibbs—ironically, an architect who got only inferior commissions from the Palladian circle—who first published designs for small country houses identified as villas (in *A Book of Architecture*, 1728).

By the mid–eighteenth century, in the model books for villa construction that began to pour from the presses in astonishing profusion (see Chapter 9), a "villa" came to be a small and unpretentious country place, launching an evolution that led ultimately to its divorce from agricultural functions and from both ancient and Palladian roots.

7 · The Landscape Garden

The preceding chapters have not been much concerned with villa gardens, mainly because few of them are preserved in their original form. But to understand the early eighteenth-century English villa one must account for the contemporaneous emergence of a radical innovation in garden design known as the landscape garden. As it evolved in the early eighteenth century, the landscape garden offered to Britain and then to the Western world a fundamentally new way of visualizing and expressing society's relationship to the natural environment. It may be England's most influential and enduring contribution to the visual arts.[1]

The interplay of art and nature, the principal theme of theorists of the arts throughout earlier centuries, was an inescapable preoccupation of the garden designer, since he worked with living materials. Renaissance and Baroque gardening subjected nature as much as possible to the rule of art, laying out geometrical parterres and walks, turning trees and hedges into cubes and hemispheres, and even giants, comic characters and chimaeras. The dominant style of the seventeenth-century garden had been fixed by

7.1 Chatsworth House and gardens. From Johannes Kip, *Britannia Illustrata*, 1727

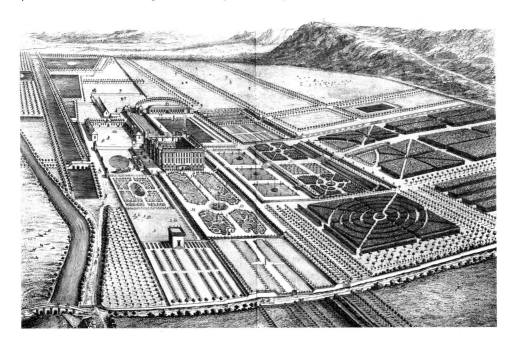

André Le Nôtre, Louis XIV's landscape designer, in the formal, Cartesian setting of Versailles, where no evidence of untamed nature was welcomed. The French garden, purified to a yet more artificial refinement in Holland, ruled English design well into the eighteenth century [7.1]. Though geometrical regularity was the normative style, in Italy (and to a much lesser extent in France) the strictly formal arrangements central to the design of gardens were sometimes accompanied by peripheral areas of groves and waterways more casually and naturally disposed. But this countercurrent largely escaped notice in England until the early years of the eighteenth century when Whig politics and Enlightenment thought gradually made the manifestations of absolutism and rigid systematization distasteful. The poet James Thomson, whose work was much engaged with the landscape, referred to gardens in the Versailles mould as "Detested forms! that on the mind impress,/Corrupt, confound and barbarize an age . . ."[2]

The British reaction against French and Dutch formality had been simmering even before the new century. An essay book on garden planning published in the last decade of the seventeenth century, William Temple's *Upon the Gardens of Epicurus: or, of Gardening, in the year 1685* (1692), concludes a discussion of formal gardens by saying:

> There may be other Forms wholly irregular that may, for aught I know have more Beauty than any of the others . . . Something of this I have seen in some Places, but hear more of it from others, who have lived much among the Chineses . . . [whose] greatest Reach of Imagination is employed in contriving Figures, where the Beauty shall be great, and strike the eye, but without any Order or Disposition of Parts, that shall be commonly or easily observ'd.

Temple says that this informality is called in China "Sharawadgi," a term that was to gain currency in England after the mid-eighteenth century, as the vogue of Chinoiserie was introduced.[3]

Temple's otherwise obscure book, however, with only this brief and peripheral passage on the subject, could not have launched a far-reaching revolution in taste. A much more influential voice was that of the 3rd Earl of Shaftesbury, a pupil of John Locke, in a series of essays published between 1709 and his death in 1713 in which he claimed that the arts and learning of any society flourish to the extent that the populace of that society enjoys liberty. This liberty, achieved by the ancient Romans during the Republican period, is, Shaftesbury says, "in its ascendant" in modern Britain. Applying his social criteria to garden design he wrote, in *The Moralists, a Philosophical Rhapsody*, of 1709:

> Your *Genius*, the *Genius of the Place*, and the GREAT GENIUS have at last prevail'd. I shall no longer resist the passion growing in me for Things of a *natural* kind; where neither *Art* nor the *Conceit* or *Caprice* of Man has spoil'd their *genuine Order*, by breaking in upon that *primitive State*. Even the rude *Rocks*, the mossy *Caverns*, the irregular unwrought *Grotto's* and broken *Falls* of Waters, with all the horrid Graces of the *Wilderness* itself, as representing NATURE more, will be the more engaging, and appear with a Magnificence beyond the formal Mockery of princely Gardens.

Shaftesbury's contemporary, the essayist Joseph Addison, who was himself an avid gardener, disseminated the new taste in his contributions to *The Spectator* and *The Tatler*. Comparing nature and art in *The Spectator* No. 414, of June 25, 1712, Addison says:

7.2 Claude Lorrain, *Landscape near Rome with a View of the Ponte Molle*, 1645

There is something more bold and masterly in the rough careless Strokes of Nature, than in the nice Touches and Embellishments of Art. The Beauties of the most stately Garden or Palace lie in a narrow Compass, the Imagination immediately runs them over, and requires something else to gratifie her; but, in the wide Fields of Nature, the Sight wanders up and down without confinement, and is fed with an infinite variety of Images, without any certain Stint or Number. For this Reason we always find the Poet in love with a Country-Life, where Nature appears in the greatest Perfection, and furnished out all those Scenes that are most apt to delight the Imagination. . . . But tho' there are several of these wild Scenes, that are more delightful than any artificial Shows; yet we find the Works of Nature still more pleasant, the more they resemble those of art: For in this case our Pleasure rises from a double Principle; from the agreeableness of the Objects to the Eye, and from their Similitude to other Objects. Hence it is that we take Delight in a Prospect which is well laid out, and diversified with Fields and Meadows; Woods and Rivers; in those accidental Landskips of Trees, Clouds and Cities, that are sometimes found in the Veins of Marble; in the curious Fret-work of Rocks, and Grottos; and, in a Word, in any thing that hath such a Variety or Regularity as may seem the Effect of Design, in what we call the Works of Chance.

Although Addison does not here apply the term "landskip" directly to the type of gardening he advocated, that usage quickly became common. The word "landscape" originally was applied only to paintings depicting the natural environment, a genre that became increasingly popular in the course of the seventeenth century. The landscapes of that era which most appealed to English *amateurs* were those known as "classical," a style best represented in the works of Claude Lorrain [7.2] and Nicolas Poussin, with those of a more "sublime" character represented in the works of Salvator Rosa and Jacob van Ruysdael. The typical classical landscape, inspired by the countryside around Rome, depicts trees, bushes and ground cover in apparently informal dispositions that disguise the orderly equilibrium of the pictorial structure—an instance of Addison's "Works of Nature [being] more pleasant, the more they resemble those of art." Cubic and cylindrical buildings of indefinite purpose often appear in clusters in the distance. The appeal of the genre rested in its capacity to evoke a poetic mood of nostalgia for the purer, more bucolic past that Virgil had described in his poetry. Accordingly, the land depicted is not cultivated, though it occasionally is used for pasture: a few cows and a shepherd support the Arcadian atmosphere. The application of the term "landscape" to garden design is due to the influence of these paintings on the patrons and designers of eighteenth-century England. At the same time, the term "picturesque" began to be applied to the design of gardens—and ultimately to works of architecture as well—that displayed the kind of naturalistic informality typical of such paintings.

Though a major inspiration for the landscape garden was from the casually designed parks and hunting preserves sometimes attached to the formal gardens of the Italian Renaissance and Baroque periods [*1.16*], these models were less clearly articulated and less transportable to northern climates than Palladian architecture.[4] Thus the earliest break from formality in a small number of British gardens of the later seventeenth and early eighteenth centuries (none of which survives) was realized in a rather selfconscious and still quite controlled deregularization of garden pathways.

In this first stage, examples of which were illustrated in the early garden books of Stephen Switzer (*Ichnographia Rustica*, 1718) and Batty Langley (*New Principles of Gardening*, 1728) the geometry of traditional designs was invaded by wiggly paths the curves of which were too carefully devised to seem natural; in fact, Langley called the style "artinatural." The first garden of Blenheim Palace (1709), by Vanbrugh, had a fortified garden in which artinatural paths were inserted into a rectilinear grid.[5]

A more decisive step toward the landscape garden was made during the 1720s in designs by the Royal Gardener under George II, Charles Bridgeman, who also made occasional use of artinatural paths. Formality in his work was relaxed, mediated by casualness, as at Stowe [*7.3*].[6] Stone pavements and balustrades began to give way to extended stretches of lawn, though strictly ordered terraces were often retained at the rear of the house. Geometric forms, straight graveled paths, circular and polygonal ponds might be bordered by freely growing greenery rather than by rigidly clipped boxwood hedges [*7.4*]. Alternatively, plant material might still be disciplined by the clippers, but paths would follow rather selfconsciously sinuous wanderings. Classically inspired architectural or sculptural incidents like those illustrated in the border vignettes of Rocque's 1736 plan of Chiswick [*7.8*] entered the design (and remained throughout the subsequent phase) to give focus and symbolic significance to every vista. Domed circular tempiettos were particularly favored for this role [*7.16*].

Horace Walpole (in the *History of the Modern Taste in Gardening*, 1771) credits William Kent with opening the way to the mature landscape garden. Kent turned to landscape design after his first projects of 1730 for naturalistic garden structures and environments in the royal park at Richmond and at about the same time for Alexander Pope's garden at Twickenham; in Walpole's words, he "leaped the fence, and saw that

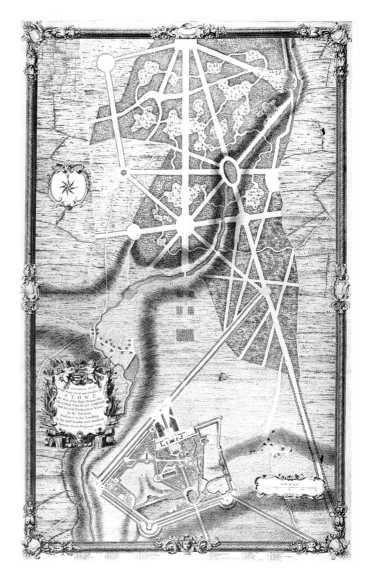

Stowe

7.3 Plan of the estate, designed by
Charles Bridgeman, 1720s. Published by
Sarah Bridgeman, 1739. The house and its
grounds are at the bottom (south)
[cf. *7.15, 17*].

7.4 View toward the house from the
oblong lake to the south [cf. *7.15*].
Drawing by Jacques Rigaud, 1746

all Nature was a garden.''[7] He was referring both to the further abandonment of geometric control over the placing and the growth of plants and to the treatment of the site so as to create an unbroken continuity between the garden and the natural countryside or pastureland beyond it. A major instrument in realizing the latter aim was the "ha-ha," a combination of grassy ditch and sunken wall separating cultivated lawns from the unmanicured fields beyond. The ha-ha, with a steep inner face to keep the grazing flocks from invading the garden, eliminated the need for fences or terraces that would destroy the illusion of an unbroken transition between art and nature.

Where designers could choose their site they sought undulating rather than flat surfaces upon which to work, and favored ground sloping to an irregular, often artificial, pond or to a winding stream or river crossed, if possible, by a Palladian or rustic bridge [6.20]. They disposed plant materials in natural though calculated groupings. The architectural and sculptural incidents of the earlier phase increased in number and significance, but were now set into freely growing greenery, often in proximity to artificial cascades or ponds [7.9]. Other strict forms gradually gave way to plantings in a natural mode; paths were no longer clearly delineated and few were of gravel or stone. Lawns began right outside the perimeter of the house. Because artifice had to be disguised if not avoided, flower beds rarely appeared. In part, this extraordinary change in the conception of gardens was due simply to boredom with rigid schemes and delight in the untrammeled workings of nature. But that attitude was itself a reflection of new literary and philosophical interests of the circle of liberal Whig patrons who had promoted Palladian architecture. The landscape garden was a highly intellectualized invention in which writers and moral philosophers played a leading role; it was an early fruit of the Enlightenment. The psychology of Locke was instrumental in encouraging designers to evoke in their garden architecture historical, ethical and other sorts of association; one's pleasure was believed to be stimulated by the ideas and recollections called up by one's progress through the garden.

The aesthetic of Shaftesbury, which extolled liberty, and which first differentiated the "beautiful" (classical, balanced) from the "sublime" (wild, awesome, exotic), suggested the possibility of inducing strong contrasts of mood by the choice of plantings and architectural incidents. Garden design was better adapted than architecture to rhetoric. Its poetic and moral—even political—message could unfold in measured time as the visitor followed a designated route through a sequence of experiences that elicited differing emotions and aroused varied associations. This dynamic progress was designed to induce changes of mood, and to introduce elements of surprise, alternations of enclosed and open prospects, each focused on a small temple or other architectural invention or on a sculpture derived from the antique—an urn, a monument, an inscription. Benches, sometimes within a sheltered structure, could be placed to encourage a pause where the most picturesque vistas had been arranged.

Such interests made literature as well as painting a muse of garden design. The "Augustan Age" of the first two decades of the eighteenth century, so named because it fostered a revival of the poets of the early Roman Empire, and particularly of the bucolic poetry of Virgil and Horace, offered intellectual justification for the emerging taste. The Augustans furthered the allegorization of the garden through monuments, urns, statues and inscriptions.[8] Above all, they initiated a century-long partnership of landscape design and literature. Alexander Pope was a major figure in the crucial years of garden development, exerting influence through his wide circle of friends among the peerage exiled from court, through his writings, and through the example of his own villa on the Thames at Twickenham, on the outskirts of London [7.5].[9] Pope's central concern as an artist was to pursue "the imitation and study of nature," and he wrote that gardening "is nearer God's work than Poetry." He contributed effectively to the development of informal principles in gardening through his writings, as in his *Epistle to Lord Burlington*:

> To build, to plant, whatever you intend,
> To rear the Column, or the Arch to bend,
> To swell the Terras, or to sink the Grot;
> In all, let Nature never be forgot.
> But treat the Goddess like a modest fair,
> Nor over-dress, nor leave her wholly bare;
> Let not each beauty ev'ry where be spy'd,
> Where half the skill is decently to hide.
> He gains all points, who pleasingly confounds,
> Surprizes, varies, and conceals the Bounds.
>   Consult the Genius of the Place in all,
> That tells the Waters or to rise, or fall,
> Or helps th'ambitious Hill the heav'ns to scale,
> Or scoops in circling theatres the Vale,
> Calls in the Country, catches opening glades,
> Joins willing woods, and varies shades from shades,
> Now breaks, or now directs, th'intending Lines;
> Paints as you plant, and as you work, designs.
> Still follow Sense, of ev'ry Art the Soul,
> Parts answ'ring parts shall slide into a whole,
> Spontaneous beauties all around advance,
> Start ev'n from Difficulty, strike from Chance;
> Nature shall join you, Time shall make it grow
> A Work to wonder at—perhaps a STOW.[10]

Pope leased the Twickenham villa in 1718, just as the suburb was becoming fashionable as a retreat for modestly wealthy Londoners. The building was undistinguished architecturally, but Pope was able to remodel it to his taste with the help of James Gibbs, a fellow Roman Catholic. His major enterprise was the transformation of the ground floor into an extensive grotto/study that formed a passage from the Thames landing to the garden behind the house. It must have been inspired by the sequence of grottoes beneath the sixteenth-century Medici villa at Pratolino, outside Florence. Pope actually used the central room as a workplace, though with its low ceilings and spring-fed fountain it must have been disagreeably damp and drafty. The grotto, which Pope compared to Plato's cave, was a metaphor of the interaction of art and nature. The imported volcanic lava of its walls was enriched by Italianate artifices: inset mirror fragments, fossils, and samples of rocks from all over Britain. But Pope altered the symbolism in 1739–40 and attempted, with the aid of a natural scientist, Borlase, to reconstruct a mine or quarry with naturalistic stratification. The change may have been intended to suggest two of his basic design principles—utility and imitation. But the

7.5, 6 Alexander Pope's villa, Twickenham, remodelled after 1718: detail of a painting by Joseph Nickolls, *c.* 1755, and plan of the garden, engraved by Joseph Serle, 1745. In the plan, the riverside garden is at the far left; a tunnel running under the house and road connects it with the rest of the grounds.

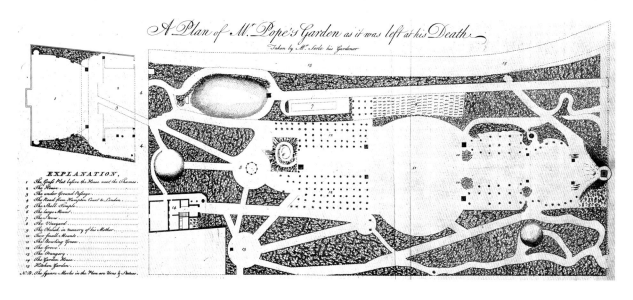

appearance of the Crown of Thorns and the Five Wounds of Christ on the ceiling near the entrance suggests a complex of allusions that remains raveled.

The narrow lawn between the house and the river must have seemed encumbered with its burden of symbolic references: a pair of reclining river gods, a swan, benches, an urn with an inscription, "Magnis ubi flexibus errat Mincius"—where great Mincius wanders in bends—that referred at once to Virgil (*Georgics*, III.14, which reads "ingens" rather than "magnis") and the Thames. Because the property was small, the garden behind the house had to be designed more in the tradition of the walled enclosures of earlier centuries than in the new landscape taste [*7.6*]. Yet Pope found room for a large mound with a spiral path leading to the top, in imitation of the Italian "paradiso" constructed at the Villa Medici in Rome and elsewhere in Italy. We know the layout only from the plan by Pope's gardener Joseph Serle, published in 1745, and from a single sketch by William Kent. The center part was formal, its main axis terminating at the post road with an obelisk in memory of the poet's mother; it looks rather dull, but Pope's authority made it exceptionally influential. The more rustic periphery, with irregular serpentine paths and a pond, was more in harmony with the sentiments Pope expressed five years before settling in Twickenham, in an essay in *The Guardian*:

> I lately took a particular Friend of mine to my House in the Country, not without some Apprehension that it could afford little Entertainment to a Man of his Polite Taste, particularly in Architecture and Gardening, who had so long been conversant with all that is beautiful and great in either. But it was a plesant Surprize to me, to hear him often declare, he had found in my little Retirement the Beauty which he always thought wanting in the most celebrated Seats, or if you will *Villa's* of the Nation. This he described to me in those Verses with which Martial begins one of his Epigrams:
>
> > Baiana nostri Villa, Basse, Faustini
> > Non otiosis ordinata myrtetis,
> > Viduaque platano, tonsilique buxeto,
> > Ingrata lati spatia detinet campi,
> > Sed *rure vero, barbaroque* laetatur.
>
> There is certainly something in the amiable Simplicity of unadorned Nature, that spreads over the Mind a more noble sort of Tranquility, and a loftier Sensation of Pleasure, than can be raised from the nicer Scenes of Art.[11]

In 1728, Robert Castell published a handsome volume, *Villas of the Ancients*, which he dedicated to Lord Burlington. It was an early effort to reconstruct the Roman luxury villa on the basis of the descriptions in letters by Pliny the Younger of his two villas, Tusci and Laurentinum [*7.7*]. (Castell had been anticipated by Jean-François Félibien's *Les Plans et les descriptions de deux des plus belles maisons de campagne de Pline le consul*, Paris, 1699 and 1706.) Pliny's descriptions give the reader some sense of the architectural and garden elements, but only inadequate clues to the villas' actual form or the relationship of their parts (see above, Chapter 2, pp. 52ff.). Castell's treatment of the buildings assumed that, being classical, they would have to be strictly symmetrical, as Palladio would doubtless have made them. (He would have done better to study the remains of Hadrian's villa at Tivoli [*2.9*], which could have helped him to visualize the agglomerative style that the Emperor inherited from antecedents like the Plinian villas.

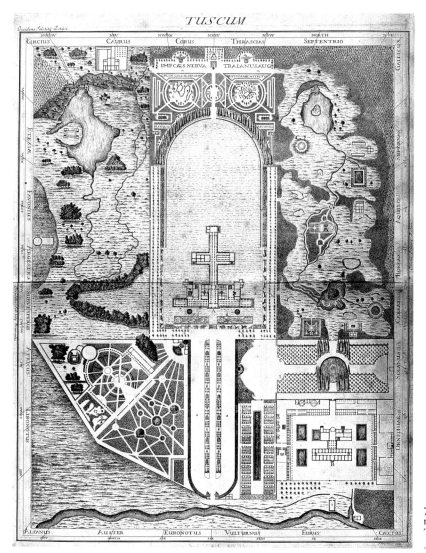

7.7 Robert Castell, reconstruction of Pliny's Tusci, from *Villas of the Ancients*, 1728

His depiction of the gardens, however, is a remarkable conflation of selfconscious naturalism, in the parks on either side, with the rigid formality of a seventeenth-century French formal garden (at the lower right), its geometry tentatively compromised by orderly clumps of trees and an "artinatural" biomorphic grove. The reconstruction does not adhere obediently to Pliny's descriptions, but follows the mixed style of Pratolino and other large Italian gardens, Marly, and their immediate English descendants. By this time, the style had almost run its course; the main role of Castell's book was to call the attention of the Palladians to the fact that informal garden elements were validated by the authority of the antique.

In his text, Castell invented an evolution of the ancient Roman garden from an initial stage of profuse and disorderly plantings, which he calls the "Rough Manner," to highly regular formal organizations and finally to a combination of the two in an imitation of nature in which the highest skill is employed to convey the impression of an artless naturalism. He arbitrarily interprets an ambiguous passage in Pliny's description of Tusci to mean that "hills, rocks, cascades, riverlets, woods and buildings, etc., were possibly thrown into such an agreeable disorder as to have pleased the eye from several views, like so many beautiful Landskips."

Castell's plans and text reflected, as might be expected, the development of the landscaping being carried out by Lord Burlington on his property at Chiswick after his return from Italy in 1715.[12] Drawings that Burlington commissioned in 1733 from Jacques Rigaud (now at Chatsworth) emphasize the geometric character of the garden, but clumps of trees, though planted in regular rows, were permitted to grow freely, and areas of the garden are less strictly separated than in the French style. Rigaud's perspective views were not adapted to representing the large areas traversed by artinatural paths that appear in John Rocque's plan of 1736 [7.8]. They apparently were designed in the 1720s by Burlington himself (with the help of Bridgeman?). Rocque enframed his engraving with vignettes illustrating the villa and the most important garden structures designed by Burlington under the influence of James Gibbs and Colen Campbell.

7.8 Chiswick House: plan of the garden, by Lord Burlington (with Charles Bridgeman?), 1720s, and William Kent, early 1730s. Engraving by John Rocque, 1736

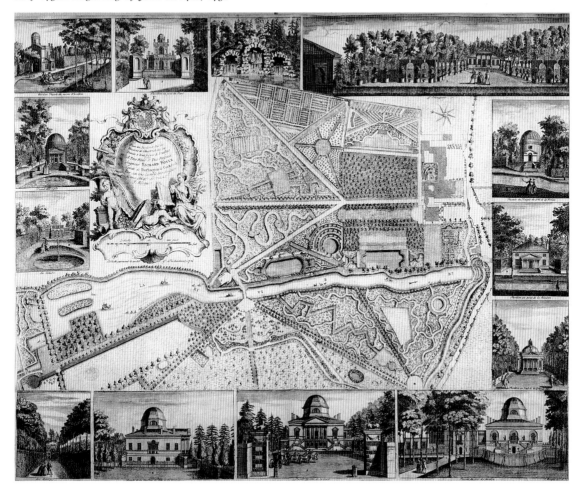

7.9 Chiswick House from the west in 1753, showing the cascade, by William Kent, early 1730s. Engraving after J. Donowell

The history of the Chiswick estate is a paradigm of the evolution of the landscape garden. Continental formality survives in the clipped box hedges bordering each path, the geometrical ponds and the small parterred private garden by the villa. The stirrings of a new naturalism are revealed in the uncontrolled growth of the trees behind the hedges, the irregular course of the river and the introduction of an artificially rustic cascade [7.8 top center, 9]. The latter is an indication of the intervention of William Kent, who is reported to have started in 1733 (the date may have been earlier) to naturalize as much as possible of his patron's geometries: Burlington's original cascade had issued from a rather prim pedimented structure.

Much of what Rocque shows had been carried out before 1730, and Kent's changes must have represented the later evolution of Burlington's taste toward a more radical diversion from tradition in the direction of the precepts enunciated by Pope in the *Epistle to Lord Burlington*. Kent preserved the principal *allées* but removed most other straight lines, eliminated the boundaries between parts of the garden by opening spaces between trees now distributed in casual rows and clumps (the impressionistic sketches [7.10] underscore Kent's informal aesthetic), and devised a naturalistic lawn sloping down to the river, which he redesigned with sinuous banks.[13] Burlington's conception had been strictly intellectual; his garden existed to display his architectural inventions, some of which were little more than facades. Kent's innovations, apart from the exedra with busts of Caesar, Pompey, Cicero, Homer and Virgil behind the villa [7.10],[14] were addressed primarily to the senses. It was his capacity to recreate the natural through artifice that launched him upon an impressive career as a landscape designer.

Kent, who had worked somewhat earlier at Carlton House for the Prince of Wales, and found his career greatly advanced by his association with Burlington, became deeply involved in landscape design as well as in architecture.[15] Rousham, near Oxford, is the best preserved of his inventions [*7.11–14*]. The twenty-five-acre estate gave him more scope than at Chiswick, though it was far more modest than the great parks like Stowe where he was also employed [*7.17*]. Rousham was inherited in 1737 by General James Dormer, a friend of Burlington; the garden at that time had followed a design of about 1725 by Bridgeman, which survives at Oxford. It shows a bowling green behind the house bordered by stone terraces on three sides, straight paths, two square pools and wooded areas with minor serpentine walks.

The Cherwell river, which marked the lower limits of the property, had been constrained to flow in a channel of straight lines with angular bends. Kent, who set to work in 1737, did not attempt to erase the basic disposition of Bridgeman's garden, but sought to soften edges and dissolve boundaries, eliminating all but a few straight lines and stone terraces and re-naturalizing the river. Even this modest program required the engagement of up to seventy laborers at a time to move earth and plants.

Rousham became decidedly more picturesque than Chiswick. Its position on elevated land sloping abruptly to the river enabled Kent to encorporate the pastures and rolling hills of adjacent properties into his design [*7.11, 12*]. Neighbors were even persuaded to permit ornamental structures to be placed on their property and changes to be made in the course of the river. The panorama from the lawn includes a fictive Gothic mill in the middle ground and an arched "eye-catcher" in the distance [*7.12*]. Kent placed

7.10 Chiswick House: project for the Great Walk and Exedra, by William Kent

7.11 Prospect from the house

Rousham, by Charles Bridgeman, *c.* 1725, and William Kent, 1737 on

7.12 The Gothic mill and "eye-catcher," by Kent

7.13 Praeneste Terrace, by Kent

7.14 The Vale of Venus, by Kent

structures at several points above the river banks—a temple of Echo, a terrace embankment of seven rustic arches called "Praeneste Terrace" [7.13] (after the Roman name of Palestrina, the site of the great hillside precinct of the goddess Fortuna Primigenia),[16] a pyramidal house—the function of which was chiefly to offer vantage points for particular vistas of the river and countryside. In each, seats were provided for the contemplative visitor: a bench in the Echo Temple (redesigned by William Townesend) is set to fix the view onto the fourteenth-century bridge over the river.

These belvederes are interspersed with more introspective images: pools and architectural incidents enveloped in trees and shrubs. The most effective of these is the Vale of Venus, commanded by a statue of Venus Pudica, where the arch of a rustic wellhead like that at Chiswick emits a cascade into an octagonal pond and is repeated in a triple arched structure below [7.14]. Kent would have seen such rustic fountains in the upper gardens of the Villa Aldobrandini in Frascati and at Pratolino. The Vale is a re-creation of an ancient Elysium, a dreamland of greenery consecrated to the gods of fertility.

Statuary was given special prominence at Rousham. Kent preserved Bridgeman's longest *allée* and focused its perspective on a copy of a Roman Apollo (called the "Colossus"). This and other statues are dramatically placed to command the full attention of the visitor. A group by the sculptor Scheemakers based on Roman precedents of a lion attacking a horse is centered at the foot of the lawn and commands attention as one looks toward the prospect beyond [7.11]. The same artist placed a statue modeled on the Capitoline *Dying Gaul* at the first resting place on the itinerary of the garden. These representations of mortal conflict may have been intended as references to the military calling of the patron or as a mortuary inference (Kent had planned to place the *Gaul* on a sarcophagus), but in general the symbolism of the garden does not seem to be especially pointed. The intention was primarily to evoke a poetic version of Roman antiquity without a definable moral message, and even this was blurred by Gothic elements.

7.15 Stowe: garden project by Charles Bridgeman—probably his definitive proposal, *c.* 1720

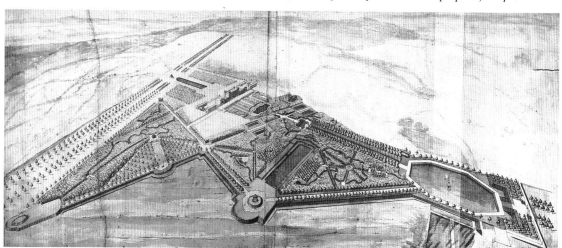

7.16 Stowe: the Rotondo, by Sir John Vanbrugh, with Bridgeman's "ha-ha" to the right. Drawing by Jacques Rigaud, 1746

Kent's attraction to scenic effects seen from pre-established positions gives his work at Rousham a theatrical quality. The visitor comes on a sequence of open and closed vistas that might have been designed as scenes for a pastoral stage comedy or masque. The effects are picturesque in the general sense though they are too eclectic, with their Gothic, rustic and vernacular elements, to associate with the paintings of Claude and Poussin that are commonly cited as the principal inspiration for the landscape garden.

At Stowe in Buckinghamshire, the ample gardens evolved through the same kind of Bridgeman–Kent sequence, and again much of the initial design was preserved in softened style under the latter's direction.[17] The proprietor, Richard Temple, a vigorous liberal Whig leader who became Viscount Cobham in 1718, was intensely involved for more than two decades in the garden program. His property was much more extensive than that at Rousham, and he began around 1713 to develop it on a grand scale with the aid of Vanbrugh and, about 1720, of Bridgeman [7.3, 15]. Before 1730 James Gibbs was employed, chiefly for architectural designs, and Kent was active throughout the 1730s. These eminent artists, and others who followed, all left their mark at Stowe and made it a permanent exhibition of the evolution of English landscape design in the eighteenth century.

The Bridgeman plan, as one would expect, is predominantly rectilinear, with a few serpentine paths enclosed by geometrically disposed walls or lines of trees. It has affinities with fortification design, and it may be from that source that Bridgeman took his early version of the ha-ha, which appears first at Stowe as a formidable defensive moat [7.16].

A contemporary observer, Joseph Spence, wrote, "Cobham began in the Bridgeman taste: it is the Elysian Fields that is the painting part of his gardens." This area, which appears in a later plan to the east of the lawn behind the house [*7.17, center*], is an elaborate version of Rousham's Vale of Venus—an opening enveloped in trees (smaller and thinner in Kent's conception than today) with a stream winding between two elevated banks. Here the patron imposed an intensely personal and contemporary symbolic message upon the vaguely Augustan associative atmosphere. In 1733 Cobham, like Burlington, had fallen out with Robert Walpole, the Whig Prime Minister, over what he felt was the weakening of democratic guarantees and civil rights. He directed Kent to design a group of buildings and monuments which would advertise his convictions—a political program that could never have been tolerated on the Continent. A Temple of Ancient Virtue, inspired by the round temple of the Sibyl at Tivoli (one of the few surviving ancient sacred groves where a building communes with nature), contained statues of Greek lawgivers and leaders who represented the respect for

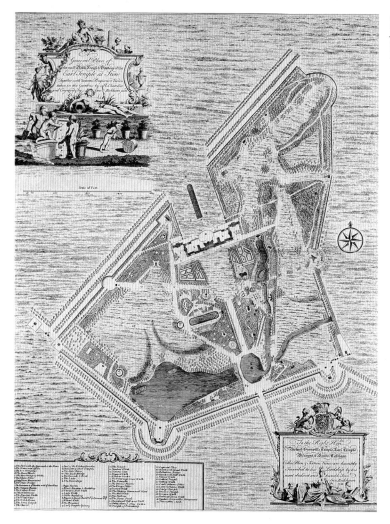

7.17 Stowe: garden plan, by J. B. C. Chatelain, 1753, showing the collaboration of Bridgeman, Kent, and Lord Cobham

7.18 Stowe: Temple of Liberty, by James Gibbs, *c.* 1741–44

constitutional rights that Cobham felt had been abrogated in George II's reign. It faced a Temple of Modern Virtue (now destroyed), which was pointedly a sham ruin containing a headless statue of Walpole, and a "Temple" of British worthies—actually an exedra with niches for portrait busts—celebrating eight great artists and scientists and eight men of action.

From the enclosed precinct of the Elysian Fields, one path leads over a steep rise toward the Hawkwell Field, an extended open plot in the form of a peaked dunce cap running parallel to the Elysian Fields. At its apex, Gibbs built the Ladies' Temple and at the base, across a winding stream spanned by a Palladian bridge, the Temple of Friendship, celebrating Cobham's bonds to others in his social and political circle (known as "the Patriots"), including Frederick, Prince of Wales. On a rise halfway between these two is the massive Gothic Temple of Liberty, also by Gibbs, which was prompted more by Cobham's propaganda aims than by the incipient romantic Gothic taste [*7.18*]. Around it were originally placed effigies of the seven "Saxon" deities after whom the days of the week are named. The Gothic style at Stowe was intended to evoke associations of northern vitality and of liberty as embodied in the ancient laws and constitutional forms reputedly brought to Britain by "Goths."[18] The inscription over the entrance (from Corneille) reads: "Je rends graces aux Dieux de nestre pas Romain,"

7.19 Stowe: Grecian Temple, later the Temple of Concord and Victory, by Kent, 1748 on

a paradoxical outburst in view of the classical allusions of the neighboring garden areas. Contemporary guidebooks, however, list other nonclassical structures at Stow—a Hermitage, a Chinese house, a Witch House, a grotto—among those that have disappeared.

The last portion of the site to be developed before Cobham's death in 1749 was the Grecian Valley on the far northern rim of the property [*7.17, upper right*], a long narrow extension of lawn, in part of which a lake was to have been excavated, framed by dense groves on either side in an intensely naturalistic mode that signalled a new phase in landscape gardening, just as the Grecian Temple of 1748 [*7.19*] at its head (renamed the Temple of Concord and Victory at the conclusion of the Seven Years' War) presaged the Greek revival of the later eighteenth century. These innovations are underscored by the absence of an architectural focus at the opposite end of the perspective (a projected triumphal arch was never built): the prospect simply runs off into unplanned fields. This change may have been proposed by Lancelot ("Capability") Brown, the assistant whom Kent left in charge in 1742, who later became the arbiter of the widely adopted succeeding phase in landscape design, in which artifice and architecture were so restrained that gardens came to look like well-kept nature.

As one visitor observed in the dialog appended to the first guide to the gardens at Stowe, "If censure was due to any thing here, in his opinion, it was to too great a Profusion of Ornament." The simplicity of Nature, he thought, was "too much pushed away."[19] While the gardens represent the maturation of the landscape style, their achievement of natural informality paradoxically became as intellectualized under Cobham's pressure as the geometric rigidity of their Continental predecessors. Such a density of symbolic structures and statuary was not attempted again. But it represented only one of Stowe's personalities; something is preserved there of every eighteenth-century mode of treating the cultivated environment.

The garden at Stourhead in Wiltshire is better preserved and maintained than Chiswick, Rousham or Stowe. It is also more coherent, since it was the realization of one man's vision.[20] Henry Hoare II was the son of the successful banker and entrepreneur, also named Henry, who had employed Campbell to build the house at Stourhead, one of the first English Palladian villas [6.18, 19]. In Campbell's design the garden, if it can be called that, was no more than an oval patch of lawn in the center of an entrance court with high walls that blocked off any view of the surrounding country. It was a curious ancestor to the most picturesque of all English gardens.

The junior Hoare, also an active banker, settled at Stourhead in 1741, and three years later began work on the garden, which he himself designed, perhaps with some assistance from his architect Henry Flitcroft. The core of the garden was to be a large lake excavated in a depression in the Stour valley [7.20–22], but in the first stage the

7.20 Stourhead: the grounds in 1785. The house is right of center, behind the hemicycle marked with the letter "A"; the village is below, near the eastern tip of the lake.

water was formed into separate ponds one of which, in front of Flitcroft's Doric Temple of Flora, was rectangular, recalling the formal style of the first stage at Chiswick, where the same architect had been employed. In the 1750s this residue of past taste was absorbed into the lake. The garden was started at the time when Rousham and Stowe were being completed and it preoccupied Hoare until the 1770s. It differs from its predecessors in being more intensely picturesque (the initial view of the Pantheon across the lake with Alfred's Gothic tower on a height behind it [7.21] is an obvious reference to paintings by Claude) and less precisely allusive; its symbolism is not primarily political or personal, but poetic and mythical: building inscriptions are taken from Virgil's *Aeneid*, and the relation to nature is more moral and religious than intellectual.

Hoare removed the walls that enveloped the Campbell villa, but he did not make his new garden an extension of it. Behind the house he provided a rather characterless open expanse of green lawn and pasture focused on a distant obelisk on the central axis. The garden itinerary begins to one side of the house and reaches its first effective prospect only after the house is no longer in sight. It is entirely independent. The manipulation of experience is more effective than in the earlier gardens, partly because the lake at the core of the composition is in a deep depression so that the encircling path offers fine elevated prospects of the opposite banks. Periodic apertures in the dense and shadowy inclines offer surprising views at the early stages of the walk along the steep slopes overlooking the water. The first of them on leaving the house is a view of Flitcroft's Temple of Apollo (1765), framed as a bright apparition through the darkness of trees and shrubs, much as architectural incidents are framed in classical landscape paintings. The pictorial chiaroscuro effects (intensified today by the importation of many new species of tree and plant) are a compelling aspect of Stourhead.

Only one major path follows the contours of the basin (high on the side toward the house and lower on the opposite bank), instead of the many artificially serpentined ones of earlier gardens. This added to the naturalness of the impression and gave the designer more opportunity to control his images. There are fewer structures than at Stowe; temples were built to Ceres (later called Flora [7.22, *left*]) and Apollo—the latter the first copy of the round temple at Baalbek in the Lebanon, published by Robert Wood in 1757. And a majestic Pantheon, dedicated to Hercules, overlooks the lake from a rise on the far shore. These classical structures alternate with rustic and exotic buildings, including a large grotto modeled on Pope's (with a sleeping nymph taken from the original in the villa of the Belvedere in the Vatican), a cascade, a Hermitage, a Gothick Convent, an artificial ruin (now really ruined) and, on a hilltop on the far side of the lake, a very high Norman-style tower–memorial to King Alfred. At the southeastern end of the lake, the remains of the ancient village of Stourton were rearranged with the Gothic parish church as the pictorial focus and a fine spire-like Gothic monument brought from Bristol, where it had marked a major street crossing [7.22]. The grotto, entered beneath an inscription from Virgil designating it as a house of the nymphs, offers the darkest setting, suggestive of the underworld, but through a large rocky aperture over the water appears an enchanting vignette of the southern bridge, the Bristol Cross, the church and village. Each of the major monuments is a resting-place from which an engaging prospect may be enjoyed, and each is the focus of numerous other prospects.

7.21 Stourhead, designed by Henry Hoare II (with Henry Flitcroft?), 1744–70s: view of the lake as approached from the house. Drawing by F. M. Piper, 1779

7.22 Stourhead: view toward the village of Stourton, 1777. The Bristol Cross is visible to the left of the church.

No garden illustrates as well as Stourhead the statement of Horace Walpole: "Poetry, Painting and Gardening, or the science of landscape, will forever by men of taste be deemed Three Sisters or the *The Three New Graces*, who dress and adorn nature." Hoare took his ethical and topographical clues from Roman poetry and his visual effects from classical landscape painting; in 1746 he bought a picture by Claude Lorrain, and he wrote much later that "the view of the Bridge, Village & Church altogether will be a charming Gasp'd picture at the end of that water" (meaning Gaspard Dughet, a more "sublime" contemporary of Claude).

Clues to the symbolic program are given by inscriptions and by Hoare's correspondence, which point to Virgil's *Aeneid* as a possible inspiration. The voyage of Aeneas to find a peaceful home in a new land was a theme that paralleled the longing of the urban man of affairs to find rest in the countryside; it had occupied Claude in many works, and his reconstructions obviously had an impact on Hoare. But Hoare was not as compelled to convey messages as Cobham had been; his symbols were generalized and, as in the case of the altered designation of the Ceres/Flora temple, adjustable.

Most of the rustic and romantic additions to the design date from the 1760s, when strict classical taste was waning elsewhere and when Hoare himself suffered the grief of having lost almost all his immediate family; in recounting to his only surviving daughter the building of the Hermitage, "lined inside and out with old Gouty and Nobbly Oakes," he added: "I believe I shall put in to be myself the Hermit." His inscription on Alfred's Tower expressed his disaffection from the aggressive policies of the Seven Years' War in terms that depict Arthur as a ruler who protected the nation from invasion, extended trade, subdued enemies, and gave "peace and rest to the Earth." The garden at Stourhead surely gave as much peace and rest to Henry Hoare and to generations of visitors as the world would permit.

If the Continental garden was an extension of architecture, the landscape garden was a celebration of the land. It permitted the artificial, cultivated disposition of plantings in the environment of the house to merge imperceptibly into the agricultural lands on its periphery. Most proprietors arranged for the appearance of cattle or deer or both in the prospect to symbolize the sources of wealth and means of recreation. In eighteenth-century England, land ownership was by far the dominant source of wealth, status and power. The peers of the realm, numbering fewer than two hundred, did not, like European aristocrats, depend on a monarch for their privileges, and could survive without loss of prestige away from court, on their estates. Their taste for an idealized nature was rooted in their affection for the soil that nurtured their wellbeing.

The ecology of Britain welcomed this enterprise; its softly contoured hills and valleys, its rich soil and, above all, its abundant rainfall, inspired and responded to the taste for tall, spreading trees, winding streams, sinuously bordered ponds, and extended areas of brilliantly green lawn.

The extent to which the landscape garden movement was related to the Acts of Enclosure is difficult to determine. Enclosure was the system that superseded the medieval apportionment of land tenure and common rights in which peasants and freeholders farmed small strips of land and shared large areas of common pasture and woodland. Through Acts that were confirmed in the course of the seventeenth and eighteenth centuries by parliaments made up primarily of owners of large estates, these holdings were consolidated and brought into the major estates, which then could be subdivided (typically by hedges or ditches) with ample fields better suited to large-scale agricultural development. In many areas this engrossment made grazing more profitable than cultivation. Woodland could be managed for effective production or turned into hunting or nature preserves. The process could be ruinous, removing the livelihood of the peasantry, impelling even independent farmers to become employees of the aristocracy and gentry and, in extreme cases, leading to the deliberate destruction of villages and dispersion of their inhabitants to create more efficient farmland or even more picturesque vistas. Oliver Goldsmith's *The Deserted Village* and the poetry of Thomas Crabbe are among the few literary treatments of country life that expose the grim underside of this change.[21]

The consolidation of agricultural holdings, however, was a necessary and inevitable consequence of the explosive growth in population and the expansion of cities during the seventeenth and eighteenth centuries. The medieval system was not adequate to feed a modern population or to effect the reforestation made necessary by the devastation of the Civil War. Moreover, enclosure was not always forced by the privileged class; villagers who failed to make a livelihood on their small allotments frequently consented to enclosure or themselves enclosed by agreement. The emergence of the landscape garden cannot be attributed directly to Enclosure: many of the formal gardens depicted in paintings and in the engravings of Kip must have been on enclosed estates, and many are as large as Stowe or Stourhead. Yet there must have been a link between legal enclosure and the visual incorporation of pastureland with ornamental and profitable sheep and cattle, and distant forests or thickets, into the panoramas of the eighteenth-century garden. The removal of visible boundaries between the lawn and the pasture made possible by ha-has can be thought of as a metaphor of Enclosure.[22]

The beauties of the English countryside as perceived by the great eighteenth-century landed proprietors and by most contemporary landscape painting and literature— witness the poetry of Thomson—were not those of an industrious peasantry working a fruitful earth but of a dreamy pastoral land protected from the plow and inhabited by an occasional shepherd and his flock: not the landscape of Brueghel but that of Claude Lorrain.

It seems contradictory that the landscape garden, which represented a rejection of formality, was the chosen setting for an architecture adhering to the strict geometry of the Palladian villa. Yet both styles represented a rejection of the Continental Baroque, an avowal of simplicity and independence in contrast to grandeur and authority. Both called upon what were understood to be the laws of nature: the garden imitated sensible nature in recreating its spontaneity and informality; the architecture, conforming to the principles of Palladio and the Renaissance tradition, undertook to obey the invisible harmony of the universe in its proportions, its symmetry and its axiality. Together they represent paired polarities of the Age of Enlightenment, romanticism and rationality.

The landscape garden was adopted abroad with enthusiasm within a generation, and in many places where geometry had once reigned: even at Versailles a corner of the garden was turned over to informality, and Marie Antoinette built a rustic *ferme ornée*, the "Hameau," in which to play the milkmaid.[23] A funerary monument to Rousseau was appropriately placed on a wooded island at the center of the quintessentially picturesque estate of the Marquis de Girardin at Ermenonville. Reversing the workings of the picturesque, the pre-Revolutionary artists Hubert Robert and Fragonard painted fantasies of manmade informal gardens and sought those Italian gardens in which the once geometric forms had grown out of control.

Eighteenth- and nineteenth-century Americans hardly ever knew an alternative to the English invention of landscape design. Today it is hard to imagine a park that is not planned, like Central Park in New York or Golden Gate Park in San Francisco, in imitation of the accidents of nature, and the same is true of the better endowed cemeteries.

Neither France nor America adopted Palladian architecture as a complement to informal gardening. It had not been part of the architectural heritage of these nations, as there had been no equivalent to Inigo Jones, and by the time the English taste had spread abroad even the English were no longer Palladian purists.

8 · Thomas Jefferson

Those who labour in the earth are the chosen people of God if he ever had a chosen people, whose breasts he has made this peculiar deposit for substantial and genuine virtue . . . The proportion which the aggregate of the other classes of citizens bears in any state to that of its husbandmen is the proportion of its unsound to its healthy parts. A barometer whereby to measure its degree of corruption. When we have land to labour, then, let us never wish to see our citizens occupied at a workbench or twirling a distaff: let our workshops remain in Europe.[1]

It seems improbable today that America could have survived as an independent nation had it followed Jefferson's conviction that industry and commerce should be abandoned in favor of agriculture. His image of a nation of citizens whose honesty and independence could be secured almost exclusively by the cultivation of the land was a pipe dream. In his advocacy of the simple life and of personal, physical involvement in farming tasks, Jefferson reshaped an attitude first articulated in the writings of another gentleman-farmer and sometime politician in Republican Rome, Marcus Porcius Cato, whose treatise on agriculture offered the proprietor a Spartan life of exacting labor as the one antidote to the evils spawned by city culture (see Chapter 2). Jefferson had read the works of Cato, as he had those of many other Roman writers; ancient authors were as formative for his concept of country life as they had been for that of his English predecessors in the preceding decades.

Jefferson's interest in architecture began before the destruction by fire of his father's simple plantation settlement, Shadwell, in 1770, when he was twenty-seven.[2] He had decided some time before to make Monticello, in the virtual wilderness of central Virginia, the headquarters of his scattered inheritance of more than five thousand acres: leveling of the hilltop had already begun there in 1768. After the Shadwell fire, which destroyed his library and papers, Monticello became the only house he possessed for several decades; while he practiced law and served in the Virginia legislature and in the federal government he rented rooms in Richmond and Philadelphia. The proceeds from farming at Monticello were to have been his primary source of income, but Jefferson could not bring himself to operate the plantation exclusively with an eye to profit. His choice of an isolated site at the crown of a high hill with steep slopes that discouraged cultivation, at some distance from the Rivanna river, was prompted more by his taste for the panorama and for a quiet retreat than by farming efficiency. His interest in the improvement of American agriculture and his scientific curiosity were more compelling than economic success; he often planted crops and garden materials untested in the area and acquired with much expense of time, effort and money.

Jefferson designed or advised on the design of a number of houses that functioned like Palladio's villas in being of modest size (though relatively elegant outside and luxurious within) and in being the working headquarters of large plantations. But in two ways they differed: the estates were in the wilderness of a virgin land, and they were worked in part by slaves. The isolation helped to determine the use of brick as a structural material (Jefferson thought that wooden architecture was inferior) since it could be made on the site, and it affected the planning of the living quarters at Monticello, especially in the enlargement that began in 1796. Because of the isolation and of Jefferson's exalted position as a politician and national hero, Monticello attracted constant visitors, many of whom had to be accommodated for days or weeks. The 185 slaves that Jefferson had inherited from his parents and father-in-law in addition to the freemen employed represented to him a responsibility that guided many of his decisions on the management of his lands: refusing to sell slaves, he undertook certain enterprises, such as the establishment of a nail factory, to make efficient use of the labor force. While the impact of slave labor on the design of the actual residence at Monticello is minimal (the household force—83 slaves and 34 freemen in 1775—as well as farm hands were housed in a village on the slopes of the hill), the two wings extending into the garden [8.5, 6] accommodate service areas adapted to a community with a high ratio of domestic servants to family members.[3]

As an educated colonial patrician, Jefferson naturally absorbed attitudes of the earlier eighteenth-century British landowners and intellectuals described in Chapter 7. His approach to the design of a country estate was similar to theirs in being grounded in classical learning, particularly Roman bucolic poetry and the villa literature. Like Lord Burlington, he was a serious amateur architect who designed buildings for himself and others in his circle and who called on professionals—Clérisseau, Latrobe, Mills—for criticism and advice. He wanted his house and grounds to represent certain Enlightenment virtues: liberty, simplicity and practicality. And, like his liberal Whig forebears, he was vigorously anti-establishment and sought an architectural style that would offer a clear alternative to the one currently favored in his social milieu.

In revealing ways, however, Jefferson rejected the Burlingtonian inheritance. He was not a member of an intellectual, philosophical and artistic circle that exerted influence over the course of architectural design. He had no interest in recalling the British national heritage and therefore no reason to reflect the work of Inigo Jones; his interest in modern French architecture would not have been acceptable in England. Unlike the earlier Palladians, and more like contemporary British architects such as Robert Adam and John Soane, his approach to design was less committed to observing precedents and rules of vocabulary and composition and less deferential to Palladian models. And finally, though he was sufficiently intrigued by the new English landscape design to study William Shenstone's "Unconnected Thoughts on Gardening" (published in 1764) and to tour the best-known examples with Thomas Whately's *Observations on Modern Gardening* (1770) in hand, his own landscape planning at Monticello adopted only the general character of informality and refrained from emulating the aspects of the sequence of diverse experiences, surprise, and the thematic treatment of separated areas.[4] His estate was not planned as an Elysium of literary allusion.

"English architecture," Jefferson wrote from Paris in 1786, "is in the most wretched

8.1 Carter's Grove, Va.: garden front, 1751–53

style I ever saw, not meaning to except America, where it is bad, nor even Virginia, where it is worse than in any other part of America, which I have seen."[5] He wrote that architecture was the only art in which the new nation could adequately express its ideals, and he was dismayed at its failure to do so. The judgment probably was less aesthetic than political and ethical: his disapproval of contemporary Virginia plantation owners, who "seated themselves below the tide water on the main rivers and lived in a style of luxury and extravagance" carried over to their plantation houses.[6] These houses, such as Carter's Grove on the banks of the James river, built in 1751–53 [8.1], are elegant and not particularly showy examples of their style, but it was a style that exemplified to Jefferson not only luxury and extravagance but Tory, anti-Republican attitudes and a lack of classical culture.

We call the architecture of Tidewater Virginia "Georgian" because it was built during the reign of the three Hanoverian Georges between 1714 and the Revolution, but it evolved from an English style that had originated in the seventeenth century, and it rarely reflected innovations of the eighteenth century.[7] The characteristic Georgian Palladian fashion in Britain was sometimes dimly reflected in the linkage of the main house to symmetrical outbuildings by closed or porticoed passages, as at George Washington's plantation house at Mount Vernon. Jefferson must have assigned Mount Vernon a place in his list of wretched architecture; it was enlarged in stages from a simple farmhouse and its facade, on which masonry blocks are imitated in wood, is asymmetrical and lacking in distinct character. Only one Tidewater mansion, Mount

8.2 Mount Airy, Va., 1758–62

Airy, of 1758–62 [8.2], overlooking the Rappahannock river, fully reflected more recent British design: it was based almost exactly on one of the more Palladian plates in James Gibbs's *Book of Architecture* (1728) and is unique among surviving structures in being entirely of stone. Gibbs had been dismissed by Burlington, no doubt for his adherence to the Wren tradition and for his insufficiently classical inventiveness, but architectural politics of that sort probably had no part in the choice made by an American colonial plantation owner.

Like Colonel Tayloe of Mount Airy, Jefferson's architectural taste was formed initially from books, without which neither would have been able to imagine alternatives to current colonial architecture. Jefferson, however, collected avidly, building an architectural library as rich as that of a British amateur of the mid-century.[8] At the start, he favored Gibbs's *Book of Architecture*, the editions of Palladio's *Quattro libri* published in London and Paris earlier in the century (he later bought three other editions) and the *Select Architecture* of 1755 by the Palladian and classical theorist Robert Morris.[9] His first notes on the construction of Monticello also refer to Perrault's edition of Vitruvius and to William Chambers's *Designs of Chinese Buildings, etc.* (1757)—the one work outside the classical tradition—from which he adapted his terrace balustrades and a design, later abandoned, for pagodalike pavilions at the corners of the terraces.[10] When remodeling Monticello after 1796, Jefferson depended rather on the more precise plates of two recent publications which he must have acquired in Paris, Fréart de Chambray's *Parallèle de l'architecture antique avec la moderne*, in a revised edition of 1764–66, and Desgodets's *Les édifices antiques de Rome* (London, 1771–95); in his copy of the former he made notes of his intention to use particular Roman orders and entablatures for the interiors of the house. Though Jefferson, writing to the proprietor of Bremo, referred to Palladio's book as "the Bible" (see below, p. 207),[11] he used it more consistently for its version of the ancient orders—especially for the proportioning of elements—than for its original dwelling projects. Except in the initial stage of the Monticello design, in which the Palladianism is mostly filtered through Gibbs, he did not reflect Palladian planning or elevation solutions. Jefferson was a designer, unlike Tayloe, and did not intend simply to adapt model projects. He used his sources selectively, and the ultimate designs of Monticello and other houses of his late years are more original than those of any strictly Palladian English architect.

Building of the first house at Monticello began in the spring of 1769 and lasted nearly a decade. Jefferson wrote from there early in 1771 that he was living in a one-room structure that may have been the basement of the future residence or the end pavilion of the southern terrace-wing [*8.5, upper left*].[12] Building progress was slow; when Jefferson married on January 1, 1772, the couple moved into the same tiny space.

The early sketches for the house done in the course of 1768–69 were variations on plans in Gibbs's *Book*—the first a square with recessed porches on each side, and later ones a rectangular plan followed by cruciform variants from which the ultimate design developed.[13] These culminate in a plan [*8.3*] that became the basis of the first elevations, of which the final version has a two-story central pedimented block flanked by lower blocks [*8.4*].[14] While the design combines the two-level central portico of the Villa

8.3 Monticello: plan project, by Thomas Jefferson, late 1760s

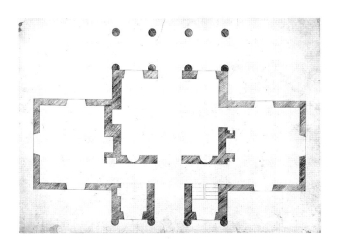

8.4 Monticello: elevation project, by Jefferson, before March, 1772 (K.23)

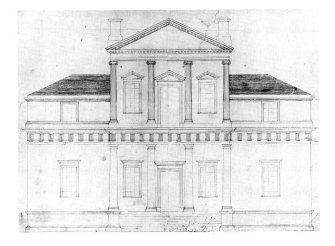

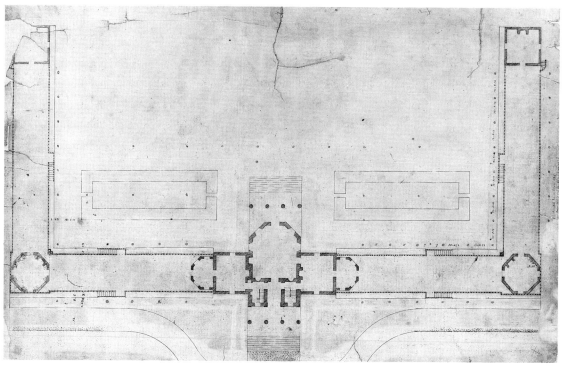

8.5, 6 Monticello: plan projects for the principal floor *(above)* and ground floor, by Jefferson, before August, 1772 (K.31, 32)

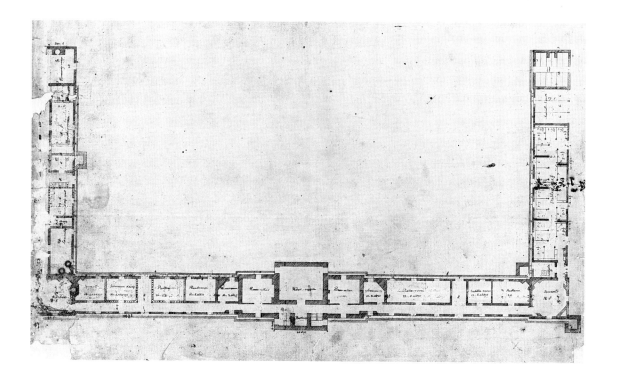

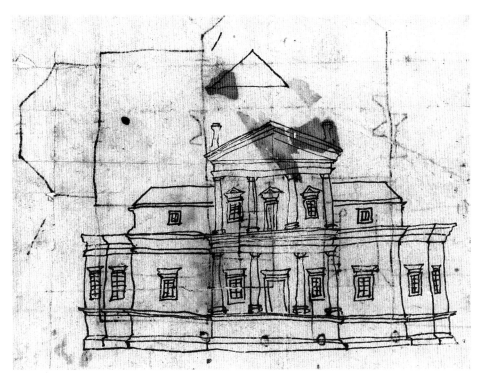

8.7 Monticello: elevation project, by Jefferson, summer 1772

Cornaro at Piombino Dese with the flanking elevations of the Villa Saraceno at Finale from Palladio's *Quattro libri*, the Doric details are derived from another of Gibbs's books, *Rules for drawing the several Parts of Architecture* (1732).[15] The illustration of the Finale villa also appears to have influenced the decision to attach L-shaped wings on either side of the main block of the residence (though Palladio's wings are porticoes at ground level, while Jefferson's have utilitarian functions housed in a Roman *cryptoporticus* at basement level and a terrace with a balustrade at the level of the house). The first in the series of plans was revised in the ensuing four years; the semi-octagonal termination of the parlor and the smaller bows on either side were last-minute additions, as is clear from the drawing. The definitive project of the summer of 1772 is recorded in two plans [*8.5, 6*] and in a lively freehand elevation of the facade [*8.7*].

These changes duplicate a very recent innovation in the design of small villas and hunting casinos in England that represented an assimilation of French planning practice. Morris's *Select Architecture* has a design for a house with an octagonal parlor projecting on one side, and Chambers favored the arrangement following his apprenticeship with J.-F. Blondel. Sir Robert Taylor's design of Asgill House in the 1760s [*8.8*] comes closest to Monticello, though it lacks the porticoes; it was published in 1767 (in volume IV of *Vitruvius Britannicus*) but there is no indication that Jefferson knew of it.[16] The inspiration could have come by other channels. Jefferson, in any case, joined elements from diverse sources in a project of striking originality that represents

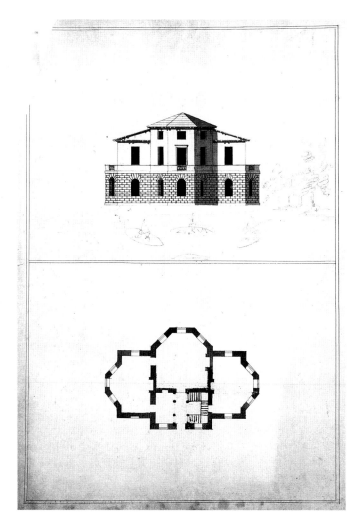

8.8 Asgill House,
Richmond, Surrey, by Sir
Robert Taylor, 1760–65

an elevation of southern colonial architecture to the level of current European design. Neither Palladio nor Burlington would have broken a facade wall by a bow of this sort because perspective effects would distort the perception of proportional relations. At the cost of classical purity the semi-octagonal spaces, filled with light and offering a panoramic view onto the garden, vary the exterior and enrich the quality of the interior. Jefferson found the motif so congenial that he used it in the majority of his remaining projects: for the Governor's Palace in Williamsburg (unexecuted), a house he rented in suburban Philadelphia, and the plantation houses at Farmington, Poplar Forest and Barboursville [8.24].[17] Comparison of Jefferson's elevation drawing [8.7] with another colonial adaptation of the double-story pedimented porch at Drayton Hall, near Charleston, South Carolina [1.5], shows the sophistication and inventiveness of Jefferson in comparison with earlier American carpenter-builders.

The utilitarian functions of the basement story are indicated by Jefferson on the ground floor plan [8.6]. The portion under the house and the south (left) terrace accommodates storage and preparation of food, the kitchen being placed at the angle under the pavilion. The north side is assigned to the stables and a room for the servants. (Neither wing, however, was built in the first campaign at Monticello; a sketch plan for insurance made in 1800 does not yet show them.) Jefferson concealed a dumb-waiter in the dining room mantelpiece to bring food and drink from the house basement to the dining room on the north. He was intent on keeping servants out of sight as much as possible.

The utility areas are linked by a vaulted corridor lit by penetrations on one side in the fashion of the ancient *cryptoporticus*, a device frequently employed in Roman villas, and described in Pliny's letter on his Laurentine villa (see above, p. 54). The corridor extended only to the angles, because the slope of the hill made it possible for the north and south arms to be open to the exterior.

The construction of the first Monticello design continued throughout the 1770s, though at a reduced pace during the Revolutionary years, and the house (except for the service wings) was substantially finished at the time Jefferson left to take up his post as Minister to France in 1784. The five years spent in Paris gave him his first experience of the ancient Roman monuments of southern France and of recent French and English architecture that he had known only through books. He was already an exceptionally accomplished horticulturist, as indicated by his identification of plant materials in the Monticello garden scheme of 1772 [*8.18*], and he visited England in the spring of 1786 primarily to make an extended tour of the best-known gardens, an experience that greatly influenced his approach to landscape design.[18] On his one trip to Italy, in 1787, he did not, surprisingly, take time to study the architecture: he was intent on gathering information on the cultivation of high quality rice in Piedmont and Lombardy, which he was eager to promote in the southern states of America. His notes from the visit are concerned exclusively with that matter, except for one, which remarks that "the Cathedral of Milan is a worthy object of philosophical contemplation, to be placed among the rarest instances of the misuse of money. On viewing the churches of Italy it is evident without calculation that the same expense would have sufficed to throw the Apennines into the Adriatic and thereby render it terra ferma from Leghorn to Constantinople."[19]

One day's travel would have brought him to the center of Palladio's activity, but he did not take the opportunity. Palladio's own buildings—apart from his studies of Roman monuments and his canon of the orders—may no longer have held Jefferson's interest; his architectural encounters were transforming him from a neo-Palladian into a neoclassicist. He confided his new passions in a letter written from Nîmes in 1787 to Mme de Tessé: "Here I am, Madam, gazing whole hours at the Maison quarée [the Republican Roman temple], like a lover at his mistress," and further on, "While at Paris, I was violently smitten with the Hôtel de Salm [*8.11*; under construction at the time], and used to go to the Thuileries almost daily to look at it."[20] Apart from what this unveiled transference of amorous engagement to architecture implies about Jefferson's inner life, it effectively emphasizes the intensity of his interest in the field. On his return to Monticello in 1794, following a brief and stormy period as Secretary of State in Washington's cabinet, Jefferson began to make studies for a radical reconstruction and enlargement of the house: his fame and his circle of acquaintances had grown to the point that his retreat had become a place of pilgrimage, and larger accommodations were needed. He finished working drawings by 1796, when he was elected Vice President, which again drew him away. Yet in March of that year he wrote, "I am now engaged in

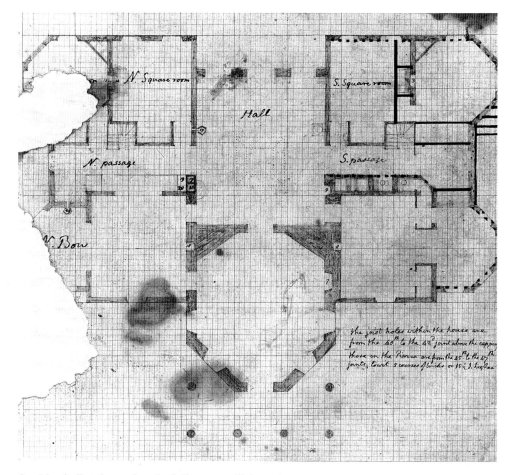

8.9 Monticello: plan project, by Jefferson, 1796? (K.150)

taking down the upper story of my house and building it on the ground so as to spread all of my rooms on one floor; we shall this summer live under the tent of heaven."[21] Though he had hoped to have the new walls ready for re-roofing by winter, he was disappointed. Yet early in 1798 he suggested to his daughter Martha that "the south pavillion, the parlor and study will accommodate your family."[22] The north side was not covered until 1801, when Jefferson's election to the presidency again kept him from attending to Monticello.

The plan of the revised Monticello is preserved in a drawing on squared paper, which Jefferson began to use on his return to France [8.9].[23] It adds to the entrance side of the house a block of approximately the same form and size as the existing one, with a corridor running the length of the building, dividing the old from the new. In this eastern tract a "Hall" echoes the parlor, and guest rooms reflect the dining room and the master's suite. The bedrooms are given bed-alcoves, a Parisian feature that caught Jefferson's fancy; in his own room, the alcove separates the dressing area from the study and is open on either side to invite the summer breezes, and to improve the light and the view in both spaces. The projections of the new bedroom alcoves leave little space in the central corridor for the two stairways; they are inconvenient to use, but Jefferson felt that they should be as inconspicuous as the staircase halls of the Tidewater mansions were grand.

The original house was significantly changed only by the blocking in of the eastern side of the parlor to complete the octagonal form and to give support to the dome which was now to rise over this area. The new plan ingeniously segregates the private areas from the public by assigning the broad central spine plus the dining room and "North Bow" to communal use, and sealing off each bedroom from its neighbor. There are four bedrooms and two other rooms on the floor above; the two sides of this floor are separated by the hall, and Jefferson joined them by a balcony over the entrance to the parlor.

Though it is not obvious from the plan, the new design represented a radical shift in style inspired by contact with contemporary French architecture. The building actually has three floors (the third being the level of the dome room over the parlor), but it appears from the exterior to have only a main floor and a mezzanine. On the entrance facade [8.10] the windows of the lower and upper levels of bedrooms are fused together and both are below the entablature, so that they seem to belong to the same floor (the third floor is quite obscured by a balustrade); this makes the upper bedrooms less

8.10 Monticello: entrance (east) facade

8.11 Hôtel de Salm, Paris, by Antoine Rousseau, 1783

agreeable, as the windows are small and reach only from just above the floor to well below eye level. Jefferson had written from Paris:

> All the new and good houses are of a single story. This is of the height of 16. or 18.f generally, and the whole of it given to rooms of entertainment; but in the parts where there are bedrooms they have two tiers of them from 8. to 10. f. high each, with a small private staircase. By this means great staircases are avoided, which are expensive and occupy a space which would make a good room in every story.[24]

The Hôtel de Salm, by Antoine Rousseau [8.11] which so engaged Jefferson, exemplifies the new style; its impact is still more evident on the garden facade of Monticello [1.26] where the drum with roundel windows and the low dome figure prominently. The octagonal saucer dome over the parlor is not in the tradition of Palladio's Rotonda [4.18] and Burlington's Chiswick [6.4], cubic buildings in which the dome covers a circular central hall at the core. It follows French tradition in being at the exterior of one of the long sides of a rectangular building, surmounting a projecting salon of the same form as the drum (the interior of the dome is not, however, like its predecessors, visible from the ground floor; the parlor has a ceiling of the same height as the rooms on either side, and a second floor at the base of the drum makes a "dome room" for which Jefferson never found a use). Jefferson's treatment of the theme remained in the pure classical tradition: it did not assimilate the refinements of contemporary Parisian architecture.

The garden side has no mezzanine because the public rooms and the master suite rise to the height of the exterior entablature. This allowed the windows of all these rooms to be extended downward to floor level—an innovation, also inspired by Parisian practice, that was to lend elegance and light to many domestic buildings of the two ensuing generations in America.

Despite importations from abroad, the second Monticello was a building of individuality and strict elegance. The home-made bricks and detailing in white painted wood carved on the site inevitably distanced the building from European models, as homespun differed from imported silks.

The interior was designed in the first years of the new century, though Jefferson's eight years as President (1801–09) caused protracted delays in construction. With the painting of the major rooms in 1809, Monticello reached nearly its present state. The interior design demonstrates Jefferson's scholarship, in its detailing, his backwoods inventiveness in its mechanical conveniences and gadgetry, and his catholic acquisitiveness in its furnishings. It has engaging qualities, particularly in the lighting, the views out from the windows, and the detailing, but the public rooms and master bedroom are too lofty and awkwardly proportioned, and the private ones too cramped.

Jefferson's notebook of the 1770s shows that he meant the decoration of the main rooms to be an illustration of the full canon of ancient orders according to Palladio's First Book.[25] Corinthian was used in the parlor since, according to the Vitruvian

8.12 Monticello: south terrace and house

tradition, it was the most elegant and festive order, but otherwise Jefferson probably did not try to apply them symbolically. In the new design, however, Palladio no longer commanded; Jefferson turned to the more accurate reproductions of ancient Roman details in Fréart de Chambray's *Parallèle* (annotating certain plates of his copy with the designation of rooms in which they were to be used) and Desgodets's *Edifices antiques de Rome*. The detailing was no longer to be generically classical but was to reproduce the decoration of specific buildings: for example, the Temple of Fortuna Virilis in Rome for the bedroom, that of Antoninus and Faustina for the hall, and the Baths of Diocletian for the north piazza. Jefferson made chaste and elegant line drawings for all the entablatures and cornices;[26] the decorative friezes he had carved directly from the book plates [*8.14, 15*]. Master joiners were brought from Philadelphia to do the work. The mantel of the dining room, with its three up-to-date blue-ground Wedgwood medallions, is an exception to the pervasive Romanism. Jefferson was otherwise cool toward the Greek Revival taste represented by the Wedgwood pieces; in fact, he set them in a frame of relief urns, probably carved on the site, that are slightly discordant in style.

The hall is the heart of circulation in Jefferson's scheme [*8.13*]: it gives access to and from the exterior, the public rooms and master bedroom, the narrow corridors that serve the bedrooms and constricted stairways on both floors, and the public privy. Because it rises the full height of the ground floor and the mezzanine, communication between the upper bedrooms on either side is provided by a ponderous and visually disruptive balcony cantilevered over the east end. The hall functioned also as a museum for the display not just of art works but, in the longstanding tradition of the European

8.13 Monticello: hall

8.14 Monticello: parlor

8.15 Monticello: interior entablature

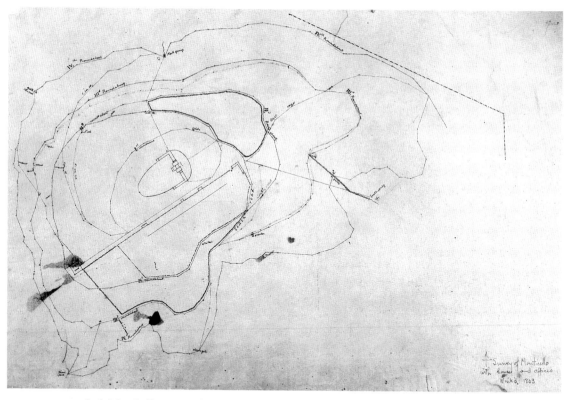

8.16 Monticello: estate plan, by Jefferson, 1803

Wunderkammer, of Indian relics, fossils, stuffed animal heads, and mementos of the Lewis and Clark expedition which first explored the American Northwest. The eighteen paintings and sculptures, imported from Europe, were partly original French, Italian and Netherlandish works and partly copies. Jefferson did not believe that the agrarian society of the new nation should take up the figurative arts, and wrote that while "architecture is among the most important arts [and] it is desireable to introduce taste into an art which shows so much," painting and statuary are "too expensive for the state of wealth among us. It would be useless, therefore, and preposterous, for us to make ourselves connoisseurs in those arts. They are worth seeing, but not studying."[27]

Monticello is an eloquent affirmation of a committed and cultivated way of life. Its situation in the wilderness, the practicality of its arrangements and its independence from the prevailing pretentiousness of colonial architectural forms reveal a will to find an architectural expression for the ideals of a new democracy. Its reaffirmation of ancient classical authority as seen through the interpretations of Palladio and later theorists and its selection of the freshest contemporary innovations from French buildings and English books reveal an aspiration to give American design a cosmopolitan outlook informed by immersion in the classical heritage.

The siting of Monticello, at the crown of a steep forested hill and not in easy reach of the river port, was unique among Virginia plantation houses [*8.16, 17*]. It must have

8.17 Monticello: prospect from the hilltop

been chosen for its isolation and its command of natural vistas. In inviting Maria Cosway to visit in 1786, Jefferson wrote of "our own dear Monticello, where has nature spread so rich a mantle under the eye? mountains, forests, rocks, rivers. With what majesty do we there ride above the storms! How sublime to look down into the workhouse of nature, to see her clouds, hail, snow, rain, thunder, all fabricated at our feet! And the glorious sun, when rising as if out of a distant water, just gilding the tops of the mountains, and giving life to all nature!"[28] Jefferson was surely influenced both by Burke's aesthetic of the sublime and the beautiful and by Palladio's description of the setting of his Villa Rotonda near Vicenza as a "theater"—suggested by the fact that *monticello* is precisely the word Palladio had used to describe his site.[29] The views outward from the porticoes of the two houses are alike in their panoramic scope [*8.17*].

Jefferson intended from the start to coordinate his design of the house and its environment on this privileged height. The earliest site plans set the house on an artificially leveled plane with a long east–west axis. His initial proposal, preceding the first house designs, envisaged a great unbroken rectangle of dependencies on the perimeter of which Jefferson drew the small square pavilions to the north and south. On the opposite side of the same sheet he drew, in 1772, a site plan with the house in the final form of the first campaign [*8.18*].[30] Now the strict rectangularity remains only in the dependent wings; the garden borders curve casually. This plan is informal but it is not

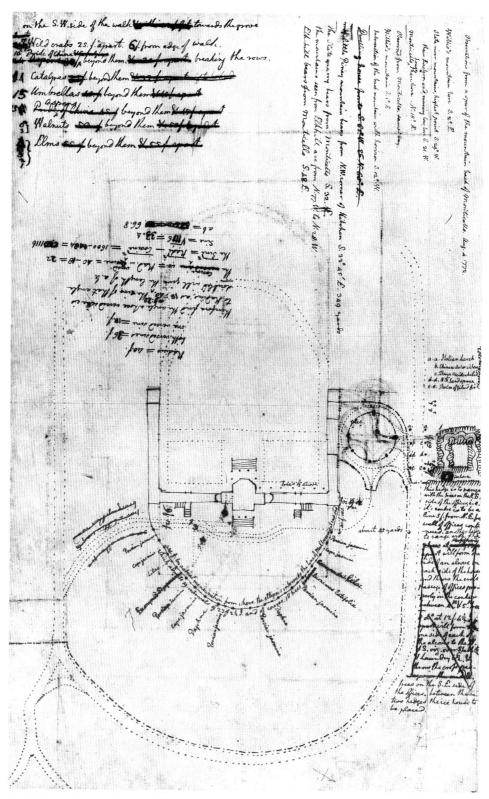

8.18 Monticello: site plan, by Jefferson, 1772 (K.34)

yet an English landscape garden; the forms may come rather, as Karl Lehmann suggested, from the ancient Roman hippodrome garden (designed in imitation of a racetrack) that constituted part of the larger ancient villas; Pliny described the one at Tusci (above, pp. 55–56). Perhaps the circular structure outside the northern wing in the drawing is based on the aviary described by the Roman agronomist Varro.[31] The notes written along the eastern arc show that even before completing the design of the house, Jefferson was fixing the species of perennial to be planted: jasmine, daphne, lilac.

That Jefferson was aware of modern English landscaping before his European travels, however, is confirmed by a long memorandum inserted into his account book of 1771, in which he contemplates selecting two sites on the property to be treated with evocative associative imagery.[32] One, a cemetery for the family and servants, in an "unfrequented vale in the park . . . among antient and venerable oaks, . . . gloomy evergreens," was to be circular in form; "in the center of it erect a small Gothic temple of antique appearance." The other involved a spring on the north side of the park, which was to be utilized either by diverting it over a cascade to a temple of which "the roof may be Chinese, Grecian or in the taste of the Lantern of Demosthenes at Athens" or, preferably, by excavating a grotto around it. Either design would have focused on the statue of a sleeping nymph, obviously a reproduction of the ancient *Ariadne* first exhibited in a villa fountain at the Vatican Belvedere, and copied in innumerable other villas, notably at Stourhead, and furnished with the same anonymous inscription: "Huius nympha loci, sacri custodia fontis/Dormio . . ." (Jefferson suggests—probably because of the gratuitous "grot"—that Pope's English translation would be more suitable for the grotto version: "Nymph of the grot, these sacred springs I keep . . ."[33]) Jefferson also mentions vistas and "seats at spots on walks most interesting for the prospect or immediate scenery," and again, "the canvas at large must be a grove of largest trees"—typical statements of English protagonists of picturesque landscape design. Jefferson's adaptation seems a rather superficial effort to keep up with the latest fashion, of which the writer had not yet had first-hand experience, and the projects were not realized.

After returning from Europe and from his tour of the great landscape gardens of England, Jefferson wrote three pages of "General ideas for the improvement of Monticello," which show a continuing interest in associative ornamental structures.[34] At the lower edge of the garden he proposes to set four boxes in the form of models of a Gothic building, the Pantheon, "cubic" architecture (the temple at Nîmes) and "A specimen of Chinese." Again he proposes a Gothic structure for the cemetery, and notes the sources in his library from which it is to be copied in stone. Greek art makes another appearance with the proposal of a reproduction of the Choragic Monument of Lysicrates from Stuart and Revett's *Antiquities of Athens*.

Several of Jefferson's drawings for ornamental garden buildings are preserved.[35] The first are temples copied from the plates of James Gibbs; later, around 1778, he sketched several others, based on an amalgam of models from his library, the most striking of which is an observation tower crowned with crenellations in the medieval style [8.19], which was quite unprecedented in American architecture, though an "Arthurian" tower of this type had been built on a hilltop at Stourhead [7.21]. Jefferson never realized any of these fantasies; they were, in fact, alien to his utilitarian inclination. And,

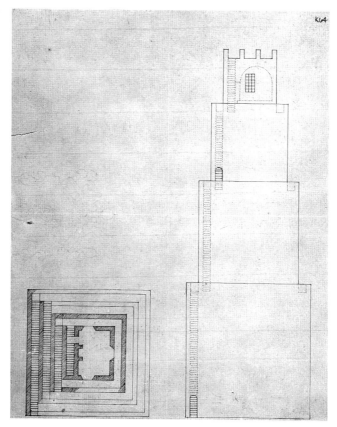

8.19 Monticello: project for
a garden tower, by Jefferson,
before 1779

unlike the English garden enthusiasts who inspired his temple schemes, he had no overall plan within which his structures would create a poetic narrative sequence. His projected small-scale reproductions of historic monuments would merely have translated into three dimensions a sequence of illustrative plates from a typical model book.

Anyhow, Jefferson cared more for planting than for such conceits; it is astonishing to discover in his *Garden Book* and horticultural correspondence the passion with which he pursued the search for new and improved flowering plants, vegetables and fruits, and the extent of his knowledge of their cultivation and of his desire to increase that knowledge through study and experiment. Horticulture remained an urgent concern even during his service as Secretary of State and President.

Soon after his tour of English landscape gardens in 1786, perhaps while he was still in France, he drew on coordinate paper a new plan for the grounds adjacent to the house [*8.20*].[36] (The house outlined on this plan is deeper than in the definitive design.) It shows the English influence in its serpentine paths enclosing an extended lawn, and in the oval pond and beds for flowering plants (the numbered horizontal lines seem to be intended to assist the executors in laying out the lawn). A note of 1808 on the drawing suggests that the project was about to be implemented at that time, toward the close of Jefferson's second presidential term. It did not supersede the one devised before the

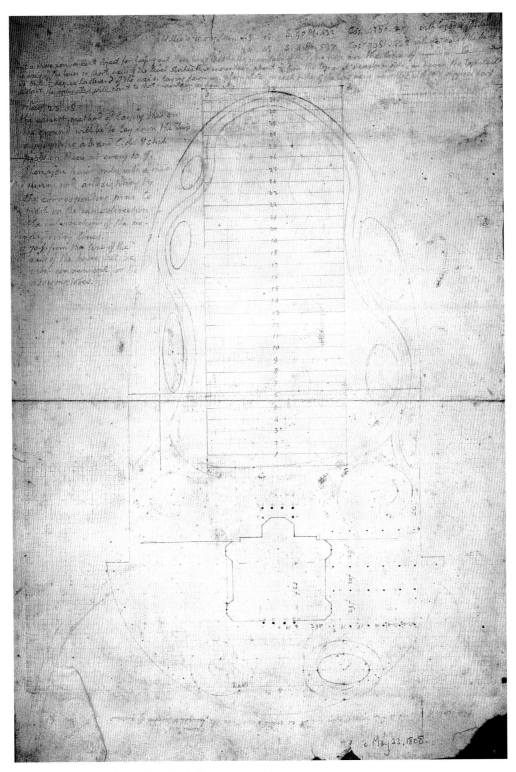

8.20 Monticello: garden project, by Jefferson, *c.* 1786–89

European trip [*8.18*], but is inscribed within the area defined there between the hemicycle east of the house and the ovular terminus at the west. With these changes, Monticello became the first American *ferme ornée* on the model of the Leasowes of Shenstone, whose writings on landscape gardening became a major source of inspiration for Jefferson. As Jefferson noted after visiting the Leasowes, Shenstone's efforts to combine a passion for design with farming had led him to financial collapse.

Jefferson was much more successful as a horticulturist than he was as a farmer: he was also permanently in debt because of the poor yield from his estates. This was due both to his frequent and extended absences (to engage in "the disgusting dish of politics") and to his inexperience in farming, an art better learned in practice than in books. Writing to his son-in-law in 1793 for advice on crop rotation, he admitted: "I am too little familiar with the practice of farming to rely with confidence on my own judgment."[37] Though he identified and imported a superior threshing machine and invented an improved plow, and though he enjoyed the economic advantage of slave labor, he could not develop successful crops to replace tobacco, which destroyed the soil and, as he wrote in *Notes on the State of Virginia*, "is a culture productive of infinite wretchedness."[38]

Yet agriculture was the keystone of Jefferson's social and ethical convictions.[39] He believed that the strength of the new democracy derived from the small freehold farmer and that the practice of farming kept men honest, vigorous and independent. The goal of his life at Monticello was not merely to enjoy the traditional escape from the tensions of the city, but to affirm his belief that labor in the earth gives health and moral strength. He did what he could through legislation to discourage the enlargement of estates, which he associated with the privileged societies of Europe. The quotation at the head of this chapter shows how earnestly he sought to maintain an almost exclusively agrarian nation (ninety percent of Americans were then farmers), though eventually piracy and enemy action at sea forced him to admit the need for home industry and artisanry.

During the forty years in which Monticello spasmodically evolved into its final form, Jefferson took on many other architectural projects. More than five hundred of his drawings for public and private buildings are recorded in the catalogue of Frederick Nichols. In the last years of his life, from 1805 on, Jefferson was occupied intensely in the most influential design of his career, the physical and academic planning of the University of Virginia at Charlottesville, on a site within a view of Monticello. And throughout his career he designed dwellings in the villa tradition for himself, his friends and occasionally for the state and federal government.

Among those in the last group, his unsuccessful competition submission for the President's house in Washington [*8.21*], of 1792, was an enlarged and revised version of Palladio's Villa Rotonda, as altered in the English edition of Palladio's Four Books [*6.16*], a project ill-suited to full-time residence (he had earlier proposed a similar scheme for the Governor's Palace in Richmond).[40] This rather submissive return to Palladio after Jefferson's European sojourn is inconsistent with the evolution of his ideas for Monticello, but perhaps he thought that a Palladian design would be more likely to meet general approval than one more congenial to his personal taste, which might have betrayed too much of the flavor of England or France.

8.21 Jefferson, project for the President's house, 1792 (K.126)

Jefferson designed at least seven more country houses between 1798 and 1817, the majority of which were variations on the Monticello scheme. Only Bremo, some thirty miles from Monticello, which its owner General John Cocke designed in 1816 with assistance from Jefferson, survives intact [8.22, 23]. Bremo is exceptional for the refined Palladian proportions of its rooms, modeled on those of the Villa Emo at Fanzolo [1.26]. It was in response to Cocke's initial project that Jefferson had commented that Palladio "was the Bible."[41] The elevations, however, are closer to Monticello in style, though not in composition. There is no dome, and there are temple porticoes at the front and two sides, while at the rear the slope of the site is used to provide an additional floor below the entrance level and wings extending from it and terminating in temple pavilions [8.23]. The projecting octagonal room, which became the hallmark of Jefferson's later architecture, is lacking at Bremo. The owner may have rejected it, preferring to adhere more strictly to Palladio, as implied in a letter from a friend who reported Jefferson's criticisms: "He [Jefferson] is a great advocate of light and air; as you predicted he was for giving you octagons. They were charming. They give you a semicircle of air and light."[42]

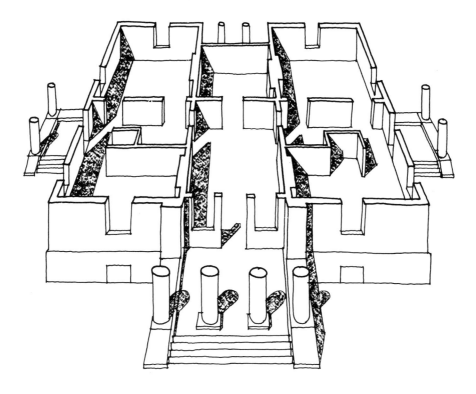

8.22, 23 Bremo, by John Cocke with advice from Jefferson, 1816: relief plan of the house, and view from the rear

In one house, Poplar Forest, a small retreat of 1804–06, Jefferson's taste for octagons produced the first of many thousands of octagonal houses built in America throughout the nineteenth century [*8.24A*].[43] A square central dining area, lit from high overhead, was surrounded by four similar polygons; the stairs were enclosed in projecting shafts on either side. Poplar Forest, for all of its light and air, must have been inconvenient, like all excessively rational buildings: nearly every room was a passageway, either to other rooms or to the stairways.

The other houses, Edgehill, designed before 1798 for his daughter, Mrs Thomas Mann Randolph [*8.24B*], Farmington (1803) for George Divers [*8.24C*], and Barbours-ville (1817) for James Barbour [*8.24D*], were variations of the Monticello concept with its projecting octagonal bows. The placement of single-flight stairs along the axis of the transverse corridors suggests that those at Monticello [*8.9*] had proved to be too constricted. The elements of the elevations came from the Monticello design, though in slightly varied arrangements: the roundel windows of the drum of Monticello's dome were employed in Farmington at the mezzanine level; the "Chinese" balustrades that crown the Monticello roof were put just over the cornice at Barboursville. But altogether these "villas" confirm the innovations of Monticello in a style that gives classical elegance and modern comfort to dwellings of modest scale.

The social and economic setting of Monticello and its progeny was unique in post-Renaissance villa history in two discordant ways: it was rooted in slavery yet committed to democracy. Jefferson, unlike most contemporaries of his class, grasped the paradox. Though he believed black people to be intellectually inferior, he vigorously opposed slavery, attempted—almost successfully—to outlaw it, and hastened his financial ruin by refusing to sell his slaves, fearing they would be mistreated (there was no legal way to free them).[44] He was a populist by conviction and a patrician in fact, and his singular political distinctions made it additionally difficult for him to escape the consequences of this contradiction, if escape were possible.

Monticello reflects this situation in its curious mixture of simplicity and elegance. It is both intimate and grand, and it was designed to hide (from the proprietor as well as from visitors) the evidence of its large cohort of servants: extensive quarters for the storage and preparation of food not only are sealed off from the dwelling, communicating only by dumb-waiter, but are concealed in subterranean chambers disguised externally as the support of the terraces for strolling. Jefferson's projects for his estate revealed the same ambiguity as they ranged from the earthy practicality of planning the optimal use of fields for cultivation and of extensive kitchen gardens and service buildings to the fantasy of Gothic temples or a stylish artificial grotto.

Yet the social underpinning of the villa culture throughout the centuries was more consistent than that of any other social manifestation in Western society over the same period. Religious or governmental structures and their environments varied, often radically, with major changes in faith and in political leadership. But the builders of country houses remained members of the patriciate with a large workforce at their disposal, whether of peasants, cheap and immobile farm labor, or slaves. They had the means to engage in large-scale agriculture while providing luxurious and elegantly appointed homes with all the comforts of city mansions. Sometimes, as in the case of Cato or Jefferson, the proprietor would be himself a working farmer proud of the dirt on

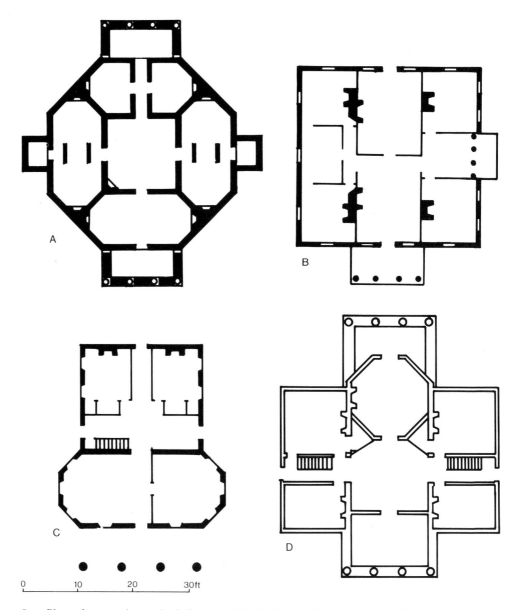

8.24 Plans of country houses by Jefferson: (A) Poplar Forest, 1804–06; (B) Edgehill, designed before 1798; (C) Farmington, 1803; (D) Barboursville, 1817

his hands; at other times he would be a fine gentleman who surveyed his estate dressed in silks and mounted on a fine Arabian steed, like the patrons of Palladio or the sitters for Thomas Gainsborough portraits; but still the similarities would have been more marked than the differences. The privileged classes shared the literary culture of Roman antiquity: Virgil's *Georgics* and Horace's country poems surely played their role in holding them all together.

Later, the tradition proved strong enough to weather the anticlassical storm of Romanticism; the villas turned Gothic without essentially altering the environments in which they were set or their social role, except that ultimately, through outside causes, the laborers were freed, proprietorship became accessible to the middle class, and villas could be wooden structures perched on half an acre of suburban property. Jefferson felt close to those ancient urbanized Romans who spoke of life in the country; he absorbed their legacy both directly by reading their works and indirectly through the study of intervening inheritors of the villa ideology such as Palladio and the English Palladians of the generation preceding his. Like all of these, Jefferson distrusted urban life and its industrial underpinnings and associated moral uprightness with working the land or at least benefiting from fresh air and exercise. Also like these, he associated country life with a closer family relationship than the city could provide and with the possibility of entertaining and conversing with one's friends. He shared with these forebears an ethic as well as an ideology of country life.

In the 1820s the first rumblings of the social evolution that brought the change about may have been partly responsible for the fact that Jefferson was unable to live on the ideology of the villa and died in bankruptcy. But his demeaning financial failure was due also to the fact that he didn't live his fantasy wholeheartedly enough. Fortunately for all of us, he was too much of a Renaissance man to spend his life making his properties profitable; he was absent for long periods, he was so much a public figure that streams of visitors and outside events constantly called his attention away from the realization of his agricultural ambitions, and, alas, he was a bad manager. These problems were compounded by the fact that Virginia's most profitable crop, tobacco, devastated the land rapidly and created a depression throughout the South. And, unlike the Romans, the Venetians or the British aristocrats who preceded him, Jefferson had no alternative sources of income. But his greatness, even as an architect, let alone as a father of his country, was sufficient to overshadow the misfortunes of his personal fate.

9.1 Richard Payne Knight, the estate as designed by Capability Brown (the "beautiful") and Payne Knight himself (the "picturesque"), from *The Landscape*, 1794

9 · The Picturesque

This chapter is intended to be not so much an autonomous study as a bridge between Jefferson and Andrew Jackson Downing—a theoretical bridge constructed to span the chasm that separated the classical from the romantic consciousness. And just as Monticello cannot be understood without reflecting on the European buildings and books that inspired it, so the appreciation of the villas published and promoted by Downing leads to a transatlantic, though now exclusively English, past.

Patrons and designers at the height of the Palladian vogue in eighteenth-century England had been able to set a strictly classical building into an apparently casually arranged environment without sensing any disharmony. The villa and its garden suggested to them two aspects of nature, the one representing the logic governing the workings of the universe, which could be expressed mathematically, and the other representing the random and fecund outcome of biological growth and geological evolution, which is not reducible to law or number. The distinction had been recognized since the Renaissance, when the first was defined as *Natura naturans* and the second as *Natura naturata*. But Renaissance and Baroque estates had been designed with gardens that mirrored the formality and regularity of their palaces; the informal English garden was radically new.

The English garden was stimulated by an appreciation on the part of literati, notably Shaftesbury and Addison, of raw nature—an awareness that the experience of rugged, awesome or overwhelming natural phenomena might have positive value (see Chapter 6). Edmund Burke took this further, and proposed a new aesthetic category, the "sublime," as a complement to the "beautiful." The first stirrings of interest in psychology, especially in the philosophy of Shaftesbury's friend John Locke, had helped to stimulate this expanse of perception, drawing attention away from objects of observation toward their effect upon the observer. Initially nobody had wanted to pursue the implications of this change because to give full value to the response of the individual psyche would have been to undermine the eternal laws and truths of the classical tradition. So the early theorists of the informal garden attempted to show that it had the authority of ancient precedent: Castell's *Villas of the Ancients* traced it, as we have seen (pp. 168–69), to Pliny's description of his villa at Tusci [7.7]. And landscape designers filled their informal gardens with ancient temples, statuary and inscriptions [7.10, 11, 21], following learned literary programs that could be interpreted only through familiarity with classical texts.

But in fact an informal garden represented the antithesis of classical principles: it could not follow rational proportions nor be judged by absolute standards. Anybody had the right to make or to evaluate a landscape design according to his own taste. Individual expression and feeling might supersede rule (an awareness that dawned in contemporary discussions of literature and painting as well). From the perspective of the classical tradition, this license opened Pandora's box, and with hindsight we can see that it was the essential precondition for romanticism and modernism. Such a radical concept was unlikely to be physically initiated in a traditionally established art such as architecture or painting. It found a fertile ground in landscape design, which previously had been considered ancillary to architecture.[1]

The idea of a villa as distinct from a country house developed gradually in harmony with the vogue for Palladian architecture in the first half of the eighteenth century in England (see Chapter 6). Toward the close of the century there began an unprecedented outpouring of literature on villa building of all kinds that lasted well into the Victorian era.[2] The phenomenon was closely linked with the social structure, and shows—as does the literature of the period—the extraordinary preoccupation of the educated segment of British society of this time with domestic life in the country, to the virtual exclusion of other architectural interests, whether urban, religious, public or commercial. The villa was perceived as one instrument by which the middle class might emulate and challenge the privilege of the aristocracy and gentry, and the design of villas in this period began to mirror the spirit of liberation from social tradition and rule.

The change was accompanied, and to some degree accelerated, by the theoretical concerns of critics and the new aestheticians. Aesthetics, in fact, was a discipline born at this very moment, when focus on the inward response to external stimuli first made the evaluation of works of art a problematic issue. This focus represented a shift of fortune in the longstanding battle in critical circles between the Ancients and the Moderns. The Ancients, guardians of the classical tradition, had been represented in architectural practice by Lord Burlington and his Palladian followers and in theory by Colen Campbell, Robert Morris and others of that circle. Their authority rested on the claim that the classical style represented not simply a venerable tradition but the very laws of nature. The Moderns whom they attacked were the representatives of English Baroque, notably Wren, Vanbrugh and Hawksmoor.

By mid-century Palladianism had waned, and interest in the Baroque style as well; now the Moderns embraced even exotic styles—Gothic, Chinese—and generally sought opportunities for invention free of the constricting rules of the classical orders and proportions. The change was fostered by a concept of artistic genius that encouraged the individual artist to seek inspired invention without regard for the conventions of established practice. Even designers like Robert and James Adam, who continued to turn for inspiration to the ancient world, looked backward from a new perspective. The introduction to the first volume of their *Works in Architecture* (1778) boasts that "we have not trod the path of others, nor derived aid from their labors." And their view of the authority of antiquity is pointedly anti-canonical:

> The great masters of antiquity . . . varied their proportions as the general spirit of the composition required, clearly perceiving, that however necessary these rules may be to form the taste and correct the licentiousness of the scholar, they often cramp the genius and circumscribe the ideas of the master.[3]

The nature to which the Ancients had appealed for its eternal laws had become a nature of individual imagination and experience. This represented the initial step toward the modern view of art and artistic creation.

In first formulating the design for Monticello, Jefferson depended on the books of Gibbs, Palladio and the English Palladians, and, like the Palladians, he planned to set his villa into an informal garden [8.20; cf. 7.6, 8] with architectural incidents such as a grotto and a medieval watch tower. But after the mid-eighteenth century in Britain the taste for locating a strictly rational architecture in a picturesque landscape setting shifted rapidly. Now buildings themselves began to reflect the irregularity and allusiveness of nature. By 1789 William Gilpin, the most influential theorist of the picturesque, would write—addressing painters:

> A piece of Palladian architecture may be elegant in the last degree. . . . But if we introduce it in a picture it immediately becomes a formal object and ceases to please. Should we wish to give it picturesque beauty we must use the mallet . . . we must beat down one half of it, deface the other and throw the mutilated members around in heaps. In short, from a *smooth* building we must turn it into a rough *ruin*. No painter, who had the choice of the two objects, would hesitate which to chuse.[4]

The initial step toward a greater naturalism in landscape design was taken by Lancelot ("Capability") Brown, who had worked as William Kent's associate at Stowe. Brown cast off the heavy literary–allegorical burden of earlier parks and the formal terraces that had separated the house from the grounds. His extended stretches of lawn that began at the very doors of the house, and were relieved by rounded trees and shrubs in scattered clumps, were virtually indistinguishable from the natural landscape, though they seemed tamer and less varied. Brown designed and modernized innumerable country estates, and by the end of the century his work became the focus of a vigorous and sometimes acrimonious theoretical debate. The controversy was sparked by three written works of 1794—the essays of two gentlemen-scholars who were more concerned with principles than with practice, Uvedale Price's *Essay on the Picturesque* and Richard Payne Knight's poem *The Landscape*, and the first of many manuals on landscape design by Brown's disciple and defender Humphrey Repton, *Sketches and Hints on Landscape Gardening*.[5]

Only a society deeply involved in the collection and connoisseurship of paintings and in the planning of country houses (in which the art collections were normally housed) and parks would have attempted to divert architectural and landscape design into the emulation of pictures. The renewed effort to articulate an aesthetic of the picturesque was prompted by the realization that one factor in the blandness of Brownian landscape design was a lack of definition of the concept. Anything could be picturesque that resembled a landscape painting of one of the admired seventeenth-century masters.[6] A major stimulus to the reformulation was Edmund Burke's influential book of 1757, *A Philosophical Enquiry into the Origin of Our Ideas of the Sublime and Beautiful*, which alerted his generation to a possible alternative to classical aesthetics. Burke's "beautiful" encompassed classical equilibrium and order and their effects—restfulness, smoothness, rationality. His "sublime" described in a favorable light the more violent aesthetic states experienced in nature such as the awe, terror, or solitude prompted by forests, chasms, wastes, stormy seas and the like. Burke was the first philosopher to grant these feelings and the artistic expression of them not just a positive value, but one on an equal footing with those engendered by the art of the classical tradition.[7] Burke's position had been anticipated by interpreters of the landscapes of Salvator Rosa and Jacob van Ruysdael, by certain passages of Shaftesbury, and above all by Addison—especially *Pleasures of the Imagination*, of 1712 (see above, pp. 160ff.). That Burke could define astonishment as "the most lofty state of the soul" was another indication of a break from the secure social and intellectual structures of the past.

Burke's "sublime" was to have an impact on literature and painting, but it was poorly adapted to architectural and landscape design because, as Uvedale Price pointed out, it involved responses to a natural environment that could not readily be built or planted. Price and Knight therefore set about reformulating the concept of the "picturesque" so that it might merge with aspects of the sublime relevant to the arts of design and constitute, like the sublime, an antithesis or complement to the beautiful.[8] This redefined picturesque isolated the irregular, intricate, and contrasting aspects of landscape pictures; in Price's words, "the two opposite qualities of roughness and of sudden variation, joined to that of irregularity, are the most efficient causes of the picturesque." Price would have the designer shun the uniform and regular; the worst building would be a block in the form of a brick. Color "may be harsh, glaring, tawdry yet please many eyes, and by some be called beautiful: but a muddy colour, no one ever was pleased with." More affective elements of the picturesque included the appearance of advanced age, neglect and decay. Knight provided a vivid image of the contrast of the beautiful and the picturesque in a pair of illustrations to his poem of 1794 [*9.1*], the one showing an estate with a classical house in a park in the style of Capability Brown, and the other the same site with an Elizabethan mansion in a rugged and unkempt setting.

The optimum architectural realization of picturesqueness, however, was not such a stately palace but the vinecovered thatched cottage, which embodied all the essential traits, and which was to exert a great influence on villa design.[9] The admission of vernacular architecture into the canon of approved styles was a sign of the lessening dependence on authority and of a momentous change in the attitude toward tradition. The acceptance of the cottage, and the actual design of cottages, sometimes called *fermes ornées*, with the intention to create picturesqueness, was soon to be followed by that of the Italian villa and the Swiss chalet. It was essentially an aestheticized version of the traditional farmhouse and its ancillary buildings; the French label indicates the origin of the concept and recalls a celebrated example, the "Hameau" built by Marie Antoinette in the park of Versailles in 1783–86. The paradigm of the villa shifted from the refinement of the Palladian country house to the humble dwelling of the laborer within a generation. That change represented a revolution as much in social attitudes as in aesthetics.

Knight began as a disciple of Price but they parted ways because he could not accept Price's attribution of the quality of picturesqueness to the object of observation.[10] Knight articulated his views in *An Analytical Inquiry into the Principles of Taste* (1805), in which he insisted that it must be supplied by the observer, since only a connoisseur of pictures could recognize what is picturesque (he was himself a collector of landscape

9.2 Downton Castle, by Richard Payne Knight, 1772

drawings by Claude Lorrain). The pleasures of the picturesque, he suggested, derive not simply from observation but from associations stimulated by the object, associations to a lifetime of experiences with pictures and pastoral poetry.[11] He admitted on this account even inconsistencies in style, citing the buildings in paintings by Claude [7.2] which, he believed, represented ancient Roman structures added to by Lombards, Goths and later generations. He also designed his own country house, Downton Castle, with a medieval exterior and a Greco–Roman interior [9.2]. The concept of association, which was already current in the previous generation, moved aesthetics one step further from classical idealism by making the enjoyment of beauty depend on the experience and psychological makeup of the individual observer rather than on absolute qualities of form inherent in the object of observation.[12] But Knight's effort to limit the application of association to the experience of pictures was artificial, because nothing could bar any train of thought from enriching the way objects are seen. The concept of association legitimized an appeal to an almost unlimited range of mental images in the design of gardens and buildings. It allowed the designer to give his work whatever character he believed to be suited to his client, the nature of the setting, or the function of the building.

A short chapter in Thomas Whately's book, *Observations on Modern Gardening* (1770), which Jefferson used as a guide on his tour of English country houses, first defined "character" as a generating component of design allied to association.[13] He must have conceived the idea while writing a book on Shakespeare which emphasized the structural role of the central character in each of the plays. After identifying two lesser types of character in gardens, the emblematical (a sign, such as a statue with an inscription) and the imitative (the reproduction of some scene), he speaks of "original" character, which may be more expressive than beauty alone, since it "affects our sensibility." Character is achieved when forms are "selected and arranged with a design to produce certain expressions; an air of magnificence, or of simplicity, or chearfulness, tranquility or some other general character."

Character, then, is a structuring force quite distinct from that of form—one that induces the observer to focus upon the elements of design through ideas and memories. The process operates affectively, stimulating associations that inevitably differ with each individual: "The power of such characters is not confined to the ideas which the

9.3 Richard Brown, "Norman, Tudor, Grecian and Roman Residences: Their Appropriate Situation and Scenery," from *Domestic Architecture*, 1841

objects immediately suggest, for these are connected to others, which inevitably lead to subjects, far distant perhaps from the original thought, and related to it only in terms of the sensations they exert."[14] Character and association are therefore inseparable: the former stimulates the latter in the individual consciousness.

Though Whately was writing about landscape design, his ideas were no less relevant to architecture. But there was confusion among later theorists on how they were to be applied: some urged designers to emulate in building the nature of the client—sometimes his personality, and sometimes his occupation; some followed Whately in seeing character as the general "genius of the place." The latter approach is illustrated vividly in a plate from Richard Brown's *Domestic Architecture* of 1841[15] [*9.3*], published late in the history of picturesque theory. Here, different characters of landscape are

matched by country houses in styles considered suited to them: Grecian on a flat plain commanded by a distant Greek acropolis; domed Roman on a sloping terrain landscaped in the style of Capability Brown; "Castellated" Norman on an elevated promontory with a sublime declivity; and Tudor at the bend of a river in the shade of casually distributed deciduous trees.

However interpreted, the concepts of character and association gave the observer a crucial role in realizing and validating the aesthetic effect of a design. This challenged the principles, the vocabulary and the system of proportions of the classical architectural tradition, all of which had claimed an absolute value independent of any observer. By granting designers potentialities limited only by the responsiveness of the viewer, character and association opened the whole repertory of the past to current use.

The often vituperative battles waged between Price, Knight and Repton obscured the fact that their goals were essentially similar. The first two started the controversy with their attack on Brown, whom Repton defended.[16] They were gentlemen-scholars (who also argued with each other) and they looked down on Repton as being below them in class and taste while he accused them of being armchair theoreticians who lacked the sobering experience of actually designing and executing parks, gardens and country houses (Repton claimed in his last book to have undertaken more than four hundred commissions). He knew from experience that nature could not literally be made to conform to pictures, and he dismissed the proposition of Price and Knight that ruin and decay contributed to the attractiveness of a landscape or of a building. He insisted that the design of buildings and grounds be based on the particular conditions involved in a commission: the topographical situation and character, the rank and aims of the client.

Though Repton was heir to the tradition of picturesque theory, he avoided reference to pictures and expressed himself in terms of the concepts the theory had articulated—variety, contrast, novelty, and intricacy. This made him a strong partisan of asymmetrical as opposed to classical architecture, and reduced all of architecture to two types: Grecian/horizontal and Gothic/vertical. He favored the Castellated Gothic because it allowed a maximum of variety and irregularity in plan which fostered the play of light and shadow, texture and color, but also because it allowed the most freedom in planning. He avoided emphasis on association and placed comfort, convenience and health above considerations of style.[17] In his emphasis on utility he heralded the practical concerns of nineteenth-century theorists, and prepared the way for the utilitarian approach of John Claudius Loudon.

Because he was not himself an architect, Repton entered into partnership with John Nash for a short period, but it was primarily through his books, attractively illustrated by aquatints from his own watercolors of his projects, that he disseminated his interpretation of the unclassical country house. Repton felt that he was at the end of a great tradition rather than at the start of a new one. He complained with undisguised snobbery that estates were passing out of the hands of the aristocracy and gentry, who had had a fine appreciation of beauty in landscaping, and were falling into the hands of a wealthy middle class concerned only with profit and efficiency. He commiserated with tenant farmers who had lost their livelihoods, and often their dwellings as well, through the Acts of Enclosure obtained by the new landlords (the old ones, he claimed, had cared for their dependants).[18] He disapproved of the proliferation of suburban villas, though

9.4 James Malton, design for a cottage for a shepherd or woodcutter, from *An Essay on British Cottage Architecture*, 1798

he was engaged to design many of them. Paradoxically, this great champion of the *ancien régime* was to become the hero of Loudon, the herald of the villa's democratic age, who celebrated his indebtedness by publishing a one-volume edition of Repton's writings in 1840.

Before discussing Loudon, however, it would be instructive to review the extraordinary outburst of villa publication that began in the last years of the eighteenth century and lasted, after a break during the Napoleonic Wars, to the 1840s. The phenomenon was unique not only in the great number of architectural books offered to the public, but in their almost exclusive engagement with villas, cottages and their gardens: there was no marked increase in the literature on civic or urban domestic architecture, though the dramatic expansion of great urban centers was a widespread consequence of the industrial revolution. The publications for the most part continued the earlier tradition of model-books, in which the text was used primarily as a support to illustrations. They enjoyed the benefits of new inexpensive reproductive techniques such as aquatint, lithography and wood-engraving (see below, pp. 240–41), which helped to make them attractive even to buyers who were not contemplating building.

James Malton was one of the first to adapt the revised concept of the picturesque to the architectural model-book, in *An Essay on British Cottage Architecture* (1798) [9.4].[19] The subtitle reveals its unconventional program:

Being an Attempt to Perpetuate on Principle, that Peculiar Mode of Building, Which was Originally the Effect of Chance. Supported by Fourteen Designs, with their Ichnography, or Plans, Laid Down to Scale; Comprising Dwellings for the Peasant and Farmer, and Retreats

9.5 P. F. Robinson, design for a "Residence in the Style of the Ancient Manor House," from *Designs for Ornamental Villas*, 1827

for the Gentleman; with Various Observations thereon: the Whole extending to Twenty-One Plates, Designed and Executed in Aqua-tinta.

In the preface (entitled "Reflections on the Necessity and Advantage of Temporary Retirement") to a later volume of the same kind, *A Collection of Designs for Rural Retreats, Principally in the Gothic and Castle Styles of Architecture* (1802),[20] Malton recommends to the upper classes the informal cottage and the simple, carefree life of the country laborer: "The wise, the virtuously independent, who prefer the pure and tranquil retirement of the country, to the foetid joys of the tumultuous city, are they who take the most likely means to enjoy that blessing of life, happiness." Some of Malton's designs represent an earnest attempt to grasp the character of the traditional country cottage [9.4], including time-worn stucco walls and decaying half-timbered construction, though their classical proportions—and in some cases classical columns and pediments—contend with the rustic effect.

At first, the production of this new genre of villa book was evenly divided between proponents of (neo-)classical architecture (John Buonarotti Papworth's *Rural Residences* of 1818 and James Thomson's *Retreats* of 1827 are major examples) and of the picturesque, but by the 1830s the latter had gained the upper hand. The most prolific of these was a devotee of the writings of Uvedale Price, Peter Frederic Robinson, who

9.6 P. F. Robinson, perspective view of a gate cottage, from *Rural Architecture, or a Series of Designs for Ornamental Cottages*, 1823

published, between 1823 and 1838, seven books on cottages, farmhouses and villas, and a series of studies of Tudor and Elizabethan mansions, some as monographs for a new supplement to *Vitruvius Britannicus*. Robinson found in the newly developed technique of lithography, which encourages a softening of line and an accentuation of tonal contrasts and textural effects, the ideal medium for conveying pictorial effects. His major contribution was his expansion of the canon of acceptable historical styles. His *Designs for Ornamental Villas* of 1827 [9.5] offers fourteen models in twelve styles (Swiss, Grecian, Palladian, Old English, Castellated, Cottage, Modern Italian, Norman, Henry VII–VIII, Elizabethan, Half-Timber and Tuscan).[21] He designed these villas to be seen from a distance as features of the landscape. "The Old English Style of Building," he writes, "is peculiarly picturesque. The high pointed gable, the mullioned window and wreathed chimney, harmonize most agreeably in scenic situations and produce effects of high interest to the painter . . ."

Robinson must have been a landscape painter manqué; the plans of his houses are assemblages of cells that show no awareness of problems of utility or spatial coherence. A cottage design in another of his books, *Rural Architecture, or a Series of Designs for Ornamental Cottages* (1823) [9.6], is packed with the icons of picturesqueness: a winding, rutted road goes past the door, leading into a village, a stream flows behind, and a tree leans over the house; the irregularity of the building manipulates light and shade. American architecture was pervasively influenced by features illustrated in Robinson's models, particularly by the verandas [9.5], which Robinson calls "Awnings,"[22] and by the scalloped bargeboards of the gables [9.5, 6]. The source of the veranda is elusive; the word—evidently not yet familiar to Robinson—comes from India, and the feature itself appears to have originated in colonial architecture of the seventeenth century.[23]

Because the landscape paintings that had done the most to inspire the aesthetic of the picturesque had been executed in Italy and depicted the Italian countryside (predominantly the Roman Campagna), the buildings depicted or invented in them exerted a powerful influence on architects [7.2]. The "Italian villa" style that began to emerge in the last two decades of the eighteenth century derived more from painted buildings than from actual ones. British architects did not go to Italy to identify and sketch traditional rustic buildings (though Karl Friedrich Schinkel's villas designed for the court of Friedrich Wilhelm III of Prussia were based on actual Italian, mostly Tuscan, prototypes),[24] but picked up the essential motifs from the paintings and

9.7 Cronkhill, by John Nash, *c.* 1802

9.8 Gilbert L. Meason, "Michael Angelo," from *On the Landscape Architecture of the Great Painters of Italy*, 1828

reproductions of them. These include cubic masses asymmetrically composed, round or square towers with open belvederes, stuccoed surfaces and tiled roofs with extended overhangs. They are exemplified in Cronkhill, one of the first examples of the style, by Repton's sometime partner John Nash, designed *c.* 1802 [*9.7*].[25] Some of the earlier nineteenth-century villa books (such as T.F. Hunt's *Architettura Campestre*, of 1827[26]) offered predominantly Italian villa designs, and others, such as Robinson's, usually included at least one.

In 1828, Gilbert L. Meason, in a book called *On the Landscape Architecture of the Great Painters of Italy*,[27] simplified their task by publishing fifty-five lithographic plates reproducing buildings from the backgrounds of Italian paintings by a variety of masters [*9.8*]. Meason's versions homogenized the structures represented by artists of the most diverse styles into a bland Claude-like repertory—to the extent that they are difficult to match with existing pictures—and thus added to the impression that there existed an actual historical source for the Italian villa style.

Loudon was a Scotsman of fabulous energy who carried on an exacting practice and published some seven books on horticulture, architecture, appliances and furnishings and edited at one time or another four journals. He was the first villa and garden specialist to see that the emerging commercial, industrial, professional and laboring classes rather than posing a threat might offer an opportunity—to democratize the villa and to raise the level of taste on a global scale.

The goals of Loudon's publications were radically different from those of his many predecessors. They are stated in the introduction to the one million-word book of 1833 that went into fourteen editions: "The main object of this ENCYCLOPAEDIA OF COTTAGE, FARM, AND VILLA ARCHITECTURE, is to improve the dwellings of the great mass of society, in the temperate regions of both hemispheres: a secondary object is to create and diffuse among mankind, generally, a taste for architectural comforts and beauties."[28] He announced the same program for *The Architectural Magazine*, which he founded in 1834 and which survived for five years. It was the first journal devoted exclusively to architecture and allied fields, and the first to publish essays by Ruskin.[29] Loudon realized that this diffusion could be amplified by innovations in the printing industry, especially the marketing of large editions by publishers (eliminating dependence on Establishment patronage) and the widespread use of wood-engraving (the expanded editions of the *Encyclopaedia* have more than 2,300 illustrations).[30] Loudon separated the villa from its agricultural origins: "*A villa*, we intend in this Book, to consider as a country residence, with land attached, a portion of which, surrounding the house, is laid out as a pleasure-ground; or, in other words, with a view to recreation and enjoyment, more than profit."[31] Loudon's ideal of the villa, like Repton's, was a grand rural residence for a member of the privileged class, but he saw that he could more easily build a reputation by addressing the more numerous members of the middle class, who were the chief clients for the suburban villa. His *Suburban Gardener and Villa Companion* (1838)[32] is devoted entirely to the advantages of building on the outskirts of major cities where, he emphasizes, owners can enjoy both the cultural benefits of urban centers (museums, theaters, etc.) and the pleasures traditionally attributed to country life. Because he was aiming at an audience of moderate and low income, he concentrated on "cottages," which actually represented in scale and flexibility of style a compromise between the rustic cottage of the picturesque model-books and the villa proper. Moreover, he gave currency to, if he did not invent, the semi-detached "villa" type that became the hallmark of the spread of the industrial metropolis.

Loudon was concerned primarily with comfort and convenience, and applied himself to problems of protection from the elements, hygiene (notably plumbing) and adequate lighting. Issues of style were secondary:

> Everything in architecture connected with use, the expression of use, and the expression of those qualities which are common to all the fine arts, can be effected without the introduction of a single form or line which is considered characteristic of any known architectural style . . . [but] by the Employment of Style in an Edifice, the Architect takes immediate possession of the prejudices of mankind [and] gains a positive beauty at once by the mere exhibition of style.[33]

He was not an accomplished theoretician and, in spite of his emphasis on taste, he was indifferent to refinement of design. Many of his models are virtually style-less; the majority were designed by others, often by amateurs. His "Beau-ideal" of the villa, which is prominently featured in the *Encyclopaedia*, is an inept and over-detailed borrowing from Elizabethan country houses that could not have contributed to the elevation of taste. By contrast, his remodeled Woodhall farm, of 1810, was simple and unornamented [9.9]: his message was addressed to those who wanted to build modestly,

9.9 J. C. Loudon, Woodhall farm, 1810, from *Observations on Laying out Farms, in the Scotch Style, Adapted to England*, 1812

and he was satisfied with almost anonymous architecture as a background for his landscape design. He was not even committed to picturesque composition: his design for his own house on the outskirts of London showed a conservative, chastely classical structure built on a plan like that of Sir Robert Taylor's Asgill House, of the 1760s [*8.8*].

Loudon emerges as the most influential of the innumerable authors of villa and cottage books of the early nineteenth century, not because of his theories, which were neither stimulating nor novel,[34] but because he identified, in the middle and working classes, new audiences for model dwellings and gardens, and effective means of attracting them. For better or worse, he altered the face of suburban Britain. He also was the inspiration for the enterprises in America of Andrew Jackson Downing, who was able to emulate his means while aspiring to more discriminating ends.

10.1 Highland Gardens, Newburgh, N.Y., by Andrew Jackson Downing, 1838, from *A Treatise on the Theory and Practice of Landscape Gardening*, 1859

10.2 Francis Goodwin, "A Villa in the Elizabethan Style," from *Rural Architecture*, 1835

10 · Andrew Jackson Downing and the American Romantic Villa

Andrew Jackson Downing was a landscape contractor and designer of Newburgh, New York, whose influence on the way Americans visualized and built their homes was greater than that of anyone in the history of the nation.

In 1838, when he built his villa at Highland Gardens overlooking the Hudson river [10.1], only some twenty years had passed from the last improvements made at Jefferson's Monticello [1.26], but a great chasm lay between the form and purpose of the two dwellings. Jefferson's plantation house had evoked the profound classical culture and the cosmopolitan interests of a proprietor from a privileged class deeply committed to farming. Downing's suburban dwelling alongside his commercial nursery on a small plot of land represented the aspirations and opportunities of an expanding middle class. Downing was also a master publicist who was able, through his books and a journal of wide circulation, to convince others of almost every class throughout the country to share his vision.

Downing's writings were not quite in the millennial tradition of villa literature in which the villa is represented as the retreat of the pressured city dweller: most of his readers were rural already. This audience also differed in not responding to the pastoral literary tradition of Virgil and Horace that had been at the core of the villa ideology; Downing simply didn't know that tradition, or the classical architecture that went with it. His importance was as a molder of taste, a wielder of the new techniques of persuasion made available just at this moment by publishers. (As late as 1837, the young New York City architect Alexander Jackson Davis had still had to finance his own publication, *Rural Residences* [10.13], and to manage the distribution.)

Downing was born in Newburgh, on the banks of the Hudson river, in 1815.[1] In 1831, after an academy education, he joined his brother, who had taken over their father's nursery and market gardening business. A few years later Downing took sole charge, and managed the firm until he sold it in 1846 in order to get more time for editing, writing and the practice of landscape design.

In 1838, following his marriage to a neighbor, Caroline de Wint, a great-granddaughter of John Adams, he designed and built a villa on a four-and-one-half acre plot alongside his father's nursery, Highland Gardens. The villa [10.1, 4, 5], identified as "Elizabethan" at the time of its sale by Downing's heirs, was adapted with modifications from a model in an English book of 1835, Francis Goodwin's *Rural Architecture*, which he owned [10.2]. Downing did not literally copy Goodwin's design. His plan was still a traditional rectangle, not strikingly different from its Greek Revival predecessors (the extension shown at the rear of the house [10.5, 0] was an office

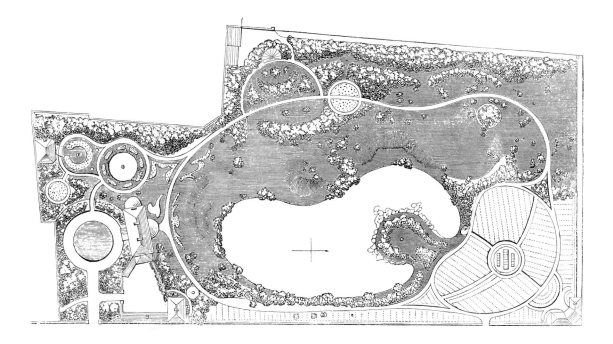

addition of 1846); he eliminated the crenellated parapet of Goodwin's porch; and he placed the windows differently. He added a veranda, an element favored by some of Goodwin's colleagues, especially P.F. Robinson [9.5, 6], and helped to make it a standard element of the American picturesque villa.[2] (Verandas proved to have little appeal to clients building in the mistier British countryside.) The exterior was of sepia sandstone, and brown tones dominated the interior, which, in the words of Fredrika Bremer—a Swedish writer on domestic architecture whom Downing had invited to visit America—made dusk of daylight.[3]

An old English atmosphere was evoked in the hall, which was decorated with antlers and feathered Cavalier hats, and the solemnity of the library was underscored by busts of Scott, Linnaeus, Milton, Dante and Petrarch. Downing, in spite of his truncated formal education, was an earnest intellectual and, in the field of horticulture, an accomplished scientist: his *Fruit Trees of North America*, published in 1845, was read throughout the Western world. He lived the life and adopted the reserved and punctilious manner of an English gentleman, though his ignorance of the classical tradition in all its manifestations would probably have been regarded as barbaric by British virtuosi.

The villa garden occupied only about a third of the property before the sale of the nursery in 1846 [*10.4*], and was enlarged and redesigned in a quite different style during the remaining six years of Downing's life [*10.5*].[4] The site, bordered by town roads on all sides, slopes gently toward the Hudson on the east. The house was placed to face the river, and the aim of the landscape design was both to enhance the river views and to screen off the nursery plantings and the road beyond. The design resembles those discussed and illustrated in J.C. Loudon's *The Suburban Gardener and Villa Companion* of 1838 under the heading "third-rate gardens." Loudon distinguishes these from the fourth-rate by their plots of two or more acres which are not so restricted that the house has to be aligned with the street. Loudon's "Villa of Two Acres and a Half in an Irregular Outline" [*10.3*] is strikingly close to the first plan of Highland Gardens [*10.4*]

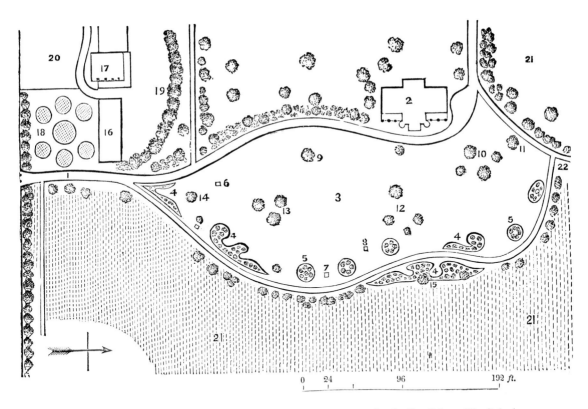

10.3 *(opposite)* J. C. Loudon, "Villa of Two Acres and a Half in an Irregular Outline," from *The Suburban Gardener and Villa Companion*, 1838

10.4, 5 *(above and below)* Highland Gardens: early plan of the garden, from the *Magazine of Horticulture*, 1841, and later plan of the garden, from *The Horticulturist*, 1853

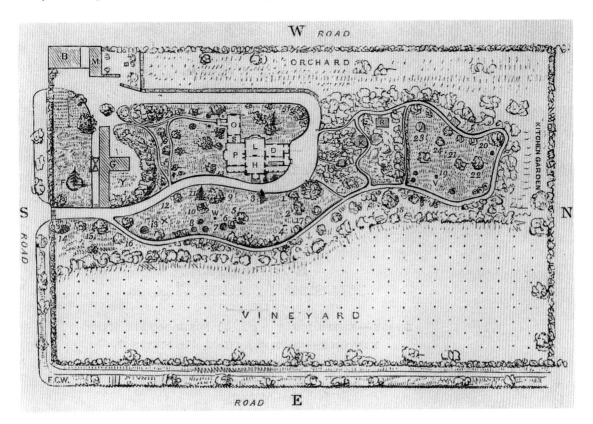

10.6 Highland Gardens: hermitage, from *The Horticulturist*, 1853

10.7 *(below)* Blithewood, by Alexander Jackson Davis, 1836. Frontispiece of A. J. Downing, *A Treatise on the Theory and Practice of Landscape Gardening*, 1841

10.8 *(opposite)* Sunnyside (Washington Irving house), Tarrytown, N.Y. Lithograph after a painting by George Harvey

in its layout and the form of the sinuous paths, the space allotted to nursery plots and the mannered amoebic flower beds (called "arabesque" in the description accompanying Downing's plan.[5]

The mature garden [*10.5*], denser in planting, and with less open area of lawn, evolved into a fully picturesque mode that Loudon and Repton never favored. The trees, more varied and exotic, are scattered with unrestrained informality. Conifers and deciduous hardwoods are mixed; indeed, the garden was planned as a private arboretum. There are numerous architectural incidents, a secluded "rock-work," a rustic "hermitage" [*10.6*], and an arbor framing an idyllic view of the river valley [*10.5, κ, R*].

Downing's was not the first picturesque villa on the banks of the Hudson. In the course of the 1830s many wealthy city dwellers began to be attracted to the heights overlooking the river—not, like generations of planters in Virginia and Louisiana, to get transportation for agricultural produce, but to take advantage of their appealing vistas, such as that at Blithewood near Barrytown, where Alexander Jackson Davis had built a villa for Robert Donaldson (illustrated in the frontispiece of Downing's first book [*10.7*]). Regular passenger steamboats linked the river settlements to New York City and to Albany, making it possible for villa dwellers to keep in contact with their urban enterprises. Thomas Cole and other painters of the river landscape stimulated a native picturesque taste [*10.17*], as the works of Claude had in England a century before, but one of a different order, divorced from classical allusion, and more literal and topographical than ideal. In the mid-1830s, Washington Irving added an asymmetrical tower, a veranda and a mixture of Tudor and Renaissance details (including Dutch stepped gables, a rare taste in this Anglophile era) to the core of a boxy post-Revolutionary house on the riverside property he called Sunnyside, in Tarrytown [*10.8*]. Though incoherent in style, the house marked a radical departure from the

prevailing classical mode of American domestic architecture, and its owner's reputation added to its impact. It must have impressed Irving's neighbor William Paulding, a wealthy New York entrepreneur who had purchased an estate of four hundred acres just north of Sunnyside with a spectacular panorama of the river. In 1838, Paulding called on Davis, who was also a friend of Irving's, to make designs for a stone villa of modest size but great elegance which was to become one of the paradigms of the new style.[6]

Davis (1803–92) had attended the National Academy of Design with the encouragement of John Trumbull, and began practice as a draftsman, making views of the major buildings of Boston and New York.

Davis's training and skill as an artist and his fascination with ornament and detail fitted him perfectly to launch a picturesque style suited to American tastes and materials. In 1829 he was invited by a well established architect, Ithiel Town, to join him as a partner, and entered a career which spanned more than half a century. Town's exceptionally large library of books and prints gave Davis access to a great repertory of historical sources, including major works of the British villa literature. The partnership with Town, who apparently left the designing entirely to his associates, lasted only until 1835, and produced buildings mostly in the Greek Revival style. Davis's first essay in Gothic was the project of 1832 for Glen Ellen outside of Baltimore, for Robert Gilmor, and in the following year he records in his account book the first project for a "Tuscan Villa."[7] He continued, however, to produce occasional classical designs, as recorded in the account book; one enchanting example, Montgomery Place, on the Hudson at Barrytown, is an 1843 remodeling of a house of the Federal period.[8]

The villa for Paulding, called Knoll, was substantially enlarged by Davis in 1865 for a subsequent owner, who changed its name to Lyndhurst [10.9–11]. Apart from its vaguely classical veranda, it was in an English Gothic style which the use of tracery and spires makes more churchy than the "Collegiate" design that Davis had put on the title page of his book of plates published in 1837 [10.13]. The interior also reflected ecclesiastical sources; it treated the entrance axis of the building as a kind of transept, and made extensive use of ribbed vaulting in the major rooms [10.11]. The daring irregularity of massing and the contrasts of light and shadow of the exterior must have astonished Americans raised in Greek Revival houses; it reflected the picturesque site as impressively as any of its English predecessors. Davis was as committed as Downing to the veranda. It provided a natural vantage-point for the addict of the picturesque view, a shaded retreat in hot weather and a fine complement to Gothic irregularity and transparency. Davis took other imaginative advantages of the asymmetry of the style to adjust the size and shapes of the various rooms to their functions, to attract daylight into the major spaces and to take full advantage of the views. The coordination of the several spaces, especially the way in which individual rooms are served by the central halls, demonstrated to future designers the advantages of the newly found freedom of planning.

Davis designed the furniture, the cabinets, and presumably the architectural sculpture (principally corbel figures supporting the ribs for the interior vault) in both the early and the later versions of the villa with his characteristic richness of invention and love of detail, and much of it is preserved in the house today. The 1865 remodeling substantially increased the size of the building and the complexity of its massing, adding

10.9 A. J. Davis, project for Knoll, Tarrytown, N.Y., 1838

a monumental tower over the library extension and the new secondary entrance, and an exceedingly elaborate dining room with bay windows at both ends. The major interior spaces of Lyndhurst are far darker than those of its predecessor, Knoll; the earlier walls were buff/gray, some of them painted to imitate stone, while the later emphasize a reddish brown. Dark interiors, perhaps due in part to Downing's influence, became increasingly fashionable after the Civil War.

The desire for extended contact with the sublime effects of nature spread further afield, and most rapidly to the Atlantic seashore, where the earliest of the surviving resort villas, called Kingscote after its second owner, was built by Richard Upjohn at Newport, Rhode Island, in 1839 [*10.12*]. Upjohn based his four-bay side elevation with a veranda (at the right in the photograph) on a plate in Davis's model-book, *Rural Residences*, issued two years before.[9] Upjohn's vocabulary of forms is close to Davis's, but he composed with wilful incongruity: the right side of the villa is an essentially classical block that contrasts with the elaborate detailing and complicated composition on the left.

10.10 Lyndhurst (formerly Knoll), Tarrytown, N.Y., by Davis, 1838 and 1865

10.11 Lyndhurst: parlor

Kingscote was built for George Noble Jones, a Georgia planter who spent summers at Newport, as did many southerners and others who sought sea air in the hot season. Earlier visitors had found lodgings in the town, as British vacationers had done since the mid-eighteenth century, but after Kingscote the spectacular Newport peninsula began to be exploited as a site for summer houses, just as the Bay of Naples had been in antiquity. Newport villas differed significantly from those on the Hudson: they were second residences for use during the summer "season," and they became part of a single-class enclave from which inelegant dwellings and commercial or industrial structures were excluded. They symbolized the counter-democratic strain in American culture, at the opposite pole from the ideals of Jefferson.[10]

Davis had anticipated Downing not only as a designer but as an author. In 1837 he published privately, with the support and collaboration of two clients, a portfolio of lithographs (intended to be expanded by later supplements) under the title *Rural Residences, etc. Consisting of Designs, Original and Selected, for Cottages, Farm-Houses, Villas, and Village Churches: with Brief Explanations, Estimates and a Specification of Materials, Construction, etc.* [*10.13*].[11] This was the first American model-book in the British villa tradition.

The brief "Advertisement," or preface, in Davis's *Rural Residences* affirms the superiority of English picturesque cottages and villas—especially those in the English collegiate style—to the "bald and uninteresting aspects of our houses," singling out those inspired by the Greek temple as poorly adapted to country life (though the plate labeled "The American House" depicts a log cabin in the form of a temple, with columns made of barked treetrunks). The remaining domestic projects include two villas, one "Oriental" and one the classical design in what might be called Empire style that Upjohn adapted for Kingscote, both perhaps inspired by J.B. Papworth's *Rural*

10.12 Kingscote, Newport, R.I., by Richard Upjohn, 1839. (Portions to the left of the main gable were added by Stanford White in 1881.)

RURAL RESIDENCES, ETC.

CONSISTING OF DESIGNS,

ORIGINAL AND SELECTED,

FOR

COTTAGES, FARM-HOUSES, VILLAS, AND VILLAGE CHURCHES:

WITH BRIEF

EXPLANATIONS, ESTIMATES, AND A SPECIFICATION

OF

MATERIALS, CONSTRUCTION, ETC.

BY ALEXANDER JACKSON DAVIS, ESQ.

AND OTHER ARCHITECTS.

PUBLISHED UNDER THE SUPERINTENDENCE OF SEVERAL GENTLEMEN, WITH A VIEW TO THE
IMPROVEMENT OF AMERICAN COUNTRY ARCHITECTURE.

NEW YORK:
TO BE HAD OF THE ARCHITECT, AT THE NEW YORK UNIVERSITY,
AND OF THE BOOKSELLERS GENERALLY, THROUGHOUT THE UNITED STATES.

MDCCCXXXVII.

10.13 A. J. Davis, titlepage of *Rural Residences*, 1837. The vignette shows a "Villa in the Collegiate Style."

Residences of 1818. Two designs anticipated and encouraged the taste for the picturesque: a grand stone "Villa in the Collegiate Style" [*10.13*] with a fifty-foot octagonal tower, and a gatehouse in the "Rustic Cottage Style," both for Donaldson, the owner of Blithewood [*10.7*].[12] The gatehouse and a few similar early works of Davis were extraordinarily influential both in type and in structure. Together with Davis's early executed designs, the gatehouse design defined in American terms the character of the cottage as distinct from the villa; and it exploited the potentialities of wood construction, most effectively in applying the siding vertically, by a board-and-batten technique that was to become standard for picturesque architecture. It also introduced a kind of scroll-sawed bargeboard in the gables that became an essential element of the Gothic cottage in America.

Davis built a number of cottages that are variants of this project, strictly symmetrical in plan; an elegant example is the Delamater house in Rhinebeck, New York, of 1843, on a small plot in the center of the village [*10.14*]. While the gatehouse offered minimal accommodations, the Delamater house shows Davis's delight in refined detail: the hood molds of the windows and doors are elegant and original, and the battens have molded edges that appealingly soften the contrast of light and dark. The ready availability of wood as a building material gave Davis and contemporary American picturesque architects an opportunity to develop a vocabulary independent of their British sources.

Rural Residences had little direct influence: Davis had to distribute it from his office, and he was left with the bulk of the five hundred copies and a large debt. But it prepared the way for Downing's spectacularly successful publications, both in its advocacy of picturesque architecture and in its ambition to elevate the taste of the nation.

Downing's great debt to Davis is acknowledged in the use of the Blithewood cottage as the frontispiece of his 1841 *Treatise on the Theory and Practice of Landscape Gardening* [*10.7*]. While still in his early twenties, Downing had decided to devote his career to the promotion of horticulture and to instructing Americans on the principles of good garden and villa design. This was to be done through writing books and journal articles for a mass public, which would combine instruction on utilitarian and aesthetic matters with theory and with engraved models for the builder and landscape gardener. Loudon, with whom he corresponded, had alerted him to the techniques of reaching a vast audience from the middle and working classes for whom increased income and low construction costs made home building possible.

Downing's unprecedented impact on Americans of almost all classes and regions was due partly to his skill and enterprise as a publicist. But it must also be appreciated as a function of a major change in the publishing industry that had started already with the British books of the later eighteenth and early nineteenth centuries (see above, pp. 215ff., 222f.).[13] These no longer required the support and subscription of wealthy patrons, which Davis still had to seek, and they could be aimed at a larger and less exclusive clientele by virtue of being cheaper to produce and to market. Nor did they need traditional engraved copper plates, which were especially costly to produce since each plate had to be printed individually by a different process from the production of the text. Several reproductive processes for the making of illustrations were fortuitously invented toward the close of the eighteenth century which made it easier for the draftsman to translate a drawing into a print—among them lithography, mezzotint and aquatint, the last of which permitted the publication in large editions of a kind of color reproduction that closely resembles painting in watercolor.

These techniques serendipitously allowed, even encouraged, the production of picturesque effects, since they made for soft chiaroscuro images [*9.5, 6*]. This was not, however, true of wood-engraving, a technique that gained great popularity among illustrators, especially in the natural sciences, at the end of the eighteenth century. But its advantages were so great that it became the favorite technique of all architectural authors who sought to reach large audiences. The wood-engraving is the "opposite" of engraving on metal in being a relief technique: the printed line is not incised, but remains on the surface, as in woodcut prints, and can therefore be set into the press together with text. This feature made it ideally suited to book illustration and ultimately to use in journals and newspapers. The pioneer of wood-engraving in America was Alexander Anderson, who began to work in the 1790s, and in 1804 reproduced the

10.14 Delamater house, Rhinebeck, N.Y., by A. J. Davis, 1843

illustrations in a zoological work by the greatest of the British wood-engravers, Thomas Bewick. Anderson was employed by Downing as an illustrator of his works whenever his services were available.

Downing's first major work, the *Treatise on the Theory and Practice of Landscape Gardening Adapted to North America; With a View to the Improvement of Country Residences . . . with Remarks on Rural Architecture*, published in 1841, had almost five hundred pages covering theory, history, landscaping, ornamental trees, architecture and "embellishments." The book was an immediate success, and was praised especially for its straightforward and engaging style. Within three years a second printing was issued and in that a third was announced.

In the architectural chapter, called "Landscape or Rural Architecture," Downing advocates English picturesque principles and is sharply critical of blocky brick houses and particularly of "glaring" white Greek Revival country dwellings and farm houses, particularly those with high temple porticoes. He discusses many styles, but favors the Italian villa and the Gothic, especially Tudor, above all others.[14]

Most of the illustrated designs are by practicing architects, and many are of the few picturesque villas by Davis, Upjohn, John Notman and others that had been executed by 1840. A letter from Downing of 1838 asks Davis for an appointment (they had not yet met) to look over the drawings in Davis's office with a view to engraving them for the projected book.[15] Downing continued to use both executed buildings and projects by Davis, at least until he entered practice himself.

Downing's interest in architecture, like Loudon's, grew out of his involvement in landscape gardening. The original impetus for this came from Repton, who had made the English country house an aspect and a reflection of the landscape. But an American landscape designer had still more reason to be involved with architecture because his normal commissions involved land that had not previously been built on.

The *Treatise* was rapidly followed, in 1842, by *Cottage Residences*. Downing later explained:

> What we mean by a villa, in the United States, is the country house of a person of competence or wealth sufficient to build and maintain it with some taste and elegance. Having already defined a cottage to be a dwelling so small that the household duties may all be performed by the family, or with the assistance of not more than one or two domestics, we may add, that a villa is a country house of larger accommodation, requiring the care of at least three or more servants.[16]

The volume presented fifteen designs of cottages and villas and of landscaped gardens and parks ranging from ample suburban lots to estates of ten or twelve acres, few of which were actually of the modest scale and cost suggested by the title. Downing's estimates (for the residence alone) averaged $6,000 and went as high as $12,000. The most modest, a bracketed "Cottage for a Poor Country Clergyman," was designed in response to a letter from the client stating that in view of his annual salary of $700 he could not pay more than $1,000 or $1,200; if we assume the clergyman's income to be one-twentieth its present equivalent and multiply the building estimates by twenty, the average Downing country house could cost $120,000 today. Even allowing generously for the inaccuracy of such calculations, we can assume that Downing's intended audience was primarily in the upper–middle income group. A few of the less expensive models are in wood which, as Downing says, was the universal American building material; but he expresses vigorous antagonism toward it: "Wood is acknowledged by all architects to be the worst material for building, and should never be employed when it is in the power of the builder to use any other."[17]

Cottage Residences was followed in 1845 by *Fruits and Fruit Trees of North America*, a handbook first issued in duodecimo format. Two years later, Downing wrote: "It has been, on the whole, the most popular gardener's book ever written; I am now correcting it for the eighth edition."

In 1846 the publisher Luther Tucker, who had been impressed by the *Treatise*, and particularly the architectural section, asked Downing to become the editor of a new journal, *The Horticulturist*. Its subtitle, *Journal of Rural Art and Rural Taste*, describes the main thrust of Downing's articles and editorial policy, though most of the contributions offered practical instruction and information. After only two months it had two thousand subscribers, and was the most widely read publication in its field.[18] At a time when the population of the United States was still eighty percent rural, agricultural and horticultural publications were in great demand, and Downing's editorials and essays pressing for a radical change of taste and attitude toward the rural

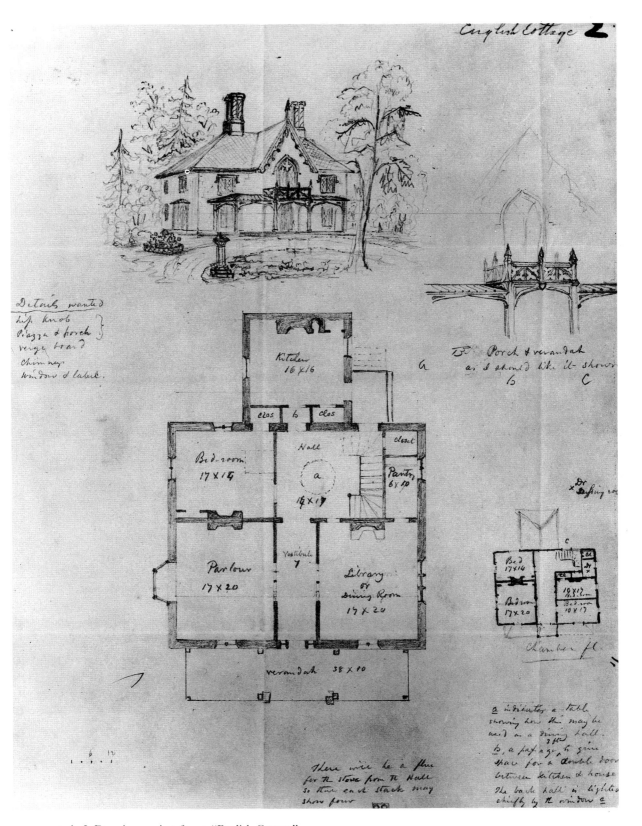

10.15 A. J. Downing, project for an "English Cottage"

and suburban home made him into a celebrity. Fredrika Bremer recorded in *Homes of the New World* her account of her visit encouraged by Downing: "Nobody, whether he be rich or poor, builds a house or lays out a garden without consulting Downing's works; every young couple who sets up housekeeping buys them."[19]

In 1848 Downing invited Davis to join him in a "closer alliance," but nothing came of the initiative, and two years later he went to England, like Jefferson, to visit the country houses where the landscape movement had originated. While there he hired a young draftsman, Calvert Vaux, who later became his partner in a firm of architectural and landscape design. No significant architectural work of the partnership has been identified to which Downing was the major contributor. Few projects can be attributed to Downing alone; he signed some sketches for the cottage and farm buildings of Matthew Vassar at Springside, near Poughkeepsie, New York, which was purchased in 1850, but these represent a modest effort short of what he would have considered suited to the residence of the owner of such a large estate.[20] The only surviving drawing by Downing comparable to those published in his books is for an "English Cottage" [*10.15*], which resembles those at Springside.

The crowning moment of Downing's career was his commission to design the Washington Public Grounds, later called the Mall. He had been campaigning for the establishment of public gardens during the 1840s, and his writings may have prompted a group of Washington leaders to get the support of Congress and President Fillmore for a comprehensive plan for both the "National Park" and the "President's Park" behind the White House.[21] Downing's scheme, which was intended "to give an example of the natural style of Landscape Gardening which may have an influence on the general taste of the Country," provided semi-separate environments which he called "distinct scenes," between each of the cross-streets, rather than the single axial project ultimately executed. The plan was approved in April 1851, and work progressed rapidly for a year, but gradually wound down after Downing's death.

In 1852, Downing drowned in the destruction of a Hudson river steamboat. It had caught fire when the crew overtaxed its boiler while racing against the boat of a rival company. Downing was traveling from Newburgh toward Washington to supervise the work there. His premature death at the age of thirty-seven was symptomatic of the change that had made his career a success. Industrialization and advances in transportation had made it possible for him and others to become professionals of national stature while living in country villas; Downing was *commuting* to work. The steamboat that killed him had extended the suburbs into the wilderness and thus made possible his enterprise of civilizing the American rustic.

The core of Downing's message was that America was now awakening to the possibilities of a life of comfort and of leisure for refined pursuits, and that there was a dramatically expanding demand for a new, less austere kind of domestic architecture in the country. Further, that an architecture of good taste could elevate the moral fiber of the nation. He was concerned only with rural buildings and gardens, and he saw the buildings as images, noble furnishings in the landscape. Invariably he presented them in scenic views, never elevations or sections from which a builder might actually work. He rarely supplied measurements and never showed an interest in proportions. The plans often seem an assembly of arbitrarily proportioned planes. By contrast, however,

Downing attended, like Loudon, to the practicalities such as toilets, sinks, contracts, materials, and architect's fees. Utility was his first principle of good design. Defining his aim, Downing said:

> So long as men are forced to dwell in log huts and follow a hunter's life, we must not be surprised at lynch law and the use of the bowie knife. But when smiling lawns and tasteful cottages begin to embellish a country, we know that order and culture are established. Whatever new systems may be needed for the regeneration of an old and enfeebled nation, we are persuaded that in America, not only is the distinct family the best social form but . . . genius and the finest character may be traced back to the farm house and rural cottage.[22]

And, in another passage,

> He who gives to the public a more beautiful and tasteful model of a habitation than his neighbors, is a benefactor to the cause of morality, good order, and the improvement of society where he lives.[23]

What, for Downing, is a good house? First, it must observe fitness, which means being useful, well functioning and healthy. Second, it must express its purpose: for example, chimneys and porches signal that it is for domestic use; finally, it must have a style that is intrinsically beautiful, one that attracts the observer's notice through the associations he is able to make with it.[24]

Fitness, purpose, style, remind us of Vitruvius's famous triad of architectural fundamentals: utility, strength and beauty. But strength—that is, the technology of building—is omitted. The picturesque building is essentially pictorial, and capable American carpenters and masons must be counted on to make it stand up.

Downing defined beauty as being of two sorts, "absolute" and "relative."[25] Absolute Beauty is produced by such abstract values as proportion, symmetry and unity; Relative Beauty involves the expression of the nature of the individual occupant, particularly of his private life, and of the national character. A building must be "indicative of the intelligence, character and taste of the inhabitants." "To have a 'local habitation'—a permanent dwelling that we can give the impress of our own mind and identify with our own existence—is the ardent wish of every man."[26]

But the villa should also reflect the scenery of the site, and in doing so it may be either beautiful or picturesque, that is, calm and classical or agitated, rough and irregular.[27] Absolute and Relative Beauty may have been Downing's distortion of the opposition of the beautiful and the picturesque proposed by Uvedale Price and Richard Payne Knight (see Chapter 9), which was illustrated by two engravings accompanying Knight's poem, *The Landscape* [9.1], engravings that Downing reinterpreted in his 1841 book on landscape gardening, altering the picturesque view by adding conifers, a Hudson river view and a garden retreat like the "hermitage" at Highland Gardens [10.6]. Downing, in assembling this collage of theory, was trying to combine the absolutes of classical aesthetics, such as proportion and unity, with the individuation of anticlassical, picturesque theory. This was just what his English mentors had sought to avoid: they devised their theories specifically to jettison absolute standards and to replace them with relative judgments grounded in individual perception and taste.

Downing did not resolve major ambiguities in his recommendations on Relative Beauty; like his English predecessors, he proposed no priority among potential representations—of the owner's character, of the site, or of the national culture. On the first point, however, he is quite specific in his last book, *The Architecture of Country Houses* (1850), suggesting that a classical scholar or a common-sense type of man must be permitted to build a Greek Revival house; the "man of sentiment or feeling" requires a house that is shadowy, with nooks about it, and cozy rooms; while men "of imagination, whose aspirations never leave them at rest" are suited to "picturesque villas, country houses with high roofs, steep gables, unsymmetrical and capricious forms." Conservative clients, he continues, "who love the past, rather with instinctive than educated affection," are best accommodated by Old English or Italian architecture, and cannot be expected to appreciate a villa "true to its own time and country." The latter he defines in terms of its modest scale, "a home in which humanity and republicanism are stronger than family pride and aristocratic feeling; a home of the virtuous citizen, rather than of the mighty owner of houses and lands."[28]

This passage is the most unequivocal statement in Downing's writing of a vigorous support for a true modern and American architecture. Earlier books had indicated that the "Bracketed" style might be suitable:

> Indeed, we think a very ingenious architect might produce an *American cottage style* by carefully studying the capabilities of this mode, so abounding in picturesqueness and so easily executed. In actual fitness for domestic purposes in this country, we think this Bracketed mode has much to recommend it. It is admirably adapted to the two kinds of construction which must, for some time, be the most prevalent in the United States—wood and brick covered by an external wash.[29]

The suggestion, from *Cottage Residences*, refers to "Design V, A Cottage Villa in the Bracketed Mode," which Downing illustrates in both masonry and wood [*10.16* is the wooden version]. The latter is republished in the 1844 edition of the *Treatise*, where the Bracketed style is described as "partaking somewhat of the Italian and Swiss features." The brackets, used to support wide roof overhangs and porch coverings, are specific to wood construction, and radically distinguish these villas from examples of the same styles in British model-books.

Downing was ambivalent about the Bracketed style. He particularly admired the masonry Italian villa of the British tradition [*1.6*], but he started his career with a strong aversion to wood as an ignoble building material. A Bracketed villa appears only once among the more elegant "Designs for Villas and Country Houses" in *The Architecture of Country Houses*. He would not have been pleased to know that his greatest impact on the course of American architecture was to be manifested in the wood architecture that Vincent Scully effectively defined as the "Stick Style" and the "Shingle Style." But in time he felt a responsibility toward less affluent families among his readers, and promoted the Bracketed mode for cottages and farmhouses for its economic and technical advantages. In the same spirit, Downing, together with Davis, launched board-and-batten construction [*10.14, 16*], arguing that its vertical emphasis was suited to the picturesque profiles of their buildings.

In his later writings—if that term can be applied to an author in his mid-thirties—Downing grafted on to his theory the concept of "Truth," which he had borrowed from Loudon and Ruskin. But he gave his interpretation little ethical import, defining it in

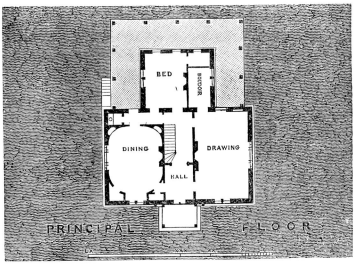

10.16 A. J. Downing, "A Cottage Villa in the Bracketed Mode," from *Cottage Residences*, 1844

terms of "Local Truth" (accommodation to the environment); "Specific Truth" (matching the design to the pocketbook); and "Truth of Materials." He did, however, move toward a more romantic and less utilitarian position in his later writings and in revisions of the *Treatise*; the change is reflected in the redesign of the gardens of his Newburgh residence.[30]

The republicanism of his last writings also expressed itself in opposition to the grandeur of European mansions:

> One would rather wish that cultivated minds should find a truer and loftier pleasure in striving to form a free and manly school of republican tastes and manners, than in wasting time in the vain effort to transplant the meaningless conventionalities of the realms of foreign cast.[31]

But Downing substituted an elite of taste for one of birth: "educated feeling" is required for the appreciation of "beauty of expression" (and in turn, a beautiful home may serve to educate the feelings).[32]

Downing's republicanism was firmly paternalistic. He wanted to persuade the less favored members of society to accept the bourgeois domestic and cultural values that he had preached from the start:

> Our rural residences, evincing that love of the beautiful and the picturesque, which, combined with solid comfort, is so attractive to the eye of every beholder, will not only become sources of the purest enjoyment to the refined minds of the possessors, but will exert an influence for the improvement in taste of every class in our community.[33]

The style repertory for domestic architecture is restricted. Downing excludes the Egyptian, Chinese and Moorish styles as inappropriate. The rest are divided into classical and romantic, the latter including Tudor, Elizabethan, Old English, and, for cottages, Rural Gothic. The Greek style would be acceptable for a scholar but fails to meet the standard of fitness because the Greeks did not use temples for domestic architecture. Castellated is inappropriate for America because it has no baronial heritage. The Italian villa, especially in its masonry (non-bracketed) versions [1.6], gets special praise: "We can hardly imagine a mode which, in the hands of a man of wealth, may produce more beauty, convenience or luxury" (note that the American version of the Italian villa came from English books and not from any Mediterranean experience).

The Tudor style, though, was Downing's favorite: he liked the irregular silhouette [10.1, 2], saying that it was "poetical and Romantic, and that it helps one to join it to enticing history, to the landscape and to the homes of our ancestors." By history I think he meant the novels of Walter Scott, which had a fabulous success in America in the 1830s.

Since Downing rarely built anything himself, many of the plans indifferently reflect the styles of the elevations. Not being particularly talented as an architect, he was forced to seek an American expression while depending on British model books. But his solution worked, because he addressed a nation with an accelerating need for suburban housing, far greater than in Britain. Americans were so engaged with their natural environment that they eagerly abandoned the classical tradition for an architecture that seemed to imitate nature in its irregularity, its materials and its colors (Downing recommended matching stone and earth in the color of houses). His genius and his influence were not as a designer but as a publicist. Adapting Loudon's techniques of mass printing for books and journals densely illustrated with the works of many architects, Downing did more than anyone else to turn a mass audience away from classicism toward an architecture of nature. He did not manage to ensure that it would be an architecture of quality, but he did set the nation on a path that would culminate in the achievements of Richardson and Wright.[34]

For all his dependence on British villa books, Downing consistently addresses the peculiar condition of life in America, pointing to the absence of large estates preserved by primogeniture and other aristocratic traditions. The nation's population was predominantly rural. The vast wilderness was quickly coming under control and the frontiersman began to demand more than a subsistence-level cabin. In many areas, new buildings came greatly to outnumber the old; they rose in an environment without a past culture.

It was a moment of crucial change, sparked by a great technological advance that bound the country together by railroad and steamboat and quickened the pace of urbanization. Economic prosperity fostered building. Political life was altered by the presidency of Andrew Jackson (1829–37), which introduced a popular democracy based on agrarian values. The Jacksonians promoted a mythology of the noble frontiersman, the *natural* man, whose simple virtues were contrasted to the effete sophistication of the European and Northeastern American city dweller.

At this moment, two issues came to the center of American consciousness. First, that of man's relation to nature, in particular the dilemma of how civilization might expand without destroying the values of the wilderness and frontier and the somewhat mythical virtues attributed to the natural man, the leatherstocking. Second, that of American self-realization, the achievement of a culture independent of Europe and of a refinement without loss of vigor. These were the issues that preoccupied Emerson and other Transcendentalists. Their response was to exalt intuition, which they called "reason," over understanding, and in this they were the indirect heirs of the British philosophers and aestheticians of the eighteenth century who had laid the foundations for picturesque theory. They sought to learn from the experience of nature, claiming that knowledge resides in the self, and that the will is more important than the intellect. Emerson's essays entitled "Nature," "Self Reliance" and "The American Scholar" are among the major articulations of the philosophy. Fredrika Bremer told of how Downing read Emerson's essays aloud to his family in the evening.[35]

Parallels may also be found in the painting of the period. Asher B. Durand's *Kindred Spirits* [*10.17*] shows the Transcendentalist poet William Cullen Bryant and Thomas Cole admiring the wilds of the Catskill mountains. The canvas is a supplement to Bryant's funeral oration for Cole, the major landscape artist of the day. All three were, like Downing, committed ruralists. In an essay on landscape painting written in 1835, Cole extolled the wildness of American scenery in contrast to that of Europe. He admits that to be absorbed in the wilderness is to forego the pleasures of association with the past, but says that Americans can enjoy associating with the future:

> In looking over the yet uncultivated scene, the mind's eye may see far into futurity. Where the wolf roams, the plow shall glisten; on the gray crag shall rise temple and tower—mighty deeds shall be done in the now pathless wilderness, and poets yet unborn shall sanctify the soil.[36]

Durand made the same observation in paint in a work called *Progress*, which shows, apparently with as much approval as he had manifested in the commemorative portrait, the wilderness giving way to buildings, railroads and mills [*10.18*].[37] But the message of this painting is ambivalent; we cannot be sure that its title is not ironic, that the artist does not feel more nostalgia for the untouched forest on the left than pride in the bustle of the railroad and factories on the right. Most Americans were deeply concerned by the accelerating passage from a simple to a sophisticated culture, from virgin forests to industrial blight. The more American pride became rooted in achievements based on the exploitation of natural resources, the more the ideology was articulated in terms of affection for the unspoiled wilderness. Artistic expression in all media reinforced the will to ignore or to hide materialism and the drive for profit. The expression of utilitarian principles, such as those of John Stuart Mill, was virtually taboo.[38] One resolution of the anxieties generated by this conflict was fostered by Jacksonian apologists. They posed the goal of "cultivation" as a mean between the primitive and the socialized American, choosing the word on the analogy of agricultural cultivation and contrasting it to the crudity or savagery of the purely natural life.[39]

The dilemma was not to be so easily resolved. Transcendental contemplation, such as that of Thoreau at Walden, could not come to terms with the exploding science and technology that constituted the most powerful forces in American culture, or with the political struggles between the claims of privilege and the voice of the common man. George Santayana claimed that the leading minds of the period formed what he called the Genteel Tradition in American thought—removed and elite in spite of their democratic claims.[40]

Downing, buttressed by the Transcendental fashion, was quintessentially genteel in his effort to raise the moral tone and the level of life of his countrymen through good taste. But he managed to democratize gentility. His vast influence over the taste of the

10.17 Asher B. Durand, *Kindred Spirits*, 1849

10.18 Asher B. Durand, *Landscape, Progress*, 1849

nation is attributable less to his message of lofty and high-minded platitudes than to his command of mass communication and to good timing: he addressed his countrymen at a moment when the middle class was expanding dramatically and when suburban living first became a practical possibility. And he conveyed his message with unexpected effectiveness in a journal of wide circulation and in books that reached a large audience through newly lowered production costs and improved means of distribution. He wrote well, and his message soothed readers with its fuzzy versions of British aesthetics and Transcendental philosophy, pointing the way to succeeding generations of American molders of taste.

The primary significance of the coming of the picturesque villa and cottage to America was not that they introduced a variety of historical styles or even that they reflected landscape paintings—the pleasures of association were a negligible factor— but rather that the approved styles favored flexible planning and composition and the adjustment of building design to the character of the environment and the taste of the individual client. The several versions of English Gothic encouraged variety and fantasy, an irregular plan and massing, and varied ornamental chimneys and scroll- work; the Italian villa offered in addition adaptability to design innovations in wood. It was an architecture suited to the desire of mid-nineteenth-century Americans to express their individuality and their freedom from the rules and the uniformity of tradition.

11.1 Frank Lloyd Wright, project for the Doheny ranch, 1922

11 · The Modern Villa
Wright and Le Corbusier

We have seen in the course of the preceding chapters an exceptional consistency in the ideology and function of the villa throughout the many centuries of Western history since the time of the Roman Republic. In the minds of its apologists, the villa has provided purity, beauty of surroundings, health and strong moral fiber, an ideal seat for the institution of the family, and above all an antidote to the city and its prolific evils. In the late eighteenth and early nineteenth centuries, the character of the villa was radically changed by social and economic developments that made country living accessible not only to the richest and most powerful citizens but also to large segments of the middle and even working classes. The democratization of the villa altered its character in shrinking its surrounding property to modest plots of land unsuited to agricultural activity. The favored sites were on the fringes of large cities, from which proprietors who could not afford a second home could travel to work or could make a living serving neighboring villa dwellers. Thus the polarity of the villa and the city was blurred. Even the term "villa" fell into disuse in the later years of the last century; it was not employed by America's two greatest masters of country residences, Henry Hobson Richardson and Frank Lloyd Wright, partly because they intended to disassociate themselves from the often tawdry production of villa structures during the romantic era.

Nevertheless, Wright and the Swiss architect Charles-Edouard Jeanneret, who called himself Le Corbusier, have been the most influential contributors to the villa tradition of our own time. Their attention, like that of villa designers throughout the centuries, focused on the task of establishing an equilibrium between nature and culture responsive to their own and to their contemporaries' feelings and convictions. Their predecessors throughout the centuries had devised solutions which fell inevitably into one of two categories: that which set itself off from nature with pure, prismatic forms and clearly defined light-washed smooth surfaces [*1.26; 6.4*], and that which reflected the informality of nature in its irregularity, asymmetry, rich texture and contrasts of color and of light and dark [*1.23; 9.6; 10.10*]. The first has adhered to the spirit and the mathematical harmonies of Greek and Roman architecture, while the second has generally been consciously anti-classical. The first best describes the work of Le Corbusier, and the second that of Wright, but both architects were attracted by, and experimented with, the opposite pole.

The history of the villa appears to have evolved by oscillating from one of these approaches to the other, as if to appeal to two mythologies. The mysterious, defensive irregularity of the early Medici villas yielded, even at the hands of the same patron and architect, to openness and cubic simplicity and purity [*3.4, 12*]. The picturesque villas of the early 1800s by Alexander Jackson Davis and his contemporaries [10.9] were offered as alternatives to the blocklike white structures of the Greek Revival. (This impulse matured into an imposing architecture a generation later in the New England country houses of H.H. Richardson [1.24], who used materials from the site itself in their original state, appropriating nature—fieldstone, unpainted shingles—as well as reflecting its character.)

The re-enactment in the twentieth century of this age-old alternation of type may be represented in the work of Wright and Le Corbusier. The contrast is perhaps more intense than ever before, since each committed all his powers not only to realizing an original artistic expression, and to reinforcing it with voluminous writing, but to endowing it with cosmic significance. This may be seen when one compares drawings for elegant villas by the two architects, Wright's for the (unexecuted) Doheny ranch in southern California, and Corbusier's for the Villa Stein-de Monzie in Garches, outside Paris [11.1, 2]. These re-state the contrast between the romantic and the classical in fresh, non-traditional terms, and they affirm a clearly defined attitude toward nature in its relation to mankind. Wright's drawing [11.1] expresses his belief in the "organic" nature of architecture; his buildings are presented as if they grew out of the earth, emerging from the contours of the dramatic site. The architecture is conceived as mass and space; it seems to have a palpable form of great density; Wright's organic metaphor usually refers rather to geological than to biological phenomena.

Le Corbusier's villa [11.2] appears as if abstracted from the environment; the geometrically exact isometric drawing, without shadows, is itself an abstraction; unlike a bird's-eye perspective, its lines do not converge at an eye-point that would give the viewer a position, and there is no implied horizon. Trees and shrubs—vestiges of a suppressed nature—are restricted to tight rectangular openings in concrete and masonry surrounds. The walls and roof are presented as two-dimensional screen-like planes (in fact, the forward parapet of the roof is presented as quite devoid of depth). There is no suggestion of texture: the same white surface signals glass, stucco and metal. The awning hung on steel rods and the tubular metal railings refer not to natural phenomena or to traditional architectural forms, but to contemporary industry.

Both architects attempted not just to make buildings but to give shape to modern life. They assumed the mantle of Renaissance artists, whose creative acts were first compared to God's. But they assumed still more authority, because they, more than their clients, defined the task, as painters and sculptors had been doing since the early nineteenth century. Twentieth-century clients have been anyhow less certain than their predecessors about their architectural goals. Rapid social changes made the well-to-do poorly prepared to guide an architect in matters of form and symbolism. Those few who have been secure enough to employ an innovative architect have usually left such decisions to him.

Wright, born in 1869, was Le Corbusier's senior by eighteen years.[1] He was raised in Wisconsin in a family of strong religious convictions and spent much of his youth doing strenuous work on an uncle's farm. His roots, like those of Jefferson and Downing, were rural and agricultural, and he did not want his country and suburban houses to be thought of as villas. He saw them simply as responses to the particular situations for which they were conceived. In part this was because, as I proposed in Chapter 1, the villa

11.2 Le Corbusier, project for the Stein–de Monzie villa, "The Terraces," Garches, 1926

type is defined in its antithetical relationship to the city, and Wright, in the tradition of American romanticism, did not think in urban terms. His scheme for urban life in America, Broadacre City, was essentially rural, assigning an acre of land to each resident—an impractical solution to accommodating a large population. But whether they are called villas or just houses, Wright's country dwellings demand consideration in the context of this study.

Wright absorbed the nineteenth-century Midwestern optimism, faith in progress and in the potentialities of individual enterprise, along with a suspicion of the European cultural heritage.

After a truncated education in engineering at the University of Wisconsin, Wright began practice in Chicago, initially as a draftsman for established architects. Of these, Louis Sullivan became his chief mentor. By 1893, when he set out to practice on his own, he had already designed several private houses, both for the firm of Adler and Sullivan and independently. Though the early residences were radically unconventional in their open plans and a-historical exteriors, his typical client was not a sophisticated connoisseur but a staid, practical businessman secure enough to want a nonconforming house rather than one from the prevailing repertory of tasteful traditional styles. The majority of these early houses were built in the rapidly growing middle-class suburbs of Chicago on lots at times large enough for a modest garden but too small to release the architect from the constraints of the street grid.[2]

The most elegant of these was the Avery Coonley house in Riverside, Illinois, of 1908 [11.3–6], which Wright called "the most successful of my houses from my standpoint."[3] This house is an exception to the general statements made above: the clients had particularly refined taste, and the grounds were unusually spacious—comparable to those of Downing's villa at Highland Gardens [10.5]—and bordered on two sides by the winding Desplaines river. Riverside was a suburban community within easy commuting distance from Chicago, with sinuous roadways laid out in the picturesque tradition by Frederick Law Olmsted together with Downing's former associates Calvert Vaux and Frank Withers in 1868–69.[4] The clients were immensely wealthy and gave Wright almost complete freedom; he designed every detail, including the furnishings and fittings, and selected the art objects.

The Coonley house marks the peak and the termination of an intensely productive eight-year period during which Wright designed or remodeled some seventy houses, mostly in the suburbs of Chicago. The sequence started with two designs of 1900 for "A Home in a Prairie Town," commissioned for publication in *The Ladies' Home Journal*, in which Wright found his stride as an architect of astonishing talent and originality. These "Prairie Houses," as Wright called them, were coherent in style, reflecting the desire to define a form responsive to the physical and cultural character of that region of unalleviated plain. Wright asserted that his emphatic horizontal accents echoed the flatness of the land; low roofs extended in broad, hovering eaves gave protection from sun and storm. The plans, many of cross-form, were generated from a masonry chimney core, from which the spacious and open areas, often lit from three sides, extended outward, as if reaching. The core was also the symbolic center: Wright invariably made the hearth/fireplace the visual and psychological focus of the major room or rooms. One space merged into another as Wright abandoned the traditional segregation of functions; in his words,

My sense of "wall" was no longer the side of a box. It was enclosure of space affording protection against storm or heat only when needed. But it was also to bring the outside world into the house and let the inside of the house go outside. In this sense I was working away at the wall as a wall and bringing it toward the function of a screen, a means of opening up space which, as control of building materials improved, would finally permit the free use of the whole space without affecting the soundness of the structure.

The climate being what it was, violent in extremes of heat and cold, damp and dry, dark and bright, I gave broad protecting roof-shelter to the whole, getting back to the purpose for

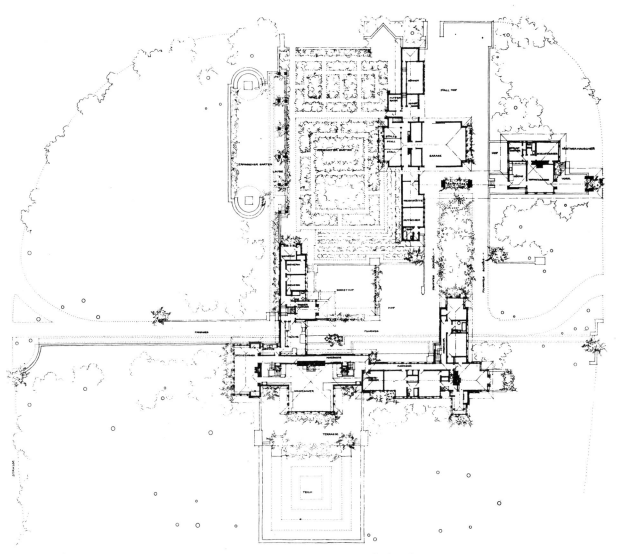

11.3 Avery Coonley house, Riverside, Ill., by Frank Lloyd Wright, 1908: site plan

which the cornice was originally designed. The underside of roof-projections was flat and usually light in color to create a glow of reflected light that softly brightened the upper rooms. Overhangs had double value: shelter and preservation for the walls of the house, as well as this diffusion of reflected light for the upper story through the "light screens" that took the place of the walls and were now often the windows in long series.[5]

By attempting to accommodate the design of Prairie Houses to the site and by rejecting formality and constriction in planning, Wright in a sense realized the aims of the picturesque theorists of a century before. But his approach was both more profound and more essentially architectural. He aimed, as the foregoing passage shows, to re-conceive *structurally* elements of architecture such as the wall and the cornice (which no proponent of the picturesque had been concerned to do) as a means of serving the basic needs of human habitation. And he saw architectural composition not just as bricks and wood but as light and color. Finally, his design was committed to a social end: the

11.4, 5 Coonley house: garden front
(right) and corner of the inner court

liberation of the American family from the cellular spatial organization and the isolation of functions in the traditional house (and with this, their liberation from the restricting formalities of behavior that traditional planning preserved).

As we have seen in the Doheny ranch [*11.1*], Wright's initial concept of the natural environment to which architecture must adjust was not the picturesque setting of trees and grass, but nature on the grand environmental scale of great land masses and of particular climates, materials and colors. The Coonley house is on a site comparable in size to those of Davis and Downing along the Hudson. The residence itself is many times larger, but it is not oriented to a view or to an immediate garden setting. In Wright's plan [*11.3*], the overall landscaping of the site is of little consequence: its purpose seems to be simply to isolate the house from the community by scattered clumps of shrubbery. Wright was, however, careful to establish an integration of architecture and nature by means of a reflecting pool and vines in masonry boxes outside the banks of windows [*11.4*]. The formal garden in the inner court [*11.5*] is incongruously traditional and classical, resembling the gardens of Wright's English contemporary Lutyens. There are other reminders of the English tradition in the service and guest wings that form the two arms of the court, and the entrance drive that passes under the kitchen on one side, through a court, and under the guest wing at the opposite side, but there is no evidence that Wright had any precedents in mind. The two facades through which the driveway passes are treated with a colorful, abstractly patterned plaster and tile surface that was new to Wright's work: perhaps it was inspired by textile designs; it was a step toward the textile block walls of some of Wright's California houses more than a decade later. Wright had avoided ornament in his early work, but now saw how to integrate it into architectural design in an enriching way:

> Heretofore, I have used the word "pattern" instead of the word ornament to avoid confusion or to escape passing prejudice. But here ornament is now in place. Ornament meaning not only *surface qualified by human imagination* but imagination giving natural pattern to structure. Perhaps this phrase says it all wholly without further explanation. Integral ornament is new in the architecture of the world, at least insofar not only as imagination qualifying a surface—a valuable resource—but as a greater means than that: *imagination giving natural pattern to structure itself*. Here we have new significance, integral indeed! Long ago this significance was lost to the scholarly Beaux Arts trained architect. A man of taste. He, too soon, became content with symbols and appliqué.[6]

The plan of the Coonley house is determined by a hierarchy of functions. The principal living area and bedrooms are all on the upper floor—a European *piano nobile*—giving a greater access to light and to garden vistas than that in earlier Prairie Houses. The primacy of the public area is affirmed in the massive chimney and in the imposing symmetry of the block that it anchors, which had complementary stairwells on either side (one has since been eliminated) linked by short corridors to the square living room, more than half of which is glazed [*11.6*]. This room is an extraordinary space enriched by light that flows in through windows with subtle patterns of leading and details of colored glass, and by such radical innovations as the complex pitching of its ceiling unified by strips of oak laid on the plaster surfaces (and in places over recessed lighting fixtures)—a fantastic, exhilarating invention.

A playroom and the two entrance halls in the core area are the only ground-floor living spaces. The modestly sized family bedrooms and a study extend in a linear sequence from this core [*11.3, right*], terminating at the master bedroom, which is marked by a chimney and extended by an open terrace. Guest rooms branch off at a right angle. This wing is reflected on the opposite side of the core by the alimentary wing, with a chimneyed dining room (with seating for only seven indicated on Wright's original plan!) and, again at a right angle, the kitchen and servants' quarters. For all the luxury and amplitude, every part of the house remains intimate and retiring. Its lack of conventional pretentiousness is signaled in the exceptional modesty of the entranceway, which, as in many of Wright's works, and notably in those to be discussed below, is virtually hidden in a recess in the darkest part of the driveway underpass (the same location was chosen for Taliesin). One's ascent from this darkness into a realm of light —the living room—was planned as a kind of spiritual progress.

The Coonley house represented a break from the pervasive fashion of elegant American country palaces of the late nineteenth and early twentieth centuries, represented by the bombastic Beaux-Arts style mansions of Newport, Rhode Island. Wright's clients employed him partly because they were not palace-builders but people of great inherited wealth who had no need to make a public statement of their position and power. They hoped to live a retired life in the midst of a personal and low-keyed

11.6 Coonley house: living room

luxury. Some, like the Coonleys, were members of the shortlived class that provided the principal protagonists of the novels of Henry James (Le Corbusier's several American villa clients of the 1920s were of the same class). They did not need to work and could devote themselves to the acquisition of refinement, sustained by the fruits of the great fortunes accumulated by later nineteenth-century entrepreneurs unconstrained by tax and trust restrictions. Like many aristocratic British villa dwellers they could enjoy privilege without the encumbrances of power, and this, more than any specific architectural influences, may explain the Englishness of the Coonley house program.[7]

While he was making the first drawings for the Coonley house, in 1907, Wright was also beginning work on plans for what might have been his grandest domestic work, for Harold McCormick, heir to the farm machinery fortune. The project [*11.7*], for a site on high bluffs overlooking Lake Michigan, was on the scale of the villas of Pliny the Younger and of the major maritime villas of the Bay of Naples [*2.11, 15*]. Like them, it extended outward by the addition of discrete elements in spurs on various levels over an uneven terrain. In spite of the unprecedented extent of the program, the architect held the individual units to the scale and style of the Prairie series, seeking intimacy rather than grandeur, which in part explains the client's rejection of the design. Perhaps the McCormicks, who were powerful members of the Chicago social establishment, felt the

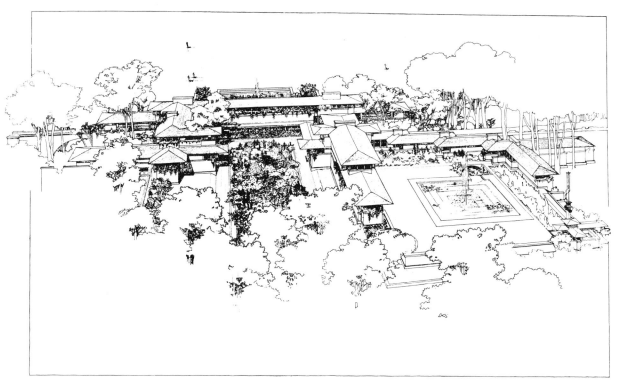

11.7 Frank Lloyd Wright, project for the McCormick residence on Lake Michigan, 1907

need for a more conventionally monumental setting. Their rejection of the Wright design may have signaled and accelerated the demise of Chicago's fledgling school of innovative modern architecture. In any case, it immediately preceded a moment of major upheaval in Wright's life and career: he abandoned his family, his practice and his debts and escaped with the wife of a client to Europe. It was a fateful and self-destructive decision for an architect who had attempted in his domestic architecture to express a traditional family cohesion as well as a modern rejection of convention. When he returned after two years he could find almost no work.

Rather than resettle in Chicago, he began in 1911 to expand a country house, which he called Taliesin, for himself, his mother and his companion at Spring Glen, in the rural Wisconsin area where his mother's Welsh father, Richard Lloyd-Jones, had settled, and where he had worked in the summers on an uncle's farm. Wright chose "Taliesin," the name of an ancient Welsh bard, to evoke the mythical aura of Celtic folklore and the castles and burial dolmens of Wales.

The site itself, on the brow of a hill that resembles a burial ground, is in a spectacular landscape—a glacial valley in some places flat and in others of rolling pasture, through which winds the Wisconsin river, a tributary of the Mississippi. The valley is bordered on either side by extended hilly ridges on which the covering of small deciduous trees is interrupted at intervals by outcroppings of yellow limestone that suggest, with their horizontal layering, the courses of masonry walls.

The house, on the edge of a hillside that rises sharply over a bend in the river, was designed to grow out of the land; it is built of the native limestone laid roughly but skilfully to match its appearance in the surrounding landscape [*11.9*], and of wood painted an earthy red. The low roofs, with eaves settling to as little as six feet from the pavement, extend protectively from the walls. One enters by passing over a stone bridge, as over a moat, and driving around the hillside as if approaching a castle, finally passing through a sequence of dark overhangs into the garden court, the core of which is small and cloister-like, enclosed partly by the house itself and partly by the gently sloping spine of the ridge. The house reaches outward from this core as if to seek contact with the river valley and ultimately to differentiate itself from the earth in which it is rooted. Behind the court, somewhat higher on the slope of the ridge, is a small, separate cluster of rooms crowned by a tower that constitutes the single vertical emphasis, as if it were the core from which all else were suspended [*1.12*]. Perhaps the tower was a homage to the *belvedere* of later Tuscan villas (Wright's previous year abroad had been spent principally in Fiesole); the intimate inner court, and to some extent the fields behind and to the south of the house, also have a Tuscan quality.[8]

The situation at Taliesin gave Wright the opportunity to fuse his most important architectural convictions, the evocation of nature, of the character of materials, and the assimilation of past cultures into a contemporary context. With remarkable success, Taliesin joins the Tuscan villa (in spirit but not in specific detail) with the topography and geological structure of Wisconsin.

Taliesin represents a fulfillment of Wright's artistic aims in ways that the earlier houses could not. The integration of architecture with nature had been hard to realize on the small and confined urban lots, isolated from a truly natural environment where most of his early houses had been built. For example, the low cantilevered eaves that were used in the Prairie Houses, by which Wright claimed to evoke the flatness of the prairie, could not, in densely settled Chicago suburbs, convincingly evoke association with the open flatlands. At Taliesin they represent a reaching out from a domestic core toward the land and water below, becoming an analog to the experience of looking out from the protected interior into the landscape around. Taliesin offered a setting in which an unbroken transition from nature to artifice—in materials, shapes, textures and color— could be achieved in the way Wright termed "organic":

> So I began to study the nature of materials, learning to *see them*. I now learned to see brick as brick, to see wood as wood, and to see concrete or glass or metal. See each for itself and all as themselves. Strange to say, this required greater concentration of imagination. Each material demanded different handling and had possibilities of use peculiar to its own nature. Appropriate designs for one material would not be appropriate at all for another material. At least, not in the light of this spiritual ideal of simplicity as *organic plasticity*. Of course, as I could now see, there could be no organic architecture where the nature of materials was ignored or misunderstood. How could there be? Perfect correlation is the first principle of growth. Integration, or even the very word "organic" means that nothing is of value except as it is naturally related to the whole in the direction of some living purpose, a true part of entity.[9]

The house was rebuilt after fires in 1914 and in 1925, and in fact was perpetually in construction, so that much was added to and altered in the original core. In one campaign, a dam was placed across a tributary that entered the river right below the

11.8, 9 Taliesin, Spring Green,
Wis., by Frank Lloyd Wright,
begun 1911: garden side *(right)* and
entrance

house, creating a picturesque lake and a waterfall. Seeing this romantic touch one feels that in the design as a whole Wright managed to fulfill the aims of the picturesque designers and architects of Downing's time better than any of them had done. They too had wanted a harmony of building and nature, but they never controlled either the form or the structural materials with the mastery that fully realized that aim, a mastery that makes Wright's home one of the most stirring examples of domestic architecture of this century.

Wright, like many of his contemporaries, was a man both deeply rooted in the vanishing American past and exhilarated by the potentialities of the industrial present and future. He spoke and wrote like a liberated Transcendentalist—in his profound response to the physical environment, his insistence on respect for the nature of materials, and in his desire to achieve an American expression free of the incubus of the Western European tradition. His early focus on family values and on the centrality of the hearth in domestic architecture echoed the concerns of Downing, but he had an infinitely greater capacity to realize them architecturally. Like Jefferson and Downing, he remained an agrarian: he wanted to abolish the modern city and to replace it with a large version of the country town in which every inhabitant could claim a right to at least an acre of land. His urban houses remained on uneasy terms with the city, demanding independence and breathing space; they were essentially villas, though he resolutely refused to call them that.

The houses discussed above were designed at precisely the apogee of the Progressive movement in American politics and society; it was a period of prosperity and self-confidence in which liberal social attitudes, rather heavily laced with Protestant moralism, began to overcome Victorian manners and the ruthless business ethic and Social Darwinism of the age of the Robber Barons. Wright has invariably been interpreted, with his own encouragement, as an individual isolated from the mainstream of American culture of his time, but the many ways in which his attitudes and achievements parallel those of other innovative minds of his time deserve consideration. John Dewey, Thorsten Veblen (both in Chicago in the early years of the century), William James, and another citizen of Wisconsin, Robert La Follette, were all, like Wright, re-examining the accepted traditions in their fields and attempting to formulate new principles not based on those established in Europe. All were aware, like Wright, that the industrial revolution and the democratic tradition distinguished life in America from that elsewhere and that the constriction of traditional modes had to be loosened— as Wright opened the plan of his houses. Wright's battle against oldfashioned attitudes toward the home was paralleled by battles of the same kind in social policy, education, sexual mores, the writing of history and the conception of the law. The evaporation of Wright's practice during the First World War period was also not an individual phenomenon, but a fate shared with Progressivism in other fields as well. The nation was submerged, first in a rigidifying patriotism and then, in the post-war period, in an orgy of relief that created an inhospitable climate for proposals of substantive change in any sphere.

The Progressives were not radicals: their Americanism led them to revere the nation's traditions. And there was no American equivalent of European modernism, the *avant garde*, with its radical rejection of bourgeois values and traditions. In Wright's case, conservatism was expressed architecturally in his Renaissance posture as the artist–creator of almost superhuman stature, and in his attachment to the handicraft aspect of design: in intricate cabinet work, in the provision, whenever the budget of the client permitted, of custom crafted furniture, fixtures and rugs. But at the same time, he was fascinated with the structural potentialities of modern industrial products, particularly steel and concrete. The extension of roofs and balconies on steel cantilevers was central to his expression. He even favored the standardization of architectural elements, though the unconventional character of his design, like Le Corbusier's, did not recommend it for mass production. But ultimately—particularly through his "Usonian" houses—his concepts helped to transform the building industry, as it produced (without recognizing the Wrightian source) millions of individual one-story tract houses on radiant-heated concrete slabs in which living, dining and kitchen areas were fused into a single space.

Le Corbusier's approach to architecture in his early work was in some ways the antithesis of Wright's. In no sense do his buildings emerge organically from the ground. They are conceived in an abstract environment and are unresponsive to their surroundings, at times even recoiling on "pilotis" (reinforced concrete columns) that minimize physical contact with the earth. Their smooth texture and gleaming whiteness affirm their utter isolation from nature. The architecture is in the spirit of Cubist painting—concerned to maintain the inviolability of the plane, bemused by the

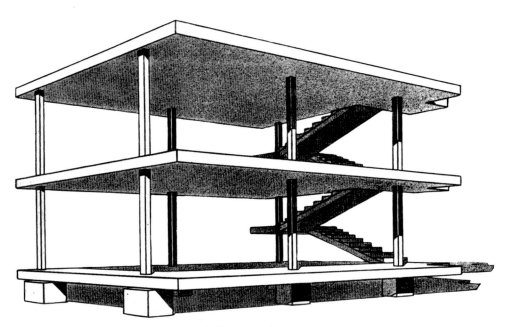

11.10 Le Corbusier, project for "Dom-ino" construction, 1914

problems of volume and modeling, preferring the appearance of the manufactured product as the painters came to prefer man-made objects (guitars, bottles, newspapers). Wright would never have thought it possible, much less desirable, to design a house, as Le Corbusier boasted having done for his parents, before searching for a suitable site.[10]

Le Corbusier was raised in a very different environment from Wright, in the small Swiss watchmaking center of La Chaux-de-Fonds, where he was born in 1887. He enrolled in the local art school to study watch decoration and, encouraged by his instructor to aim for a career in architecture, left home in 1907 to wander about Europe. At the time he was attracted mostly to medieval monuments and showed little interest in contemporary architecture. In 1908 he arrived in Paris and found a place in the atelier of Auguste Perret, the pioneer of modern design in reinforced concrete, where he stayed only a year before setting out on a two-year voyage through Europe and the Near East. From 1912 to 1917 (when he returned to Paris to settle) Le Corbusier was again in La Chaux-de-Fonds, where he practiced architecture and began his prolific career as a pamphleteer of art, architecture and urbanism.

At this time (1914) he published his drawings for the "Dom-ino" house [11.10], which was intended to serve as a model or type rather than as the project for an actual structure.[11] The name refers to the rectangular domino-like reinforced concrete slabs as well as to the Latin word *domus* (house). The structural technique illustrated in the drawing was inspired by industrial structures and public buildings since the late nineteenth century, in which steel rods in the core of the columns are bent around into the formwork of the floor slabs before the concrete is poured, making it possible to fuse the floors, stairways, ceilings and piers, and to build with a minimum of supports, eliminating the need for either exterior or interior load-bearing walls.

The Dom-ino model, however, only appears to conform to this sytem; Le Corbusier's floors were of pot tile held with steel rods and required a complex scaffolding. The floors and piers were not fused, partly because the architect believed in separating elements (because of his admiration for the Parthenon?), and partly because it was technically impossible to join the columns to the floors without some kind of mushrooming "capital" at the juncture. But if the technique was problematic, the model had radical implications for the conception of small structures and, he hoped, for the production of mass housing in the postwar period. It demonstrated that the building could be raised off the ground on minimal foundations, that the exterior face could be a screen rather than a wall, that the roof might be flat and thus provide the inhabitants with usable outdoor space, and that the interior plan could be either entirely open or subdivided freely without having to resort to the customary partitions to support the weight above.

The principles were further developed in a series of designs for "Citrohan" houses (1920–22), small dwellings intended for mass production [*11.11*].[12] Though they are rendered as if in a rural setting or a suburban development, the houses evoked industrial architecture, as did their name, which suggested that of a successful automobile manufacturer, Citroën. Le Corbusier was attempting to emulate the economic efficiency and the formal simplicity of those standardized mass-produced machines not yet complicated by the application of good taste, and particularly machines designed to enclose the user: aircraft and steamships in addition to motor cars. He found support in traditional architectural forms—not those of the major historical styles, but of vernacular architecture. The exterior staircase placed against the side of the building is a feature of southern French farmhouses; the *parti* with a two-story living room at the front and bedrooms on a mezzanine balcony at the rear was suggested to him by the plan of a Parisian café which he and the painter Ozenfant frequented at the time. The facade dominated by industrial glazing was a feature of Parisian artisans' shops and artists' studios.[13]

Neither the Dom-ino nor the Citrohan model exploited the freedoms available in theory. The houses based on them were essentially boxes, and the interior plans proposed by Le Corbusier put smaller boxes within them. Though perspectives of the Citrohan houses show them in a setting of trees and grass, they are essentially urban, with side facades having minimal openings, as if they had been projected as row houses. It turned out that the model had its apotheosis as an apartment unit in Le Corbusier's later projects for high-rise housing, notably in the Unité d'habitation in Marseilles and elsewhere.

One of the first villas of Le Corbusier that realized his principles was built in 1926–27 at great expense at Garches, on the outskirts of Paris, for Mme de Monzie and her daughter and for Mr and Mrs Michael Stein, art collectors with a special taste for Matisse [*11.2, 12–15*].[14] Le Corbusier was repeatedly faced with the paradox that solutions he had conceived as a basis for mass-produced housing came to be realized for clients of great wealth whose interest in abstract art and other aspects of avant-garde culture predisposed them to the forms of his work.[15]

The architect called the Garches villa "The Terraces" to call attention to the open areas provided on each of the upper floors intended to encourage a close connection

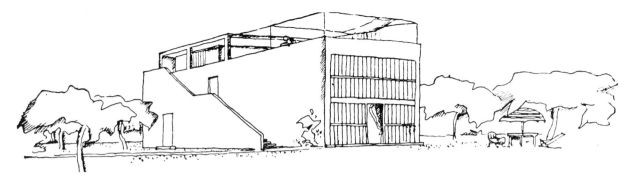

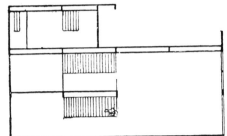

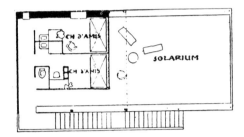

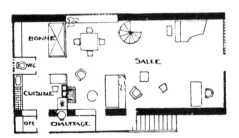

11.11 Le Corbusier, project for a
"Citrohan" house, 1920: two views; section
(above); and plans of (from bottom to top)
the ground floor, upper floor, and roof
terrace

11.12 Stein–de Monzie villa, Garches, by Le Corbusier, 1926–27: entrance front, seen from the driveway

between the interior and the exterior—a closed-in garden. The villa occupies a long, narrow plot. The distant shot of the front [*11.12*] shows how Le Corbusier impresses his concepts on the whole environment, leaving nothing to the unaccountable ways of nature. The slab of the driveway is integral to the building design, indicating the ground plane as well as defining a perspective focused on the secondary entrance, which is set off from the center of the facade (the principal entrance is marked by an odd canopy suspended on steel struts).

The entrance facade is ambiguous [*11.2, 12*]: it is both classically centered, with its fourth-story balcony, and asymmetrical, with differently articulated ground-floor entrances on either side of its unaccented center. One identifies the left door as the service entrance only by deducing that the plane hovering over the other door is a machine-age *porte cochère*. But these asymmetries are assimilated into a unity by a geometrical–arithmetical network of organizing "tracés régulateurs" (lines drawn diagonally across the elevation of the facades and apertures). The bays alternate in a 2–1–2–1–2 sequence characteristic of some Renaissance buildings (e.g., Alberti's Tempio Malatestiano in Rimini); the diagonals from the upper right to the lower left of the facade, the upper balcony aperture, the garage door, and the central ground floor window are all parallel, creating similar rectangles.

11.13 Stein–de Monzie villa: garden front

The garden facade [*11.13*] has the external stair proposed earlier in the Citrohan model, leading to the terrace of the main floor. In order to ensure that the rise of the external stairway would be parallel to the diagonal as drawn on the entrance facade, Le Corbusier raised its base above the garden level on an artificial mound. Here the strip windows, terrace-garden and free plan are essential elements of what Le Corbusier defined as the new architecture. The pilotis, another of his basic elements, are hidden behind the facade—not within the wall, as in earlier architecture, but freestanding. The facades, "bearers of light," Le Corbusier boasts, are mere skins of glass and masonry *hung* from the floors to which they are fused by the ferroconcrete armature. They do not touch the ground, he says.[16]

The main floor, containing the living and dining areas, kitchen and library, illustrates the free plan in its openness and in the curved partition that marks off the dining area [*11.14*]. The lower terrace is one one side, opposite the kitchen. The latter is closed only because this is a ménage with numerous servants. The interior view [*11.15*] illustrates what the architect called the "architectural promenade." He explains:

You go in. The architectural spectacle offers itself to your eye at once; you follow an itinerary, and a very varied sequence of vistas unfolds; you play with the flood of light illuminating the walls or creating shadows. The windows give views of the exterior, where you discover that the architectural unity is maintained.... The inside of the house ought to be *white*, but for this to be effective, there must be a well regulated polychromy. . . . Here, alive again under our modern eyes, are the architectural events of history: the pilotis, the strip windows, the roof-garden, the glass facade. *But you have to know, when the time comes,* how to recognize what is available, and how to give up things you have learned in order to pursue truths that are growing inescapably out of new techniques and under the impulse of a new spirit born out of the profound upheaval of the machine age.[17]

Le Corbusier writes of the natural environment as an adjunct to architecture; the sun serves to illuminate the walls, and the view from the windows reveals architectural unity.

This passage does not present the promenade as an organized itinerary through a determined sequence of spaces, but as the scattered impressions gathered by an observer in motion. The organization is obviously related not to traditional symmetrical order but rather to the kind of unfolding equilibrium of dissimilar elements, to the revelations of light, that Le Corbusier admired at the Acropolis in Athens.[18] Le Corbusier's domestic designs of the 1920s experimented with new ways, such as ramps and interior bridges, to open up interior circulation through the major public spaces and, as a climax, onto the roof-garden: "all of family life is directed toward this high part of the house. *The plan is turned around* (the interior disposition); one flees from the street; one goes toward the light and pure air."[19]

The opening of the plan and the penetration of the wall (except for the bedrooms, which were conventionally boxed in) represented a radical innovation not only aesthetically but also in style of life, breaking down the cellular containers that

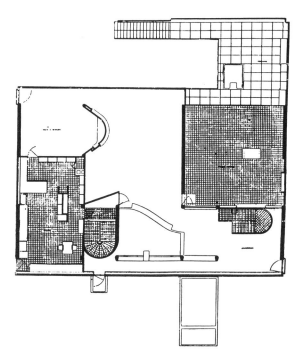

11.14 Stein–de Monzie villa: plan of the main floor. The dining area is at the top left, next to the kitchen (below left); the covered terrace is at the top right.

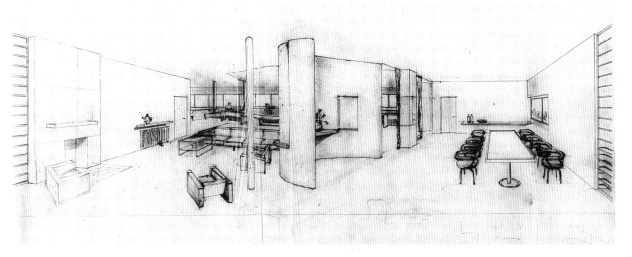

11.15 Stein–de Monzie villa: drawing by Le Corbusier showing the living room (left) and dining area

segregated different domestic functions—stairwells, corridors, living and dining areas. Le Corbusier sought to replace the somber, confined interiors and overstuffed furnishings of the typical middle-class house with light-bathed areas equipped with lean furniture, much of it bent wood or metal tubing. He substituted built-in cabinets beneath the strip windows for the heavy storage pieces of traditional interiors. This new concept of the interior anticipated the time when families rich enough to build villas would have to make do without numerous live-in servants (at Garches there were still four rooms for servants), but Le Corbusier obviously had difficulty in combining the need to segregate the living space and circulation routes of a domestic staff with the principle of openness.

The classic Le Corbusier country residence of the 1920s is the Villa Savoye at Poissy, an hour's drive from Paris, of 1928–30 [*1.7; 11.16–18*]. Sited on a squarish plot, it offers a sharp contrast to its environment.[20] Its gleaming white stuccoed exterior facades are raised off the ground on pilotis that mark a grid of 4×4 bays. These thin supports are revealed on three sides (on the fourth, entrance, facade only one bay at either end is open) and hold the principal living quarters aloft over the shadowy spaces of the ground floor, as if to reduce their contact with the earth. The entrance foyer, servants' quarters and garage on the ground level are set back one bay from the plane of the external pilotis, partly to reinforce the impression that the stories above rest on a void, and partly to make room for automobiles. Cars enter the right-hand bay of the entrance facade, continue around the oval curve of the foyer walls, and park diagonally in stalls on the far side. The module of the plan was tied to the turning radius. This accommodation of the automobile within the house and the adjustment of the plan to its turning radius had a symbolic value, underscoring Le Corbusier's mystique of the machine and paying homage to the role of the automobile in facilitating a new style of country living. It is comparable to Palladio's symbolic use of colonnaded villa wings adapted from local farm structures.

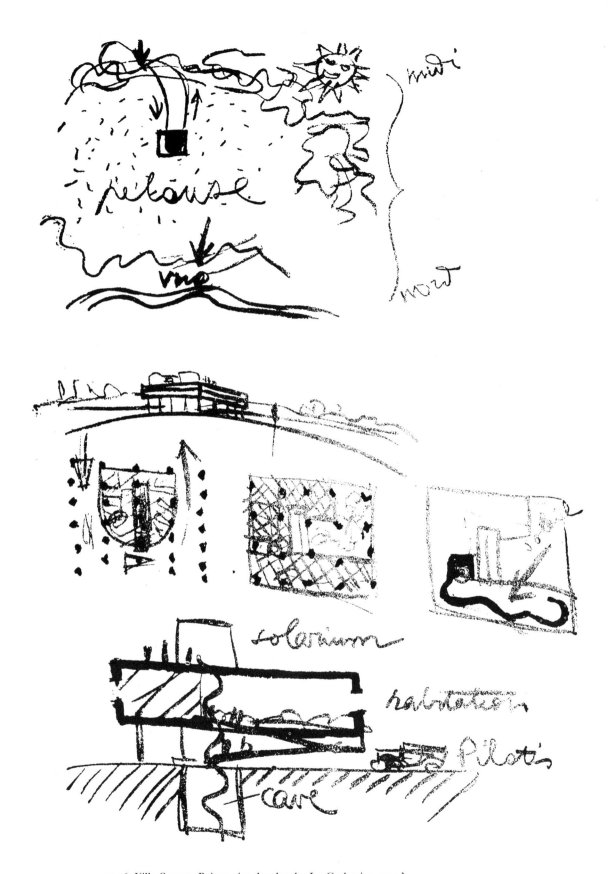

11.16 Villa Savoye, Poissy: site sketches by Le Corbusier, 1929?

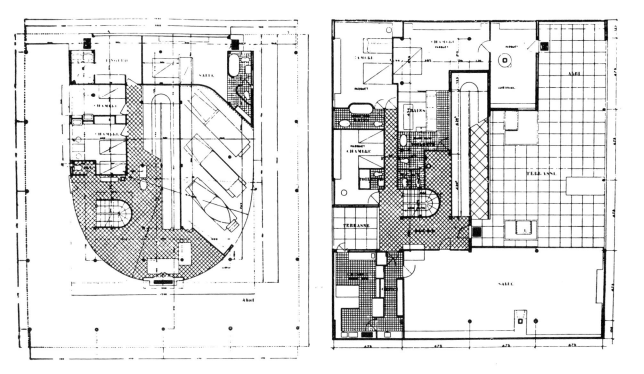

11.17 Villa Savoye, Poissy, by Le Corbusier, 1928–30: plans of the ground floor and upper floor

In a lecture called "The Plan of the Modern House,"[21] delivered during the construction of Villa Savoye, Le Corbusier analyzed the design, starting with the observation that visitors have been baffled by the building, "finding nothing in it that they could call a 'house.' They feel as if they were in something else entirely new. And . . . they aren't bored, I bet!" The text is accompanied by some explanatory drawings [11.16]. The topmost shows the sun as a major protagonist; arrows indicate the route of autos arriving and departing and, at the bottom, the direction of the principal view. The next sketch shows the house to be "a box in the air, pierced all round, without interruption, by a strip window—no more hesitation about making an architectural play of solids and voids." The plans show how the grid of pilotis permits great variation in each successive floor, and the bottom drawing shows how one rises by "a gentle ramp [which] leads, almost without one's having perceived it," to the main floor, while a spiral stair, indicated as a serpentine line (a "pure vertical organ"), joins all levels from the basement to the roof-garden. Le Corbusier explains:

> The plan is pure, responding to the most exact needs. It is in the right place in the rural landscape of Poissy.
> But at Biarritz it would be magnificent. If the view is different, on either side, or if the orientation differs, the terrace-garden would simply be modified.[22]

The ramp is an element much favored by Le Corbusier as a feature of the architectural promenade; its purpose appears to be primarily to enhance the experience of passage and to make one more aware of the play of architectural forms. Another ramp leads from the terrace-garden of the main floor onto the roof-garden [*11.18*].

The local situation affected the design of the villa so little that Le Corbusier later designed for an Argentine developer a garden-city project with seventeen Villas Savoye dispersed in different orientations within a fairly restricted area. The above quotation, and the passage quoted on p. 14, suggest that if a Corbusier villa did not respond specifically to the character of the site, it could be accommodated to a view. The architect insisted, however, on subjecting the view to an architectural order; at Poissy, the open terrace is walled in like a room; one looks outside through the rectangles of unglazed strip "windows" regularly punctuated by the verticals of the structural armature. This is illustrated in a sketch [*11.19*] made four years earlier for another villa client. The view (of the Folie St-James, an eighteenth-century park on the edge of Paris) is framed like a painting.[23]

By contrast, the roof-garden is shut off by curvilinear walls that look like the shapes in Le Corbusier's Purist still-lifes, so that there is little visual access to the surroundings.

The villa was occupied only briefly by the Savoye family, in part because the many innovations in structure and detailing caused exasperating technical failures. But this was an inevitable price paid for setting the traditions of building on a completely new path; in later decades what had been almost insuperable obstacles for Le Corbusier became, in part through his leadership, standard planning and practice.

After serving as barracks and a hayloft, the villa has been restored to something like its original condition, though its rural setting has been destroyed by tall housing blocks that hover over the original plot. But its authority is undiminished; it declaims with the severe intellectual rigor of geometrical proportions and classical reference while seducing the viewer with unique and varied experiences of light that unfold as one

11.18 Villa Savoye: terrace

11.19 Le Corbusier, view through a strip "window" of the roof-garden, from the second project for a villa for Mme Meyer, 1925.

advances along the ramps, modeling forms and defining spaces. Color plays a significant role in giving each image of the interior its character; a sky-blue or gray and a salmon-buff are used for interior walls, in some cases within the same room; doors are matte oxblood red, and steps and railings gray-black. The Villa Savoye is cerebral and sensual in equal measure.

If Le Corbusier insisted on dominating most aspects of nature, he was himself controlled by the sun. Throughout his writings, he referred repeatedly to the effects of light, and almost never to the terrain or to landscape elements. He saw sunlight as affecting architectural form in a way that abstracts it from the phenomenal world and effectively isolates a building from its setting, for example:

> Architecture is the skillful, exact, and magnificent play of volumes assembled in light. Our eyes are designed to see forms in light; shadow and light reveal forms; cubes, cones, spheres, cylinders, and pyramids are the great primary forms so well revealed by light; their image is exact and tangible, free of all ambiguities. This is why they are *beautiful, the most beautiful forms*. Everyone agrees on this point, children, primitives, and metaphysicians. It is a prerequisite of plastic art.[24]

And again,

> Light is for me the basis of architecture. I compose with light.[25]

The Poissy villa realizes the seven innovations the architect announced in his lecture on house planning of 1929: 1, free plan; 2, free facade; 3, independent skeleton; 4, strip or plate-glass windows; 5, pilotis; 6, roof-garden; 7, built-in furniture to free the interior. (These were immediately consolidated, for publication in the *Oeuvre complète*, into Le Corbusier's celebrated "Five Points," by eliminating items 3 and 7 and the plate glass.) The "Points" are the summation of the models and experiments of the preceding years; with the exception of the roof-garden they relate to structure and are detached from aesthetic considerations. They are not theoretical but simply define some potentialities of reinforced concrete construction. The widespread adoption of these elements in architecture since 1930 has probably been due more to the publication of Le Corbusier's work than to their influence as axioms. But the construction of the Villa Savoye was a disaster; it involved huge extra costs. The clients found it uninhabitable and abandoned it after a few visits.

Le Corbusier's concept of plastic art had developed, in the course of a decade, toward increasing emphasis on transitions from light to dark. This is illustrated at Poissy by the sculptural roof-garden elements and shadowy ground floor, which invite the modeling of sunlight as opposed to the sharp light–dark contrasts generated by the strictly cubic shapes of the early work. The change paralleled Picasso's emergence from the planes of synthetic Cubism to the ponderous, modeled classical figures of the 1920s. Color also played a significant role—as it had at Garches—not evident from photographs: the underside of the main floor was painted dark green, lighter green and gray were used on the walls, and the exterior window frames were a brick red. On the curvilinear protective walls of the sun deck, steel blue and rose alternate on the inner and outer faces, underscoring the relationship of the forms to Purist still-life painting.

Le Corbusier sought, as Wright had, to realize a domestic architecture that would liberate society from the confinements and traditional applied ornamentation of the bourgeois house. He wrote to a client, Mme Meyer, in 1925:

> We have dreamed of making you a house that would be smooth and compact like a well proportioned box and that would not be injured by a multiplicity of details which create an artificial and illusory picturesqueness, and which are distorted by the light and only add to the confusion of the surroundings. We are opposed to the fashion for complicated houses full of clashing elements that is afflicting us here and abroad.[26]

Le Corbusier's mix of tradition and modernity differed from Wright's. In his early years he had been, like Wright, a provincial; both had been avid readers of Ruskin, a vigorous proponent of medieval architecture, and when Le Corbusier first traveled in Italy, he had eyes only for medieval monuments and he drew them in a deft Ruskinian style. In Vienna, he overlooked the radical new architecture of Hoffmann and Loos. But ultimately he chose to turn, like so many of the great Western European architects, to his classical roots, as his drawings show and as we can see throughout his work. He remained sensitive to all of past architecture, and was never carried away by his futuristic enthusiasm for the machine to the point of rejecting the lessons of history.

His modernism manifested itself in two distinct ways: first, in his effort to use new building technologies to free his clients from the confinements of traditional architecture, and particularly to provide enriching light, open space and ease of movement; and secondly, in his affinity with and practice of contemporary abstract art, particularly Cubism, which gave him inspiration for what he called the magnificent play of forms in light.

Building concepts realized in the villas of the 1920s were essentially conceived for city dwellings—the open ground-floor plan, the block raised on pilotis, the strip window, and the roof-garden. Le Corbusier's early works stand alone in the history of the villa by affirming rather than rejecting the conditions of urban life.

Like many European modernists, he had socialist political tendencies (later transformed into support of the Vichy government), which moved him to a deep concern for the design of cities and of mass housing. But his city schemes were as autocratic as any of the age of absolutism, and he had difficulty in coming to terms with the practicalities of workers' housing.[27] He was eventually less successful than Wright in reducing the cost of dwellings, and his clients were frequently tortured by technical failures and cost overruns. The buildings I have illustrated, like those of Wright, were for very wealthy clients.

Le Corbusier's clients were as different from the villa builders of earlier centuries as those of Wright, but they also bore no resemblance to Wright's moderately prosperous Midwestern patrons. Many were in fact Americans who had the means to live a deracinated existence as intellectuals supported by private means in France. For them, the millennial villa ideology no longer obtained, because their country residence was not an escape from the intense preoccupations of city affairs. Yet the villa remained for them an alternative to urban life made possible by the development of the motor car, which could provide the benefits of sun and fresh air for a weekend stay or, in the case of the Steins, access from their suburban location to Parisian cultural events. They could enjoy the best of the two contrasting worlds depicted by the Roman poets of antiquity. The clients who turned to Le Corbusier tended to be adventurous and in some way eccentric: mainstream French culture was particularly conservative. For those who bought art, a house by the architect may have represented an object in their collection, and they were willing to forego some of the comforts and proprieties of traditional living to be seen as supporters of an obviously revolutionary innovation in the history of architecture.

During the 1930s, the two architects extended the potential of their vision by, in certain respects, crossing paths. Le Corbusier cast aside the machine aesthetic and began to use the native materials and techniques of the site and Wright exploited the possibilities of reinforced concrete cantilevers to achieve a free plan with weightless walls of glass.

Le Corbusier dismissed the revolutionary principles of the early villas—the Five Points, the industrialized symbolism—even while the Villa Savoye was under construction.[28] In drawings of 1930 for the Errazuriz house in Chile [11.20] the ramp and the floor are of uncut masonry loosely laid in mortar as in traditional building; the mezzanine and apparently the roof are supported by a timber post-and-lintel system. Perhaps the problems experienced by the architect in getting builders to follow his instructions in France made it seem prudent to adopt more conventional structural means for a distant site—though the house was never built.

The roof of the Errazuriz house slants downward from the outer walls to form an uneven V—an inversion of the normal pitched roof that later became standard usage in

11.20 Le Corbusier, project for the Errazuriz house, 1930

suburban dwellings in the United States. One of Le Corbusier's sketches shows the villa in its rugged setting, suggesting that the profile of the roof is intended to echo the mountains behind—a far cry from the abstraction of the drawing for Garches [11.2]. The piers, presumably of masonry, seem heavier than necessary, announce the future phase of the architect's work in which dense and massive forms replace the light curtain walls of the 1920s. Perhaps the inspiration for the Chile design came from Le Corbusier's lecture tour in Brazil in 1929, when he made many sketches of the landscape, the Indians, and vernacular dwellings that seem infinitely distant from his earlier obsession with the modern machine. Le Corbusier's interest in the French Syndicalist movement, which emphasized local and regional diversity, also played a role in his changed approach of the 1930s.

Two designs of the same period, the villa for Mme de Mandrot near Toulon (1930–31)—the first of the new type to be executed—and the seaside villa at Les Mathes (1933–37), show that the regionalism of the Chile design is not due entirely to its exotic distance. They have load-bearing walls of fieldstone laid in irregular courses in thick beds of mortar. There are no pilotis, strip windows or sun roof. Both are basically shoe-box shaped structures, with tightly designed, relatively open plans that serve a maximum number of functions in a minimal space. In this respect they resemble Wright's low-cost Usonian houses from 1937 on.

In Le Corbusier's most radical villa design of the 1930s, for a weekend retreat outside Paris, of 1935, three concrete pavilions ranked side-by-side are covered by slightly

11.21 Le Corbusier, project for a "maison de weekend" outside Paris, 1935

curved ceiling-roofs supported only by corner posts [11.21]. The infill between the posts is partly glass brick and partly masonry. The vaults were designed to carry a layer of sod in which grass and shrubs might be planted. This country cottage, though suburban, rejects any relationship to the architect's concepts of the city and industry. It represents a return to the millennial myth of the villa as a retreat from urban ills.

At the same time, Wright began to use reinforced concrete as an essential element in a domestic design for the first time in his career, in a work that seems today to be the most unprecedented and imaginative villa of this century, Fallingwater at Bear Run, Pennsylvania, for Edgar J. Kaufmann, a wealthy Pittsburgh merchant and entrepreneur [1.23; 11.22–24].[29]

Bear Run is a stream that flows through a sloping forested property. The client planned to build a weekend retreat on the bank opposite the waterfall, and was astonished to find in Wright's first drawings that it had been placed directly over the fall and was to be founded on a great boulder (engineers engaged to study the feasibility of the proposed foundations reported that they were insufficiently sound, and the architect, on hearing this, told the client that he did not deserve a Wright building).

Wright's purpose was to make the house an evocation and extension of the site. Because of its "organic" conception, Fallingwater has no facades in the usual sense of the word, and no major axes; there is no one point from which it was designed to be viewed. The structure is treelike in conception. Rough masonry-faced piers emerge like trunks from the rocks and generate limblike cantilevers that support floors and terraces.

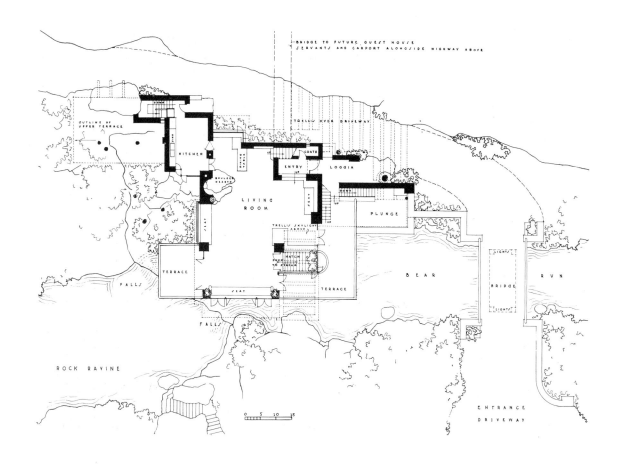

The masonry verticals that reflect the rockiness of the site contrast abruptly with the smooth cement parapets, seeming to express at once a contrast and a partnership of the natural and the industrial. Wright actually wanted the parapets to be painted gold, adding another dimension—one of fantasy—to the partnership, but the clients refused. These allusions are strictly symbolic; the reality of the ferroconcrete musculature that makes such daring possible is invisible.

The approach is by a path that descends the far bank, bridges the stream, then flanks the house and makes a sharp turn into a shadowed, gulf-like corridor between the house and a high, rustic retaining wall. The entrance sequence is like a voyage of the spirit from darkness into light. Trellises between the house and the cliff darken the passage; the entrance, midway along the corridor, is in a cavelike recess. On entering, one's attention is drawn through the unbroken bands of window on the far side of the low-ceilinged living-room to the light and the expanse of the woods beyond [11.24]. The floor of local stone draws the outdoors into the interior of the house; as in Wright's early work, an imposing fireplace is the core of the living room. From the living room a flight of suspended steps descends to a pool in the rocks under a terrace. It hardly serves a practical purpose (the client asked to have it eliminated), but Wright insisted upon it as an evocation of communion with the stone and water.

His achievement was more profound and more complete than that of the designers of picturesque architecture a century earlier. They sought to emulate the informal

11.22–24 Kaufmann house, Fallingwater, Bear Run, Pa., by Frank Lloyd Wright, 1936: plan *(opposite)*, exterior, and living room

character of the natural and the designed landscape in the style of country buildings. Wright made his buildings evolve out of and within nature to the point at which nature and structure become merged in a new landscape. At Fallingwater there is no designed landscape other than the essential access pathways, and exceptional efforts were made to avoid changing the pre-existing state of the site.

Wright continued to design country houses throughout his career with undiminished inventiveness. But he had little impact on the succeeding generation because he was unique and inimitable, and because society and its values had changed at an unprecedented rate. Younger architects could not re-establish the fervor of his romantic nineteenth-century Americanism. They could much more easily follow the Europeans because they promulgated clear, teachable rules, and because Americans had always bowed to the authority of European culture. Moreover, in the years after the Second World War, American architectural intellectuals and planners focused attention on pressing problems of urban renewal and large-scale housing, which were not strong areas of Wright's legacy. While the practice of residential architecture continued to flourish into the 1960s (when it began to lose its economic viability), it became as isolated from the major issues of urban design as suburban dwellers were isolated from the inner city. The great achievements of Wright were occasionally acknowledged but rarely emulated.[30]

Even with the recent reaction against abstraction and reaffirmation of richness and variety in architecture, Wright's achievement has not been re-evaluated. That of Le Corbusier, on the other hand, has been constantly taken as a source of new invention. There was a revival of Le Corbusier's early villas in American domestic architecture starting in the late 1960s and early 1970s and continuing vigorously today.[31] But the architecture changed tone and message. It is no longer an affirmation of the machine age and of the freedoms it brought, but a stylish and sophisticated quotation that one understands as a homage to the master's manner rather than to his convictions. The issues of contemporary architecture revolve more around style and association—and for a few architects around the abstract essence of architecture—than around society, technology and nature.

I pointed out earlier the tendency of Western architecture to oscillate between purist classical modes and pictorial, irregular ones, and recently this pattern has been repeated. The austerities of European modernism have been countered by a variety of efforts to restore the richness and allusion of earlier centuries. Robert Venturi was a pioneer in proposing such a shift in a book of 1966 called *Complexity and Contradiction in Architecture*, and in the course of the 1970s there emerged across the world the mode of historical allusion that critics have ineloquently labeled the postmodern style.

It has seemed on first sight (and the impression has been fostered by many of the architects themselves) that postmodern architects intended to return to classical forms, but I believe that, nonbearing Doric columns and Palladian plans notwithstanding, this architecture has resumed the postures of the late eighteenth- and early nineteenth-century promoters of association and character. In a sense it is picturesque as well, though this time the pictures don't exist. It represents, in short, a new romanticism, an escape from the ideals and social commitments of the modern European masters and from the grave intensity of Wright. Also, because true romanticism is not possible in these days when every tradition is being diluted and a plausible return to past craftsmanship is unachievable, it is practiced with irony. Irony is our form of self-protection.

It is difficult for me to interpret the villa of today with the confidence I feel when, with the advantage of historical perspective, I discuss those of earlier times. No historian can see his own time clearly because he cannot stand back from it sufficiently to distinguish its truths from its ideologies. Moreover, the villa has become an exceedingly rare phenomenon because the cost of custom building has outstripped the financial resources of all but the exceedingly rich. It is easy to see that today's villa builders are no longer motivated by the pastoral images of the landscape and country life inherited by earlier generations from the classical poets and also, for a time, from the painters of landscape. Agriculture and an agrarian faith no longer draw many of the wealthy into the country. They build, as always, to have a refuge from the city, because they can afford it, and because of the fresh air and informality. It seems that the traditional ideology that imputed spiritual and moral values to country life has finally been lost, and with it a link between the villa and the social, political and economic life of our time.

Postscript

Frank Lloyd Wright, who was antagonistic to urbanization, wanted to address the relation of the dwelling to the land, and found vocabularies and syntaxes largely independent of those of historical Western architecture. Le Corbusier wanted in his villas to address at once the promise of industrialization and the ideals of the European classical tradition. But while these two diverged widely in their agendas, they were always closer to one another than to unselfconscious traditional builders because they believed, and desperately wanted to persuade others to believe, that through design they could make a better world, physically and spiritually. What distinguishes a villa from a farmhouse or a country cottage in their buildings, as in the whole of the history of Western architecture back to the time of Horace and Pliny, is the intense, programmatic investment of ideological goals. This, I believe, has always been more true of the design of villas than of any other building type, because the image of a refuge in the country focuses not so much on the accommodation of clearly defined rural functions as on a cornucopia of values absent or debased in the city. The city, as the locus of social interaction, is inevitably mundane and temporal, while the country, in exacting confrontations with the immanent brute forces and sensuous enchantments of nature, prompts inspired responses.

NOTES

AB   *The Art Bulletin*
AR   *The Architectural Review*
BCISA   *Bolletino del Centro Internazionale di Studi di Architettura "Andrea Palladio"*
JRSA   *Journal of the Royal Society of Arts*
JSAH   *Journal of the Society of Architectural Historians*
JWCI   *Journal of the Warburg and Courtauld Institutes*

1 The Typology of the Villa (pp. 9–34)

1. Since the very beginnings of the genre of villa literature, there has been an ambiguity as to whether "villa" refers to the estate, the buildings on the estate, or just to the residence. In antiquity, the owner's residence was called the 'villa urbana' to distinguish it from an agricultural building which would be called a "villa rustica," while Palladio calls the former a "casa di villa," the "villa" being the whole estate. It will be more convenient here to accept contemporary usage in which "villa" means the main residence.

2. I am much indebted for the articulation of villa ideology to the innovative treatments of R. Bentmann and M. Müller, *Die Villa als Herrschaftsarchitektur: Versuch einer kunst- und sozialgeschichtlichen Analyse*, Frankfurt a. M., 1970, and of Grazia Gobbi, *La villa fiorentina*, Florence, 1980. See also the essay "Villa" (1908) by the poet and critic Rudolf Borchardt, *Prosa*, III, Stuttgart, 1960, pp. 38–70.

3. See the comments of Girolamo Priuli, a Venetian writing in the early years of the sixteenth century, quoted on pp. 92–93. I believe this phenomenon to have been different from that of the nineteenth century in that the unprivileged small landholders did not build proper villas with the symbols of the ideology, but shacks and farmhouses. For an overview of the types, see Martin Kubelik, *Die Villa im Veneto: zur typologischen Entwicklung im Quattrocento*, 2 vols, Munich, 1977.

4. An impressive example, relevant to this study, is Fernand Braudel's *The Mediterranean and the Mediterranean World in the Age of Philip II*, New York, 1972.

5. A similar arcaded podium has been discovered recently in the Roman villa of Settefinestre [2.4, 5]; this villa is also cubic in plan: see below, pp. 45 and 84.

6. I have dealt with this problem in a paper: see James Ackerman, "Sources of the Renaissance Villa," *Papers of the Twentieth International Congress of the History of Art* (1961), II, Princeton, 1963, pp. 6–18. Several authors have pointed to the role of vernacular farm buildings as a source of Renaissance villa design: see especially K. Forster and R. Tuttle, "Back to the Farm: Vernacular Architecture and the Development of the Renaissance Villa," *Architectura*, I, 1974, pp. 1–12, and Claudia Lazzaro, "Rustic Country House to Refined Farmhouse," *JSAH*, XLIV, 1985, pp. 346–67.

2 The Ancient Roman Villa (pp. 35–61)

1. Horace's most revealing comments on the benefits of country life appear in his *Odes* (*Carmina*), III.i and III.xiii; *Satires*, I.vi and II.vi (source of the country mouse passage); *Epistles*, I.x, I.xiv, I.xvi and V.xvi; and *Epode* II.

2. K. D. White has compiled a useful anthology of ancient writings on rural matters in *Country Life in Classical Times*, Ithaca, 1977; see also Evelyn, Countess Martinengo-Cesaresco,

The Outdoor Life in Greek and Roman Poets, London, 1911.

3. See Jean-Marie André, *L'otium dans la vie morale et intellectuelle romaine*, Paris, 1966.

4. See A. Foucher, "La vie rurale à l'époque de Caton d'après le *De agricultura*," *Bull. de l'Assoc. G. Budé*, 1957, pp. 41–53; Alan Astin, *Cato the Censor*, Oxford, 1978, esp. pp. 240–66; René Martin, *Recherches sur les agronomes latins et leurs conceptions économiques et sociales*, Paris, 1971; Kenneth White, "Roman Agricultural Writers, I: Varro and his Predecessors," *Aufstieg und Niedergang der römischen Welt*, I, pt iv, Berlin/New York, 1973, pp. 439–97.

5. For the ownership of country properties in the late Republic and Empire, see Elizabeth Rawson, "The Ciceronian Aristocracy and its Properties," and M. I. Finley, "Private Farm Tenancy in Italy before Diocletian," in M. I. Finley, ed., *Studies in Roman Property*, Cambridge, 1975. For the evolution of Roman agricultural economy, see Cedric A. Yeo, "The Development of the Roman Plantation and the Marketing of Farm Products," *Finanzarchiv*, 13, 1952, pp. 321–42.

6. Cedric A. Yeo, in "The Economics of Roman and American Slavery," *Finanzarchiv*, 13, 1952, pp. 445–85, shows that the *latifundia* declined in the course of the first century AD when the need for grains caused a return to tenant farming.

7. See Egon Maróti, "The Vilicus and the Villa-System in Ancient Italy," *Oikumene*, I, 1976, pp. 109–24.

8. I have found useful the discussion of Virgil's approach to the countryside in Friedrich Klinger, "Über das Lob des Landlebens in Virgils *Georgica*," *Hermes*, 64, 1931, pp. 159–89; Gilbert Highet, *Poets in a landscape*, London/New York, 1957, pp. 50–74; Martin, *Recherches*, pp. 109–210 (the most comprehensive); A. Cossarini, "Le Georgiche di Virgilio: ideologia della proprietà," *Giornale filologico ferrarese*, I, 1978, pp. 83–93; and André, *Otium*, pp. 500–533.

9. Pt II, ll. 458–96. A prose equivalent close in spirit to Virgil can be found in Cicero's salute to Cato, *De senectute*, XV. 51.

10. *Recherches*, pp. 109ff.

11. This designation does not appear to be related to the Vitruvian *pseudourbana*, which I take to be a formal type—the compact villa block with a central axis of the kind found at Pompeii [2.7]—as distinguished from villas with more loosely organized assemblages of parts; it means nothing more than "residence," and is sometimes called *domus*.

12. Velleius Paterculus, *Res gestae Divi Augusti*, II. xxiii. 4; see also the comment of Pliny the Elder, *Nat. Hist.*, IX.170; Plutarch, *Life of Lucullus*, XXXIX.

13. The most thorough and up-to-date treatment of ancient villas in Italy may be found in Harald Mielsch, *Die römische Villa: Architektur und Lebensform*, Munich, 1987. See also R. J. Carrington, "Studies in Campanian Villae Rusticae," *Journal of Roman Studies*, XXI, 1931, pp. 110–30; B. Crova, *Edilizia e tecnica rurale di Roma antica*, Milan, 1942; A. Mansuelli, "La villa romana nell'Italia settentrionale," *Parola del passato*, LVII, 1957, pp. 444–58; Jens E. Skydsgaard, *Den romerske Villa Rustica*, Copenhagen, 1961; K. D. White, *Roman Farming*, Ithaca/London, 1970, pp. 415–41; J. J. Rossiter, *Roman Farm Buildings in Italy* (British Academy in Rome International Series, 52), Oxford, 1978. The majority of the remains were excavated before the period of scientific archaeology, and few of the more recent excavations have been adequately reported.

14. Felice Barnabei, *La villa pompeiana di P. Fannio Sinistore*, Rome, 1901. The name given to the villa appeared on the urn

excavated there. There is no proof that that gentleman was the proprietor.

15. M. Aylwin Cotton and Guy P. R. Métraux, *The San Rocco Villa at Francolise*, New York, 1985. Originally reported in P. von Blanckenhagen, M. A. Cotton and J. B. Ward-Perkins, "Two Roman Villas at Francolise, Prov. Caserta; Interim Report on Excavations, 1962–64," *Papers of the British School in Rome*, 33, 1965, pp. 57ff.

16. A. Carandini, ed., *Settefinestre: una villa schiavistica nell'Etruria romana*, 3 vols, Modena, 1985; also A. Carandini and T. Tatton-Brown, "Excavations at the Roman Villa at 'Sette Finestre' in Etruria, 1975–79: First Interim Report," in K. Painter, ed., *Roman Villas in Italy*, London, 1980, pp. 9–17.

17. See John d'Arms, *Romans on the Bay of Naples: a Social and Cultural Study of the Villas and Their Owners from 150 B.C. to A.D. 400*, Cambridge, Mass., 1970; idem, "Proprietari e ville nel golfo di Napoli," *I campi flegrei nell'archeologia e nella storia (Accad. naz. dei Lincei, Atti dei convegni*, 33) Rome, 1977, pp. 347–63.

18. H. Drerup, "Die römische Villa," *Marburger Winckelmann-Programm*, 1959, pp. 1–24; a useful and well illustrated summary of the discoveries is Theodor Kraus, *Pompeii and Herculaneum*, New York, 1975, esp. pp. 65–96.

19. A. de Franciscis, "La villa romana di Oplontis," in B. Andreae and H. Kyrieleis, eds, *Neue Forschungen in Pompeii*, Recklinghausen, 1979. For a contemporary villa of comparable scale near Rome, see M. Moretti and A. Sgubini Moretti, *La villa Volusii a Lucus Feroniae*, Rome, 1977.

20. Guido Mansuelli, "La villa nelle *epistulae* di C. Plinio Cecilio secondo," *Studi romagnoli*, 24, 1978, pp. 59–76.

21. H. Winnefeld, "Tusci und Laurentinum des jüngeren Plinius," *Jb. des Kaiserl. Deutschen Archäologischen Instituts*, VI, 1891, pp. 201–17; a collection of earlier reconstructions, an indifferent translation and a new proposal were published by Helen Tanzer in *The Villas of Pliny the Younger*, New York, 1924. Recently a competition for the reconstruction of Laurentinum was held in France among distinguished contemporary architects and produced a new group of proposals [2.11]: Institut français de l'architecture, *La Laurentine et l'invention de la villa romaine*, Paris, 1982.

Archaeologists are presently excavating some of the many villa remains in the area designated by Pliny as the site of Laurentinum, and some claim to have discovered the villa; for one claimant, see Eugenia Salza Prina Ricotti, "La cosi detta Villa Magna. Il Laurentinum de Plinio il Giovane," *Atti della Accad. naz. dei Lincei, Rendiconti della classe di scienze morali, etc.*, ser. VIII, XXXIX, 1984, pp. 339–58.

22. Interpretation of the texts and of their arcane vocabulary has been much furthered by the painstaking analysis of A. N. Sherwin-White, *The Letters of Pliny*, Oxford, 1966, pp. 186–99 and 321–30, and Karl Lehmann-Hartleben, *Plinio il giovane: lettere scelte*, Florence, 1936, pp. 43–57.

23. The "formam . . . pictam," according to Lehmann-Hartleben (*Plinio*, p. 51) and Sherwin-White (*Letters*, p. 323), is a map; Mansuelli ('Villa nelle *epistulae*," p. 68) rejects this reading, reaffirming the traditional one that it is a landscape painting.

24. As suggested in the perceptive interpretation of Eckhard Lefèvre, "Plinius-studien I: Römische Baugesinnung und Landschaftsauffassung in den Villenbriefe," *Gymnasium*, 74, 1977, pp. 519ff. In addition, as suggested by Heinz Kähler in *Hadrian und seine Villa bei Tivoli*, Berlin, 1950, the long axes described by Pliny move through a sequence of doorways leading to a view-window; these doorways function like stage *coulisses*, and a viewer at the beginning of the axis cannot visualize the intervening spaces. Similar collapsing of space by successive planes occurs in Pompeian wall-painting.

25. e.g. the passage already quoted, *Epist.* II.xvii. 21, goes on: "tot facies locorum totidem fenestris et distinguit et miscet."

26. See n. 17.

27. Examples cited by Mielsch (*Römische Villa*, pp. 50ff.) are villas at Sperlonga, Anzio, Capo di Massa and Punta near Sorrento.

28. M. Rostovtseff, "Die hellenistisch-römische Architekturlandschaft," *Mitt. des Kaiserl. Deutschen Archäologischen Instituts, Röm. Abteilung*, XXV, 1911, pp. 1–185; Paul Zanker, "Die Villa als Vorbild des späten pompeianischen Wohngeschmacks," *Jb. des Deutschen Archäologischen Instituts*, 94, 1979, pp. 461–523.

29. As Mielsch suggests (*Römische Villa*, pp. 64f.), these changes may have been stimulated by the innovations of the vast complex of the Golden House of Nero in Rome.

30. Anton Gnirs, "Forschungen über antiken Villenbau in Südistrien I: Die Grabungen in der antiken Villenlage von Val Catena," *Jahreshefte des Österreichischen Archäologischen Institutes in Wien*, XVIII, 1915, pp. 101–46.

31. N. Lupo, "La villa di Sette Bassi sulla via Latina," *Ephemeris Dacoromana*, VII, 1937, pp. 117–88.

32. There were exceptions in the late Empire, such as the villa of Diocletian at Spalato, a four-square, compact, but huge walled town.

3 The Early Villas of the Medici (pp. 63–87)

1. The most relevant of Petrarch letters on rural life are: *Familiarium rerum libri*, XIII. 4, XIII. 8, XVII. 5, XIX. 16; *Senilium rerum libri*, XV. 3. My interpretation of Petrarch is indebted to Bernhard Rupprecht's fundamental article on the ideology of the villa, "Villa. Zur Geschichte eines Ideals," *Wandlungen des paradiesischen und utopischen: Studien zum Bild eines Ideals (Probleme der Kunstwissenschaft, II)*, Berlin, 1966, pp. 210–20. In emphasizing Petrarch's anti-political rhetoric, however, Rupprecht undervalues the irony implicit in the powerful attraction he felt to the centers of power, an attraction shared by virtually all writers on villa life.

2. Giovanni Villani, *Cronica*, in *Croniche storiche di Giovanni, Matteo e Filippo Villani*, III, Milan, 1848, p. 326. For a general treatment of the pre-Renaissance villas, see also B. Patzak, *Palast und Villa in Toscana*, I, *Die Zeit des Werdens*, Leipzig, 1912. For commentary on the social and economic aspects, see Renato Stopani, *Medievali "case da signore" nella campagna fiorentina*, Florence, 1977; Grazia Gobbi, *La villa fiorentina*, Florence, 1980. For a general treatment of the early Medici villas, see Hartmut Bierman, "Lo sviluppo della villa toscana sotto l'influenza umanistica della corte di Lorenzo il Magnifico," *BCISA*, XI, 1969, pp. 36–46. An important and richly documented source for information on the contemporary Florentine villas and farm properties of families other than the Medici is Amanda Lillie, *Florentine Villas in the Fifteenth Century: A Study of the Strozzi and Sassetti Country Properties*, diss., Courtauld Institute of Art, University of London, 1986.

3. *Le vite de' più eccelenti pittori, scultori ed architetti* [hereafter *Vite*], ed. G. Milanesi, II, Florence, 1906, p. 442. On the villa and its dating, see Miranda Ferrara and Francesco Quinterio, *Michelozzo di Bartolomeo*, Florence, 1984, pp. 168–72, with a review of earlier literature. Their date of 1427–33 is based on documented visits there by members of the family escaping the plague of 1430 and by Cosimo and his brother Lorenzo in 1433.

4. The chronology of the Medici villas at Trebbio, Cafaggiolo and Careggi, which is vague in the literature of the last generation, was first clarified by Mario Gori Sassoli, "Michelozzo e l'architettura di villa nel primo Rinascimento," *Storia dell'arte*, 23, 1975, pp. 5–51, and has been further refined by Ferrara and Quinterio, *Michelozzo*. Many new documents have been brought to bear on the problem since the earlier work of Patzak, *Palast und Villa*, II, 1913, pp. 68–82. For the Palazzo Comunale in Montepulciano and other works of Michelozzo's conservative style, see H. Saalman, "The Palazzo Comunale in Montepulciano," *Zeitschr. für Kunstgeschichte*, XXVIII, 1965, pp. 1–46. Presumably the tile(?)

roofing shown in Saalman's Figs. 1 and 3 is a fifteenth-century innovation, because it would inhibit the use of the machicolated parapets for defensive purposes and its wooden framework would constitute a fire hazard in the event of a military attack.

5. Vittorio Franchetti Pardo and Giovanna Casali, *Medici nel contado fiorentino*, Florence, 1978, pp. 48–53; in the tax declaration of 1433 (Archivio di Stato, Florence [hereafter ASF], *Medici avanti il Principato* [hereafter *MAP*], 88, 382) Cosimo's cousin Averardo di Francesco is listed as having "Uno abituro atto a fortezza posto in mugello nel popolo della pieve di S. Giovanni in Petroio luogho detto chafagiuolo con fossato intorno" with twenty-one farms.

6. ibid., pp. 52, 56, from ASF, *Possessioni medicee*, vol. 4112, of 1456.

7. See Daniela Mignani, *Le ville medicee di Giusto Utens*, Florence, 1982. Fourteen lunettes were commissioned as decorations for the sixteenth-century villa at Artimino.

8. Ferrara and Quinterio (*Michelozzo*, pp. 176–83) rediscovered the document on the visit of Eugene IV and favor the pre-1434 date, while L. H. Heydenreich and W. Lotz (*Architecture in Italy, 1400–1600*, Harmondsworth, 1974, p. 332, n. 16) propose 1430 for Trebbio and *c.* 1450 for Cafaggiolo; Gori Sassoli ("Michelozzo," pp. 39ff.) dates Trebbio in the period of Michelozzo's church at Bosco ai Frati, 1427–36, and Cafaggiolo in the period following the close of that work. Like Ferrara and Quinterio, he suggests that since Medici family decisions were made communally, commissions did not necessarily have to await the official transfer of property; but it seems unlikely that Cosimo would have ordered building at Cafaggiolo before the property was inherited by his branch of the family.

9. In 1485 Lorenzo di Piero di Cosimo de' Medici, "The Magnificent," the sole heir of Cosimo following the murder in 1478 of his brother Giuliano in the Pazzi conspiracy, sold Cafaggiolo to his cousins Lorenzo and Giovanni di Pierfrancesco de' Medici to settle a longstanding debt to their father. Its dependencies at the time included 66 *poderi*, 20 *case*, 3 *mulini*, and *fornaci* (Franchetti Pardo and Casali, *Medici*, p. 58, from ASF, *MAP*, 150, n. 39; 104, n. 48, col. 457). The price was 37,350 fl., of which the palace was estimated at 6,000 fl.

10. On the evolution of the post-feudal system of landholding in Tuscany, see Giovanni Cherubini, *Signori, contadini, borghesi: ricerche sulla società italiana del basso medioevo*, Florence, 1974, especially ch. 2; exhaustive statistical studies have been made by Elio Conti, *La formazione della struttura agraria moderna nel contado fiorentino*, Rome, I; III, 2, 1965.

11. See Gobbi's chapter entitled "Origine e sviluppo della villa suburbana nel contesto dell'economia fiorentina dall'età comunale al regime signorile," *Villa fiorentina*, pp. 9–19; Franchetti Pardo and Casali, *Medici*, p. 12ff.

12. Leone Battista Alberti, *I libri della famiglia*, ed. C. Grayson, Bari, 1960, pp. 194ff.; translation from Renée Neu Watkins, *The Family in Renaissance Florence*, Columbia, S.C., 1969, pp. 187ff.

13. The Sforza letter is reproduced in B. Buser, *Die Beziehungen der Mediceer zu Frankreich*, Leipzig, 1879, p. 347. In the tax declarations of 1427 and 1433 the property appears as "A place we live in with a court and garden and farms for our use . . . with numerous cultivated properties and vineyards." The annual yield from "nostra parte" of the *mezzadria* contract is estimated at 2,906 fl. (Franchetti Pardo and Casali, *Medici*, pp. 48, 54–56, from ASF, *MAP*, 83, n. 89; 165, cols. 78–81).

14. Vasari, *Vite*, loc. cit. (above, n. 3); Ferrara and Quinterio, *Michelozzo*, pp. 245–51; Gori Sassoli, "Michelozzo," p. 41. The eastern (far right) wing may have been added in the program of Alessandro de' Medici in the 1530s, but in any case before 1598, when it appears on a plan of the villa by Giorgio Vasari the Younger (illustrated by Ferrara and Quinterio, p. 249, and Gori Sassoli, p. 24, fig. G).

There is an anonymous later eighteenth-century drawing from the archive of the Ospedale di Santa Maria Nuova (illustrated

without commentary in Philip Foster, *A Study of Lorenzo de' Medici's Villa at Poggio a Caiano*, 2 vols, New York, 1978, pl. I B; the original was kindly located for me by Annamaria Petrioli Tofani), which is labelled "Veduta e pianta della villa di Careggi vecchio di S.A.R." ("S.A.R." indicates the elevation of the Medici dynasty by the Pope to royal privileges in 1699: Harold Acton, *The Last of the Medici*, Florence/Edinburgh, 2nd ed., 1980, p. 222). This drawing is, as Howard Saalman reminded me, a pendant to one showing the villa roughly as it is today (". . . villa di Careggi novo di S.A.R."; published by O. Morisani, *Michelozzo architetto*, Florence, 1951, fig. 72) and appears to be an effort to reconstruct the pre-Michelozzian villa based on lost visual evidence. A low tower in the style of those in the Mugello villas rises at the northeast corner and there is a projecting turret on the corner toward the road. Other evidence for the tower is found in the thickening of the walls at this corner of the villa revealed in the plan published by Ferrara and Quinterio and referred to in their text, p. 248. The entrance to the villa is not from the road but in the center of the garden front (labelled "ingresso primo"), and this was probably the case in Michelozzo's project.

15. Giuseppe Marchini, in *Giuliano da Sangallo*, Florence, 1942, p. 91, attributes the loggia on the garden side to Giuliano. It is not likely to have been built after the expulsion of the Medici from Florence in 1494. The two loggias appear to be the ones that Vasari (*Vite*, VI, pp. 280f.) tells us were being frescoed by Pontormo and Bronzino for Duke Alessandro de' Medici at the time of his assassination in 1537. The plan drawing of Giorgio Vasari the Younger cited in n. 14 shows the two existing projecting loggias at the rear (north) of the building.

16. The ambivalence of Michelozzo's style in its conservative and progressive aspects has been brought out in studies by L. H. Heydenreich, "Gedanken über Michelozzo di Bartolomeo," *Festschrift Wilhelm Pinder zum sechzigsten Geburtstage*, Leipzig, 1938, pp. 264–90 (republished in *Studien zur Architektur der Renaissance*, Munich, 1981, pp. 83–99); H. Saalman, "Palazzo Comunale"; G. Marchini, "Aggiunte a Michelozzo," *La rinascità*, 7, 1944, pp. 24–51.

17. Excerpt from a letter in Latin published without date or source by Angelo Fabronio, *Magni Cosmi Medicei Vita*, I, Pisa, 1789, p. 137. (An English translation was published by Janet Ross, *Lives of the Early Medici*, London, 1910, p. 73, without citation of Fabronio.)

18. The quotation, from the letters of Bartolomeo Scala, was published by Alison Brown, in *Bartolomeo Scala, 1430–1497*, Princeton, 1979, pp. 17f. (I thank Dale Kent for the reference). It makes an estimate of the date more precise than that suggested in the art-historical literature, most recently in Ferrara and Quinterio, *Michelozzo*, pp. 252–55; their dating (1451–57) was based on the absence of any mention of the property in the *catasto* tax declaration of 1451 and a full description including a "chasa overo chasamento" in 1457; Patzak (*Palast und Villa*, II, pp. 88–92) had suggested a date after 1457.

19. Our present knowledge of Michelozzo's designs is based on the publication and interpretation of the details from the Ghirlandaio fresco and from pl. 42 of Zocchi's *Vedute delle ville e altri luoghi della Toscana* by Clara Bargellini and Pierre de la Ruffinière du Prey in "Sources for a Reconstruction of the Villa Medici, Fiesole," *Burlington Magazine*, CXI, 1969, pp. 597–605. To these Ferrara and Quintero (*Michelozzo*, p. 254) have added a detail of an *Annunciation* by Biagio d'Antonio in the Accademia di San Luca in Rome.

20. *Vite*, II, pp. 442f. The 1492 inventory has been transcribed from ASF, *MAP*, CLXV, fol. 83ʳ, by Lillie, *Florentine Villas*, p. 449, n. 124.

21. Alberti, *De re aedificatoria*, ed. G. Orlandi and P. Portoghesi, Milan, 1966, IX, 4, p. 809. The editors (p. xii) date the compilation of the first half of the text to 1443–45 and the second to 1447–52.

22. Quoted by Foster, *Study of . . . Poggio a Caiano*, I, pp. 30f.; II, n. 94, from *Angeli Politiani et aliorum virorum illustrium*

epistolarum libri duodecim, Basel, 1522, lib. X, epist. 14. Poliziano was resident in Fiesole in 1479 and 1483–84.

23. André Chastel, *Art et humanisme à Florence au temps de Laurent le Magnifique*, Paris, 1959, pp. 148f.; Foster, *Study of . . . Poggio a Caiano*, I, p. 21, from *Opera Omnia*, Turin, 1959, I, 2, pp. 893f.

24. Quoted by Foster, *Study of . . . Poggio a Caiano*, II, n. 58, from A. Wesselski, ed., *Polizianos Tagebuch [1477–1479]*, Jena, 1929, p. 3: "Cosimo predetto solera dire che la casa loro di Cafagiuolo in Mugello vedera meglio quella di Fiesole, perche? ciò che quella vedera era loro, il che di Fiesole non arrevia."

25. Vasari, *Vite*, III, p. 498; S. Sandström, "The Programme for the Decoration of the Belvedere of Innocent VIII," *Kunsthistorisk Tidskrift*, XXIX, 1960, pp. 35ff. See also Anthony Blunt, "Illusionist Decoration in Central Italian Painting of the Renaissance," *JRSA*, 107, July, 1959, pp. 309–26; Juergen Schulz, "Pinturicchio and the Revival of Antiquity," *JWCI*, XXV, 1962, pp. 35–55.

26. Angelo Poliziano, *Le selve e la strega: prolusioni nello studio fiorentino (1482–1492)*, ed. I. del Lungo, Florence, 1925: "Rusticus," p. 64, ll. 557–69; "Ambra," pp. 105ff., ll. 590–625. The Cascina is described in an undated letter of the humanist Michele Verino, as the foundations of the new villa were completed (transcribed by del Lungo, p. 108; English translation, Foster, *Study of . . . Poggio a Caiano*, I, p. 68). (These and other contemporary descriptions are transcribed in J.-M. Kleimann, *Politische und humanistische Ideen der Medici in der Villa Poggio a Caiano*, diss., Heidelberg University, 1976, pp. 148–56.) The letter also gives an account of the entire area before the building of the new villa. On the Cascina see also the following note.

The villa is discussed by P. G. Hamburg in "The Villa of Lorenzo il Magnifico at Poggio a Caiano and the origin of Palladianism," *Idea and Form: Studies in the History of Art*, I, 1959, pp. 76–87; Hartmut Bierman, "Lo sviluppo della villa toscana sotto l'influenza umanistica della corte di Lorenzo il Magnifico," *BCISA*, XI, 1969, pp. 36–46; idem, "Das Palastmodell Giuliano da Sangallos für Ferdinand I, König von Neapel," *Wiener Jb. für Kunstgeschichte*, XXIII, 1970, pp. 154–95; Foster, *Study of . . . Poggio a Caiano*; H. Bierman and Elmar Worgull, "Das Palastmodell Giuliano da Sangallos für Ferdinand I, König von Neapel: Versuch einer Rekonstruktion," *Jb. der Berliner Museen*, XXI, 1979, pp. 91–118; S. Bardazzi and E. Castellani, *La villa medicea di Poggio a Caiano*, 2 vols, Prato, 1981. See also Chastel, *Art et humanisme*, pp. 151ff.

27. The circumstances of Lorenzo's acquisition of the Rucellai property (apparently against their will) are recounted by F. W. Kent in "Lorenzo de' Medici's Acquisition of Poggio a Caiano in 1474; and an Early Reference to His Architectural Expertise," *JWCI*, XLII, 1979, pp. 250–57. On the Cascina see P. Foster, "Lorenzo de' Medici's Cascina at Poggio a Caiano," *Mitt. des Kunsthistorisches Institutes in Florenz*, XIV, 1969/70, pp. 47–66. Marvin Becker, in a paper read at a symposium on Poggio a Caiano at the University of Michigan in April 1985, estimated that ninety percent of Lorenzo's income derived from agriculture and mining, whereas fifty percent of Medici income at mid-century derived from business.

28. Vasari's account: *Vite*, IV, p. 270. In September 1485 Lorenzo asked a correspondent to "remind Giuliano da Sangallo to complete my model." This has been assumed (by Mario Martelli, "I pensieri architettonici del Magnifico," *Commentari*, XIII, 1966, pp. 107–11, and subsequent writers) to be the Poggio model, but the recent discovery by Piero Morselli and Gino Corti (*La chiesa di S. M. delle Carceri in Prato*, Florence, 1982, pp. 15ff.) of documents of that date for the Prato model makes identification with the latter more probable. For the chronology of the villa, see Foster, *Study of . . . Poggio a Caiano*, ch. 4, pp. 108–67. A short review of the evidence and recent interpretation is given by Andreas Thönnesmann, *Der Palazzo Gondi in Florenz*, Worms, 1983, pp. 103–08. See also the splendid photographic survey by

Paolo Brandinelli in S. Bardazzi and E. Castellani, *La villa medicea di Poggio a Caiano*, 2 vols, Florence, 1982. For Michele Verino's letter see above, n. 26.

29. For evidence of Lorenzo's architectural expertise, see Kent, "Lorenzo de' Medici"; Martelli, "Pensieri," pp. 107–11; and Morselli and Corti, *S. M. delle Carceri*, pp. 24–31. Alberti's manuscript had been finished in the early 1450s (see above, n. 21) but was not published until 1485. On the letters to Mantua and Urbino, see Morselli and Corti, p. 24 (citing *Protocolli del carteggio di Lorenzo il Magnifico per gli anni 1473–74*, Florence, 1956, p. 333), and Giovanni Gaye, *Carteggio inedito d'artisti . . .*, I, Florence, 1839, p. 274. Giuliano's lack of previous architectural experience is documented in Thönnesmann, *Palazzo Gondi*. For Lorenzo and the Naples palace see below, n. 34.

30. *De re aedificatoria*, IX, 4, p. 809: "Fastigium privatis aedibus non ita fiet, ut templae maiestatem ulla ex parte sectetur. Vestibulum tamen ipsum fronte paulo subelatiori atque etiam fastigii dignitate honestabitur." Vitruvius was unclear about the meaning of *vestibulum*. Daniele Barbaro, in his Vitruvius edition, represented it as the forecourt of a large urban house, which would not be required in a villa. The sources of the temple front motif and the interpretations of *vestibulum* are discussed by Bierman in "Das Palastmodell."

31. G. Fiocco, "La casa veneziana antica," *Atti della Accad. naz. dei Lincei, Rendiconti della classe di scienze morali, etc.*, CCCXLVI, 1949, pp. 38ff.; J. Ackerman, "Sources of the Renaissance Villa" (above, Chapter 1, n. 6); Wolfgang Wolters, "Sebastiano Serlio e il suo contributo alla villa veneziana prima del Palladio," *BCISA*, XI, 1969, pp. 83–94; Martin Kubelik, *Die Villa im Veneto: zur typologischen Entwicklung im Quattrocento*, 2 vols, Munich, 1977. On the origins of the Renaissance villa see also the other works cited in Chapter 1, n. 6.

32. See Janet Cox-Rearick, *Dynasty and Destiny in Medici Art*, Princeton, 1984, pp. 65–86; Chastel, *Art et humanisme*, pp. 218–25.

33. Vasari, *Vite*, IV, p. 271. For the Villa Tovaglia, see Beverley L. Brown, "Leonardo and the Tale of Three Villas: Poggio a Caiano, the Villa Tovaglia in Florence, and Poggio Reale in Mantua," *Atti del Convegno di Firenze e la Toscana dei Medici nell'Europa del Cinquecento*, Florence, 1983, pp. 1053–62 (proposing that the vault there, though the first large example to be built, was based on the project for the Poggio *salone*). The Palazzo Scala vaults are discussed by Linda Pellecchia, "Observations on the Scala Palace: Giuliano da Sangallo and Antiquity," diss., Harvard University, 1983, pp. 138–86.

34. On the Florence project, see G. Miarelli-Mariani, "Il disegno per il complesso mediceo di Via Laura a Firenze," *Palladio*, XXII, 1972, pp. 127–62; Caroline Elam, "Lorenzo de' Medici and the Urban Development of Florence," *Art History*, I, 1978, pp. 43–66. On the Naples palace, see Bierman and Worgull, "Das Palastmodell." They suggest that Lorenzo may have attempted to recreate a columnar hall called the *oecus* which Vitruvius mentions as an element in the Roman private house (VII, iii. 8–9). This might explain the painted columnar articulation of the hall under Leo X. See also Bierman, "Sviluppo," p. 41.

35. At the four corners of the podium that supports the villa are sketched little bastion-like extrusions. These are too small even to look like bastions; either they were sketched in for fun or they were intended as decoration. The moat may have had a real defensive function. As the villa was being constructed, a madman made an attempt on Lorenzo's life, and Lorenzo's friends expressed fear that he might be assassinated at Poggio (Foster, *Study of . . . Poggio a Caiano*, pp. 60f., 70). Miarelli-Mariani, "Via Laura," n. 54, reports Marchini's claim in conversation to have discovered proof that the walled enclosure with four towers was executed in the original building campaign. In the absence of this evidence, the delineation of the site in the present drawing appears to demonstrate that the enclosure was not built.

36. See below, Chapter 4, n. 4.

37. Amedeo Maiuri, *La villa de' misteri*, Rome, 1931. The significance of ancient villa and temple podia for the conception of Poggio a Caiano is discussed in Bierman, "Das Palastmodell," pp. 168ff.
38. See above, Chapter 2, n. 15.
39. Pietro Ruschi, "La villa romana di Settefinestre in un disegno del XV secolo," *Prospettiva*, 22, July, 1980, pp. 72–75.
40. Discussed by Fiocco and myself in the works cited in n. 31.

4 Palladio's Villas and their Predecessors
(pp. 89–107)

1. *I quattro libri dell'architettura, ne' quali, dopo un breve trattato de' cinque ordini, & di quelli avertimenti, che sono piu necessarii nel fabricare; si tratta delle case private, delle vie, de i ponti, delle piazze, de i xisti et de' tempii*, Venice, 1570.
The earliest of the villa studies, partly superseded by subsequent scholarship, is Fritz Burger, *Die Villen des Andrea Palladio*, Leipzig, 1909. The style was discussed in Rodolf Wittkower, *Architectural Principles in the Age of Humanism*, pt iii, London, 1949, and the function first in Georgina Masson, "Palladian Villas as Rural Centers," *AR*, 118, 703, 1955, pp. 17ff. Scholarship on Palladio and the villas of the Veneto greatly intensified after 1965: see James Ackerman, *Palladio*, Harmondsworth, 1966, ch. 2, and later edns; idem, *Palladio's Villas*, New York, 1967; G. G. Zorzi, *Le ville e i teatri di Andrea Palladio*, Vicenza, 1968; Bernhard Rupprecht, "L'iconologia della villa veneta," *BCISA*, X, 1968, pp. 229ff.; Manfredo Tafuri, "Committenza e tipologia nelle ville palladiane," *BCISA*, XI, 1969, pp. 120–36; F. Barbieri, "Palladio in villa negli anni quaranta," *Arte veneta*, XXIV, 1970, pp. 68–80; Lionello Puppi, "Dubbi e certezze per Palladio construttore in villa," *Arte veneta*, XXVIII, 1974, pp. 93–105; Howard Burns, ed., *Andrea Palladio 1508–80: the Portico and the Farmyard*, London, 1975, esp. pp. 163–204; and the villa sections of L. Puppi, *Andrea Palladio*, Boston, 1975. Many valuable contributions to the subject have been made in articles published by specialists of several countries in the *BCISA*.
On the villas of the Veneto prior to the period of Palladio, see B. Rupprecht, "Ville venete del '400 e del primo '500: forme e sviluppo," *BCISA*, VI, 1964, pp. 239–50; Marco Rosci, "Forme e funzioni delle ville venete prepalladiane," *L'arte*, 2, 1968, pp. 27–54; L. H. Heydenreich, "La villa, genesi e sviluppi fino al Palladio," *BCISA*, XI, 1969, pp. 11–22; W. Wolters, "Sebastiano Serlio e il suo contributo alla villa veneziana prima del Palladio," *BCISA*, XI, 1969, pp. 83–94; Wolfram Prinz, "Studien zu den Anfängen des oberitalienischen Villenbaues," *Kunst in Hessen und am Mittelrhein*, XIII, 1973, pp. 7–45; Kurt Forster and R. Tuttle, "Back to the Farm: Vernacular Architecture and the Development of the Renaissance Villa," *Architectura*, I, 1974, pp. 1–12; Martin Kubelik, *Zur typologischen Entwicklung der Quattrocentovilla in Veneto*, Aachen, 1975.
On villas of the Veneto in general, G. F. Viviani, ed., *La villa nel Veronese*, Verona, 1975; Michelangelo Muraro, *Venetian Villas: the History and the Culture*, New York, 1986.
2. The bulk of surviving Palladio drawings is in London, at the Royal Institute of British Architects, Burlington–Devonshire Collection (a catalog by Howard Burns is in preparation); a small group is preserved in Vicenza at the Museo Civico; and a few other institutions in Europe and America possess one or two each. See G. G. Zorzi, *I disegni delle antichità di Andrea Palladio*, Venice, 1959; Howard Burns, "I disegni," in R. Cevese, ed., *Mostra del Palladio* [Milan, 1973], pp. 131–54; C. Douglas Lewis, *The Drawings of Andrea Palladio*, exh. cat., Washington, D.C., 1981.
3. Manuela Morresi, *La villa Porto Colleoni a Thiene*, Milan, 1988.
4. M. Botter, *La villa Giustinian di Roncade*, Treviso, 1955; Carolyn Kolb Lewis, *The Villa Giustinian in Roncade*, New York, 1977.

5. See Angelo Ventura, *Nobiltà e popolo nella società veneta del '400 e '500*, Bari, 1964; idem, 'Aspetti storici-economici della villa veneta," *BCISA*, XI, 1969, pp. 65–71; James Ackerman, "The Geopolitics of Venetan Architecture in the Time of Titian," in D. Rosand, ed., *Titian: His World and His Legacy*, New York, 1982; Manfredo Tafuri, *Venezia e il Rinascimento*, Turin, 1985.
6. Roberto Cessi, "Alvise Cornaro e la bonifica veneziana del secolo XVI," *Atti della Accad. naz. dei Lincei, Rendiconti della classe di scienze morali, etc.*, ser. VI, XIII, 1936, pp. 301–23; Daniele Beltrami, *Saggio di storia dell'agricoltura nella repubblica di Venezia durante l'età moderna*, Venice/Rome, 1955; S. J. Woolf, "Venice and the Terraferma . . ." in B. Pullan, ed., *Crisis and Change in the Venetian Economy in the Sixteenth and Seventeenth Centuries*, London, 1968.
7. Priuli, *Diarii*, as quoted by Alberto Tenenti, "The Sense of Space and Time in the Venetian World," in John Hale, ed., *Renaissance Venice*, London, 1973, p. 11.
8. *I dieci libri dell'architettura di M. Vitruvio tradotti & commentati da Mons. Daniel Barbaro eletto Patriarca d'Aquileia . . .*, Venice, 1556, bk VI, 9, p. 298.
9. As quoted by Ventura, "Aspetti," p. 66. See also the work by Ugo Soragni cited below, Chapter 5, n. 1.
10. From his *Discorsi intorno alla vita sobria*, I, in G. Fiocco, *Alvise Cornaro, il suo tempo e le sue opere*, Vicenza, 1965, p. 179. See also Lionello Puppi, ed., *Alvise Cornaro e il suo tempo*, exh. cat., Padua, 1980, and, on Cornaro as a land reformer, Cessi, "Alvise Cornaro."
11. Lionello Puppi, "La villa Garzoni di Pontecasale di Jacopo Sansovino," *Prospettive*, XXIV, 1961, pp. 51–62; idem, *BCISA*, XI, 1969, pp. 95–112; Bernhard Rupprecht, "Die Villa Garzoni des Jacopo Sansovino," *Mitt. des Kunsthistorischen Institutes in Florenz*, XI, 1963, pp. 1–32; Manfredo Tafuri, *Jacopo Sansovino e l'architettura del '500 a Venezia*, Padua, 1969, pp. 99–131.
12. For Sanmicheli's villas, see Piero Gazzola, ed., *Michele Sanmicheli*, exh. cat., Venice, 1960, pp. 153ff.; Bernhard Rupprecht, "Sanmichelis Villa Soranza," *Festschrift Ulrich Middeldorf*, Berlin, 1968, pp. 324–32; Camillo Semenzato, *BCISA*, XI, 1969, pp. 113–19. See also C. Douglas Lewis, "The rediscovery of Sanmicheli's Palace for Girolamo Cornaro at Piombino," *Architectura*, VI, 1976, pp. 29ff. The Villa delle Trombe in Agugliaro (Vicentino) is generally accepted as Sanmicheli's: see R. Cevese, *Ville della provincia di Vicenza*, Milan, 1971, II, pp. 285ff.
13. William Bell Dinsmoor, "The Literary Remains of Sebastiano Serlio," *AB*, XXIV, 1942, i, pp. 55–91; ii, pp. 113–54; H. Günther, "Studien zum venezianischen Aufenthalt des Sebastiano Serlio," *Münchner Jb. der bildende Kunst*, 32, 1981, pp. 42–94.
14. Munich, Staatsbibliothek, Cod. Icon. 189, commentary by Marco Rosci, *Il trattato di architettura di Sebastiano Serlio*, 2 vols, Milan [1967]; New York, Columbia University, Avery Library, commentary by Myra N. Rosenfeld, *Sebastiano Serlio on Domestic Architecture*, New York/Cambridge, Mass., 1978; Dinsmoor, "Literary Remains."
15. See above, Chapter 1, n. 6.
16. *I quattro libri*, bk II, ch. xii, p. 45: "Del sito da ellegersi per le fabbriche." On Lonedo, see Paul Hofer, *Palladios Erstling, die Villa Godi Valmarana in Lonedo bei Vicenza*, Basel/Stuttgart, 1969; Ursel Berger, *Palladios Frühwerk: Bauten und Zeichnungen* (diss., Munich University), Vienna, 1978, pp. 30–42.
17. G. Mazzariol, *Palladio a Maser*, Venice, 1965; N. Huse, "Palladio und die Villa Barbaro in Maser: Bemerkungen zum Problem der Autorschaft," *Arte veneta*, XXVIII, 1974, pp. 106–22.
18. *I quattro libri*, II, xvi, p. 69.
19. See Heinz Spielmann, *Andrea Palladio und die Antike*, Berlin, 1966; Erik Forssman, "Palladio e l'antichità," *Mostra del Palladio*, pp. 15–26.
20. See n. 8.

21. R. Cocke, "Veronese and Daniele Barbaro: the Decoration of Villa Maser," *JWCI*, XXXV, 1972, pp. 226–46.

22. *I quattro libri*, II, xiv, p. 51.

23. Michelangelo Muraro, "Feudo e ville venete," *BCISA*, XX, 1978, pp. 203–23; and, more extensively, idem, "La villa palladiana dei Repeta a Campiglia dei Berici," *Campiglia dei Berici: storia di un paese veneto*, Campiglia, 1980.

24. Cf. Tafuri, *Sansovino*, pp. 128ff.

25. *I quattro libri*, II, xiv, p. 61.

26. G. P. Bordignon Favero, *La villa Emo di Fanzolo* (*Corpus Palladianum*, V) Vicenza, 1970.

27. *I quattro libri*, II, xiv, p. 55.

28. ibid., p. 56.

29. ibid., iii, p. 19. See Wolfgang Lotz, "La Rotunda, edifizio civile con cupola," *BCISA*, IV, 1962, pp. 69–73. C. A. Isermeyer, "Die Villa Rotonda von Palladio," *Zeitschr. für Kunstgeschichte*, 1967, pp. 207–21 (redating the villa from 1550–53 to 1566–70); C. Semenzato, *La Rotonda di Andrea Palladio* (*Corpus Palladianum*, I), Vicenza, 1968.

5 The Image of Country Life in Sixteenth-Century Villa Books (pp. 108–23)

1. I was alerted to this literature and to its value for the interpretation of the Renaissance villa by two innovative studies, Bernhard Rupprecht, "Villa. Zur Geschichte eines Ideals" (see above, Chapter 3, n. 1), and R. Bentmann and Michael Müller, *Die Villa als Herrschaftsarchitektur* (above, Chapter 1, n. 2); brief excerpts from some of the texts were published by the latter authors in "Materialen zur italienischen Villa der Renaissance," *Architectura*, II, 1972, pp. 167–91.

Recent studies of the villa literature have greatly expanded our awareness of the material: P. L. Sartori, "Gli scritti veneti d'agraria del Cinquecento e del primo Seicento tra realtà e utopia," *Atti del convegno "Venezia e la Terraferma" attraverso le relazioni dei Rettori (1980)*, Milan, 1981, pp. 261–310; Ugo Soragni, "L'agricoltura come professione: trattatistica, legislazione e investimenti in territorio veneto (sec. XVI)," *Storia della città*, 24, 1988, pp. 25–44; and Manuela Morresi, *La villa Porto Colleoni a Thiene*, Milan, 1988, pp. 81ff.

Studies in north Italian agronomy have been much aided by the recent opening to the public of the library "La Vigna" at the Centro di Cultura e Civiltà Contadina in Vicenza, where I found several of the works consulted for this chapter.

2. Anton Francesco Doni, *Le Ville*, ed. Ugo Bellocchi, Modena, 1969, pp. 29, 31. This volume contains, in parallel columns, the texts of manuscripts in Reggio and Venice, written some time after 1557, and the very rare edition printed in Bologna in 1566; my excerpts are from the Reggio version, which is mostly the clearest, unless otherwise indicated.

3. The descriptions, however, are of types of accommodation and do not permit us to visualize the buildings, so I have not reproduced any.

4. Serlio, manuscript at Columbia University, Avery Library, cf. facsimile ed., ed. Myra N. Rosenfeld, fols. xlviii, xlix. A manuscript in Munich, Cod. Icon. 189, has also been published in facsimile. For both facsimiles see above, Chapter 4, n. 14.

5. *Le ville*, pp. 62ff., 90ff.

6. The following is a list of the North Italian agricultural writings of the fifteenth and sixteenth century that I have been able to compile in addition to the four on which I am focusing. I have consulted those mentioned in the text; the titles of those I have not examined are taken from Sartori, "Scritti veneti." Daniele di Villa, *Regula d'agricoltura* (late sixteenth century?), Venice, Bibl. Naz. Marciana, ms. Marc. It., classe ix, cod.ci–6862 (publ. by Morresi, *Villa Porto Colleoni*); Antonio Venuto, *De agricultura opuscula*, Venice, 1541; G. B. Tatti, *dell'agricoltura. Libri cinque*, Venice, 1560 (a compilation of Roman sources); A. Clementi, *Trattato dell'agricoltura*, Venice, 1572; Camillo Tarello da

Lonato, *Ricordo d'agricoltura*, Mantua, 1577; M. Poveiano, *Il fattore. Libro d'arithmetica, et geometria praticale*, Bergamo, 1582; G. M. Bonardo, *Le richezze dell'agricoltura*, Venice, 1590; G. B. Barpo, *Le delitie et i frutti dell'agricoltura e della villa. Libri tre*, Venice 1633; G. Agostinetti, *Cento e dieci ricordi, che formano il buon fattor di villa*, Venice, 1679; V. Tanara, *L'economia del cittadino in villa*, Venice, 1680.

7. The chapter I have reproduced in translation in the Appendix, from *Le dieci giornate della vera agricoltura e piaceri della villa di M. Agostin Gallo, in dialogo*, Venice: Giovanni Bariletto, 1566, is titled "Ragionamento fatto tra i nobili M. Gio. Battista Avogadro, e Messer Cornelio Ducco. Nel mese di Maggio. 1553. Sopra le cose dilettevoli della villa: e quanto è meglio habitarvi, che nella Cittade." The Brescia edition of 1564 (Bozzola) is apparently the first (M. S. Aslin, *Catalogue of the Printed Books on Agriculture*, Aberdeen, 1926?, refers to a 1550 edition that has not been confirmed in other catalogs). This edition was followed in 1566 by *Le tredici giornate della vera agricoltura . . .*, Venice: Bevilacqua, and in 1569 by *Le sette giornate dell'agricoltura*, Venice: Perchacino. The fullest version is of 1569: *Le vinti giornate dell'agricoltura, e de' piaceri della villa*, Turin: Bevilacqua. The chapter on the pleasures of the villa remained substantially unchanged in the expanded editions. I am grateful to Susan Halpert of The Houghton Library, Harvard University, for bibliographical assistance.

8. The page citations I shall give are to the original texts, except for the references to Gallo in the Appendix. The Falcone references are to the edition of Venice, 1628.

9. *Le vinti giornate* (above, n. 7), Day XX, p. 383.

10. Angelo Ventura, *Nobiltà e popolo nella società veneta del '400 e '500*, Bari, 1964, chs. 4, 6; idem, "L'agricoltura veneta nei secoli XVI–XVIII," *Studi storici*, IX, 1968, pp. 675–722. See also the brief commentary of Giorgio Simoncini in *Città e società nel Rinascimento*, I, Turin, 1974, pp. 162ff., and the studies by Enrico Basaglia, Francesco Vecchiato, and Angelo Ventura in the volume *Atti del Convegno "Venezia e la Terraferma"* (above, n. 1).

11. See P. S. Leicht, "Un movimento agrario nel Cinquecento," *Scritti vari di storia del diritto italiano*, Milan, 1943; Peter Blickle, *The Revolution of 1525*. Baltimore, 1981. A brief survey of the condition of the peasantry in northern Italy during the Renaissance is given by Ruggiero Romano, *Tra due crisi: Italia del Rinascimento*, Turin, 1971; Romano suggests that the declining fortunes of the agrarian worker led to a virtual "refeudalization."

12. See Domenico Merlini, *Saggio di ricerche sulla satira contro il villano*, Turin, 1894.

13. Adelin Fiorato, "Rustres et citadins dans les nouvelles de Bandello," *Ville et campagne dans la littérature italienne de la Renaissance, I: le paysage travesti*, Paris, 1976, pp. 77–138; A. Bignardi, "Squarci di vita contadinesca nelle pagine di Giulio Cesare Croce," *Economia e storia*, 4, 1976, pp. 452–85.

14. Eugenio Battisti, "Dal 'comico' al 'genere'," *L'Antirinascimento*, Milan, 1962, pp. 278–313; the arts elsewhere in Europe generally maintained an intransigent antagonism or condescension toward the peasant throughout the century: see Stephen Greenblatt, "Murdering Peasants: Status, Genre and the Representation of Rebellion," *Representations*, I, 1983, pp. 1–30.

15. Ludovico Zorzi, ed., *Ruzante: Teatro*, Turin, 1967; Mario Prosperi, *Angelo Beolco nominato Ruzante*, Padua, 1970. For a similarly sympathetic understanding of the plight of the peasant see also the contemporary, anonymous, *Alfabeto dei villani*, in E. Lovarini, ed., "*L'alfabeto dei villani* in pavano nuovamente edito e illustrato," *Il libro e la stampa*, IV, 1910, pp. 125–42.

16. In this respect, Doni (*Le ville*, p. 43) differs from the rest, in his account of a group of ladies swimming nude in a pool deep in the villa garden. This occurs, however, in the description of the aristocratic or princely villa; the mores of noblewomen apparently permit greater freedom of action.

17. Falcone also prohibits priests and peasants from hunting, the latter lest it replace time spent in cultivating the villa of the

padrone. This prohibition, which was enacted into law, was the cause of much unrest during the Renaissance, because it denied sustaining food to peasant families, and increased the threat of famine.

18. See the comparison of medieval and Renaissance attitudes in Joan Kelly-Gadol, "Did Women Have a Renaissance?," in R. Bridenthal and C. Koonz, eds., *Becoming Visible: Women in European History*, Boston, 1977, pp. 137–64. The Renaissance repression of women was already well established in the cities of fourteenth-century Italy: see David Herlihy, "Some Psychological and Social Roots of Violence in the Tuscan Cities," in L. Martines, ed., *Violence and Civil Disorder in Italian Cities, 1200–1500*, Berkeley, 1972. Renaissance attitudes, as reflected in literature, are documented in Ruth Kelso, *Doctrine for the Lady of the Renaissance*, 2nd ed., Urbana, 1977. For women as workers, see Judith Brown, "A Woman's Place Was in the Home: Women's Work in Renaissance Tuscany," in Margaret Ferguson, Maureen Quilligan and Nancy Vickers, eds., *Rewriting the Renaissance: The Discourses of Sexual Difference in Early Modern Europe*, Chicago, 1986, pp. 206–24. For the Renaissance roots of feminism, see Joan Kelly, "Early Feminist Theory and the *Querelle des Femmes*," *Signs*, 8, 1982, pp. 4–28.

19. The portico mentioned is apparently an independent barn structure with an open colonnade, like the Venetian *barchessa*. Falcone (p. 31) mentions two, "un bello, & lungo portico, avanti la casa del Padrone, e del Massaro: sotto di cui, si starà all'inverno, e terrà asciuto l'usci delle case, e sotto pure si vi porteranno mille cose a [= sotto] tetto, & in governo. . . . Poi dietro alla casa, verso niun'hora, sagli un'altro portico per le botte, tine, e per far i vini, e sia murato d'ogni intorno, per sicurezza del tutto, e che d'inverno per le pioggie, e d'estate pe'l gran caldo, vi stiano sotto in governo carri, arati: erpico, con un luogo particolare, per vanghe, zappe, seghe, con arme rusticane."

If the first portico serves to keep the entrances to the dwellings of master and bailiff dry, it must run across the facades of both in a fashion quite different from those of Palladio and his contemporaries, which flank the facade of the master's house (though at the Villa Barbaro in Maser [*4.10*] the *salone* is entered from under the northern arcade).

6 The Palladian Villa in England (pp. 135–58)

1. On the Palladian villa, see John Summerson, "The Classical Country House in Eighteenth-Century England," *JRSA*, 107, July, 1959, pp. 539–87 (reprinted in Summerson, *The Unromantic Castle and Other Essays*, London/New York, 1990, pp. 79–120), especially the third, "The Idea of the Villa," pp. 570–87; idem, *Architecture in Britain 1530–1830*, Harmondsworth, 1977, pt iv; John Harris, *Georgian Country Houses*, Feltham, 1965; idem, *The Palladians*, New York, 1982; Rudolf Wittkower, *Palladio and English Palladianism*, London, 1974. John Harris is preparing a book based on the Mellon Lectures of 1980 on this subject.

2. On Baroque architecture in England, see Christopher Hussey, *English Country Houses: Early Georgian, 1715–60*, London, 1955; Kerry Downes, *English Baroque Architecture*, London, 1966; Summerson, *Architecture in Britain*, pt iii.

3. See John Charlton, *A History and Description of Chiswick House and Gardens*, London, 1958; Christopher Hussey, "Chiswick House Restored," *Country Life*, 124, July, 1958, pp. 228–31; Kerry Downes, "Chiswick Villa," 164, October, 1978, pp. 225–36; Richard Hewlings (for English Heritage), *Chiswick House and Gardens*, London, 1989.

4. On Burlington, see James Lees-Milne, "Lord Burlington in Yorkshire," *AR*, 98, July, 1945, pp. 11–18; idem, *The Earls of Creation*, London, 1962, pp. 103–72; Wittkower, *Palladio* ("Lord Burlington and William Kent," pp. 115–34; "Lord Burlington's Work at York," pp. 135–46; "Lord Burlington at Northwick Park," pp. 147–54); Nottingham University Art Gallery, *Apollo of the Arts: Lord Burlington and his Circle*, ed. John Wilton-Ely,

Nottingham, 1973. Margot Wittkower is preparing a study of Burlington as a patron.

5. 1st ed.: vol. I (10 pp., 100 pls), London, 1715; vol. II (8 pp., 100 pls), 1717; vol. III (8 pp., 100 pls), 1725. Vol. I was reissued in 1717; vol. III, with two additional plates, in 1725 (?) and 1731. See Paul Breman and Denise Addis, *Guide to Vitruvius Brittannicus*, New York, 1972 (vol. IV of the facsimile); and John Archer, *The Literature of British Domestic Architecture, 1715–1842*, Cambridge, Mass., 1985, p. 240f.

6. John Pinto, "The Landscape of Allusion: Literary Themes in the Gardens of Classical Rome and Augustan England," *Smith College Studies in History*, XLVIII, 1980, pp. 97–113.

7. *The Twickenham Edition of the Works of Alexander Pope*, III, 2: *Epistles to Several Persons*, ed. F. W. Bateson, London, 2nd ed., 1961, p. 154.

8. Revealed by Kent's *Journal* in the Bodleian Library, Oxford, as reported by Leopold Schmidt, *Holkham Hall, Studien zur Architektur und Ausstaltung*, diss., Freiburg i. Br. University, 1980, n. 148.

9. Margaret Jourdain, *The Work of William Kent, Artist, Painter, Designer and Landscape Gardener*, London, 1948; Michael Wilson, *William Kent: Architect, Designer, Painter, Gardener, 1685–1748*, London, 1984.

10. See above, Chapter 4, n. 2.

11. Wittkower, *Palladio*, pp. 114–34.

12. Chesterfield's opinion of Burlington's practice appears in a letter of 1734: "For the minute and mechanical parts of [architecture], leave them to masons, bricklayers and Lord Burlington; who has, to a certain degree, lessened himself by knowing them too well." Quoted by Schmidt, *Holkham*, p. 57.

13. Matthew Brettingham, *The Plans, Elevations and Sections of Holkham, etc.*, London, 1773; Schmidt, *Holkham*, and idem, "Holkham Hall, Norfolk," *County Life*, 167, January 24, 1980, pp. 214ff. Brettingham says (p. v): "The Earl [of Leicester] continued with uncommon diligence to improve and elucidate the first sketches of the plans and elevations concerted with the Earl of Burlington and Mr. Kent . . . guided by Palladio and by Jones."

14. On Campbell, see Howard Stutchbury, *The Architecture of Colen Campbell*, Cambridge, Mass., 1967. On Houghton Hall, Isaac Ware, publ., *The Plans, Elevations and Sections of Houghton in Norfolk*, n.p., 1735.

15. Schmidt (in *Holkham* and "Holkham Hall") published drawings by Brettingham in the British Museum which document an early design in which the main block stands alone, without the attached pavilions. The change was made in the late 1720s.

16. John Summerson first defined the origins and terminology of the English villa in the three papers cited in n. 1.

17. For the translation of musical consonances and harmonies into architecture, see Rudolf Wittkower, *Architectural Principles in the Age of Humanism*, London, 1962, pt iv, "The Problem of Harmonic Proportion in Architecture."

18. Kenneth Woodbridge, *Landscape and Antiquity: Aspects of English Culture at Stourhead, 1718–1838*, Oxford, 1970; idem, *The Stourhead Landscape*, 2nd ed., n.p., 1982. On Stourhead see also below, Chapter 7, n. 20.

19. Lees-Milne, *Earls of Creation*, pp. 79–92; anon., *Marble Hill House, Twickenham*, London, 1969; English Heritage (rev. Julius Bryant), *Marble Hill House*, n.p., 1988. Mrs Howard received £11,500 toward the building costs from the Prince of Wales. The original property of eleven acres was later expanded by eighty acres, and Charles Bridgeman designed a garden of which nothing remains.

20. The Palladian style, notably the combination of a central block linked to two smaller wings by curved quadrant colonnades, enjoyed a great efflorescence in Ireland where the vogue continued past mid-century. There are well-preserved examples at Newberry Hall (1750s–60s?) and Lodge Park (1773–75), both in Co. Kildare, and Colganstown House in Co. Dublin (1760s? see the Knight of Glin, "Architectural Books and 'Palladianism',"

Quarterly Bull. of the Irish Georgian Soc., V, 1962, pp. 9–35). A larger Palladian mansion is Powerscourt, Co. Wicklow, executed in *c.* 1760–62.

21. Robert Morris, *An Essay in Defence of Ancient Architecture; or a Parallel of the Ancient Buildings with the Modern: Shewing The Beauty and Harmony of the Former, and the Irregularity of the Latter*, London, 1728 (facsimile, Westmead, 1971), quotations from pp. 14f.; idem, *Lectures on Architecture. Consisting of Rules Founded upon Harmonick and Arithmetical Proportions in Building, Designed As an Agreeable Entertainment for Gentlemen . . .*, London, 1734 (facsimile of the 1736 ed., Westmead, 1971), quotations from Lecture V, pp. 63–76 of the 2nd ed. For a bibliographical study and commentary on Morris's writings, see Archer, *Literature*, pp. 575–87, no, 213.

22. Pope, *Epistles*, pp. 139–40.

23. The link with Venetian religious and political ideas has been suggested by Stutchbury, *Campbell*, pp. 8f.

24. Mark Girouard, *Life in the English Country House*, New Haven/London, 1978, esp. chs. 6, 7.

7 The Landscape Garden (pp. 159–84)

1. Of the ample and excellent bibliography on the early eighteenth-century landscape garden, I have found the following works most useful: H. F. Clark, *The English Landscape Garden*, London, 1948; idem, "Eighteenth Century Elysiums: the Role of 'Association' in the Landscape Movement," *JWCI*, 6, 1943, pp. 165–89; W. G. Hoskins, *The Making of the English Landscape*, London, 1956; John Dixon Hunt, *The Figure in the Landscape*, Baltimore, 1976; idem, *Garden and Grove. The Italian Renaissance Garden in the English Imagination: 1600–1750*, London, 1986; idem and Peter Willis, eds., *The Genius of the Place: the English Landscape Garden, 1620–1820*, London, 1975; Christopher Hussey, *The Picturesque: Studies in a Point of View*, London, 1927; idem, *English Gardens and Landscapes*, London, 1967; S. Lang, "The Genesis of the English Landscape Garden," *The Picturesque Garden and its Influence Outside the British Isles*, ed. Nikolaus Pevsner, Washington, D.C., 1974; E. Malins, *English Landscaping and Literature, 1660–1840*, London, 1966; G. C. Mingay, *English Landed Society in the Eighteenth Century*, London, 1963; A. Parraux and M. Plaisant, *Jardins et paysages: le style anglais*, 2 vols., Lille, 1977; Nikolaus Pevsner, "The Genesis of the Picturesque," *Studies in Art, Architecture and Design*, I, London, 1968; Horace Walpole, *Horace Walpole Gardenist: an Edition of Walpole's "The History of the Modern Taste in Gardening"*, ed. Isabel W. U. Chase, Princeton, 1943; R. Williams, *The Country and the City*, New York, 1976; Peter Willis, ed., *Furor Hortensis: Essays in the History of the English Landscape Garden in Memory of H. F. Clark*, Edinburgh, 1974; idem, *Charles Bridgeman and the English Landscape Garden*, London, 1976; Rudolf Wittkower, "English Neo-Palladianism, the Landscape Garden, China and the Enlightenment," *Palladio and English Palladianism*, London, 1974, pp. 176–92; Kenneth Woodbridge, "William Kent as a Landscape Gardener: A Reappraisal," *Apollo*, 100, 1974, pp. 126–37. On the influence of the early landscape garden on the theory of Robert Morris, see David Leatherbarrow, "Architecture and Situation: a Study of the Architectural Writings of Robert Morris," *JSAH*, XLIV, 1985, pp. 48–59.

2. James Thomson, "Liberty," bk. V, l. 681 (*Poetical Works*, ed. J. L. Robertson, London, 1908, p. 412).

3. See Nikolaus Pevsner, "A Note on Sharawaggi," *Studies in Art, Architecture and Design*, London, 1968, pp. 102–07. The text of Temple and those that follow are taken from Hunt and Willis, *Genius of the Place.*

4. For the Italian sources of English landscape design, both formal and informal, see Hunt, *Garden and Grove*. The Italian precedents most likely to have been known to English patrons and designers were the sixteenth-century garden of the Medici villa at Pratolino outside Florence, noted for its naturalistic cascades and

varied grottoes (since destroyed)—which may have influenced the design of Sir William Temple's garden at Moor Park, Surrey, of before 1698 (see fig. 5 in John Harris's article cited in the following note)—and the Roman parks of the Villas Borghese, Medici and Doria Pamphili and those of Frascati, especially the Villa Aldobrandini.

5. The role of the artinatural style, and of the examples cited here, has only recently been revealed by John Harris, "The Artinatural Style," *The Rococo in England: a Symposium*, ed. Charles Hind, London, 1986, pp. 8–20.

Paradoxically, British garden designers may have been inspired by a work of the designer most identified with the deplored French formal garden, Le Nôtre. This was a rustic segment of Louis XIV's garden at Marly (after 1679) called the Bosquet de Louveciennes, conceived in the conviction that a mixture of formal and informal areas had been a feature of the gardens of ancient Rome, and in particular of Pliny's Tusci. See Betsy Rosasco, "The Sculptural Decorations of the Garden at Marly: 1679–1699," *Journal of Garden History*, IV, 1984, p. 103, cited by Harris.

6. On Bridgeman see Willis, *Bridgeman.*

7. Kent's designs of 1730, preserved in his drawings, are discussed by Cinzia Maria Sicca, "Like a Shallow Cave by Nature Made: William Kent's 'Natural' Architecture at Richmond," *Architectura*, 16, 1986, pp. 68–82.

8. See John Pinto, "The Landscape of Allusion: Literary Themes in the Gardens of Classical Rome and Augustan England," *Smith College Studies in History*, XLVIII, 1980, pp. 105ff.

9. Pope's grotto and garden are discussed by Maynard Mack, *The Garden and the City*, Toronto, 1969, and by Frederick Bracher, "Pope's Grotto: the Maze of Fancy," *The Huntington Library Quarterly*, XII, 2, 1949, pp. 141–62; Morris Brownell, *Alexander Pope's Villa* (Greater London Council exh. cat.), London, 1980; Hunt, *Figure in the Landscape*, ch. 2; Naomi Miller, *Heavenly Caves*, New York, 1982, pp. 81–84. In a letter of 1738, Kent claims to have designed Pope's garden: quoted in Wilson, *William Kent* (above, Chapter 6, n. 9), p. 196.

10. loc. cit. (Chapter 6, n. 7), pp. 141–43. See also Mack, *Garden and City*; Hunt, *Figure in the Landscape*, ch. 2.

11. Reproduced in Hunt and Willis, *Genius of the Place*, pp. 204ff.

12. On the garden at Chiswick, see Jacques Carré, "Lord Burlington's Garden at Chiswick," *Garden History*, I, 3, 1973, pp. 23–30; idem, "Architecture et paysage: le jardin de Chiswick," in Parraux and Plaisant, *Jardins et paysages*, I, pp. 69–84; idem, "Through French Eyes: Rigaud's Drawings of Chiswick," *Journal of Garden History*, II, 1982, pp. 133–42 (Carré's reconstruction of the plan of the garden at the time of Rigaud's visit lacks the artinatural paths shown in Rocque's engraving of 1736 [7.8] but he does not offer evidence that they were not contemporaneous with the more geometrical elements); Cinzia M. Sicca, "Lord Burlington at Chiswick: Architecture and Landscape," *Garden History*, X, 1982, pp. 36–68; Hewlings, *Chiswick House* (above, Chapter 6, n. 3). For the attribution to Bridgeman, see Willis, *Bridgeman*, p. 64.

13. John Harris has kindly called my attention to a landscape garden anticipating Kent's naturalism in a design entirely devoid of formal vestiges, at Westcombe in Kent, started in 1729 and portrayed in paintings by George Lambert in 1732. Here lawns extend from the house to informal shrubbery borders beyond which the natural landscape extends. The owner, Henry, Lord Herbert, later Earl of Pembroke, was as passionate for architecture as Burlington, and Harris has identified designs for the garden by his hand. His architect Roger Morris may also have participated.

14. In the final design, the Exedra was replaced by a clipped yew hedge behind the five busts. Kent later employed the Exedra design for the Temple of British Worthies at Stowe. Sicca ("Lord Burlington," pp. 61ff.) interprets the five busts as a commentary on Burlington's resignation from court service in 1733, in protest at Walpole's policies: Caesar and Pompey represented civil discord and Cicero the voice of reason; the poets indicated Burlington's intention to cultivate the arts rather than politics.

15. For a general treatment of Kent's career as a gardenist, see Woodbridge, "Kent as a Landscape Gardener," pp. 126–129; Wilson, *William Kent*, ch. 8. For Rousham, Woodbridge, "William Kent's Gardening: the Rousham Letters," *Apollo*, 100, 1974, pp. 282–91; John Fleming, "William Kent at Rousham, an Eighteenth-Century Elysium," *Connoisseur*, 157, 1963, pp. 158–65; Mavis Batey, "The Way to View Rousham by Kent's Gardener," *Garden History*, XI, 1983, pp. 125–32; David Coffin, "The Elysian Fields of Rousham," *Proc. of the American Philosophical Soc.*, 130, 1986, pp. 406–23. In his second article Woodbridge published the original garden plans of Bridgeman and Kent, which provide a vivid image of the differences in style.

16. Several of the Palladio drawings in the Burlington-Devonshire Collection (above, Chapter 4, n. 2) are reconstructions and fanciful variations of the grand, many-terraced structure of Praeneste that extends over a mountainside, and may have influenced Kent's design.

17. On Stowe, see Laurence Whistler *et al.*, *Stowe: a Guide to the Gardens*, Stowe, 1968; George Clarke, "The Gardens of Stowe," *Apollo*, 97, 1973, pp. 558–65; idem, "William Kent: Heresy in Stowe's Elysium," *Furor Hortensis*, Edinburgh, 1974, pp. 48ff.; idem, "Grecian Taste and Gothic Virtue: Lord Cobham's Garden Programme and its Iconography," *Apollo*, 97, 1973, pp. 56ff.; Willis, *Bridgeman*, pp. 106–23.

18. The interpretation was suggested by George Clarke, "Gardens of Stowe."

19. Anon. [William Gilpin], *Stow: The Gardens of the Right Honourable Lord Viscount Cobham*, 5th ed., London, 1748.

20. See J. Turner, "The Structure of Henry Hoare's Stourhead," *AB*, LXI, 1979, pp. 68–77; Kenneth Woodbridge, "Henry Hoare's Paradise," *AB*, XLVII, 1965, pp. 83–116; idem, *Landscape and Antiquity: Aspects of English Culture at Stourhead, 1718–1838*, Oxford, 1970; idem, *The Stourhead Landscape*, 2nd ed., n.p., 1982; idem, "Stourhead in 1768: Extracts from an Unpublished Journal by Sir John Parnell," *Journal of Garden History*, II, 1982, pp. 59–70; Malcolm Kelsall, "The Iconography of Stourhead," *JWCI*, XLVI, 1983, pp. 133–43.

21. See John Barrell, *The Idea of Landscape and the Sense of Place, 1730–1840*, Cambridge, 1972; Hoskins, *Making of the English Landscape*; Williams, *Country and City*; J. A. Yelling, *Common Field and Enclosure in England 1450–1850*, London, 1977 (who points out, however, that more villages were destroyed under Henry VII than in later centuries). An instance of the impact of the picturesque aesthetic on rural society (not necessarily related to enclosure) is found in county maps of the area of Stourhead of 1722 and 1785 (Woodbridge, *Landscape and Antiquity*, pls. 9a, 9b) showing that several houses were removed from the village of Stourton to improve the pictorial composition.

22. Gardens were not the only diversion of the privileged classes to be affected by enclosure: the large fields bounded by hedges or ditches and spotted with thickets and groves were essential to channeling the sport of hunting (and ultimately the quarryless steeplechase) away from the larger animals towards the fox. See John Patten, "The Chase and the English Landscape," *Country Life*, 150, 1971, pp. 660–62, 736–38.

23. For the spread of the landscape garden from England to America, see Adrian von Buttlar, *Der Landschaftsgarten*, Munich, 1980.

8 Thomas Jefferson (pp. 185–211)

Basic bibliography:

JEFFERSON'S WRITINGS

The Papers of Thomas Jefferson, ed. Julian P. Boyd, 21 vols to date (up to 1791), Princeton, 1950–82; *Thomas Jefferson's Garden Book, 1766–1824*, ed. E. M. Betts, Philadelphia, 1944 (includes Jefferson's horticultural correspondence); *Thomas Jefferson's Farm Book*, ed. E. M. Betts, Philadelphia, 1957.

SECONDARY SOURCES

William Howard Adams, *Jefferson's Monticello*, New York, 1983; Fiske Kimball, *Thomas Jefferson Architect*, Boston, 1916, facsimile ed., New York, 1968 (drawings catalogued in this are cited below as "K." followed by the figure number); Karl Lehmann, *Thomas Jefferson, American Humanist*, New York, 1947; Dumas Malone, *Jefferson and his Time*, 6 vols, Boston, 1948–81; Frederick D. Nichols, *Thomas Jefferson's Architectural Drawings: A Massachusetts Historical Society Picture Book*, Boston, 1960; idem, *Thomas Jefferson's Architectural Drawings*, 2nd ed., Boston and Charlottesville, 1961 (drawings catalogued in this are cited below as "N." followed by the catalog number); idem and James A. Bear, Jr, *Monticello: A Guidebook*, Monticello, 1967; idem and Ralph Griswold, *Thomas Jefferson, Landscape Architect*, Charlottesville, 1978; William B. O'Neal, *Jefferson's Fine Arts Library*, Charlottesville, 1976; Burford Pickens, "Mr. Jefferson as a Revolutionary Architect," *JSAH*, XXXIV, 4, 1975, pp. 257–79; William H. Pierson, Jr, *American Buildings and Their Architects: the Colonial and Neoclassical Styles*, New York, 1970.

1. Jefferson, *Notes on the State of Virginia* (1787), Chapel Hill, 1953, p. 165.

2. For the building history of Monticello, see Adams, *Monticello*; Gene Waddell, "The First Monticello," *JSAH*, XLVI, 1987, pp. 5–27; Kimball, *T. J. Architect*, pp. 57–61, 68–70, 73; Nichols and Bear, *Monticello*; Pierson, *American Buildings*, pp. 287–316.

3. For the size of Jefferson's estates and the number of slaves, see *Farm Book*, p. xv; for his attitude toward slavery, *The Jefferson Cyclopedia*, New York/London, 1900, *sub voce* "Labor," "Laborers," "Slavery," "Slaves," also the works cited in n. 44.

4. On Shenstone and Whately see below, pp. 206 and 217ff.

5. *Papers*, IX, p. 445.

6. I have been unable to locate this comment on Tidewater life quoted by Erik Erikson, *Dimensions of a New Identity*, New York, 1974, p. 19.

7. On southern Colonial architecture preceding Monticello, see Pierson, *American Buildings*, ch. 3; Fiske Kimball, *Domestic Architecture of the American Colonies and of the Early Republic*, New York, 1922; Thomas T. Waterman, *The Mansions of Virginia, 1706–1776*, Chapel Hill, 1946.

8. O'Neal, *J.'s Library*; E. Millicent Sowerby, *Catalogue of the Library of Thomas Jefferson*, 5 vols, Washington, D.C., 1952–59. See also below, n. 32.

9. For Jefferson's use of Gibbs, see Waddell, "First Monticello"; of Palladio, James Ackerman, "Il presidente Jefferson e il palladianesimo americano," *BCISA*, VI, 1964, pp. 39–48; of Morris, Clay Lancaster, "Jefferson's Architectural Indebtedness to Robert Morris," *JSAH*, X, 1951, pp. 3–10. See also Kimball, *T. J. Architect*; Nichols, 1961; Pickens, "Revolutionary Architect."

10. A subsequent study for these pavilions proposed an octagon (cf. *8.5*, *6*) with, he notes, "domes, resembling that of Ld. Burlington's house at Chiswick: Jones' designs pls. 70, 71, 72, 73" (his reference is to William Kent's *Designs of Inigo Jones with some Additional Designs*, London, 1727).

11. Reported in a letter of February 23, 1816, from Isaac Coles to John Cocke, proprietor of Bremo, cited by Fiske Kimball, "The Building of Bremo," *Virginia Magazine of History and Biography*, LXVII, 1949, p. 8, and in the introduction by F. D. Nichols to the facsimile edition of Kimball, *T. J. Architect*, p. vii.

12. The date and the basement dwelling have been proposed by Waddell, "First Monticello," p. 19.

13. For the matching of early projects to Gibbs, see Waddell, "First Monticello," figs. 4, 7 (K.37 and Gibbs, pl. 67); figs. 5, 6, 8 (K.11, 18, and Gibbs, pl. 84); figs. 10–12 (K. 29, N.45, and Gibbs, pl. 68).

14. On the sequence of elevations, ibid., pp. 14–18.

15. ibid., p. 15.

16. For the projecting parlor or hall and Morris, see Lancaster, "Jefferson's Indebtedness to Morris," p. 4 and figs. 3, 4, 9; and Chambers, see William Chambers, *A Treatise on Civil Architecture*, London, 1759, unnumbered end plate; and Taylor, see Marcus Binney, *Robert Taylor*, London, 1984, pls. 45, 46 (Asgill), 32, 39, 40, and *Vitruvius Britannicus*, IV, London, 1767, pl. 74 (Asgill). Soane also favored the device: see Pierre de la Ruffinière du Prey, *John Soane*, Chicago, 1982, pp. 270ff.

17. Jefferson's drawings with projecting bays are: Williamsburg, Governor's Palace, K.98–100, N.425–27; Richmond, Governor's Palace, K.101, N.285; Philadelphia house, K.120, N.251; Edgehill, K.170–74 (171–74 listed as for Shadwell), N.7–10; Farmington, K.182–83, N.13–14; Poplar Forest, K.194–95, N.262–63; Barboursville, K.205–06, N.4–5. See also Farmington in Louisville, Ky, which vaguely follows K.189–90, N.19–20 (Fiske Kimball, "Jefferson's Designs for Two Kentucky Houses," *JSAH*, IX, 3, 1950, pp. 14–16).

18. For the first Monticello garden plan, see K.34, N.61. For Jefferson's notes on his tour of English gardens, *Garden Book*, pp. 111–19; *Papers*, IX, 1954, pp. 369–75.

19. For the trip to Italy, see *Garden Book*, pp. 120–29; for the comment on Milan Cathedral, etc., *Papers*, XIII, 1956, p. 272.

20. Letter of March 20, 1787, *Papers*, XI, 1955, p. 226.

21. For the rebuilding of the house, see *Garden Book*, pp. 248, 260; Duc de La Rochefoucauld-Liancourt, "Travels through the United States of North America . . .," London, 1799, excerpted in Henry Randall, *The Life of Thomas Jefferson*, II, New York, 1858, pp. 302ff.

22. Letter to Martha Randolph of February 8, 1798, *The Family Letters of Thomas Jefferson*, ed. E. M. Betts and J. A. Bear, Columbia, Mo., 1966, pp. 155f.

23. K.150, N.135. The interior is richly illustrated in Adams, *Monticello*, pp. 83–144.

24. Letter to John Brown of April 5, 1797, Kimball, "Kentucky Houses," p. 15.

25. K.68–92, N.97–123.

26. K.158–60, N.173–74, 157.

27. "Notes on Objects of Attention for an American," *Papers*, XIII, 1956, p. 269.

28. Letter from Paris of October 12, 1786, *Papers*, X, 1954, p. 44. Compare the description by Margaret Smith of her visit to Jefferson (*The First Forty Years of Washington Society*, New York, 1906, p. 66): "We began to ascend this mountain, still as we rose I cast my eyes around, but could discern nothing but untamed woodland, after a mile's winding upwards, we saw a field of corn, but the road was still wild and uncultivated. I every moment expected to reach the summit, and felt as if it was an endless road; my impatience lengthened it, for it is not two miles from the outer gate on the river to the house. At last we reached the summit, and I shall never forget the emotion the first view of this sublime scenery excited. Below me extended for above 60 miles round, a country covered with woods, plantations and houses; beyond, arose the blue mountains, in all their grandeur. Monticello rising 500 feet above the river, of a conical form and standing by itself, commands on all sides an unobstructed and I suppose one of the most extensive views any spot on the globe affords. The sides of the mountains covered with wood, with scarcely a speck of cultivation, present a fine contrast to its summit, crowned with a noble pile of buildings, surrounded by an immense lawn, and shaded here and there with some fine trees."

29. "E sopra un monticello de ascesa facilissima": *I quattro libri dell'architettura*, Vicenza, 1570, bk II, p. 18. I have no idea how Jefferson came upon the Italian word, since his Palladio editions were in English and French; Leoni's translation—dated 1715ff.—renders the word as "hillock" (bk II, p. 8). The "theatre" passage in Leoni reads: "On the other side it is surrounded by several hills, that seem to form a great Theatre, and which besides are all of them cultivated . . . so that having the advantage of fine prospects on all sides, some confin'd, some more remote, and some farther than the sight can reach, I have made Portico's to all the four fronts . . ."

30. For the rectangular site plan, see K.12, N.34; the 1772 site plan, K.34, N.61.

31. Marcus Terentius Varro, *Rerum rusticarum*, III.v.

32. *Garden Book*, p. 25. F. D. Nichols and R. E. Griswold, *Thomas Jefferson Landscape Architect*, Charlottesville, 1978, p. 95, state (without source) that in 1765 Jefferson acquired the *Works* (London, 1764) of the English landscape gardener William Shenstone, containing his influential "Unconnected Thoughts on Gardening." Though the book is included in Jefferson's library inventory of 1815 (as are the British garden books of Whately and of Heely—which describes Shenstone's garden at the Leasowes), it is in the third edition of 1773 (Sowerby, *Library of T. J.*, IV, p. 486, no. 53; for Whately and Heely, pp. 380, 387).

33. Pope's verses are found in a letter to Edward Blount of June, 1725, quoted in E. Malins, *English Landscaping and Literature, 1660–1840*, London, 1966, p. 35. For this, and for earlier garden adaptations of the sleeping nymph, see Elizabeth B. MacDougall, "The Sleeping Nymph: Origins of a Humanist Fountain," *AB*, LVII, 1975, pp. 357–65.

34. K.160–61, 164, pp. 69f.; N. 171; *Garden Book*, pls. XIX, XX.

35. Ornamental buildings, K. 35–37, N. 62–64; observation towers, (Georgian) K. 38–39, N.65–66; (medieval) K. 62–64, N. 91–93. See also William Beiswanger, "Jefferson's Designs for Garden Structures at Monticello," *JSAH*, XXXV, 1976, pp. 310–12.

36. K. 138, N. 136.

37. *Garden Book*, p. 196.

38. pp. 166ff.

39. For Jefferson as a farmer and agricultural theorist, see A. Whitney Griswold, *Farming and Democracy*, New York, 1948.

40. For the President's house, see K. 125–29, N. 397–401; for the Governor's Palace, Richmond, K. 105, N. 284.

41. See n. 11 above.

42. For the letter to Cocke from Coles see n. 11 above. On the Bremo design, which Cocke discussed with Jefferson, but apparently executed himself, see Kimball, "The Building of Bremo," pp. 7–13. The lost drawing for Bremo cited in Alexander Lambeth's 1913 monograph on Jefferson's architecture as being Jefferson's design for Bremo and cited by Kimball, *T. J. Architect*, p. 74n., turned up in 1963 and proved to be by Cornelia Randolph after Poplar Forest (Nichols, introduction to facsimile ed. of Kimball, p. vii).

43. On projects for other houses, see n. 17 above, esp. Kimball, "Kentucky Houses."

44. For Jefferson's attitude toward blacks, see *Notes on the State of Virginia*, pp. 138ff.; Erikson, *Dimensions*, pp. 23f.

9 The Picturesque (pp. 213–27)

1. It would be fruitless to attempt to provide representative items from the extensive literature relevant to this change. I found particularly useful W. J. Bate, *From Classic to Romantic: Premises of Taste in Eighteenth Century England*, Cambridge, 1946, esp. ch. 3; M. H. Abrams, "Art as Such: A Sociology of Modern Aesthetics," *Bull. of the American Academy of Arts and Sciences*, 38, 1985, pp. 8–37. Abrams shows that the ground for the change was prepared by the interest of a leisured class in establishing taste as a basis for the validation of works of "fine" art, and ultimately the democratization of taste through museums, concert halls, and the opening of country houses and parks to the public.

2. This phenomenon has been cataloged and extensively interpreted by John Archer, in *The Literature of British Domestic Architecture, 1715–1842*, Cambridge, Mass., 1985 (items cataloged in this are cited below as "A." followed by the catalog number). See also Christopher Hussey, *The Picturesque: Studies in a Point of View*, London, 1927; the essays of Nikolaus Pevsner in *Studies in Art, Architecture and Design*, I, London, 1968; Rudolf

Wittkower, "The English Literature on Architecture," *Palladio and Palladianism*, London/New York, 1974, pp. 94–112; Colin Rowe, "Character and Composition," *The Mathematics of the Ideal Villa and Other Essays*, Cambridge, Mass., 1976, pp. 60–87.

3. *The Works in Architecture of Robert and James Adam*, London, 1778, preface, pp. 4–5. The concept of genius, as it has been used since the generation of the Adams, was formulated in aesthetic writings of the mid-eighteenth century. The most influential British contribution was Alexander Gerard's *An Essay on Taste*, London, 1759. "The first and leading quality of genius is *invention*," Gerard writes (p. 173), "which consists in an extensive comprehensiveness of imagination, in a readiness of associating the remotest ideas, that are in any way related." See Archer, *Literature*, p. 42.

4. William Gilpin, *Observations relative to Picturesque Beauty made in the year 1789 in several parts of Gt. Britain, particularly in the Highlands of Scotland*, London, 2 vols, 1789, I, p. 193, as quoted by H. F. Clark, "Eighteenth Century Elysiums: the Role of 'Association' in the Landscape Movement," *JWCI*, 6, 1943, p. 187.

5. The appearance of Repton's book was delayed by the publisher until 1795 and the author took the opportunity to answer the attacks on Brown and himself in notes and in a closing letter addressed to Price.

6. Hussey, *Picturesque*; Walter John Hipple, Jr, *The Beautiful, The Sublime, and The Picturesque in Eighteenth-Century British Aesthetic Theory*, Carbondale, 1957; Nikolaus Pevsner, "The Genesis of the Picturesque," *Studies*, pp. 78–101.

7. For the impact of Burke's *Philosophical Enquiry* see Hipple, ch. 6 and pp. 74f., 93, 272f. Burke actually found in one classical philosopher, Longinus, an inspiration for this anticlassicism: see *The Works of the Right Honourable Edmund Burke*, Boston, 1865, I, p. 124.

8. The theories of Price (best represented in *Three Essays on the Picturesque*, London, 1810; the quotations below are from vol. I, pp. 50f., 200) and of Knight (best represented in *An Analytical Inquiry into the Principles of Taste*, London, 1805) are reviewed in the volumes quoted in n. 6 and by Pevsner in *Studies*: "Uvedale Price," pp. 126–37, "Richard Payne Knight," pp. 108–25.

9. Knight, in *The Landscape*, London, 1794, p. 35, ll. 254ff., wrote: "Blessed is the man, in whose sequestered glade / Some ancient abbey's walls diffuse their shade . . . / Nor yet unenvied, to whose humbler lot / Falls the retired, antiquated cot:— / Its roof with weeds and mosses cover'd o'er, / And honey-suckles climbing round the door / And clust'ring ivy decks the chimney's head . . ." James Malton, in *An Essay on British Cottage Architecture*, London, 1798, p. 4, referring to the traditional definitions of the cottage by "Dr. Johnson" and "Dr. Watts" as a "mean house in the country," observes: "But with great deference to such high authorities, I have led myself to conceive very differently of a cottage; which may, I think, as well be the habitation of a substantial farmer or affluent gentleman as the dwelling of the hedger . . ." A parallel change in attitude is found in the "ferme ornée," an eighteenth-century invention reflected in John Plaw's *Ferme ornée; or Rural Improvements*, London, 1795 (A. 259).

10. The difference in the two viewpoints are revealed in a volume published by Price in 1801, called *A Dialogue on the Distinct Characters of the Picturesque and Beautiful*, in which he and Knight are interlocutors. Price naturally favoured his own position.

11. The second and major part of Knight's book of 1805 was entitled "Of the Association of Ideas," and was divided into chapters entitled "Of Knowledge," "Of Imagination," and "Of Judgment." He must have been aided in his articulation of the concept by the doctrine of association developed in Archibald Alison's *Essays in the Nature and Principles of Taste*, Edinburgh, 1790.

12. See Clark, "Elysiums," pp. 165–89; John Archer, "The Beginnings of Association in British Architectural Aesthetics,"

Eighteenth Century Studies, XVI, 1983, pp. 241–64; idem, "Expression and Affectivity: Theories of Character and Association," *Literature*, ch. 3, pp. 46–56.

13. Facsimile ed., New York, 1932, ch. xlviii; Whately's role in promoting the concept of character is defined in John Archer, "Character in English Architectural Design," *Eighteenth Century Studies*, XII, 1979, pp. 348ff.; see also Rowe, "Character."

14. Whately, *Observations*, p. 54.

15. A. 24.

16. On the controversy, see E. Malins, *English Landscaping and Literature, 1660–1840*, London, 1966, ch. 6, pp. 123ff.; on Repton, Hussey, *Picturesque*, pp. 160ff.; Pevsner, "Humphry Repton, 1752–1818," *Studies*, pp. 138–55; Dorothy Stroud, *Humphry Repton*, London, 1962, pp. 82–92. See also n. 5 above.

17. Repton, *Fragments on the Theory and Practice of Landscape Gardening Including Some Remarks on Grecian and Gothic Architecture Collected from Various Manuscripts in the Possession of the Different Noblemen and Gentlemen for Whose Use they were Originally Written the Whole Tending to establish Fixed Principles in the Respective Arts*, London, 1816, p. 16 (A. 277): "Antiquarian effort can interfere with comfort."

18. *Fragments*, p. 204.

19. A. 197 and n. 9 above.

20. A. 196.

21. A. 293; the following quotation is from the text to design no. v.

22. We cannot be sure that Robinson, rather than another villa author, was responsible for transmitting these elements to America: see below, Chapter 10, p. 230 and n. 2.

23. The *O.E.D.* records the use of the term in England in 1711.

24. K. F. Schinkel, *Sammlung architektonischer Entwürfe*, 2 vols, Berlin, 1866, *passim*. David Watkin and Tilman Mellinghof (*German Architecture and the Classical Ideal*, London, 1987, pp. 105f.) propose that in designs for the court gardener's house at Charlottenhof of 1829–33 Schinkel was inspired by pl. XVII of Papworth's *Rural Residences* (1818) as well as "reminiscences of his Italian tour of 1803–04."

25. See John Summerson, *The Life and Works of John Nash, Architect*, rev. ed., Cambridge, Mass., 1986, pp. 46ff.

26. A.153.

27. A.203.

28. A.184. The quotation is from p. 1. On Loudon's publications, see "John Claudius Loudon, a List of His Publications," in Elizabeth MacDougall, ed., *John Claudius Loudon and the Early Nineteenth Century in Great Britain*, Washington, D.C., 1980, pp. 127–33; also below, n. 30.

29. A.182. Ruskin's fourteen contributions, published under the pseudonym Kata Phusin, were entitled "The Poetry of Architecture; or the Architecture of the Nations of Europe Considered in its Association with Natural Scenery and National Character."

30. On the evolution of British architectural publication in the course of the century, see Archer, *Literature*, pts i and ii, "Architecture and the Book Trade" and "Format and Content"; and on Loudon and his contemporaries, Ray Desmond, "Loudon and Nineteenth-Century Horticultural Journalism," in MacDougall, *Loudon*, pp. 79–101.

31. *Encyclopaedia*, p. 763.

32. A.190.

33. *Encyclopaedia*, p. 1122.

34. Archer (*Literature*, pp. 519f.), however, emphasizes the innovative nature of Loudon's proposition that a building can be appreciated only in terms of its own geographical and historical context (in contrast to earlier associationists' focus on the observer).

10 Andrew Jackson Downing and the American Romantic Villa (pp. 229–51)

1. The definitive study of the life and works of Downing is unfortunately unpublished: George Tatum, *Andrew Jackson*

Downing, Arbiter of American Taste: 1815–1852, diss., Princeton University, 1949 (University Microfilms International). See the same author's introduction to the facsimile ed. of Downing's *The Architecture of Country Houses* (1850), New York, 1968, pp. v–xvii. There are two excellent critical studies of Downing and his contemporaries: Vincent Scully, "Romantic Rationalism and the Expression of Structure in Wood: Downing, Wheeler, Gardner and the 'Stick Style', 1840–76," *AB*, XXXV, 1953, pp. 121–42, and William H. Pierson, Jr, *American Buildings and Their Architects: Technology and the Picturesque, the Corporate and the Early Gothic Styles*, Garden City, 1980, ch. 7. My view of Downing is also indebted to an unpublished paper by Peter Fabry.

2. The house and garden are discussed in detail by Arthur Channing Downs, "Downing's Newburgh Villa," *Archives of Preservation Technology*, IV, 3–4, 1972, pp. 1–113. Downing had read Robinson's *Designs for Ornamental Villas* (1827) and *Rural Architecture* (1823), along with the books of Goodwin, Lugar, Hunt and Loudon (see above, Chapter 9), all of which he recommends to readers of his *Treatise on the Theory and Practice of Landscape Gardening*, New York/London, 1841, p. 387.

3. Fredrika Bremer, *The Homes of the New World: Impressions of America*, I, New York, 1853, p. 20.

4. Downs, "Newburgh Villa," pp. 6–19, described the development of the grounds at Highland Gardens and assembled the visual documentation. As Ann Gilkerson has pointed out to me, Downing's approach to the traditional antithesis between the beautiful and the picturesque changed in the course of the 1840s. In the 1841 first edition of the *Treatise* he refers to the former, which he calls "graceful," as "the most beautiful and perfect" (pp. 58f.), while in the 1850 edition he leans toward the picturesque (pp. 76f.).

5. The "third-rate" gardens are described on pp. 409–547; Loudon's "Villa" plan is on p. 514. The book may not have influenced Downing's design, since it appeared as his house was being completed, but Loudon had published extensively on the subject previously (see above, Chapter 9, n. 28).

6. Walter Creese gives an ample account of the development of villa properties along the Hudson river valley, and an assessment of the development of a taste for the natural landscape, in *The Crowning of the American Landscape*, Princeton, 1985.

On A. J. Davis, see Jane B. Davis, *sub voce*, *Macmillan Encyclopedia of Architects*, I, New York, 1982, pp. 505–14, with a checklist of works; Edna Donnell, "A. J. Davis and the Gothic Revival," *Metropolitan Museum Studies*, V, 1934/36, pp. 183–233; Roger H. Newton, *Town and Davis, Architects*, New York, 1942; Pierson, *American Buildings*, ch. 6. Pierson gives the house for Paulding (Knoll, later renamed Lyndhurst) an extended and perceptive study, pp. 308–48.

7. New York, 1837; facsimile ed., New York, 1979, with a useful introduction by Jane B. Davies. According to Davies, the first four plates and accompanying text were completed by 1836 but publication was delayed in the hope of receiving a preface by Washington Irving. The client-sponsors were Robert Donaldson and James A. Hillhouse, for whom Davis designed villas near Barrytown (Blithewood [*10.7*]) and in New Haven. On Davis and Downing, Donaldson later wrote to Davis, "My recollection of the *initial* steps (taken in 1834 or 1835 by the late *Mr. Hillhouse & ourselves*) sometimes recurs to me—of the rural Architecture and Villa embellishments which have since gone on—to the great *improvement of country life* notwithstanding the overdone ginger-bread work & be-gabled houses which abound. *Downing stole your thunder*, for a while—but I always, on suitable occasions, claimed for you the *seminal* ideas which have been so fruitful."

8. Donnell, "Davis," fig. 14. The plan of Glen Ellen shows a classical niched rotunda as the central room. The "Tuscan Villa" entry is in the Metropolitan Museum, New York, Print Room, Davis Coll., vol. I, 24.66.1400, p. 39.

9. Wayne Andrews, *Architecture in New York*, New York, 1969, p. 34.

10. Pierson, *American Buildings*, pp. 366ff. Davis's plate showed a villa for David Codwise that is classical, not picturesque; the style could be defined as Empire.

11. The planned garden suburb was another setting for the mid-nineteenth-century villa. One example, Llewellyn Park, New Jersey (1853–57), was a 350-acre scheme developed by Llewellyn Haskell, a friend of Downing who had the forested site laid out on Downing's principles of landscaping. Davis built a number of the villas there, including one for himself.

12. The "Villa in the Collegiate Style" was projected for another estate, at Fishkill, but was not built. The site at Blithewood is occupied by an equally grandiose Baroque Revival villa on the campus of Bard College, in Allendale.

13. See above, Chapter 9, n. 30.

14. *Treatise*, pp. 340ff.

15. Tatum, *Downing*, pp. 53f.

16. *Architecture of Country Houses*, p. 257.

17. *Cottage Residences*, p. 7; in his last statement on the subject, Downing wrote: "We miss in all our wooden farm-houses, that substantial, solid, real look, that harmonizes so well both with rural life and pastoral scenery, and which is always felt on seeing farm-houses well built of solid stone or brick" (*Horticulturist*, VII, July, 1852, p. 331).

18. Tatum, *Downing*, pp. 62ff. At this time, the increasing pressure of correspondence and the preparation of new books (and revised editions of those published) led Downing to sell his nursery.

19. Bremer, *Homes*, p. 46.

20. Tatum, *Downing*, pp. 191ff., based on Benson Lossing, *Vassar College and Its Founder*, New York, 1867. The buildings have recently been burned down by vandals except for the gatehouse.

21. Daniel Reiff, *Washington Architecture, 1791–1861: Problems in Development*, Washington, D.C., 1971, pp. 113ff.

22. *Architecture of Country Houses*, p. v.

23. From *Rural Essays*, a collection of Downing's essays (mostly from *The Horticulturist*), ed. G. W. Curtis, New York, 1853, p. 212.

24. *Treatise*, pp. 300–305; *Cottage Residences*, pp. 2ff.

25. *Architecture of Country Houses*, pp. 10–25. In *Treatise*, pp. 61ff., the principle of Relative Beauty is not yet developed.

26. *Treatise*, pp. 339f.; the opinion is specified more fully in *Architecture of Country Houses*, pp. 261ff. See also *Horticulturist*, VI, 1850, p. 11.

27. *Treatise*, p. 341: "Buildings of almost every description, and particularly those for the habitation of man, will be considered by the mind of taste, not only as architectural objects of greater or less merit, but as component parts of the general scene."

28. *Architecture of Country Houses*, pp. 262–70.

29. *Cottage Residences*, pp. 89f. The passage goes on to cite ease of construction as an additional advantage. See also *Treatise*, p. 363, where Downing adds: "We hope to see this Bracketed style becoming every day more common in the United States, and especially in our farm and country houses, when wood is the material employed in their construction."

30. *Architecture of Country Houses*, pp. 30ff. Roger Stein, *John Ruskin and Aesthetic Thought in America, 1840–1900*, Cambridge, Mass., 1967, pp. 47ff., has suggested a more significant role for Ruskin in accounting for changes between the utilitarian aesthetic of Downing's first two books and the more romantic emphasis of the last, especially in Downing's development of the concept of Relative Beauty (paralleling Ruskin's Vital Beauty), and in his greater emphasis on social and psychological factors.

31. *Architecture of Country Houses*, p. 264.

32. ibid., p. 24.

33. *Treatise*, p. 378.

34. The path is imaginatively traced by Vincent Scully, *The Shingle Style and the Stick Style: Architectural Theory and Design from Downing to the Origins of Wright*, New Haven, 1971.

35. Bremer, *Homes*, p. 27.

36. "Essay on American Scenery, 1835," in John McCoubrey, *American Art, 1700–1960: Sources and Documents*, Englewood Cliffs, 1965, p. 109.

37. David Lawall, *Asher Brown Durand: His Art and Art Theory in Relation to His Times*, New York/London, 1977, p. 261.

38. See Perry Miller, "Nature and the National Ego," *Errand into the Wilderness*, Cambridge, Mass., 1956, pp. 206–15. For an exceptional contemporary expression of the utilitarian position, see Charles Caldwell, "On the Moral and Other Indirect Influences of Rail-Roads," *New England Magazine*, II, 1832, pp. 288ff.

39. See John William Ward, *Andrew Jackson: Symbol for an Age*, New York, 1953, ch. 3; Leo Marx, *The Machine in the Garden*, New York, 1964, ch. 1.

40. George Santayana, "The Genteel Tradition in American Philosophy," *The Genteel Tradition*, ed. D. L. Wilson, Cambridge, Mass., 1967, pp. 37ff.

11 The Modern Villa: Wright and Le Corbusier
(pp. 253–85)

1. Robert Twombly, *Frank Lloyd Wright, an Interpretive Biography*, New York, 1973; Wright's *An Autobiography*, New York, 1932, rev. ed. 1943, 1977 (my citations are from the 1977 printing) is the major source for his theory as well as for the events of his career and private life, presented in a vivid and powerful style.

2. Major monographs on Wright's work are Henry-Russell Hitchcock's pioneering study *In the Nature of Materials: the Buildings of Frank Lloyd Wright*, New York, 1941; Grant C. Manson, *Frank Lloyd Wright to 1910: the First Golden Age*, New York, 1958; Norris Kelly Smith, *Frank Lloyd Wright: A Study in Architectural Content*, New York, 1966, rev. ed., Watkins Glen, N.Y., 1979; and the brief essay of Vincent Scully, *Frank Lloyd Wright*, New York, 1960; see also H. Allen Brooks, *The Prairie School*, Toronto, 1972.

3. Manson, *Wright*, pp. 87–97.

4. On Riverside, a model for many suburban designs of later decades, see Walter Creese, *The Crowning of the American Landscape*, Princeton, 1985, pp. 219–42.

5. *Autobiography*, p. 165.

6. ibid., p. 372.

7. On Wright's clients, see Leonard K. Eaton, *Two Chicago Architects and their Clients: Frank Lloyd Wright and Howard van Doren Shaw*, Cambridge, Mass., 1969; Robert Twombly, "Saving the Family: Middle-Class Attraction to Wright's Prairie House, 1901–09," *American Quarterly*, XXVII, 1975, pp. 57–72.

8. The relation of Taliesin with the Welsh poetic tradition and prehistoric and rural stone structures has been studied by Thomas Beebe, "The Song of Taliesin," *Modulus*, I, 1980–81, pp. 3–11. The significance of the Italian influence was suggested to me by David Van Zanten and Neil Levine. See also Crease, *Crowning*, pp. 241–60, valuable for its old photographic records.

9. *Autobiography*, p. 172.

10. Le Corbusier, *Une petite maison* (*Les carnets de la recherche patiente*, 1), Zurich, 1954, p. 9: "je prends à plusieurs reprises le rapide Paris-Milan ou l'Orient-Express (Paris-Ankara). J'emporte un plan de maison dans ma poche. Le plan avant le terrain? Le plan d'une maison pour lui trouver un terrain? Oui."

11. Le Corbusier and Pierre Jeanneret, *Oeuvre complète*, I, *1910–1929*, ed. W. Boesiger and O. Stonorov, Zurich, 1937 (and other eds), pp. 23–26. On Le Corbusier's early career and intellectual background, see Paul Turner, *La formation de Le Corbusier: idéalisme et mouvement moderne*, Paris, 1987.

12. *Oeuvre complète*, I, pp. 45–47.

13. Reyner Banham, "Ateliers d'artistes. Paris Studio Houses and the Modern Movement," *AR*, 120, 1956, pp. 75–83; idem, *Architectural Theory in the First Machine Age*, New York/London, 1967, pp. 216–19; Stanislaus von Moos, *Le Corbusier, éléments*

d'une synthèse, Paris, 1971, pp. 64f.

14. *Oeuvre complète*, I, pp. 140–49; S. Giedion, "Le problème du luxe dans l'architecture moderne," *Cahiers d'art*, 3, 1928; Henry-Russell Hitchcock, "Houses by Two Moderns," *The Arts*, XVI, i, September, 1929, pp. 33–38; Colin Rowe, "The Mathematics of the Ideal Villa: Palladio and Le Corbusier Compared," *AR*, 101, March, 1947, pp. 101–04 (reprinted in *The Mathematics of the Ideal Villa and Other Essays*, Cambridge, Mass., 1976, pp. 1–28); Tim Benton, "Villa les Terrasses," *Les Villas de Le Corbusier et Pierre Jeanneret, 1920–1930*, Paris, 1984, pp. 165–89; *The Le Corbusier Archive*, ed. H. Allen Brooks, III, New York, 1982, pp. 367–469; William Curtis, *Le Corbusier: Ideas and Forms*, New York, 1987, pp. 79–84.

15. See Lauren Soth, "Le Corbusier's Clients and their Parisian Houses of the 1920s," *Art History*, VI, 1983, pp. 187–98.

16. *Oeuvre complète*, I, p. 140. The Garches facades do not touch the ground.

17. ibid., p. 68.

18. Suggested by Sanford Anderson, "Architectural Research Programmes in the Work of Le Corbusier," *Architectural Design*, 5, no. 3, 1984, pp. 151f., and Richard Etlin (in a talk at the 1985 meeting of the Society of Architectural Historians); the latter proposed that Le Corbusier's perception of the use of asymmetry may have been prompted by the books of Choisy.

19. *Oeuvre complète*, I, p. 63.

20. On the Villa Savoye, see *Oeuvre complète*, I, pp. 186ff.; "Explication des Planches: Villa, à Poissy," *L'architecture*, n.s., 7, September, 1930, pp. 69–76; Tim Benton, "Villa Savoye," *Villas*, pp. 190–207; idem, "Villa Savoye and the Architect's Practice," *Le Corbusier Archive*, VII, 1984, pp. ix–xxxi; Curtis, *Le Corbusier*, pp. 93–98.

21. *Précisions sur un état présent de l'architecture et de l'urbanisme: Collection de l'esprit nouveau*, Paris, 1930, pp. 123ff. The quotations that follow are on pp. 136f.

22. ibid., p. 138.

23. ibid.; and see the quotation on p. 14 above.

24. Le Corbusier, *Vers une architecture*, Paris, 1923, p. 16.

25. *Précisions*, p. 132.

26. *Oeuvre complète*, I, p. 89.

27. See Brian B. Taylor, *Le Corbusier at Pessac*, Cambridge, Mass., 1972; idem, *Le Corbusier's Prototype Mass-Housing: 1914–1928*, diss., Harvard University, 1974; Philippe Boudon, *Pessac de Le Corbusier: 1926–1967*, 2nd ed., Paris, 1985; and the account in Benton, "Villa Savoye."

28. For villas of the early 1930s, see *The Le Corbusier Archive*, IX (for 1930), New York, 1982, pp. 3ff. (Errazuriz), 411ff. (Goldenberg), 419ff. (de Mandrot), XII (for 1933–37), 1983, pp. 393ff. (Paris, "petite maison de weekend"), 503ff. (aux Mathes); James Stirling, "Garches to Jaoul: Le Corbusier as Domestic Architect in 1927 and 1953," *AR*, 118, September, 1955, pp. 145–51; Peter Serenyi, "Le Corbusier's Changing Attitude Toward Form," *JSAH*, XXXIV, 1965, pp. 15–23; Curtis, *Le Corbusier*, pp. 108–17. The sketches made in Brazil in 1929 are reproduced in *Le Corbusier Sketchbooks, I, 1914–48*, Cambridge, Mass., 1981; note especially fig. 243.

29. Donald Hoffmann, *Frank Lloyd Wright's Fallingwater: the House and its History*, New York, 1978; Edgar Kaufmann, Jr, *Fallingwater: a Frank Lloyd Wright Country House*, New York, 1986 (exceptional photographic coverage).

30. Except for the influence of his early work on Europe before the First World War.

31. See the work of Richard Meier, of Gwathmey and Siegel, and of Peter Eisenman [*1.8*], and the early houses of Michael Graves, illustrated in monographs on their work and in Arthur Drexler, Colin Rowe and Kenneth Frampton, *Five Architects: Eisenman, Graves, Gwathmey, Hejduk, Meier*, New York, 1972. Le Corbusier's influence on housing and public building was pervasive from the 1940s on.

SOURCES OF ILLUSTRATIONS

The author and publishers gratefully acknowledge the following individuals and institutions:

1.1 Deutsches Archäologisches Institut, Rome; 1.2 Photo courtesy of the Fogg Art Museum, Harvard University; 1.3 Courtesy the Duke of Beaufort, photo Marlborough Fine Arts Ltd; 1.5 Frances B. Johnston; 1.7 Fondation Le Corbusier/ SPADEM, Paris; 1.8 Peter Eisenman; 1.9 Reconstruction by Maiuri, courtesy Istituto Poligrafico e Zecca dello Stato, Rome; 1.10 Courtauld Institute of Art, London; 1.11 Copyright © 1982, David King Gleason; 1.12 Visual Services, Loeb Library, Harvard University; 1.13 Philip Trager; 1.14 Museo Firenze com'era, Florence, photo Soprintendenza alle Gallerie di Firenze; 1.15 After Kahler, courtesy Gebr. Mann Verlag, Berlin; 1.18, 19 James Ackerman; 1.20 Redrawn by Barbara Shapiro; 1.21 After Fouet, courtesy of C.N.R.S., Paris; 1.22 By permission of the Houghton Library, Harvard University; 1.23 Neil Levine; 1.24 as 1.12; 1.25 as 1.14; 1.26 Photo copyright Sandak Inc.; 1.27 Phyllis Massar; 2.1 Fototeca Unione, Rome; 2.2 From Axel Boethius and J. B. Ward-Perkins, *Etruscan and Roman Architecture*, 1970, courtesy Penguin Books, Harmondsworth; 2.3 Courtesy Professor Guy Métraux; 2.4, 5 After M. Medri, courtesy Edizioni Panini s.p.a., Modena; 2.6 as 1.20; 2.7 After Drerup, courtesy University of Marburg; 2.8 By Professor Wilhelmina Jashemski, courtesy Aristide Caratzas Publishers; 2.9 as 2.2; 2.10 as 1.20; 2.11 Courtesy Leon Krier and The Canadian Centre for Architecture; 2.12 as 1.20; 2.13 Anderson 40855/Art Resource; 2.14 Museo Nazionale, Naples, no. 9479, photo Fototeca Unione; 2.15 Museo Nazionale, Naples, no. 9480, photo Villani/Art Resource; 2.16 Bardo Museum, Tunis, photo Deutsches Archäologisches Institut, Rome; 2.17 Computer generated from plan by Gnirs; 2.18 as 1.1; 3.1 as 1.2; 3.2 Mansell/Alinari; 3.3, 4 as 1.14; 3.5 Courtesy Mario Gori Sassoli; 3.6, 7 as 1.18; 3.8 as 1.22; 3.9 After Ferrara and Quinterio, copyright Libreria Salimbeni, Florence; 3.10 as 1.18; 3.11 Paul Birnbaum; 3.12 Soprintendenza alle Gallerie di Firenze, Florence; 3.13 Pierpont Morgan Library, New York; 3.14 Paolo Brandinelli; 3.15 Drawn by Norman Newton; 3.16 Gabinetto dei Disegni degli Uffizi, Florence, photo Soprintendenza alle Gallerie di Firenze; 3.17 Alinari; 3.18 as 3.14; 3.19 as 1.18; 3.20 as 3.16 (Arch. 1640); 3.21 Biblioteca Comunale, Siena, S.IV.8; 3.22 as 3.16; 3.23 Biblioteca Comunale, Treviso, Pergamene Giustinian, n. 4, photo courtesy Douglas Lewis; 3.24 Biblioteca Mediceo Laurenziana, Florence, Ashburnham, App. 1828, c.97, dis. 143; 3.25 as 1.18; 4.1 After Kubelik (see Ch.4, n.1); 4.3 as 3.17; 4.4 Rijksmuseum, Amsterdam; 4.5 G. Paolo Marton; 4.7 Avery Library, Columbia University, New York; 4.8 as 1.18; 4.10 as 1.27; 4.11 as 1.13; 4.13 Giacomelli, Vicenza; 4.14, 15, 17, 18 as 1.13; 6.1, 2 A. F. Kersting; 6.3 Historic Buildings and Monuments Commission for England; 6.4, 5 as 6.1; 6.6 Royal Commission on the Historical Monuments of England; 6.7 Reproduced by permission of the Trustees of the Chatsworth Settlement, photo Courtauld Institute of Art, London; 6.8 Royal Institute of British Architects; 6.10 as 6.1; 6.11 Dumbarton Oaks Research Library; 6.12 as 6.6; 6.13 as 6.8; 6.14 as 1.22; 6.15 as 6.1; 6.16 as 1.22; 6.17 as 1.20; 6.18 as 6.1; 6.19 Photo courtesy of John Harris; 6.20 as 6.1; 7.1 as 1.22; 7.2 City Museum and Art Gallery, Birmingham; 7.3 British Library, London; 7.4 The Metropolitan Museum of Art, New York, Harris Brisbane Dick Fund, 1942 [42.79(2)]; 7.5 Yale Center for British Art, New Haven, Paul Mellon Collection; 7.6 as 7.3; 7.7 as 1.2; 7.8, 9 as 7.3; 7.10 as 6.7; 7.11, 12 Copyright *Country Life*; 7.13 Edwin Smith; 7.14 Mr C. Cottrell-Dormer, photo Courtauld Institute of Art, London; 7.15 Bodleian Library, Oxford, Gough Drawings A4, fol. 46; 7.16 The Metropolitan Museum of Art, New York, Harris Brisbane Dick Fund, 1942 [42.79(7)]; 7.17 as 7.3; 7.18, 19 as 7.11; 7.20 Reproduced by permission of the Wiltshire Record Office; 7.21 The Royal Swedish Academy of Fine Arts, Stockholm; 7.22 as 6.6; 8.1 as 1.26; 8.2 Photo copyright © Wayne Andrews/Esto; 8.3–6 Coolidge Collection, Massachusetts Historical Society, Boston; 8.7 Manuscript Department, University of Virginia Library; 8.8 Courtesy Clarendon Gallery Ltd, London; 8.9 as 8.3; 8.10 Photo Thomas Jefferson Memorial Foundation, Inc./James Tkatch; 8.11 Lauros-Giraudon; 8.12 Langdon Clay; 8.13 Photo Thomas Jefferson Memorial Foundation, Inc.; 8.14 H.A.B.S.; 8.15 as 8.12; 8.16 as 8.3; 8.17 as 8.12; 8.18–21 as 8.3; 8.22 Fogg Fine Arts Films; 8.23 Photo Joseph Farber; 8.24 as 1.20; 9.1 as 1.2; 9.2 Alistair Rowan; 9.3 as 1.2; 9.7 as 7.13; 9.8 as 1.2; 9.9 as 1.22; 10.2 Yale University Library; 10.4–6 Museum of Comparative Zoology Library, Harvard University; 10.8 Photo New York Public Library, Eno Coll. 486; 10.9 The Metropolitan Museum of Art, New York, Harris Brisbane Dick Fund, 1924 [24.66.70]; 10.10, 11 as 8.14; 10.12 as 8.2; 10.13 Library of Congress, Washington, D.C.; 10.14 as 1.18; 10.15 The Metropolitan Museum of Art, New York, Harris Brisbane Dick Fund; 10.16 as 1.2; 10.17 The New York Public Library; 10.18 The Warner Collection of Gulf State Paper Corporation, Tuscaloosa, photo Hirschl & Adler Galleries, Inc.; 11.1 Frank Lloyd Wright Memorial Foundation; 11.2 Fondation Le Corbusier/SPADEM, Paris; 11.3 From *Ausgeführte Bauten und Entwürfe von Frank Lloyd Wright*, Wasmuth, Berlin, 1910; 11.4 Loeb Library, Harvard University; 11.5, 6 as 11.1; 11.7 as 11.3; 11.8 Graduate School of Design, Harvard University; 11.9 as 10.12; 11.10 From Le Corbusier, *Oeuvre complète 1910–65*, Artemis, Zurich, 1967; 11.11 From Le Corbusier, *Oeuvre complète*, I, *1910–1929*, Les Editions d'Architecture, Zurich, 1965; 11.12 Lucien Hervé; 11.13 F. R. Yerbury, courtesy the Architectural Association, London; 11.14 as 11.10; 11.15 as 11.2; 11.16 From Le Corbusier, *Précisions sur un état présent de l'architecture et de l'urbanisme*, 1930; 11.17 as 11.10; 11.18 as 11.12; 11.19 as 11.11; 11.20 as 11.2; 11.21 From Le Corbusier, *Oeuvre complète*, III, *1934–38*, Les Editions d'Architecture, Zurich, 1964; 11.22 as 11.1; 11.23, 24 Photo copyright © Ezra Stoller/Esto. We acknowledge the Fondation Le Corbusier/SPADEM, Paris, for images of works by Le Corbusier.

INDEX

Figures in *italic* type indicate pages on which illustrations appear; there may also be textual references on these pages.
References to the notes give the page on which the note appears, followed by the chapter and note number.